WORDS WITHOUT PICTUR

NOVEMBER 2007–FEBRUARY 2009
Los Angeles County Museum of Art

CONTENTS

CONTENTS

CONTENTS

--

QUESTIONNAIRE responses appear occasionally throughout the text.

WORDS WITHOUT PICTURES was conceived as a year-long project with monthly themes that were formulated by an editorial team in tandem with contributors to the wordswithoutpictures.org website. The aim was to create spaces where thoughtful and urgent discourse around very current issues for photography could happen. Each month, beginning at the end of November 2007 and concluding in November 2008, an artist, educator, critic, art historian, or curator wrote a short, un-illustrated and opinionated essay about an aspect of photography that, in his or her view, was either emerging or in the process of being rephrased. Each essay was available on the website for one month and was accompanied by a discussion forum focused on the specific topic. Over the course of its month-long "life," each essay received invited and unsolicited responses.
The essays were proposals, from which the respondents picked up and created new strands of inquiry, thereby demonstrating the multidimensionality of each topic.

Wordswithoutpictures.org's discussion forum functioned as a very slow and considered form of weblog, with long posts from people clearly invested in and willing to engage with the issue at hand and to develop the scope of the discussion in meaningful ways. Similarly, a series of panel discussions were hosted at the Los Angeles County Museum of Art during the course of the year as a way of bringing the conversations off-line and into the space of the museum. The live discussions were a chance to further explore some of the site's themes with a diverse group of contemporary artists whose thinking and engagement with the medium of photography reflected differing viewpoints and practices. These events often resulted in the invited guests and members of the audience travelling offsite to a local diner where the discussions were continued late into the night.

The project facilitated conversations and discussions between a variety of people who might otherwise not come into contact with each other. The project aimed to be as inclusive as possible so as to create a space where artist writings, critical examinations and informal commentaries could intersect. Thus, the tone of the writing varies from the informal and conversational to the creative and academic. It was our feeling that if we are to honestly talk about the state of photography in our contemporary landscape, it is imperative to reach across disciplinary boundaries. Students, photographers active in the commercial sector, bloggers, critics, historians, artists of all kinds, educators, publishers, and fans of photography all came together to consider the issues at hand. At every level of the process we aimed to remain accessible, acting as facilitators, instigators, and participants.

In addition to the live panel discussions we organized a series of longer, mostly undirected conversations between artists, two of which are included in this volume. At the same time, we asked Lester Pleasant to send out questionnaires with a small number of pertinent questions about the contemporary experience of photography to people working in the photographic arena. A sampling of these questionnaire responses appear sporadically throughout the book. We initiated public and private conversations between artists that revolved much more broadly around what it means to work with photography at this present moment. Running alongside wordswithoutpictures.org was its sister site, pictureswithoutwords.org, which used a continuous word counter to generate abstract pictures configured by the multiple uses of particular words and allowing us to ultimately include a particular form of picture-making in our consciously un-illustrated endeavor.

One of the challenges of the project was the question of how to translate the experience of the web and live conversations into book form. The editorial process attempted to preserve as much of the informal, loose, and lively nature of the discussions as possible in accordance with the temporal experience of the project, while striving for a satisfying after-the-fact experience. For the most part, the publication follows the chronology of the project as an organizational model. We hope that the reader will have the flexibility to choose to experience the content as it unfolded this past year, or to select discrete sections of focused inquiry. The book includes all 12 essays, a selection of the responses in the discussion forums, excerpts from a series of related panel discussions, two conversations between artists, and selections from the responses to the questionnaires.

All of these manifestations of WORDS WITHOUT PICTURES are summarized and compiled in this book, and we hope that the project will continue to be a stimulus to thinking about photography today. We want to thank all of the people who gave up their time to get passionate, speak plainly and openly, and to participate in this record of what some of us were thinking about photography over the course of this project.

Charlotte Cotton and Alex Klein

Qualifying Photography as Art, or, Is Photography All It Can Be?

CHRISTOPHER BEDFORD

With medium specificity a passé historical concern confined chiefly to the pages of art history, it may seem prosaic and anachronistic to question the position and relative validity of a single medium—photography—within the world of contemporary art. In addition, the same question may seem patently irrelevant to those who might justifiably point out that many of the most eminent, critically lauded, and well-collected artists of the twentieth century—Thomas Demand, Jeff Wall, Bernd and Hilla Becher, Cindy Sherman, and Andreas Gursky, to name a few—all use the camera as their primary instrument. Furthermore, the status of photography as art is rarely drawn into question, and the market currency of the medium is beyond dispute. But does it necessarily follow that the fundamental ontology of photography as a practice has been fully interrogated, understood, and integrated into the discourse of contemporary art, assuming its rightful place alongside traditional media such as painting, sculpture, and drawing, as well as new media such as installation and video? In other words, does photography exist as photography in art history and criticism today? And if not, why not? Is photography—and by derivation photography criticism—all it can be?

Not surprisingly, one of the most astute theorizations of this quandary was offered—albeit obliquely—by

Michael Fried in a wide-ranging essay on Thomas Demand published in 2005. Discussing Demand's by now familiar technique of fabricating and photographing sculptural models of judiciously chosen, historically charged sites, Fried summarizes the results of the artist's exacting enterprise as follows: "Simply put, he aims above all to replace the original scene of evidentiary traces and marks of human use—the human world in all its layered-ness and compositeness—with images of sheer authorial intention, as though the very bizarreness of the fact that the scenes and objects in the photographs, despite their initial appearance of quotidian 'reality,' have all been constructed by the artist throws into conceptual relief the determining force (also the inscrutability, one might almost say opacity) of the intention behind it." While seizing on a timely vernacular to capture and critique the ineffable heterogeneity of the world has been and will likely remain the fundamental charge of the most ambitious painters and sculptors, that same world arrives in the hands of the competent photographer—assuming he or she possesses the requisite instinct for detail, composition, and topicality—as a readymade of sorts. The camera provides the language, and the world at large is a rich well of potential subjects. Fried seems keenly aware of this rather problematic dialectic, and equally keen to establish photography's currency as a more determined, intention-laden industry than is commonly presumed.

Throughout his generally laudatory account of Demand's achievement, Fried argues that the artist's critical value issues directly from his resistance to the observational, documentary impulse. Demand's concomitant embrace of a harder-won, multi-faceted process, Fried suggests, operates in arch, critical relation to the assumption that a photograph is an indexical cohort with reality. Demand's working method interrupts this neat indexical relation, forcing the viewer to think explicitly about the intention of the maker and conjurer with an additional layer of interpretive difficulty. Fried notes that photography per se is not important to Demand, just the conclusion brought to bear on the artist's process. Demand's photographic practice does not direct our attention to the subject captured or to the technical aspects of photography, but to the artist's tyrannical control of his process, which ultimately brings order and conceptual coherence to the project. The ultimate referent is, therefore, not the form or content of his images, but the authorial concept. This being the case, the onus on Fried to develop a sophisticated understanding of the relationship of form to content, and of facture to ultimate effect in the photographs themselves, is somewhat mitigated, since purpose and meaning have been located so convincingly elsewhere.

In the context of the present essay, it is important to cite Fried, who, for many contemporary art curators, has offered a convincing and select entry point into the vast and diverse terrain of photography. Fried's emphasis rests upon intention. For although we as an art critical community no longer use artistic intention—the most outmoded of methodologies—as the infra-logic for interpretation, we do place an implicit premium on intentionality, and we take it for granted that an object arrives in a gallery or museum saddled with some degree of authorial purpose, even if that intention does not figure vitally in the meaning of the work as enumerated by the viewer, critic, or scholar. Demand's work is thick with explicit indices of intention, intellectual reflection, and considered action, all of which—in a sense—mimic the minute decisions and adjustments that take place during the execution of a painting, for example. Every detail, therefore, may be understood as intentional and vigorously interpreted as such. This, of course, leads to a rich critical record, but Fried's emphasis on Demand's pre-photographic processes also leads the reader further and further away from the specific objecthood of the photograph.

So what is lost in this interpretive account? Fried's essay is characteristically suggestive and fertile, but it rests on issues removed from a close analysis of photography as a specific technical practice that mediates and directs understanding. How Demand's photographic methods actually operate in the context of his conceptual scheme gets distinctly short shrift. Instead, the currency of his practice is defined by the various stages of production that precede the execution of the photographic image. In effect, it is these discrete, mappable phases that make Demand's photographs intelligible and critically potent; there is no need to look carefully at the image itself. Demand's photographs, then, achieve legibility and encourage art critical exegesis principally as a result of their non-photographic features. Demand is just one example of an artist/photographer—other obvious examples include Cindy Sherman and Jeff Wall—who has achieved prominence and whose work generates interest because process and concept can be located in the work that precedes the moment a photograph is taken. The photograph is simply the incidental conclusion, the polished index of a more complex back-story to be researched and unpacked by the viewer/critic. In this sense, the photograph is not independently productive of meaning, but is rather the document that records and implies the extended process behind the image.

Fried's account of Demand's work is an unusually sophisticated and provocative example of art critical writing on photography. More often, what passes for photography criticism in major art magazines discounts issues of facture and ontology entirely in favor of a descriptive mode that slyly ignores questions raised by medium. Generally speaking, the nuances of the photographic process are poorly understood in the art critical community—the present author included—and this shortfall radically limits the discourse. The effects of this situation can be measured through brief reference to the discourse surrounding painting in the twentieth century.

Through the 1960s, Clement Greenberg's Kantian understanding of the central imperatives of modernist painting remained the yardstick against which contemporary abstraction was measured. According to Greenberg, the essence of modernist painting "lay in the use of the characteristic methods of [the] discipline to criticize the discipline itself, not in order to subvert it but in order to entrench it more firmly in its area of competence." As a result of Greenberg's position, critics and artists were compelled to evaluate the fundamental ontology of painting, a compulsion that resulted in a hermetic, highly self-reflexive discourse that bore down ruthlessly on the relationship between a given canvas and Greenberg's maxims. This contention framed the discourse around painting for at least two decades and set the stage for the Minimalists, whose principal goal was to subvert the logic of Greenberg's system through objects that relied not on the relationship between their constituent parts, but on the interaction between object and viewer. Though medium specificity is no longer a salient issue in contemporary art practice, the discourse of Greenbergian modernism, and the various dissenting positions that emerged in its wake, has provided today's critics with the language and critical tools to describe and evaluate an artist's use of media, and to apply this understanding when interpreting the way a given object makes meaning. In this sense, the inheritance of Greenbergian discourse is both obsolete and invaluable.

Unfortunately, no such model exists for evaluating photography as a specific medium in art critical circles, and so the majority of art critics writing today lack the requisite descriptive vocabulary and technical understanding to account for and evaluate the appearance of a photograph, and to relate those observations to the critical rhetoric of the image. This deficit in understanding is readily explicable, deriving in part from the simple fact that the technical aspects of advanced photographic practice are elusive to all but those who consistently operate a camera and produce pictures. More importantly, perhaps, the relative opacity of facture in photography—the absence of the artist's hand—means that the much-vaunted consonance (or dissonance) of subject and form, so often the lynchpin of successful painting and sculpture, is much harder to bear down on and evaluate in the case of a photograph. While there is room for improvisational descriptive language and speculation in characterizing the way a painting was executed, no such possibility exists when describing, for example, a photograph by German-born Florian Maier-Aichen, whose large-format photographs are obviously manipulated, but utterly opaque to the lay viewer. As a result, the meaning of a given work is often located in what can be easily discerned simply by looking, leading all too frequently to facile observational descriptions that do not account for the ways in which the conditions of production inflect how we interpret content. The elusiveness of photography as a medium and the relative invisibility of process, therefore, have resulted in a radically impoverished mode of criticism.

Photographers who have been greeted with the most emphatic critical endorsements—Wall and Demand, for example—have, generally speaking, achieved notoriety by folding into their photographic programs additional processes that mitigate the necessity to evaluate their photographs alone. Photographers who instrumentalize photography as one component of a broader practice have therefore accrued far more critical and commercial traction than photographers who hew more closely to the essentialist, "observe and record" model of photography, simply because their work is more accessible and intelligible to art critics. The latter process of seeing, electing, and shooting is too connoisseurial, too ineffable, and too intuitive to qualify as an intelligent and intelligible conceptual strategy according to the imperatives of the contemporary art world, where a premium is placed on conceptual sophistication. As Maurice Berger has noted, such work is assumed to be "weak in intentionality."

However, the presumption that this essentialist model of photographic production relies on intuitive knowing rather than on rigorous thinking can only undermine the credibility of so-called "traditional" or documentary photographers in the context of art criticism because no adequate framework exists by which to measure the achievements of these photographers. And no commonly acknowledged measure exists because the ontological understanding of photography and its methods among art critics is far less sophisticated than is the case for painting, sculpture, and performance art. Demand's work, for example, is uniquely conducive to the logic of narrative exegesis and seems to presuppose its own theorization; rather predictably, therefore, his photographs have spawned a vast literature. Standard photographic practice, on the other hand, is not so easily parsed and theorized; its ontology is comparatively elusive. The key, then, is to enumerate even the most prosaic aspects of conventional photography (the physiognomy of an individual photographer's practice, the ebb and flow of intentionality through the process from choice of film or digital back through to print type and size); to claim these considerations and procedures as the basic ontological condition of photographic work; and to re-theorize the ways in which these factors shape the image, direct the viewer's attention, and contribute to the production of meaning. In effect, it is necessary to remake the technical and conceptual discourse around traditional photography within art criticism. Such a process would not only throw into high relief the fundamental nature and limits of the medium, as well as the achievement of photographers' photographers such as James Welling, Christopher Williams, Jean-Marc Bustamante, and Thomas Struth, but it would also radically enhance—and perhaps recast—our understanding of photographers already entrenched firmly in the canon of art history.

Ultimately, there is only one effective, long-term remedy for the instrumentalization of photography in the broader context of art production, and that remedy begins with the production of advanced criticism that addresses photographs with a deep awareness of both the technical conditions of photographic production, and the concomitant conceptual implications of these technical processes. If photography is to be understood as a medium always and deliberately productive of meaning in the same sense as painting, this will require a rich and thorough understanding of the myriad decisions that precede the production of a photographic image, ranging from the conceptual and obtuse to the mundane and pragmatic. Such technical awareness is the necessary precondition for the production of art critical writing that operates with a full ontological awareness of photography as a unique medium. Only then will an advanced and, dare I say, medium-specific discourse emerge that mines the rich territory between fact and facture, process and product, form and content, sign and signified. The development of such a self-aware critical discourse will signal photography's equal passage into the world of contemporary art, and only then will the problems and questions posed in this essay be truly anachronistic.

--

DISCUSSION FORUM
WWW.WORDSWITHOUTPICTURES.ORG

--

Subject: Cyclical Interests
Date: 27 November 2007 22:03:57
From: CHARLOTTE COTTON

I applaud Christopher Bedford's honesty in offering a perspective onto the shortcomings of art criticism and its appraisal of photography as well as the problems that photography faces in overcoming this. I've been thinking about why Chris might have chosen Greenberg, writing in the 1960s and Fried in the 2000s as his two main authors who impact on the critical explanation of photography as art and its partial validation within art's realm. Actually, what it made me think of was a passage in Lewis Baltz's essay "American Photography in the 1970s: Too Old to Rock, Too Young to Die" when Baltz paraphrases the former director of the Leo Castelli Gallery, Marvin Heiferman, about how the art world and art criticism (and perhaps I would include *Artforum* here) has only a cyclical interest in photography—one that reaches infatuation point about every thirty or forty years. This kind of first love syndrome of art criticism comes with all the amnesia of fresh emotions that you might expect. Each high point of Baltz and Heiferman's cycle inherently calls for the degree of projection that all great love affairs require at their start, and no promise that this burst of imaginative energy will turn into something sustained, or even destined to go beyond the surface.

I think Chris nails the art critic's problem with photography when he says in his essay that "the presumption that [an] essentialist model of photographic production relies on intuitive knowing rather than rigorous thinking is only enough to undermine the credibility of so-called 'traditional' or documentary photographers in the context of art criticism because no adequate framework exists by which to measure the achievements of these photographers." There's no room in the cyclical model of temporary art adoration that allows for photography with a character set that would frighten off a new suitor—ambiguity, luck, and magic, even; these concepts just don't give over the reassurances that notions such as intentionality and legibility offer. But, then again, I don't think that processes outside of photography that garner parallel uncertain, unauthored outcomes or marks are somehow excluded from the discourses of contemporary art for these reasons alone. I agree with Chris that most photography manifests deeply unfashionable and seemingly uncritical qualities such as chance or a lack of clear authorship. But the idea that this stands in the way of photography being accepted on its own terms as an entity within current art discourse is deeply distressing. Notions such as luck or happenstance are hardly new concepts in art or art criticism since the 1960s. I just wonder if, when they are coupled with the medium of photography, art critics get suspicious of its validity as worthwhile art. I suspect that even though Chris hints at the lack of transparency (for an art curator) of technique, he just doesn't like the way some photographs look, especially when they patently reveal a technique that isn't especially labored or that lacks high production values.

Templates for writing about photography within art today are set by Fried and Greenberg, who have brought their visual and critical intelligence to bear on a field that admittedly seems to prefer not to foreground its own more sustained, seriously academic discourse. To stretch the love-at-first-sight analogy even further, I think that the two critics were captivated by the surface appearance and high-octane authorship of the most spectacular specimens of contemporary art photography. It is innate to the work of some of Fried's favorites, for example Thomas Demand and Jeff Wall, that the extent to which a photographic surface can hold so many layers of process and intellectualization is the main talking point. I'm sure James Welling was pleased to join Fried's pantheon of photographic masters; I was pleased to see him there. But it is a little like saying that the election of a female president would bring about women's emancipation. I think it's wonderful that great writers such as Fried make intensely academic justifications for some (mainly intensely academic) photographers. But I don't see this as creating a pathway for how contemporary art curators engage with photography in ways that are well suited to much of photography's practice or, indeed, to more than one moment about every thirty or forty years.

--

Subject: Photography's Destinations
Date: 27 November 2007 03:29:10
From: ARTHUR OU

That photographs are semiotic monads perpetually linked to the temporal moment of their exposure is an inherent characteristic that differentiates photography from other depictive mediums such as painting and drawing. This axiom not only applies to non-art photographs of the vernacular, quotidian types but also to the ones with full artistic intentions—photographs produced and intended to be art. Because of this coupling to time, photographs, although indexically anchored to their illuminated referent, become like time itself, always in constant flux, anxiously inserted back into the flow from which they initially came. Unlike painting, drawing, and sculpture, photographs can never reach an ultimate finality (perhaps this is even more true with digital processes). Therefore, they remain propositions that suggest an idea or what something looks like at a given, chosen moment. In other words, they are propositions of the potentiality of the subject; they point towards the possibility of meaning.

In Roland Barthes's essay "Death of the Author," the reader is given power and precedence to give meaning to a text and to generate interpretative impressions, which consciously severs the umbilical thread that connects the work to its authorial origins. Barthes writes, "The reader is the space on which all the quotations that make up a writing are inscribed without any of them being lost; a text's unity lies not in its origin but in its destination." There is a fundamental similarity between photographs and text. When a viewer is confronted with a photograph (as a reader is with a text), he/she is presented with a proposal to arrive at another destination. Whether it's a geographical place, a cerebral place, or otherwise, the viewer/reader, while observing the content and formal aspects of the image/text, must depart from the site from which his/her eyes have rested and go elsewhere for its meaning. Like text, photographs, ranging from the candid to the most determined, are all embedded with this elusive slippage. The question that seems to consistently challenge the status of photography as art is directly linked to photography's own elusiveness as an innate autonomous object. But these continual attempts at validation and revalidation of photography's artistic claims are no more than tautological circles within which practitioners, curators, critics and art historians perform their awkward dances. Photographs are like no other objects. In the capitalistic sense, of course, every object—manufactured or natural—will at some point in time reach expiration. But no other object, except other indexical objects such as audio recordings and video, bears the imprint of time as its core structure. Like text then, and unlike paintings or other autonomous art objects, photographs cannot be "deciphered," but are rather "disentangled" from the temporal morass that binds them.

In the expanding fields of contemporary photographic practices within the sphere of globalization, notions of the photographic are being extended towards and beyond other mediums, while at the same time being co-opted and reoriented within cultures outside of the Western centers of art production. As a result, in viewers' engagement with photographs it becomes increasingly difficult to locate destinations of meaning other than the one intended by the photographer/artist/author, or even from possible origins of meaning through the canonical models from Western art history and criticism. What seems necessary is for the viewer to knowingly reinsert or reinstate the photographs encountered into a broader cultural discourse that acknowledges an increasingly interrelated web of ideas and practices wherein material and intellectual factors simultaneously coincide and collide. The destination of meaning is in the viewer, but it becomes the task of the viewer to not only have knowledge of the technical, historical and conceptual conditions of photography, but to also expand this awareness into the wider cultural and political implications that these particular types of images always bear. Instead of positing and bounding photography in existing categories (such as art), perhaps it is more illuminating to consider photographs as something inherently different and always changing. As Barthes states, "... By refusing to assign a 'secret,' an ultimate meaning, to the text (and to the world as text)," the reader/viewer "liberates what may be called an anti-theological activity, an activity that is truly revolutionary since to refuse to fix meaning is, in the end, to refuse God and his hypostases—reason, science, law." If photographs are propositions, then they are constantly in flux, necessitating a viewer that can also adapt and change, to be able to arrive at destinations that are heretofore not yet determined.

--

Subject: Photography and its discontents
Date: 28 November 2007 15:07:05
From: PHILLIP PRODGER

Those of us who work with photographs for a living trudge daily through a swamp of prejudices and prejudgments, many of which are carried over from the 19th century, others of which have been absorbed uncritically from film and camera manufacturers' marketing campaigns, and still more of which were scripted as gallery sales pitches. Of course, photography is also somewhat unique in that pretty much everybody does it, or has done it; so, unlike painting and sculpture, photographs are read and interpreted in terms of personal experience. Your basic amateur photographer is of the point-and-shoot school—what you see is what you get, minus the odd technical flaw. So it's only natural that when visitors see a photograph in a museum or gallery, they subconsciously assume it was made in much the same way. This is one reason for the medium's powerful resonance.

But here is a question for you: Does Thomas Demand make photographs of his intricate constructions as some sort of wry, nuanced critique of material culture, as a layered, self-referential ontological dance imbued with distinct meaning, or is it just the fact that he can sell the things? Sure, it's cool that his works are photographs and all that. Using photography invites us to think about what it means to absorb the conventions of mundane visual communication in the name of artistic expression. See that? It's a photograph. You know them. They're in magazines; I make art out of them.

But take other artists who use photographs as "indices," as Bedford describes them. Would we accept that Andy Goldsworthy adds special meaning to his landscape interventions by photographing them? Or, here's a trickier one, what do we say about a Marina Abramović or a Vito Acconci or any one of the artists whose work began with performance—ephemeral, evanescent, unpredictable—only to find it didn't pay the rent. Enter the photograph, infinitely reproducible, eminently quantifiable. And, well, saleable.

Demand could sell his original constructions for six times what he charges for each photograph in an edition of six, and he'd come out the same financially, more or less. Of course, there is more to it than that. Demand is so accomplished in using the limitations of photography—yes, the limitations—that his images work brilliantly in that medium alone. Photographs don't let you see around corners, use your stereovision, or peek behind the surface to test verisimilitude. Ironically, it is these illusionary qualities—our inability as viewers to authenticate what we see—that make his pictures tick.

So much the better. In a Demand photograph, or a James Casebere, Zeke Berman, or Jan Groover, the savvy viewer is treated to 31 flavors of meaning. The works exist as concept, in the artist's mind; as rhetoric; as constructs, separate to the finished work of art but nevertheless very real; and as finished products—photographs. My point is not that photography and all its baggage are unimportant when it comes to a Goldsworthy, an Abramović, or a Demand, rather that it is convenient. And that is worth remembering.

There is a curious idea in visual art that every step that an "art object" is removed from the circumstances that gave rise to it the more compelling it becomes. This is only true of visual arts, if you think about it. Are films of a ballet more interesting than performers on stage? Are MP3s more evocative than a night in a dance club? Because photography translates one corporeal reality into another, and because we are trained to evaluate art in similar frames of reference, photography retains a unique and peculiar traction.

A generation or two from now, I don't doubt these same tensions will be discussed and rehashed. Why not—we've already been talking about them in one form or another for 150 years or so. And yet, as time goes by they will seem increasingly quaint. It strikes me forcefully that a typical Chelsea art gallery samples visual culture but doesn't even begin to understand it—its occupants inhabit rarified air, and at the same time, the artists they elevate wrestle with old questions and tired conceits. They do this because this is what people want to buy, or at least what they are habitually fed. Being "cutting edge," but at the same time a little behind the curve, is a solid economic proposition for an art gallery. But my friends—dear, sweet, misguided friends—that is so *yesterday*. Still images—and I mean *all* still images—are already old-fashioned, and have been for some time. What use will they have in a world swarming with high-def video and film and cell phone electronica? Photographs have already lost their bite, and now exist principally to reassure us, in much the same way oil paintings do.

One of the great ironies of the early 21st century museum world is that just as photography is losing its potency, curatorial positions dedicated to the form are sprouting like mushrooms. It is not a coincidence. Declaring a medium worthy of serious institutional attention in its own right is something of a death knell, because it is only when something is no longer dangerous that we clutch it to our collective bosom, like a giant teddy bear. Art is a relic culture, and photography has become the ultimate relic. It is the T-shirt you wear from a city you never visited.

Bedford's appeal to fortify photographic criticism is absolutely on target. And yet, I believe photography is not the only medium that escapes thoughtful analysis; nor is photography so distinct among media that we should allow it to be ghettoized. The contextual rigor Bedford prescribes is appropriate to art in all its forms. So let us not be content to settle for circumspection in the way photographs are seen and discussed. Let's reinvent the way *art* is understood—the whole lot of it.

--

Subject: A Response
Date: 30 November 2007 22:55:59
From: ALEX KLEIN

It makes sense that Christopher Bedford begins his essay by expressing reservations about retrograde terms such as medium specificity and intentionality. Surely this is not the time or place for a rehashing of Greenbergian modernism, and not simply because of its outmodedness within contemporary art discourse. As others have noted, the battles fought by Greenberg and his acolytes primarily centered on what was at stake in painting and sculpture. A true photo-criticism, if there is such a thing, must, first and foremost, start with photography. We have seen where attempts to historicize and break down photography using models from other mediums have lead us. Specifically, these investigations signaled a return to pastiche—a mode of photography that embraced the tableaus of history painting under the rubric of postconceptualism and postmodernism. A similar dilemma has arisen when an essentialist program for photography has been mapped diagrammatically as an "expanded field" from which several intermedia branches extend. This is where we encounter the frustrating category of "the artist using photography."

Curiously enough, here perhaps it is worth recalling a canonical essay by Rosalind Krauss that offers a key to the simultaneously problematic and liberating potential of the photographic medium. In "Photography's Discursive Spaces," Krauss articulates some of the fundamental misconceptions underpinning the art critical historicization of photography. I am not suggesting that we take Krauss as the model for photographic criticism (or her subject, Eugène Atget, as the prime example), merely that the critical language and institutional categories that we use to build histories around images are themselves constructed, even as they organize the ways in which we remember and misremember. It is precisely photography's numerous contexts and types of functionalities that make it fascinating and confusing.

In this light, it is useful to cite Bedford's example of Demand, whose work perfectly addresses many of the complications within contemporary photographic practice, but I do so for reasons other than the ones that Fried implies. The strength of Demand's images lies in the very fact that they are photographs. Re-imagined from an archive primarily drawn from popular media, Demand's paper constructions require an erasure of detail in order to hint at something remembered, and not in an effort to disclose any laborious back-story or intentionality. It is only when the sculptures take the form of photographs that they can begin to re-circulate as images and thereby tap into something approaching collective memory. Photography, for all of its verisimilitude, is an adaptable, ambiguous, slippery thing. Undeniably populist and multifaceted, it is necessarily always pointing outside of its own frame. It can never fold in upon itself in the manner of a Greenbergian, medium-specific object because it must always be about other pictures, temporalities, and modes of representation.

Indeed, even when photography is liberated from the burden of traditional representation and concerns itself with material investigations that explore and dismantle the interaction of light, paper, and photochemical processes, we do not and cannot reach its essence. In the most interesting examples of such work the impulse and the impact reach far beyond a vogue in the market or a simple exploration of photography's mechanical supports. Perhaps it is little wonder that we see a retreat from the real and a return to photographic abstraction at our current moment of extreme geopolitical crisis, when depiction seems somehow unsatisfactory and, at best, unstable. Nevertheless, the call for a criticism grounded in a reduction of photography to a mere set of technical concerns is misguided and would return us to equally outmoded debates around craft and technique. As our copies of *The Contest of Meaning* begin to yellow, I wholeheartedly agree that it is time for a revaluation. But in an era when it is standard for students to learn both black-and-white printing and Photoshop in high school, it is ridiculous to approach the camera as if it were some kind of mystifying magic box. Although we may never be satisfied with the words we use to investigate photographic pictures, maybe it is worth taking a look at the extensive criticism on photography that we *do* have and asking how *it* can be expanded.

--

Subject: Ontological Flexibility
Date: 4 December 2007 01:47:56
From: NICHOLAS GRIDER

This is an interesting way to look at the ontology of photography, but there are a few implicit assumptions in Bedford's essay that ultimately sabotage the idea of instrumentality being useful as a way of looking at photography-as-art.

The main assumption is that the labor involved in "art" is ontologically prior to the existence of the art itself. With something such as a painting, any given canvas brings with it an implied linear history of labor: an artist started with a blank space, so to speak, and worked on it until, at some point, it became art.

But the fascinating thing about the ontology of photography is that its instantiation of this kind of labor means that the labor is produced alongside or after the "art." Florian Maier-Aichen's work is a good example of a case where the labor happens somewhere between "taking a photo" and printing it. Jörg Sasse also comes to mind, and so does Soo Kim. In fact, ever since James Welling started sticking his hands under the enlarger lamp, the materiality of the photograph as an object has been a given.

What this instantiation does, though, is problematic, because it tends to pose the photographer as either someone who stumbles across an already-made "image" waiting to be captured, or as a strange brand of filmmaker or performance artist who is responsible for creating the worlds he or she then appears to stumble across (Wall, Gursky, et al.).

And cleaving content from form by means of time divides things too neatly into documentary (content-based) photography on one hand and form-based "art" on the other, thereby overvaluing the labor prior to product at the expense of photography's flexible ontology.

The other, seemingly minor problem is in fact a bigger one: by assuming that art is the condition to which photography does or should aspire, there's a real danger of eliding the demotic and industrial/commercial base of actual photo-production. This is kind of a shame, because rather than wondering how photography can be positioned within the terms of the art market, it may be more interesting to explore in more detail how photography manages the balancing act, more than any other contemporary medium, of simultaneously being both art and non-art—both "the thing itself" and a record of that thing.

--

Subject: Let's don't throw the baby out with the bathwater . . .
Date: 6 December 2007 13:23:18
From: KEN ABBOTT

Christopher Bedford's article and the equally illuminating responses to it are a good indication that photographic discourse and criticism are, despite reports to the contrary, still alive and kicking. This discussion reminds me of one of my favorite rants: that the art world success of conceptually based photography (as opposed to the essentialist, "observe and record" mode) is mostly due to the fact that nowadays to teach you have to have an MFA or other academic pedigree. (Unless otherwise noted, all quotes are taken from

Bedford's article.) It's clear to me that teaching art students to think up interesting ideas and imaginative schema for their presentation is easier to work into a syllabus than a method that relies for success, at least in part, on " . . . ambiguity, luck, and magic, even" (from Charlotte Cotton's response, above). Academics must publish (exhibit) or perish, and this fact provides all the fodder necessary for keeping the "shoe gazers" busy, and the accomplishments "measurable."

I recall a field trip when I was an undergraduate student in a photo class being taught by a visiting professor, Frank Gohlke. We were heading to Santa Fe, NM, from Colorado Springs, "to photograph." (About the only blessed conceptualizing Frank did was to suggest that in photographing we were creating new things, and that those things were evidence of a new reality that we were creating.) I was driving Frank and several students; in an idle moment, I asked Frank what he said when people asked him, "Is photography really art?" (Okay, this conversation took place about thirty years ago, and if you're old enough you may remember those heady days when there was still considerable debate about this.) At any rate, I was taken aback by Frank's reply. It went something like this: "When I'm feeling feisty, I might even make the argument that photography is better than art." Hah! Take that! Wow! That hadn't occurred to me. But a correlate to Frank's suggestion crystallized quickly. In suggesting that perhaps photography is better than art, Frank was implying that perhaps it also was something different than art, to be judged on its own terms and not considered any less important for that fact.

I think it's worth considering that "determined, intention-laden industry" doesn't necessarily make for better pictures, and "interpretive difficulty" isn't necessarily a plus. Could it be argued that photography has been co-opted by the "contemporary art world," and its talents made to serve a false god? Another teacher, Richard Benson, used to say, "The world is a more interesting place than our ideas about it." I'd like to note of Benson and Gohlke that neither holds an MFA in photography. I don't think MacArthur Fellow Benson even went to grad school, and Gohlke got his Masters in English Literature.

--

Subject: art as photography
Date: 10 December 2007 16:30:46
From: COLIN WESTERBECK

> "I would like to see photography make people despise painting until something else will make photography unbearable." —Marcel Duchamp

The "cycle" of art criticism's "infatuation" with photography that Charlotte Cotton speaks of in her response to Christopher Bedford's essay seems to me to have a longer span than the "thirty or forty years" she suggests, though the rate of repetition may be accelerating. The big push to have photography accepted as a major art form, spearheaded by Alfred Stieglitz and crossover critic Sadakichi Hartmann about 100 years ago, was, all things considered, a flop. Photography continued to languish in a dusty corner of prints and drawings departments, or at best as a separate and segregated department all its own, until late in the 20th century. Then, in an ironic historical twist that added insult to injury, photography burst upon the art scene full-force when a new generation of artists took it up, not because they revered it as an art form, but because they despised it as a vulgar and debased mass medium.

The co-opting of photography by postmodernists left in the lurch those who wanted to continue to meditate on the methods, history, and aspirations of traditional art photography, which had been thrown into a parallel universe where everything was now reversed as in a mirror. To continue to pursue a traditional program in photography now made one a bit of a simpleton, somebody who was out of it, rather than the aesthetic sophisticate that he or she might have seemed in the esoteric, connoisseurial photo world of an earlier era. A double consciousness was now necessary to pursue artistic ambitions in photography that would have seemed de rigueur before.

Whereas Bedford, while wondering whether our definition of art in photography is comprehensive enough, focuses on Thomas Demand's career (and on an essay that Michael Fried wrote on Demand), I might have been tempted to look instead at another photographer on whom Fried has written illuminatingly, but who is mentioned only in passing by Bedford: James Welling. I remember that when I once confessed to Welling that I did not know what to do with him in my photo history survey course, he seemed pleased. Though a pretty low-key guy, he was almost enthusiastic about being an enigma. It's a distinction he has in fact sought, with his shifts in genre, his explorations of process, and his modest—or is it deadpan?—choice of subject.

Thomas Crow has pointed out that artists are now writing art criticism and art history with their work, thereby making the old dichotomy between artists and critics obsolete, and perhaps making the critics themselves redundant. Certainly Welling would be a prime example of someone whose work has been a prolonged meditation on photography's history. There is an assumed naiveté in taking pictures of flowers and creating photographic abstractions post-postmodernism, or else it is an unexpected sophistication cleverly disguised as naiveté. The darkness in Welling's photographs on which Fried's essay remarks is the photographer's way of acknowledging the dimness into which not only historic subject matter, like locomotives or H. H. Richardson's architecture, but photographic history itself is now cast. In Welling's work, the old-fashioned art photographer becomes the subversive, and it is always with a renewed subversiveness that the cycle of which Cotton speaks in photographic history begins again.

Is Photography Really Art?

Los Angeles County Museum of Art
Participants: Arthur Ou, Michael Queenland, Mark Wyse
Moderator: Charlotte Cotton

Is photography really art? Now this is an intentionally dumb question. We are sure that everyone knows that the war is over and believes that photography can most definitely be art. The goal of this first Words Without Pictures discussion was to begin to think through the parameters of what exactly makes some photography part of contemporary art, while much photography is not even on the art radar.

How are artists who work with photography asked or conditioned to categorize themselves and their practices? What does it mean for a photograph to be categorized as "contemporary art"? Is something indeed lost or misunderstood about the plurality of photographic practice when viewed through the lens of contemporary art? How might an art context actually have the effect of confining or redefining the history of photography? These are just some of the questions posed to the three panelists.

ARTHUR OU: Hello everyone. The piece that you've been looking at is a collage piece that's made of paper and tape, and the design is derived from a Chinese window screen. Embedded in the screen is the word *Aufheben*. It is a German word with a threefold meaning: it simultaneously means to preserve, to elevate, and to cancel. When I think about this word I immediately think of its analogy to photography, and how apt and perfect these three meanings are to describe photographic activity. The word literally embodies the transformation that the camera imposes on its subject. The very urge to photograph stems from a desire to preserve a subject, whether it is a moment, a building, or a person. Through that decision to record or to preserve, the subject is elevated, chosen out of a flux of moments or subjects. And in that very moment of elevation, the subject is also canceled or even annihilated, because it has crossed over to a two-dimensional representation, trapped within a photographic illusion. So this word has been the driving subtext of much of my recent work.

. . . I think, for me, photographs are almost automatically archeological, whether they are made candidly or set up. I'm interested in making photographs because I'm interested in the idea of making artifacts that could perhaps situate my own history within a larger existing history.

. . .The title of this piece is *On Every New Thing There Lies Already the Shadow of Annihilation*, which is a line taken from W. G. Sebald's book *Rings of Saturn*. These ceramic sculptures began as photographs made of objects that people collected in their homes, on shelves and in cabinets. They are things that have already been transformed into the realm of collected objects, so they are functionless. I made one frontal photograph of each of these objects and sent the photographs to a factory in Shenzen, China, to be made into three-dimensional objects again. This is a factory that makes mass quantities of products, and I was interested in using this manufacturing process to make so-called art objects. Around the same time that I was working on this project, I read a story about the counterfeiting industry in China, where factories that were authorized to produce DVDs of Hollywood films would continue their production after hours. But the DVDs produced after hours were considered illegal because they were made outside of the contractual agreements. I was interested in this binary status of an object due to external factors, which is a phenomenon that I think is also apparent in the photographs.

. . .

MICHAEL QUEENLAND: I am going to focus on just two shows. This first slide is from a show I did at Daniel Hug Gallery here in Los Angeles in 2005, titled *XX*. This show came out of a book, or, rather, the beginning of this work came out of a Dover Press book on Shaker furniture, a sort of bible, a how-to manual. It includes measurements of actual furniture pieces. The author went around to several Shaker communities and measured the furniture and made technical drawings, and in the book were these very cheap photographic reproductions of the furniture pieces in their natural settings in different Shaker communities. I was really interested in the reproductions of this furniture and in how poorly the photographs were taken, how there was a sense of earnestness about trying to capture the spirit of Shaker groups. And then I started doing more research. Basically the project turned into me taking this book as a challenge and then remaking the furniture. That was a tough decision, because there were over 80 pieces of Shaker furniture. In this image, the sculpture in the center is about seven feet high. All of the pieces were enlarged about 45 to 50 percent.

. . . When I moved to New York, I was in a residency, and I was trying to think of what I would do for the show that culminated at the end of the residency. Because I had moved to New York, I thought it would be a perfect opportunity to do some research on the Shakers and their communities. Coincidentally, I was invited by curator Toby Kamps to do something at the Institute of Contemporary Art at Maine College of Art. Coincidentally, the last remaining Shaker community is about 45 minutes outside of Portland, Maine. . . . So, it turned out that I was able to meet Shakers and visit them pretty often, and the project culminated in me shooting these sculptures in their original buildings throughout. In a sense I was copying these photos I'd seen in the Dover Press book. There are a lot of heavy shadows and bad lighting in these photographs, and I'm playing with scale, and also a sense of space and emptiness in some of these images . . . The whole show dealt with the idea of practicality and how things that were once threatening become appropriated over time. In the case of Shaker furniture—and these Ikea chairs we are sitting in are a perfect example—the influence of that movement has become so watered-down and appropriated that it has lost its impact. So, I was also thinking of the Minimalists and their relationship to the Shakers, and a return to this kind of puritanical, reductive form.

This is a show I did this year in New York at Harris Lieberman, entitled *Bread and Balloons*. It goes beyond the scope of this talk, so I'm just going to focus on the images. This image is called *Mademoiselle Pogany*, and it is named after a Brancusi sculpture . . . I work in a lot of different mediums, so I don't really make distinctions between sculptural work and photographic work, or drawings and collages. I wanted to reproduce the idea of an artist's studio versus a gallery or a collector's house. This photo is inspired by Brancusi who took photographs of his sculptures in his studio, and also took pictures of people coming to visit his studio. So this is Mademoiselle Pogany coming to visit the studio, and she has a bread purse. The bread and balloons are also dealing with the idea of a reductive forms; they are like a cheaper version of Brancusi's reduced forms. This is a photo called *Studio*, and again, it represents Brancusi and is inspired by images of his studio.

These photographs—there are about 70 of them—I took with my digital camera. What I love about digital photography is the fact that I took 76 of these images in a period of 15 minutes. It was the first snowfall in New York last year, and I was trying to photograph something that is unclear. I was photographing the wire between my building and the building across the street from me. There was this build-up of snow on the wire, and I was also smoking at the same time, so smoke was drifting in and out of the snowflakes. The whole grouping of the images moved from feeling like you're underwater, looking at Titanic debris, to feeling like you're in space. In a sense this was a moment of stepping outside from the world of the studio.

MARK WYSE: One of the reasons I'm so attracted to

photography is that I have this compulsion to always want to break things down, to try and understand them, and with photographs I find that impulse or that desire to be rather frustrating. It is frustrating in the sense that photographs' meanings are so often tangled between the real world and the intentions of the photographer.

. . . What I want to talk about is that photographs, for me, often provide an experience of being inside oneself and outside oneself at the same time. I think that this often gets overlooked. So often we talk about the photograph's meaning in terms of its subject, but we often don't talk about the experience of being in someone else's body, feeling like you're looking through it. In a lot of my work, I'm interested in that sensation, that pull between this presence that is felt and not seen.

In a painting that presence is seen; it is automatic and you're aware of it. In photography, you feel it, in a sense, and that tension butts up against the meaning. These photographs are from a recent show called *Marks of Indifference*. In each of the photographs, "Marks of Indifference" is in the title. I was trying to make photographs in which their meanings were caught between reflecting on the nature of photography itself, and being depictions of the world at the same time. The viewer would oscillate between being aware of the photograph's presence or its materiality and its nature of being a representation. Then, in other photographs, you would be seeing through it and engaging the subject in a direct and visceral way.

. . .

CHARLOTTE COTTON: One of the reasons that Alex Klein and I invited the three of you to come together to talk about the subject "Is Photography Really Art?" is that all of you, in very different but I think complementary ways, grapple in your processes with the idea of what is photographic practice. It seems, in the way that all of you have talked, that it is clearly something that you are working through at the point at which you're conceiving of a project, an idea.

Or maybe that's a question. If you're working through, in a very critical way, the idea of what is photographic meaning—what it means to take pictures—what values does this medium have in terms of your practice? Does it feel like a cold, unemotional thing to make photographs? Or, do you think that there is a part of you that, in an unconstructed way, just wants to see what things look like as pictures?

WYSE: It is a huge source of anxiety for me. I mean it is weird how it is split in my head between these intellectual concerns and this desire that doesn't respond to those intellectual concerns. I'm always grappling with those two. I get stuck in between and I just accept, or try to explore that.

To me, photography is a good model of one's relationship to reality. I usually think of it in that sense, of not necessarily *what* I'm representing, but as some kind of relationship *between* two things. After making a body of work, I can see those things that are revealing of oneself. For example, why was I so concerned with these intellectual concerns, or why was I not? Or, why was I trying to articulate them here, and not articulate them there?

OU: When I started making artwork, I started making straightforward pictures. I think that now the meaning of photography becomes this kind of propositional tool. It is very different from other mediums in that photographs are always coupled with time. Because of that inherent nature, they become similar to inquiries or questions, and I love that aspect of using this medium.

QUEENLAND: I would say that I have a much more practical relationship to photography. When I first started making art, I started doing photography because I didn't have a formal art education, and I didn't have a studio, so photography offered a way I could access art. I could take pictures of things and think about them. As I started getting access to a studio and those sorts of things, then I was able to not just be within the frame of a photograph. That came full circle, as I work more intensively with photography now.

But now it really is a practical relationship. A lot of times, it is just like using it as a documentary sort of thing, while also acknowledging the transformative power that a photograph has, and its relationship to time, which is different from seeing something in person.

. . .

COTTON: Last night at dinner, when we were discussing what we suspect the contemporary art world sees in contemporary art photography, it seemed necessary that we categorize it to a certain extent, because the idea of photography in contemporary art tends to be concerned with the highly authored school of staged photographic practice. None of you are actually working in that world, but you consider your work to be part of contemporary art.

OU: I think that in even the contemporary art world there seem to be so many different strata of photographic production. There are the directorial artists that you mentioned, but there are also artists who use photography in relation to other mediums. And there is also the photo world within the contemporary art world that seems to have its own kind of inner relations. For example, the photo world has its own art fairs, and so on.

. . .

WYSE: I intentionally engage some kind of transparency of photography in a way that can be misinterpreted. I love that aspect of someone overlooking the complexity of the work and saying, "That's just a picture." And I'm quite invested in all of these ideas from photography, and what photographs are in a complicated way. But there is something there. I don't know why, but I have a problem with articulating intentionality in photographs.

COTTON: *Your* intentionality, or do you mean reading intentionality *in* photos?

WYSE: I have a feeling that one of the anxieties of the contemporary art world not accepting this "other" kind of photography is that photographs get overlooked in the sense that their intentionality is seen in a very visible, articulated way. At its essence, meaning in photographs is conceptualized, but not always visible; it doesn't always have to be registered visually to be articulated. I think that those things get overlooked and neglected. So, I'm trying to make bodies of work that engage those ideas. I showed the pictures from *Marks of Indifference*, which is also the title of a Jeff Wall essay. There are a lot of people in the art world who take Wall's essay as the beginning of contemporary photography. I'm invested in the same kind of ideas that Wall is exploring, but I intentionally made my photographs in a way that didn't work in the way Wall's do, or in the way that the work of the artists Wall is talking about does.

. . .

QUEENLAND: I think one thing that we talked about a little bit that helps to distinguish this question of how confusing it is to define boundaries between what is art and what is photography is the intention. I think, like we said, we're in a period right now where art is in an expanded field of practice. For example, there is a questioning of the ready-made right now, and people making gestures like chewing gum and sticking it on the wall. So, it is hard to ask, "Is photography art?" when you have someone sticking gum on the wall that's begging the same question. I think it is really a strange period, although there always has been a questioning of what the art object is. But it has never been so unstable as it is right now. I guess I like exploring that confusion in my work. I think, just naturally, I've been drawn to it; it is like a playground. I want to eke out these other things that are maybe not recognized in photography, or haven't been recognized in photography.

COTTON: Actually, what I believe Michael is saying is that he's infusing a photographic-ness, which is an ambiguity, into all areas of practice. In a way, I think that is what's so interesting in his practice.

QUEENLAND: Well, that may be because you have a photographic agenda, because I think someone else could say that there is a sculptural agenda behind the photographs. I'm definitely interested in making everything an equal playing field . . .

WYSE: I was just thinking that you were talking, in essence, about where the meaning was located, and Michael is saying that it is not located in photography. I'm actually also saying that it is not located in photography, even though in essence, yes, it has to do with these kind of relationships. It is not embedded in the object itself, either. Meaning is not embedded in the readymade itself, it is in this kind of intentionality that's going on behind the scenes, whether that intentionality is visual, or whether it is extracted in a way that's not. Whether the artist is questioning ideas of representation, or just being expressionistic, I think all those things are invisibly going on in the background. I'm invested in these ideas photographically, but even when the meaning is located in the form of the photographs, it is still me pulling the strings behind the scenes in ways that would be parallel to working with sculpture.

. . .

OU: Do you think that is a modernist approach to making pictures? I mean modernism is this self-awareness of the medium. It seems like a lot of photographs are made with that kind of intent, or at least with that kind of approach, which makes the process much more difficult; it makes the materiality of the image more difficult.

. . .

COTTON: I think we're entering into a phase where you can't take as a given that anyone other than photographers and photo curators see photographic prints on a daily basis. So, I think that's another kind of shaping of the context of why it might be a time when I don't feel like an entrenched modernist if we talk about the form of the photographic print, or abstraction. These kinds of things that have been taboo in terms of talking about photography could re-emerge because of the fact that a photographic print is no longer a default position; it is an act of will to make a photographic print.

. . .

QUEENLAND: I would agree with that. It is just that my attitude is, as an artist, you use whatever sort of tool you can. I hate saying that—photography as a tool—but yeah, tool. I think it is basically whatever the artist's relationship to whatever medium it is, and the specific climate that they are in is always going to inform the photograph or the sculpture or the painting, whatever it is. And I think that, when I first heard the title of this talk, "Is Photography Really Art?," the question that came to my head was, "Well, what is art?" I think we're in a period right now where a lot of artists using photography in their work have been shut down as far as what they can do, and I think that speaks to a larger climate of what's happening in contemporary art right now. I think there is a general malaise. A lot of artists are working and trying to come to terms with modernism, postmodernism. You know, all of those big words.

. . .

COTTON: But, you know, the history of photography is littered with the greatest photographers being quoted as having maximum disdain for the medium. I mean, Man Ray made the same kinds of statements about photography.

I would like to ask James Welling, who is in the audience, a question. Are there too many people out there taking pictures that look like your pictures?

JAMES WELLING [AUDIENCE]: Not yet. But I had an observation that I would like to turn into a question. I think it is an interesting situation about photos passing for art. The question that I had was about the idea of photography as a tool. I was thinking, what's the difference between photography and sculpture? Because a lot of you—Arthur and Michael—were talking about sculpture. I realized that sculpture isn't a tool. Photography, when you say that it is a tool, it is like saying it is a chisel. In discussions of photography-as-art, I feel like photography was sucker-punched by art, and it is trying to catch up somehow.

QUEENLAND: It is not a tool. Maybe I misspoke. My camera is a tool. My computer is a tool. Photography itself is an idea. It is information.

WELLING: This intense condition of ambiguity is something that differentiates it from something like sculpture or art. Photography is ultimately this very ambiguous thing, and that's something I think all of you are participating in, in this condition of ambiguity.

QUEENLAND: I would say about asking this question—is photography art—why even ask the question? If photography truly does have the ability to still be so jarring, ambiguous and evasive, then why try to tie it down?

COTTON: It is a type of gentrification. Does photography really have to gentrify itself? Institutionally, we face that all the time. One of the big decisions when I came here to LACMA was am I going to try and battle for that corridor that leads to the toilet, which could be the history of photography? Or, am I just going to say, "No, we're going to do incendiary, explosive things in the main exhibition program, and in the auditorium, and have these debates around the fact that photography's pluralism is something that should not be contained"?

WHAT ARE SOME OF YOUR OBJECTIVES AS A PHOTO EDUCATOR AND IN WHAT WAYS HAVE THEY CHANGED IN RECENT YEARS?

The first and most important is to articulate my love and understanding of photography as clearly as I can to my students. Recently, the purity of this ambition has been blurred by the evolution, and ever-expanding success, of a gallery system that seems determined to expose young photographers well before most of them have had a real chance to develop their work beyond the limits of their M.F.A. thesis portfolios. But, fortunately for me, the students themselves seem happy to take what they can from where they can, whether it's my perceptions about the great past of photography, or the seeming-promise and blandishments of the ever-seductive art world.

WHAT ARE SOME OF THE CURRENT TOPICS AMONG YOU AND YOUR STUDENTS?

Hmmmm. From my point of view, the major topic is why don't more young photographers take on the world around them as a subject, particularly when that world is so obviously fraught with pain and deep confusion. Our country is at war, and poised at the beginning of what could be a long, and possibly terrifying, slide into relative inconsequence, and yet young artists and photographers today are, in general, content to study themselves in a mirror.

In answer, they seem to say that it's simply too difficult now to be out in the street (or in the city, or on the road) with the aim of photographing it, and that all they really know is the color-saturated, self-regarding world of television and the personal media that so effortlessly connects them together. They're correct, of course. But that shouldn't exclude an effort to break out and away from what, in general, are little more than solipsistic concerns. As Robert Frost said: "The best way out is always through."

WHAT DO YOU SEE AS BEING IN STORE FOR THE MEDIUM?

I'm not particularly sanguine about it all: après Photoshop, le deluge. At the very least, photography as an independent creative medium will be remembered—or, more likely, casually dismissed—as a quaint niche-practice of the past. Art, art-process, and artists will have finally absorbed it utterly: if any photograph can be anything at all (given the ability of digital manipulation to make it so), what logical relation will such a picture bear to those produced within the severe and limited practice of classic, "conventional" photography? What an end, Photography finally Art!

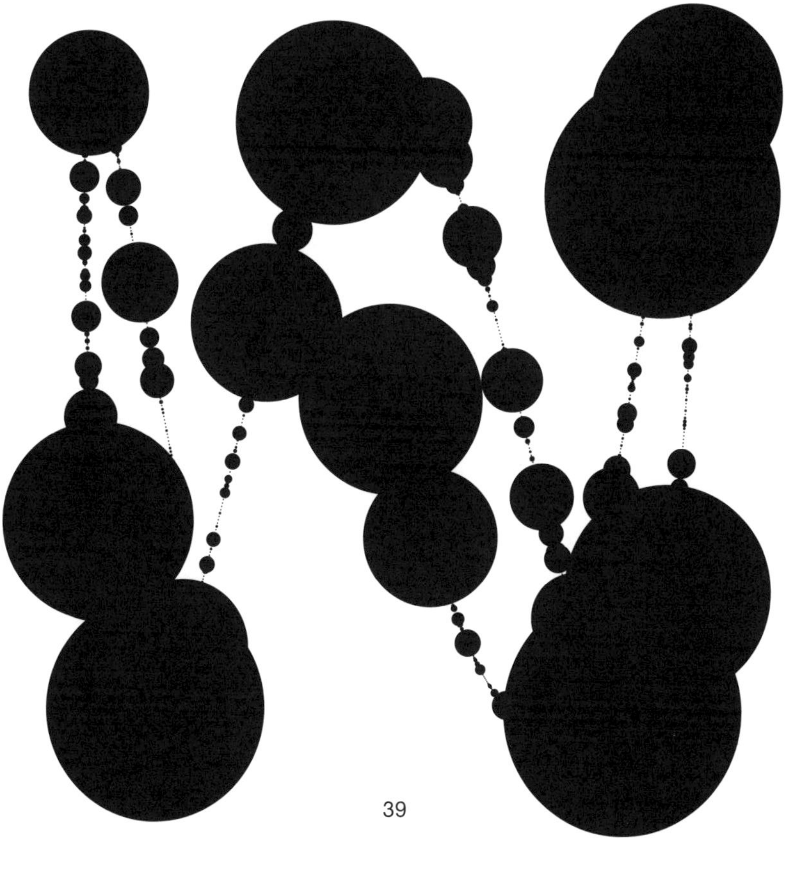

Online Photographic Thinking

JASON EVANS

Photography travels. Photographic images customarily appear on coffee mugs, t-shirts, and front pages, and this capacity to roam continues to be one of the defining characteristics of our slippery medium. This essay addresses the context of the Web for photography. It's a new frontier that, from the standpoint of an independent practitioner, doesn't seem to have fulfilled its potential, given photography's phenomenal recent expansion as a contemporary art form, as well as its over 150-year-old track record for multiple expansions. Thus far, I am underwhelmed by photography's presence online and the lack of innovative explorations of the new medium. I want to ruminate on why that might be—on what conditions might have led to an underwhelming response by serious and independent photographers to the potential of the Internet.

First, let me contextualize myself. I am a 39-year-old photographer/educator living an hour from London. My own work, I like to think, is experimental and often takes photography as its subject. I have regularly operated in the editorial, fashion, and music industries. I studied fine art in the late 1980s, when computers were just finding their way onto campus. In those days, my idea of innovation was Brian Eno's wonderfully plodding "Mistaken Memories of Medieval Manhattan" (1981), in which the monitor, at that time almost solely linked to a televisual experience, was turned on its side to accommodate an image generated by a camera in equivalent condition.

This anachronism may seem simplistic by contemporary standards, but it proposed an important dialogue with the imposed system of image reception, a subtle "détournement" that informed my own engagement with media systems, both in integral and formal ways.

My own work, which had previously consisted largely of self-obsessed street photography, made the hop from the page to the screen in 2001. As a big budget flaneur for British Telecom, I filed daily image and text reports as I drifted through pedestrian precincts. I shot on film, mailing handwritten notes to a Web designer in Soho. In 2002, the cosmetics giant Shiseido commissioned "Beauty Where You Find It," a two-month circumnavigation with a remit to photograph things I found beautiful. This developed my antenna for idiosyncratic fancies, from a knitted bicycle cover in Myanmar to the retro-utopias of Brasilia and Chandigarh. For this project, I worked with a Sony Cyber-shot (still my favorite capture palette) and a laptop from which I emailed images to the Paris La Beauté gallery for immediate display, as well as to be uploaded to their website constructed for this purpose.

The following year manifested a similar process for Nick Knight's SHOWstudio in a project called "New World," made on a camping trip through New Zealand. By then the technology fit in my pocket, as a clunky camera phone that afforded me freedom from cyber-café negotiations. The tool of delivery had changed radically in three years, with a particular emphasis on reduced cost and size along with increased speed. The new technologies gave me license and encouraged me to deliberate less about whether or not to actually take a picture. Liberated from the worry that the film in my camera would run out just as I stumbled across the best observation of the day, and from the fear of "wasting" valuable film in the process of experimentation, I developed a confidence and a flippancy that allowed me to take new sorts of pictures and not be too precious about my practice.

However, I'm conscious of the contradictory ways in which I've responded to digital photography. For some projects, I've become slower and I take fewer pictures. I launched TheDailyNice.com in October 2004. The project has channeled a few personal anxieties towards catharsis. I show one picture at a time, uploaded at bedtime. There's no archive of previous days' images; when it's gone, it's gone. At a point in photographic history where commodification offers new challenges to practitioners, I wanted to kill my darlings one by one, which has been a cause of anxiety for many viewers. The images are always of something that was its own reward and that made me happy at the moment when I found it. Real beauty is not about perpetuity. It seems that there are a few people out there (34,000 visits per month in the winter months and 32,500 in the summer) who enjoy a website that is dedicated to a happy moment in each day. It's a good news page, and by harnessing the ephemeral aspects of photography, I now come across more "nices" than I can show. In a society that discourages such behavior, I have owned and shared my happiness.

Without the World Wide Web, I could not make such a project happen. The site has generated an international audience and dialogue. (Visitors respond with everything from haiku to rambling essays on aesthetics.) The other great advantage of this Internet-based project is the ratio between the numbers of visitors and my own expenditure in launching and maintaining the site. Magazine, book, or gallery projects just can't compete on this level. There is the quality versus quantity debate, but I like to think that I have that down, too. I've reached the biggest audience of my life with no content compromise and an entirely affordable process. There is no coffee table book in the pipeline, for which I am glad. Contemporary collectors seem only to discuss what they own, rarely the content. My work is no longer hemmed in by the deadening, hyper-accelerated capitalist objectification of magazine advertising as in my editorial days. I feel free.

Creating TheDailyNice site has encouraged me to think about other applications of my pictures online. I'm making book-type projects now that paper publishing has a different imperative. Like many photographers in the mid-1990s, I was sucked into a sense of inadequacy from not having a monograph by the time I was thirty. In the early 2000s, I started talking to publishers and hearing what a hard time they were having; stories of editions of a thousand barely shifting half the print run. In 2007, I launched TheNewScent.com, and it had 3,700 visitors in its first month. If an audience is what you prefer (as opposed to a physical thing like a book or a show as the testimony to your photographic talent), then the Internet is for you. How the perceived populism and the lack of exclusivity of my online presence places me in relation to, say, the gallery system has yet to be determined.

In the inevitable and frankly tedious digital versus analog debate, my position is one of either/and. Both systems offer distinct possibilities, but I ultimately believe that they are just different sides of the same coin. Photography's comparatively brief history is littered with mechanical revelations and methodological revolution. I see the digital as nothing more than the most recent of these. Those who whine about the demise of Kodachrome rarely bemoan the lack of popularity or common usage of the cyanotype. Those fuzzy thinkers seldom make the connection between a beloved aesthetic and the motivations of the corporation that created it. We are not having our choices taken away from us by the usurping of analog by digital; we just have to expand what photography can be.

Changes in "capture" characteristics, particularly the preview screen, have had an essential impact. In the "good old days," when we shot in the dark with intuitive reliance on a sense of skill, a serendipitous selection of "happy accidents" informed the development of the medium. With the preview screen, we are more likely to delete immediately anything that doesn't look like a picture we formally recognize—that is, photography that looks like photography as we used to know it. I'm an advocate for not pressing the delete button too readily—for leaving the (analog-born) door open for finding a new direction or cause for thought in your photography through retrospective editing.

Many of us come from a position of having learned to create photography with analog tools and outcomes. An interesting thing about the digital is that it does us good (mentally, anyway) to sometimes put aside the seductive "thing-ness" of photography (the crumpled papers, the hassles of framing and hanging) and engage directly with the image. I'm not saying, of course, that online/digital photography doesn't have form, or that there aren't already stylistic conventions emerging on the Web, but rather that the issues of form and aesthetics that are rightly heavy or serious ones for a photographer working in print form become lightened and are less the focus of my creative energy when thinking "WWW." When making work, we usually operate from a tangible experience that still seems to matter like hell when that same work becomes intangible. These are good buttons for us photographers to press.

In the recent scramble to establish the new cultural frontier that is "contemporary art photography," there has been a shift away from defunct ideas about visual "democracy," wide circulation of the "image," and the re-establishment of the photograph as object. Art market credo limits many of the defining characteristics of the photographic medium, simultaneously rendering "serious" work less likely to reveal itself with any real intent in the populist and, dammit, free realm of the Internet. The prospect of all of those uncalibrated monitors is going to be a turn-off for any photographer who has labored with specific tools and palettes to produce particular effects. Compare the "image" impact of a Gabriel Orozco to the "picture" production values of a Gregory Crewdson, and ponder which translates better to the Internet.

I know that this means that the Internet is not the place for everyone's photography. But editorial photographers are a pragmatic group of people and, taking cues from photography's analog past, we have learned stoicism when dealing with the reproduction quality of our work in books and magazines. The same quality won't be delivered by 35-mm film as an 8 by 10 view camera, but it delivers nevertheless. The argument that photographic imagery doesn't "work" on screen need only be directed to how well the Web's fleshly offerings serve their clients. There were 260 million porn websites last year, which implies that certain images can and do work rather well on the Net.

I've found myself shifting some of my browsing from the library to the Web, getting lost and found in digitized photography. At its most satisfying, I stumble across both intentionally and unintentionally brilliant photographs and ideas. The way Internet search engines work will always be a mystery to me, but I trust that they are like libraries with well-reasoned taxonomies and filing systems that I feel an obligation to subvert. Just like a library shelf organized along the lines of book height or accession date, the brilliant coincidences of what sits next to what on a Google search is food for my imagination. To round up these thoughts on Web-based photography, I want to describe some of the projects that inform and brighten my experience of photography on the Web.

I've never been very interested in qualitative judgments brought to bear on photographs; all photographs can work given the right context. A good example of this and of "bad" digital photography would be http://www.usefulphotography.com, which culls images from eBay—where sellers have attempted, with varying degrees of success, to illustrate their wares. These are pictures you will not be finding at a swap meet in twenty years' time.

For lovers of the vernacular, Squareamerica.com is a gift. This humanely curated collection of "found" images overshadows recent paper publications on similar themes. It gives real insights into the collection, and the sense of humor that resonates through the selections is unique. The site's warm-hearted lightness of touch is a terrific pick-me-up.

During my cruise of Flickr, the online photographic social site, I came across the postings of Zimbaman. His collection is made up of vernacular images of fit and handsome young men, which have a contemporary homoerotic charge when seen en masse. Viewed in another way, this collection could be seen as a glimpse into the nature of masculine stereotyping in Israel; some of the photographs show young men in army training or posing in situations where flags and images of war machines are displayed. Others offer intimate bathroom posturing and poolside horseplay in which a besieged secular national identity apes a more liberal, relaxed lifestyle. Either way, the collection offers the fascinating and poignant prospect of a vernacular form that could be seen as an accidental version of the highly intentional speculations of Collier Schorr.

It might not be currently fashionable to make the kind of street pictures that you can see at In-public.com, with their dependence on mid-twentieth-century photographic standbys like timing, luck, and loitering. However, it's great to have a site that makes such a good bid at convincing us that the genre is alive and well, rather than threatened by institutional paranoia about uncontrolled imaging and its potential destinations at a time when nearly everybody has a camera on his or her phone.

Also poignant is the site of a talented but reticent, recently graduated young photographer Kevin Beck. Unlikely to rise through existing channels of photography promotion anytime soon due to a lack of ambition rather than talent (sometimes the art system supports those who are good at networking and form-filling) is http://www.kevinbeckphotography.com. This Web format offers critical closure in what is otherwise an unstoppable stream of image production.

For me, Tim Barber's refreshing labor of love, http://www.Tinyvices.com, beats all other photography sites hands down. The volume, quality, and diversity of this altruistic selection is staggering and it offers an "intimate" view of a range of work that one simply would not be able to access otherwise. The organic parameters defined by Barber's unswerving and kindly instinct shift and accommodate notions of photographic pluralism that would be hard to find elsewhere. His own blog is interspersed with images of and by (becoming) famous friends as well as the awesome "submissions" gallery and a huge collection of submitted folios of work, with contact details. Barber draws no income beyond occasional sales and hosts no advertising on this site, which lends a refreshingly un-corporate, DIY air to the proceedings. (He does, however, have plans to use the site as a springboard to publishing artists' books.)

I'm not arguing that the Internet should be considered as the only new frontier for serious and independent photography, any more than I subscribe to the anxiety that I need to choose between digital and analog photographic capture and output. Instead, I believe that complementary versions of photographic thinking can be played out at this interesting moment in the medium's history and that it's time for any photographer with public, discursive ambitions to shape our online context.

Imagine if the Internet had emerged in the early twentieth century. The majority of those "-ists" would have had a field day—imagine Andy Warhol and the Internet. I guess it is simply a matter of time before a generation not weaned on paper and chemicals sees the manufactured bubble of "art photography" for what it is, and begins to explore the potential of an inclusive, affordable distribution network and its inherently interesting formal qualities for presentation and distribution.

--

DISCUSSION FORUM
WWW.WORDSWITHOUTPICTURES.ORG

--

Subject: Not Yet
Date: 3 January 2008 14:37:52
From: AMIR ZAKI

I interpret Mr. Evans's essay to be expressing his frustration that more "serious and independent photographers" are not making more interesting work for the Internet as an alternative to gallery and museum installations. Why is this the case? Why haven't they? Why not?*

Well, one somewhat boring reason may be because it is just not time yet. These sorts of things seem to happen organically and with a sense of critical urgency—I'll even say necessity—not wishful thinking or desire. My interpretation is that, despite the imperfections within the "art world proper" (the gallery and the market), it

is nonetheless a finite forum that has some sort of system of checks and balances, problematic as they may be. There is an evolving structure in place. Artists that choose to participate within
ing its faults and potential
doing so because of a shared
f a language, a history, and
ing contemporary art dialog
hibitions, critics, journals,
tc. For me, as one of these
s, the potential for failure
important as aspects of criti-
support. In short, there is

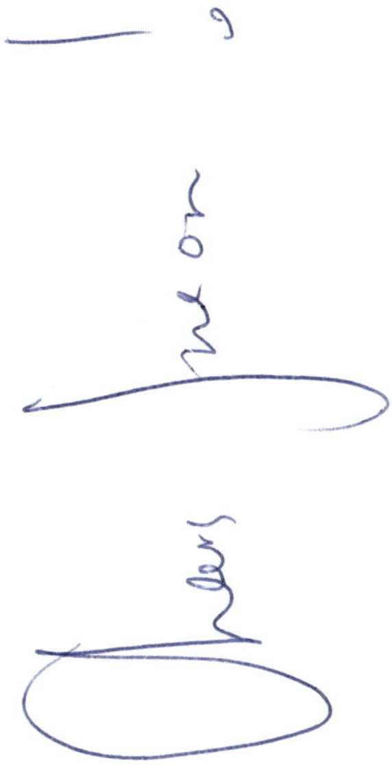

made for the Internet, there
. There is no such system or
s, there is no such potential
. If no one "hits" your web-
ly one who knows or cares. If
ross the site and wishes to
sort of critical response,
of blogs and comments, which
t this point. (I think "OMG"
ly the most popular responses
online.) There is very little
it's very safe. And, as
is free. It is democratic.
vinced that democracy, in
it, is a system that is best
of cultural production. In
st a democratic art world if I
ke it seriously.

omparison, please imagine that instead of art, we consider the field of philosophy, a relatively parallel mode of creative cultural production. There are contemporary philosophers, mostly academics, who participate within a rich history of rigorous dialog and debate in the world of ideas. Most of the time peers in academic journals and books review their work. It is scrutinized, torn apart, refuted, dismantled, challenged, praised, and expanded upon. There is a community and structure in place. And, if it is like many other fields of study or inquiry, it is not perfect. There is probably nepotism, feuding camps, some injustice, etc. Despite these ills (like a close family with its own problems and difficult relationships) organized groups function better than nomads. Certainly, there must be some independent philosophers philosophizing online without any of these constraints, right? I'm sure some of the content is also incredibly rigorous and interesting. However, at this point, there isn't nearly as much of this serious work happening as there is nonsense and "philosophy-lite" ranting or opining.

Similarly, within the realm of contemporary art, I think there is some incredibly engaging and serious work that has a final destination on the Web. However, at this point, there are infinitely more examples of terrible and uninteresting, albeit VERY popular, imagery floating in cyberspace. The majority of Myspace.com is but one example. Countless videos of people doing "face-plants" on YouTube.com or Break.com are certainly entertaining if one is in the mood to comfortably revel in the low resolution, excruciating pain of others, but it isn't good art, no matter how many thousands of "hits" these sites get. When considering the benefit of having a potentially much larger audience online than in the gallery or museum venue, Mr. Evans states, "If an audience is what you prefer (as opposed to a physical thing like a book or a show as the testimony to your photographic talent), then the Internet is for you." With this logic, one could stand on a freeway overpass holding up a large photograph during rush hour and could have an incredibly large audience. But what does that mean? Personally, it means more to me to have 10 people intentionally spend 20 minutes each seriously engaging with my photographic installations in actual space than it does to know that 100 people happened upon my website, half of whom got there by accident when Googling their favorite guitar virtuoso who happens to share my name, and spent five seconds or less before they were on to yet another adventure.

I understand that the potential that Mr. Evans

describes for much more interesting work to exist on the Web is there. I happily welcome these expansions of the medium, both formally and conceptually. However, we have many historical examples of artists who begin by working outside of the fuzzy boundaries of what is then accepted as art. Their ultimate success is not so much in forcing (or even caring about) a dramatic alteration in the existing structure, it's in the structure's ability to slowly grow, adapt and absorb that work within its boundaries. Mr. Evans invokes Andy Warhol as a pioneer, which he certainly was. (One could easily replace Warhol with Marcel Duchamp or several others in this example.) However, the reason Warhol's radicalism took hold is because it was time for it to do so. Had he made the same work 50, 15 or even 5 years earlier, there is no guarantee that the response would have been as strong. All the wishful thinking and desire one can muster won't make a difference.

I suspect that Mr. Evans is foreshadowing in some way an inevitable evolution in contemporary artistic production and public reception. I suspect that the art world, sort of like the commercial music industry already has done with some success, will eventually incorporate more art that exists as digital information in addition to discrete objects. As with the music industry, it will happen when it absolutely has to, when all parties and the technology are ready. It will be later than its pioneering participants wish, and I bet it won't be free.

* "Why Not" was the working draft title of Mr. Evans's essay.

--

Subject: The Buck Does Not Stop Here
Date: 7 January 2008 01:21:32
From: NICHOLAS GRIDER

It seems that the nervousness that underlies both Evans's original essay and Zaki's response is not ultimately one of the quality, seriousness, or ontology of photographs circulating on the Internet, but the equally serious question of how to profit from it. Digital technology has reached a state of expansion and the contemporary art market has reached such a state of attenuation that, for an unknown artist like myself, the Internet offers a paradox: it's easier for me to distribute work on the Internet than it is for me to print it, assuming that I actually have a reason to do so.

Or, put in a better way, the focus of the photograph on the Internet is not on the photographer, but on the image and the context, which is both immediate and less direct. This is almost completely the opposite of the art world proper, which operates by marketing artists, not their work (which is more or less a loss-leader for investment in an artist's career). This is why online distribution models for photographs will never replace or subsume the current art market; there's no way to control where a faceless and unknown audience is supposed to look, and what names it is to remember.

What the Internet is very good at is information. A site not mentioned by Evans but one I check at least once a day is iheartphotograph.blogspot.com. Don't let the title fool you. It's a serious endeavor to promote photography worldwide, and while there's a definite post-market lack of care for whether the photographer is an art student in Ohio or a food designer from France, the site (for me, at least) acts as Flickr with a critical intelligence.

For someone like myself, coming of age without preference for analog or digital and, like many people my age, without access to an increasingly shuttered art world, what the Internet offers is not a utopia but something even better: an overwhelming amount of undifferentiated information. What the impersonality of the Internet offers is that I can at least get the feeling, at times, of having some measure of agency over where to look and how to work.

--

Subject: __________
Date: 28 January 2008 04:30:55
From: DAVID CAMPANY

A wonderful essay, Jason.

One observation. Current photography publishing tends toward serial repetition; look at the first three pages of most contemporary photo books and you know what the next 60 are going to be. It's connected to the fact that most (but not all) gallerists and curators want this from photography/ photographers. They trust repetition, since it's the easiest way to "look like you mean it," and it takes the anxiety out of confronting the radical plurality of the medium and what's possible with it.

If I were generous, I'd say that the kinds of websites you are drawn to represent the opposite of this—images loaded up on a case-by-case basis with no apparent agenda other than curiosity about the medium and its subject matters. I'm sympathetic to this. But, speaking from my own viewing experience here, I feel these sites lead to their own kind of repetition, a kind of auto-leveling of experience in which the un-hierarchical display of heterogeneous photos can lead to a new kind of homogeneity. Perhaps the immaterial form of the Internet screen has found a perfect photographic analogy in the stream of interesting but replaceable photos that tend to erase the preceding ones as they materialize with a mouse's click and vanish with the next. Is photography on the Net able to reflect on this condition?

I don't know the answer, but I sense there's a problem.

--

Subject: __________
Date: 29 January 2008 20:26:03
From: DAVID WEINER

DAVID: Thanks for the response. It neatly sums up what I've been thinking about this as well, and since I've been incapable of neatly summing up what I've been thinking, it allows me to jump in anyway.

What I think is interesting about this sort of dichotomy (images in a series/images with less obvious connections) is what I think is also interesting about Jason Evans's original essay: context. While Evans goes to some effort to contextualize himself in the opening of the essay and provides some context for the sites he links to, the sites themselves go pretty far to decontextualize the images they present, both in terms of what comes before and after them and in the more basic context of the production. Of course, Google is always there to apply some context. Without much effort I can go from the temporality of TheDailyNice to Evans's portfolio site and make a connection from there to "this guy also shot Radiohead," and from there all kinds of context can be added in. The "risk" of this is that Jason Evans no longer really controls the context and I'm free to make all kinds of associations that may or may not be productive to appreciating his work. But then how different is that from real life?

Well, I think it's pretty different in some important ways and the difference is unfortunately a bit of a high/low argument that I'm not very comfortable with, but I'll make it anyway. I see the Web as more of a mass medium, most similar to television, and it has a way of erasing value difference that is quite televisual. This can be good for all kinds of things where the vacuum of critical dialog is an advantage, but it can be difficult to evaluate art in that kind of a vacuum. I think commercial photography has taken great advantage of the ability to establish its own context and drive its own meaning, and at least superficially what I see on the Web as the most popular photography projects are ones that adhere most closely to the commercial paradigm of decontextualized imagery.

The type of decontextualized imagery I'm thinking of here is not the same as non-serial imagery, though. Personally, I'm a strong believer in working against serialized imagery, but to sustain a work of non-serial, non-narrative images takes far more effort on the part of the artist and the viewer. I think this type of work requires a contextualization, and benefits from both a historical perspective and a sustained look. The stats that Jason Evans presents are as good an illustration of this as any. He cites ~34,000 monthly visits, but doesn't mention the more pertinent stat of duration. What his site and many sites based on photography offer is the ability to take a look at an image and move on. In fact that's all that TheDailyNice offers; in that respect it's a perfect vehicle for that type of image consumption.

So, for me, the question becomes whether or not the type of viewing that the Web can sustain is compatible to the type of viewing that I associate with non-commercial photography. At least for right now, I'm thinking that there's no context online for a sustained look.

--

Subject: Re: New Photographic Thinking
Date: 31 January 2008 03:21:18
From: LESTER PLEASANT

Photography changes and evolves whether or not we like it or choose to recognize it. We can hold on to rusty models of thinking about images and disregard the fluid present reality if we want, but the photographic is constantly moving and changing regardless of which theories and ideas we subscribe to. Isn't it inevitable that the theory will always be several steps out of sync with the current possibilities the practice offers at any given moment anyway?

This reminds me of the previous essay on this website, in which Bedford suggests that photography critics have failed to comprehensively address the medium and how this situation has limited the discourse and therefore the possibilities of the medium itself. It makes me wonder, if they can't do it, who can? If the allegedly most educated and "aware" critics, curators, and historians are unable to fully comprehend how photography functioned yesterday, why should we believe they will be able to do it tomorrow? (Luckily, there are plenty of critics, curators, and historians who have done an incredible job of taking on the challenge.) As practitioners, we can either wait around for someone else to write history for us or we can be active participants in its evolution now.

This leads me to believe that practitioners today have a responsibility to be aware of these shifts and new possibilities as much as possible in order to define their own positions and come to their own conclusions. Unfortunately, in our ever-accelerating situation, it's going to be much easier to see what we want rather than what is actually happening—especially if the reality threatens to contradict or undermine the foundations of our ideas. So it will be a challenge and there will be growing pains. Maybe this is why it might have to wait for a generation that is free from our peculiar baggage to truly open the doors wide and walk on through instead of nervously peering though the keyhole into the darkness beyond. Will it be similar to the moment when the conceptual-artists-using-photography of the '60s and '70s—who had little interest in or allegiance to the conventions of the photo world at the time—proceeded to bend and re-write the rules of what was possible with photography in the process?

Ultimately, we create our own reality and set our own rules and limitations, even if that reality is simply settling for the default modes that have been handed down to us unquestioned from the academy and our cultural institutions. (And you don't have to get an MFA to inherit default perspectives, BTW.) Many of these same institutions have admitted that they are struggling themselves to maintain a position of relevance in the current situation. So maybe it's a case of the blind leading the blind . . .

In any case, I don't think we should dismiss Jason's call to arms lightly. We have a window to new realities before us, and the question of what form the photographic possibilities of the Web will consist of will be answered by our own actions. The time could be now, if we choose to embrace it. But we might have to risk venturing beyond the known.

--

Subject: other online thinking
Date: 31 January 2008 14:26:19
From: PENELOPE UMBRICO

The Internet presents a complicated relationship to what I think of as "photographic." For me, there is an analogous experience in viewing something through my computer window and viewing something through a camera viewfinder, while there is a kind of dialectical inversion in the position of the photographer and Web surfer. The photographer moves about, gathering information and making it available to others, whereas the position of the gathering Web surfer, for whom information moves through the field of screen-based computer vision, is static. But both practices provide access to other realities; both allow us to offer up our ideas and images; both make the local global, and the global local; both foster a pseudo-intimacy of sharing private aspects of life; and both work by remote tactile control mediated by machine. And, most interesting to me, both function as an indexical record of our culture (of what we think, and of our concerns). Since all these aspects of the Web are created and managed by us, the myriad visual representations there become a visual index of ourselves—a constantly shifting auto-portrait.

In the context of this glut of imagery everywhere, the post production practice of pulling together sets of pre-authored images and information is as much an act of creation as making the images oneself.

I view the characteristics inherent in all photography—appropriation, and by extension questioning authorship; multiple production, and by extension questioning uniqueness and individuality; mediation, and by extension questioning perception and truth; decontextualization; fragmentation; ubiquitous dissemination; and the loss of aura—to have extended into the very essence of the Web.

So to speak in terms of the potential of the Web to circulate photography, for me, is only a tiny part of the equation. Assuming Net neutrality continues, the concepts of open source and free distribution become valuable in their own right, and I'd like to think, somewhat revolutionary. The idea of exchange and engagement with the platform itself (creating work on, with, and for this platform) is where the interesting space on the Internet is for me, with regard to photography. I am inspired by the many artists' projects on the Web that use the Web and its technology to produce the work. My favorite websites are the ones that support these projects (Rhizome.org, Turbulence.org, and Ars Virtual on Second Life, to name a few). By addressing the shifts in meaning that result from the shifts in content and context inherent on the Web, artists are finding agency by utilizing the potential of the Internet as a tool for making, as well as circulating.

QUESTIONNAIRE / FIA BACKSTRÖM

DO YOU ENJOY LOOKING AT PHOTOGRAPHS ONLINE?

I almost only look at photography online, although I enjoy very much real, physical prints. I think the online experience obviously is the most prevalent these days, and contributes to the distributability and shape-shifting appearance of photography.

WHAT FACTORS DETERMINE THE VALUE OF A PHOTOGRAPH TO YOU?

Its news value. I am very interested in photo journalism. But mostly its use-value, how I could re-use the image, or what kind of generation of ideas it could be part of. What kind of cultural production could I move it to from where it originally occurred?

QUESTIONNAIRE / TODD HIDO

DO YOU ENJOY LOOKING AT PHOTOGRAPHS ONLINE?

Yes, very much so. I see hundreds of photographs a day online. You cannot ever beat the ease of how things are just out there for viewing. However, there is nothing like a really great print on a wall. The right image presented the right way can literally hold a room.

I feel it is important to see that all these spaces in which we view photographs—the Web, the book, and the wall—are all really different; not every image works well in all the spaces. I think it is harder to make things for the wall. In my own practice as an artist I will always use the wall as a benchmark for whether an image works or not.

WHAT WOULD YOU CONSIDER SOME OF THE MOST IMPORTANT CHANGES THAT PHOTOGRAPHY HAS UNDERGONE IN THE LAST FEW YEARS?

I feel the most important positive change in the

medium is that it is now possible for almost anyone to distribute photographs to a worldwide audience, in some cases in moments. That is the biggest and best change that has happened.

WHAT DO YOU SEE AS BEING IN STORE FOR THE MEDIUM?

Great things. Lot of things. The fact that anyone can post anything or get a book printed on demand is fantastic. But with more things being produced there will be many, many more not so good things being made as well.
I feel it is harder to wade through all the sites and blogs that are being produced. We'll see how it all shakes out in a few years. I think the cream will still rise to the top.

QUESTIONNAIRE / PAUL GRAHAM

WHAT WOULD YOU CONSIDER SOME OF THE MOST IMPORTANT CHANGES THAT PHOTOGRAPHY HAS UNDERGONE IN THE LAST FEW YEARS?

If you are talking about the art of photography, it is the recognition of the medium by the art world. This is a great thing, but has been somewhat partial, confused, and off-target on occasion. It has skewed the field a lot, but will hopefully work itself out in time, as people come to understand the core qualities of this medium, instead of trying to see what it does only in the familiar terms of other traditional art forms.

QUESTIONNAIRE / JAMES WELLING

WHAT ARE SOME OF YOUR OBJECTIVES AS A PHOTO EDUCATOR AND IN WHAT WAYS HAVE THEY CHANGED IN RECENT YEARS?

I don't have any objectives as a photo educator apart from getting through the eight hours of my class and stimulating my students to think "in the moment."

Incidentally, I teach art classes (as I am

right now) as well as photo classes and most of my students are not doing photography. I've been bringing in a lot of visitors to class (Joyce Campbell, Kristen Calabrese, Mark Owens, Warren Neidich, Mark Allen of Machine Project) to stimulate discussion and new ways of working.

WHAT ARE SOME OF THE MOST NOTABLE WAYS DIGITAL TECHNOLOGIES HAVE CHANGED YOUR PRACTICE?

I have spent an inordinate amount of time not making work and futzing with all things digital.

WHAT WOULD YOU CONSIDER SOME OF THE MOST IMPORTANT CHANGES THAT PHOTOGRAPHY HAS UNDERGONE IN THE LAST FEW YEARS?

Historical amnesia has grown rampant.

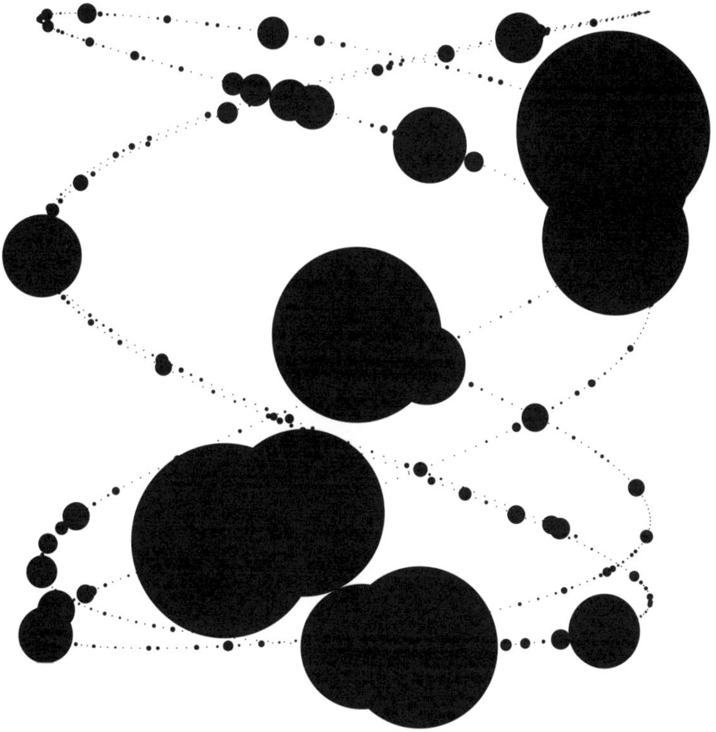

foRm

KEVIN MOORE

Interest in form is everywhere in photography these days, but the word itself remains little used, if not consciously avoided. Form and its institutional counterpart, Formalism, are so out of date as terms that their very mention conjures images of moldy painting surveys from the 1950s. Yet what other terms do we have to describe the phenomenon that's happening in current art photography, in which "photographers" seem to be exploring the basis of the medium through photograms and smoke-and-mirror abstractions? Meanwhile, some non-abstract photographers have admitted lately to being interested in—in their own words—"formal beauty."

It's all very old-fashioned sounding, at least to old-timers and art historians. One has to ask if these contemporary artists (who are artists, not "just" photographers) do not know about Alvin Langdon Coburn, László Moholy-Nagy, or Aaron Siskind. Surely, they must. Or maybe they don't. In a certain sense, it doesn't really matter, because what is happening is something that does not adhere precisely to the avant-garde model of continuous innovation. Nor can we presume a narrow track of influence, with photographers responding to photographers and building upon a canon of established approaches, techniques, and ideas in a linear fashion. That system fractured long ago (though it remains surprisingly intact in some places, particularly in museums). There's something curious to me in the timing of the death of such Modernist ideas, which I associate with the death of former MoMA curator John Szarkowski last year, and the rise of interest in Modernist forms. You wouldn't want to call it a revival, because the contemporary artists conjuring new life from the ashes are smarter than that. But there might be just a hint of nostalgia in the impulse, a yearning or admiration for a vision of the world as a whole and purposeful place. That, at least, is part of the reference: a use of form to invoke the Modernist era.

Form, it seems to me, is now being incorporated into art-making as an element, a referent, a token of past histories and practices. Form is being spoken again as a language, though that's a bit like saying that modern Italians speak Latin—which isn't to say that they speak it badly, but that they speak it differently and use it to talk about more contemporary issues. The current form-patois is infused with Conceptualist ideas. Indeed, it might be more accurate to say that artists are using the language of Conceptual Art, as has been the reigning practice for years, but peppering their speech with "form words." "Hey, hand me the silver salts, I need a little Christian Schad here." Would it be fair to say that form seems cool and rich as an idea and practice to artists, whereas to scholars and critics it invokes a completely outmoded way of thinking about art—one that smacks of universal mysticism and a lack of politics, and thus threatens the hard-won rigor of contemporary art criticism and history? There seems to be both a taboo against the "F-word" and a lack of other terms with which to adequately describe what one is seeing in art-making these days—a pair of conditions that are equally hobbling in terms of our ability to assess much of contemporary art, not just that which is photography-based.

While there's been some talk in recent years of "beauty," "concrete photography," and new forms of "objectivity," as well as other terms referring to "the visual," none of these has really gotten to the heart of the matter. Like the visual references that artists make, language has a nuanced history. If form, both visual and verbal, has historical underpinnings—meaning that certain forms and words gain certain currencies in certain eras and continue, more or less, to invoke those eras as their use continues and their meanings evolve—then to speak of form is, on some level, to speak of mid-twentieth-century art and criticism. Form is thus not only a general term for the dimensional character of something; it's also a reference to a historical aesthetic system, and I think that in light of the kind of work now being produced by artists such as Walead Beshty, Eileen Quinlan, Anthony Pearson, and many more, it is an accurate term. It's meaning, however, could be better understood. So what do we mean when we say "form"?

SOME GENERAL HISTORY

Formalism as a critical discourse arose some time after the comparable practice in painting. British art critics Roger Fry and Clive Bell began talking about form in the early decades of the twentieth century as a way to explain Impressionism and Postimpressionism, Paul Cézanne's work in particular. Impressionism, of course, was all about formal innovation (and about vision and social realism, too), so it might seem odd that a parallel vocabulary did not develop contemporaneously in art criticism. Discussions of form came only in the decades that followed, when the work itself was starting to look historical and formalism in linguistics had had a run in Russia. This brings me to my first point: form as a critical discourse and form as an artistic practice should be understood as being askew, like two neighborhoods that occupy the same town but sit on a fault line: you can look across to the other side and perhaps cross over by footbridge, but the streets don't line up.

The idea as it was established in art criticism was that form could speak on its own, that its role in painting was primary, and in the idea's purest renditions, that form was all that mattered, as opposed to recognizable content that conveyed a symbolic or social value associated with that content. This is the basis for abstract art, which enjoyed an end run in the U.S. during the middle part of the century, with Clement Greenberg as a sort of Howard Cosell in the press box. What is interesting here is that Greenberg's ideas, when he first started asserting them in the 1940s, were highly politicized in nature. Writing about Abstract Expressionist painting in *Partisan Review* in 1948, he drew an overt connection between art and politics, proclaiming: "The main premises of Western art have at last migrated to the United States, along with the center of gravity of industrial production and political power." Greenberg is better known for a more astringent line on painting, in which he talks not about politics but "self-criticism," "aesthetic consistency," and "intelligible continuity." This is Greenberg hitting his stride in 1960, in "Modernist Painting," in which he creates his own Mark Rothko painting in words, reducing all of painting to the "ineluctable flatness of the support." It seems curious that this kind of critical pronouncement would replace the other during the 1950s, a time of political and social unrest in the U.S., and one wonders whether (as some assert) McCarthyism and the Cold War changed both the way art was made and how it could be talked about in the United States. Formal abstraction and its subsequent criticism might in that sense be seen as a form of political escapism, emerging at a time when there was much to escape from—not just politics but also a consumerist malaise that many felt was descending on the country. To talk of art in formalist terms both steered away from strident politics and elevated the discussion above a landscape of mindless consumerism.

Even though Abstract Expressionist painting did not seem to be about anything more than painters emoting from some private psychic core, historians since have been quick to argue that the works were in fact highly political. Despite what various artists said about their own work and despite their evident obsession with formal ideas and processes, their work embodied not simply the essence of an individual artistic sensibility but Individualism with a capital "I"—a major American export. Just consider all the traveling exhibitions of these works, sent to countries such as Russia and France during the 1950s, with the intention of promoting ideas of American liberty, daring, and sophistication. My second point: although form-based work, especially abstraction, may seem politically detached, it generally is not.

SOME HISTORY OF PHOTOGRAPHY

Photography had a more problematic relationship with the terms of these arguments as formulated for painting, but that didn't stop anyone from adopting the approach, almost wholesale, to enduring effect. The problem for photography is that it is a literal medium, transcribing directly what is illuminated and passed through a lens. Related to the formal explorations occurring in painting from the first decade of the twentieth century onward, photography showed similar promise, particularly in the realm of abstraction. One could throw the camera out of focus, or shoot from unconventional angles or really close up, defamiliarizing the ostensible subject. Or one could dispense with the camera altogether and get into the chemistry, exploring the more primitive capabilities of the medium. Further still, cut the picture apart, collage it, montage it, draw on it, and re-photograph the results. Such transgressive experiments, made by Coburn and Schad in the teens, and Moholy-Nagy and Man Ray in the twenties, were, significantly, some of the most innovative practices in photography at that time. Yet were such practices "true" to photography—true to a medium that did things other mediums couldn't? You couldn't paint a Walker Evans photograph; well, you could, but it wouldn't be the same act of perspectival genius and social perspicacity. Long before Modernist thought in photography hit its stride in the 1960s (relatively late, to be sure), there was a separatist spirit afoot in the land, calling for a strict division of mediums—*différance*, to plunk the theoretical term onto it. In the U.S. in particular (the good-old, practical U.S.), the mandate for a documentary aesthetic in photography took hold, favoring a certain kind of form in photography, one that held the medium fast to its unique transparency, celebrating insightful arrangements of hats and hands but not, say, blobs and squiggles. In orthodox photographic circles (including many current museum photography departments), this attitude remains entrenched.

Despite fears expressed at the time of an increasingly mechanized and dehumanized modern world, experimental photography of the 1920s, which was where much of the formal vocabulary of modernism first developed, was actually quite individualistic and humanistic in its practice. The photograms of Moholy-Nagy, for example, had a machine cadence and aesthetic, which perfectly summoned the emerging industrial utopia, but they also contained much that was personal. In and of themselves, such images were acts of individual expression, pure gestures of formal experimentation, not so unlike expressionist paintings of the previous generation. Moreover, such images often contained traces of sentimental ephemera, such as images of Moholy-Nagy's wife Lucia, or of the artist's own hands, a motif that insisted on preserving the human-organic within the rational-mechanistic. For Man Ray, the photogram was used in an equally dichotomous fashion, observing on one level the Surrealist fascination with psychological revolution (and by extension, social/political revolution, another path toward another kind of utopia), while incorporating in the process the personal effects of an enviably complicated sex life.

By mid-century in the U.S., such explorations had to contend more directly with the force of abstract painting. Two conditions made abstraction a compelling yet compromised choice for art-photographers. Abstraction proclaimed a seriousness of purpose, one that dovetailed with serious ideas, both personal and aesthetic; psychic and formal investigations into the photographic medium were conducted side by side. Moreover, as with Abstract Expressionist painting (more so, in fact), the political climate in the U.S. made certain forms of social documentary photography a tough row to hoe, especially for the politically minded photographer working outside the sunny, lobotomized environment of the picture magazines. On the downside, the road to photographic abstraction was troubled by a parallel thoroughfare traveled by the painters. If the political climate and the potential of formalist aesthetics made abstraction compelling, the threat of being compared unfavorably to trends in painting—a copycat movement in a lesser medium, which is what Pictorialism had been called at the turn of the century—sullied the option.

Siskind struck out most boldly and made the most distinguished body of abstract photographs at a surprisingly early date, starting in the late 1940s—significantly predating similar looking paintings by his close friend Franz Kline. This direction is particularly surprising because Siskind had been a key member of the New York Photo League, an organization with strong leftist political convictions and a belief in photography as an agent of social change. The reasons for his radical shift have not yet been fully explored, but it is intriguing to note that Siskind's first abstract works appeared just as the League was being menaced by investigations from the McCarthy administration. The League was shut down in 1951, the same year Siskind exhibited a large-scale, abstract photograph with The Club, an artists' group comprising Kline, Willem de Kooning, and other young Abstract Expressionist painters, on 9th Street in New York. An abject image of bubbles and drips on an anonymous wall, *Gloucester 2* (1949), was the only photograph in the show.

A similar kind of evasion-within-progression may be seen in contemporaneous photographs by Minor White, a preacher of sorts for a certain form of revelatory photography (a Pollock to Siskind's Kline). Whereas Siskind seemed to be evading political persecution in his choice of abstraction, White revealed (and simultaneously guarded) a torrent of feelings, many of them sexual feelings for young men. Although White's rhetoric, appearing in numerous articles published in *Aperture* (a journal he helped to found and later edited), advocated a vision of photographic practice modeled on the meditative practices of Eastern religions (or Western notions of the same), White's personal diaries reveal a man tormented by his sexuality and driven to destruction by loneliness. It's hard to look at all those sequences, with their alternating views of crashing waves and embryonic male navels, without hearing the whimpers of the artist amid the cries of seagulls and the sound of one hand clapping.

Then there's the much chillier Frederick Sommer, a universalizing mentality attempting to fuse all the physical and philosophical systems of the world into palimpsests of forms and references, and often breaking with the notion of media purity in the process. For Sommer, a fastidious encyclopedist and philosopher by nature, this sort of approach represented an audacious attempt to register all of human knowledge on so many sheets of photographic paper. Third point: historically, abstraction in modernist photography embodies many purposes and meanings, even within a single image, but generally speaking these works are driven by the elevated twin goals of progress—for both society and the photographic medium—and the heroic artist-individual, seen as a pioneer of such progress.

Such ideas had run their course by the end of the 1960s, but they may still be glimpsed in the embers of works by Robert Heinecken, one of the most important and undervalued photographers of the second half of the twentieth century. Radically experimental and politically irreverent, Heinecken managed to adopt (and even advance) many of the familiar tropes of photographic abstraction. However, he applied this language to aspects of contemporary life such as politics, consumerism, human sexuality, and the media's role in shaping these discourses. In Heinecken, we find a sensibility similar to—though not exactly the same as—ours today, in which abstraction mediates a personal and political point of view but does so through a deconstructive process. Rather than conjuring a veiled world, Heinecken scrambled the existing one, flushing out insights by a different tack.

SOME THOUGHTS ON THE HISTORY OF PHOTOGRAPHY'S RELEVANCE TO CURRENT ART PRACTICE AND INTERPRETATION

Now, as the modernist principles that shaped the history of photography as an academic discipline fade away, that history finds itself in the position of having to justify its relevance to contemporary art. This is not an altogether bad thing. I think of photography as the preeminent modern medium, one that still deserves a more central role in the history of modern art; it should be integrated. For all the good it did in elevating photography to a distinct art form with its own history, modernist thought did so at a cost. By isolating the medium in order to define both its unique character and its particular historical development, many of the most fruitful and provocative passages in the medium's history, both distant and recent, have been overlooked or swept aside—or, more optimistically, are waiting to be written as the hegemony of the documentary tradition is challenged by interest in other aspects of photography's history.

Today people talk about digital technology signaling the death of analog photography. But is it not more accurate to say that the basis of modernist thought—that modern romance of utopian politics and individual heroism—was finally overtaken by the realities of a much bigger, messier world? Technological explanations always seem too reductive. Before photography was a modern art form, it was many things: a scientific curiosity, a business scheme, a tool for artists, a tool for policemen, a window to the Orient, the precious remains of a loved one, an erotic aid, a picture of the moon, a picture of a disease, the basis for all film, news, advertising . . . Photography never stopped being those things, and it is interesting now to see such uses appearing within the framework of contemporary art, as artists reference photography of different historical uses and contexts—including formalist art photography of mid-century—in order to invoke different elements of the modern period. Today's visual literacy depends on an even larger collective databank of cultural memory. It is here that one meets those references to modern forms, rich in optimism and psychological promise, yet looking a little careworn and naïve—museified, perhaps—in their contemporary setting, whispering of a deflated modernism and in the same breath promising everlasting renewal.

Now is a different moment from the 1920s, 1950s, or 1970s for choosing abstraction. Art-making has become heterogeneous, the boundaries between the different mediums have been all but demolished, and many artists move fluidly between painting, photography, sculpture, and video. In that sense, to choose photographic abstraction today is to choose something very specific: a historical episode from photography's past. To what purpose are such choices made? Typical of today's sensibility, there is at once a sort of wiseacre worldliness and a willful naiveté—something I like to refer to as a "suspension of cool"—in which artists seem to have naturalized post-modernism's deconstructive tendencies while passing on its nihilism (Jeff Koons would be the patron saint of this attitude). So when Beshty chooses the photogram, producing images that bear a striking resemblance to works by Moholy-Nagy albeit on a much larger scale, he is invoking a tenuous utopian moment, one in which technology is seen to be both a path toward salvation and also a threat to basic human existence. Moholy-Nagy's writings are full of anxieties about the outcome of "technical civilization" and, in this instance, I don't doubt one bit that Beshty knows that history of ambivalence and is carrying it through to the contemporary moment, in which the photogram's mysterious beauty also references airport x-ray technologies and the grimmer realities of international security. The work almost serves as an homage to Moholy-Nagy's own half-articulated fears.

To hazard an interpretation of an equally cryptic body of work, Quinlan's *Smoke and Mirrors* series seems both to invoke the dewiness of past formal explorations (riffing, perhaps, on Fred Sommer's *Smoke and Cellophane* works of the 1960s or more recent work by Barbara Kasten), and to foreclose on any sort of profound revelation beyond immediate visual pleasure, as the series title suggests. Yet the title itself is curiously pleasurable and teasing, causing this viewer's brain to flip-flop: "Oh, it's just smoke and mirrors. It's smoke and mirrors. Oh, it's just smoke and mirrors." In that sense, the work seems conceptual and literal, cynical and marveling at the very same time.

One wants to draw parallels to the current cultural moment, abstract though such comparisons may be. It is interesting to note that, historically, radical formalism seems to occur most emphatically during periods of radical change, when technology, politics, and social mores seem to be morphing at dizzying speeds. What is the world becoming? What promise does the future hold? What solace from past traditions will remain? Today's formalism seems to me an anxious attempt to both visualize something new and to keep something of the familiar. It is an exercise in fortunetelling that desires as much to see the past as to know the future. Just as the fortuneteller intuits the hopes and fears of the rube, using such insight to create a plausible and emotionally satisfying vision of the future, the artist looks to the world and negotiates a fate.

--

DISCUSSION FORUM
WWW.WORDSWITHOUTPICTURES.ORG

--

Subject: Notes in Response to foRm by Kevin Moore
Date: 1 February 2008 15:29:14
From: CARTER MULL

Are we just sifting through the past, upturning graves and exhuming the dead? Was modernism the height of Western culture? Is the collective West now like post-Baroque Italy? Do the best of us only rival Canova? I hope not.

All educated artists working now are (or should be) aware of their direct historical precedents as well as the other artists on the horizon of their own practice. When I think of my colleagues' work, I think of influences such as the films of Michael Snow, the early appropriation work of Richard Prince, the practice of Stan Douglas, Barbara Kasten's photographs of the late 1970s, Baroness Elsa von Freytag-Loringhoven's assemblages, and Brancusi's photographs, more so than Moholy-Nagy or Christian Schad. In considering the variety of these sources, one should also note that the diversity of historical drives intersecting many practices today constitutes a compost pile more than a teleological imperative. This entropy of information can in some large way be attributed to the enhanced place of individual, everyday data browsing in our lives. Still, the sense of "the modern" is in certain practices. When interesting, it is articulated as a critical yet complicit nod to contemporary décor or stylistically employed to engage issues of history. When poor, it is tired and retrograde. Yet, despite exhibitions of work that attempt to frame contemporary photographic practice in terms of the Modernism of the teens and twenties, the most overarching influence on a younger generation of photographers is the work of James Welling. His meta-historical practice looms large.

Welling is a complex artist whose work cannot easily be reduced to any one idea. The heterogeneity of his practice still pushes the development of many unique and evolving photographic minds. Interestingly, Welling's first important bodies of work were made while he was living in New York in the late 1970s, at a time when Postminimalism was soon to fade as a dominant force in the galleries, and a moment when the Pictures Generation began to emerge as the new paradigm. Two early Welling series employed different yet specific materials to make constructions in front of the lens for the purpose of making photographs. The scattered philo dough over drapery and the formed and crinkled tinfoil are not unlike miniature, postminimal sculptures built in front of the camera. At the same time, their forms as silver gelatin prints are not unlike romantic seascape paintings or all-over abstractions. Within these early works there is a dynamic between material construction and articulation in front of and in-camera, paired with a consciousness of other images.

Welling's relationship to the Pictures Generation is unusual. He showed at Metro Pictures early on and was associated with the gallery artists, yet his notion of how one image could relate to another was not entirely constructed around ideas of simulation and cultural critique. Instead, there is a wider range of associative reads for his early abstract work, some of which were articulated in contemporaneous interviews and press releases. The dynamic between a sense of materiality on one hand, and an awareness of how images relate to other images (historical, commercial, or contemporary) on another, is what characterizes a strong facet of contemporary photographic practice—more so than a relationship to early modernism.

The sense of materiality in contemporary photography usually occurs in front of the lens, within the formal structure of a work or within the printing and presentational modes. On the one hand, this interest in process and the material construction of a photograph could be seen as an assertion of fact within the making of an image. On the other hand, the interest in materiality could be thought of as an outgrowth and continuation of the concept of a constructed image. Both of these concerns may be seen as working in response to the contemporary realities of American image politics. There were the presidential election scandals of 2000 and 2004; the theater of lies used to invade Iraq, and the echo of the spectacularization of the September 11, 2001, events. With these realities in mind, it seems valuable to note the porous boundaries between the potential of intellectual productivity and the deflating inevitability of commoditization that any photograph, object or even experience negotiates at this point in late capitalism. We are in a state of shifting mirrors. In this light, the recent work of Christopher Williams, with its intense relationship to commercial photography, deserves closer examination. Also, in the face of these complexities, a return to the old-school documentary politics of an artist like Allan Sekula seems somehow less adequate as a mode of operation. Instead, the potential of constructed photography, where the work is not only concrete but also depictive, and where the sense of construction is somehow present, not transparent, seems to be a more viable and effective strategy. Kevin Moore's comment about smoke and mirrors seems accurate at this hour.

That said, the art historical baggage of the term formalism and the brand modern need to be shelved to their proper place, either as limiting nomenclature or inaccurate default labels. In turn, we as artists need a more accurate framework that can productively speak to the dialogue between materiality and the forms of appropriation that are at play in much work today. It is the artist's job to stay ahead of the curve, producing complex and nuanced works that advance discourse. And it is the critic's job to see the contained, not the container, and to produce a more accurate and generative framework for understanding the diversity and complexity of contemporary photographic practices.

We have *Words Without Pictures.* And we now more than ever need a new discursive term that can be put in play to accurately reflect the contentions produced by the friction between the material realities of the photographic arts and the complexity of our relationship to the image-written world we inhabit.

To the critics and writers around us: Can you make these words? Please do so, and we will continue to further the possibilities of pictures.

--

Subject: Re: Notes in Response to foRm by Kevin Moore
Date: 1 February 2008 17:26:43
From: CHARLOTTE COTTON

Carter, I really enjoyed your response to Kevin's

essay and the topic of form and photography in general. I want to start by responding to your response. I'd like to avoid drawing a line in the sand between critics and curators who are observing issues of form, and practitioners such as you who are shaping its current visual discourse. Plus, well, you clearly don't need writers and critics to give you the words to very eloquently talk about one of the subjects that your work addresses.

I also wanted to respond to your response rather than start a separate thread of discussion because I think critics' and artists' impulses and investigations are connected, especially when it comes to underdeveloped contemporary discourses such as form in photography, with a particular weighting towards abstraction. Maybe those of us who are using this forum to think aloud and intelligently will develop quite a list of figures from photography's near and distant past who are on our radars and seem pertinent, before we forget.

I don't think the reasons that curators, writers and practitioners are initially attracted to photographic genres and moments are so very different because we are all, at first, acting intuitively and having our curiosity tweaked. Perhaps we are, collectively, following a highly predictable pattern of being especially interested in the time when a previous generation was young and curious, the creative context into which we were born. In the context of this discussion, maybe we are getting back to modernism in generational leaps: El Lissitzky and Aleksandr Rodchenko, via Minor White and Aaron Siskind, via Jim Welling and Barbara Kasten. In the context of this forum, we are unlikely to be battling it out for a platonic understanding of the lineage of form or the top ten most influential abstract photographers, and I am not making that invitation here. Instead, what I would love to investigate with you—qualify, disqualify and elaborate upon—is Kevin's sage unpacking of some enduring and emergent issues for how we talk about subjects that we are psychologically drawn to and what this means for contemporary practice, regardless of whether we primarily make or view photographs.

The first big issue that resonated with me comes about four pages into Kevin's essay, where he cites Clement Greenberg and his critical writings about Abstract Expressionist painting. Kevin reminds us that the political resonance and politicization of abstraction is something very useful for us to consider while thinking about the history of abstraction in photography and the likely testing ground of its contemporary manifestations. I read this passage of the essay as a timely challenge to my interest in abstract photography. It was a reminder that there is a fuzzy line between political and critical abstract art and politicization of and theorizing about abstraction. How am I distinguishing between pertinent and critical uses of abstraction and merely the decorative versions? How would I explain the differences, and where do the differences become evident? How do we tell the difference between a Walead Beshty photogram and the amiable and lovely counterparts of a West Coast, Sunday photographer? What impact does it have upon a practitioner's criticality to work with such noodle-y, craft-based versions of photography?

I'm sure it's a unique balance for every photographer who is seriously working with abstraction right now. Can you successfully appropriate the field of abstraction and the theories that surround it without falling into the retro-style-over-substance trap, and simultaneously induce the criticality increasingly implied by your working with forms that are transparently driven by your active choices?

--

Subject: Re: Notes in Response to foRm by Kevin Moore
Date: 12 February 2008 02:07:02
From: ALEX KLEIN

In a 1923 letter to the poet Hart Crane, Alfred

Stieglitz wrote, "I know that there is more of the really abstract in some 'representation' than in most of the dead representations of the so called abstract so fashionable now." While I do not mean to divorce this historically contingent quotation from its original context, it reminded me of the catalogue for James Welling's *Abstract* exhibition (2002), which is striking for its inclusion of so many photographs that in a strict sense are not abstractions. For me, this points (to quote Rosalyn Deutsche by way of David Joselit) to an "erosion of the security of any presumed boundary between abstract and figurative representation."

This is perhaps a tangent to take from the topic of "form," but I believe it is an essential component of the discussion, especially with regard to influences and to a number of the points touched on in Carter's response. Which is to say that part of the significance of Welling's work lies precisely in a formal heterogeneity (although I would argue that it is unified in terms of its investigatory concerns) that has launched a younger generation of artists in seemingly disparate directions. I think Kevin Moore is right to question the direction of formal inquiry in current photographic practices, if only to underscore Carter's insistence that there is no overarching "teleological imperative" at play.

In our present moment of the historicization of photographic experimentation, it is important to think about how these newer works function and to question whether the differences between them will be legible as we move further away from the moment of their creation. There are certainly artists working today for whom form, materiality, and abstraction have political implications and for whom a meditation on the medium's support speaks to present concerns, rather than retrograde specificities. Nevertheless, there is also a contingent of these investigations that suggests ulterior motives that are trendy, market-savvy, and scarcely disguised by a veneer of easily digestible theory. The seeming freshness of much of this work thus begs the question of the difference between a quotation of modernist aesthetics and a critical appropriation of its terms.

To close, I want to return to another point in Carter's response that struck a chord with me. It seems significant that he mentions "data-browsing" within the context of a discussion of the potential ramifications of abstraction. Instead of the simplistic dialectic of analog versus digital, this remark points to something approaching Baudrillard's "ecstasy of communication." What I take from this is that the very way in which we process images has ruptured—and I do not just mean the Internet. That the perceptual world around us has broken down into an abstracted media mash-up in which to look is to be overwhelmed is now something of a cultural given.

Thus, in light of our present moment of geopolitical crisis, abstraction that could be interpreted not just as a formal inquiry but as a symptom of the very breakdown of autonomous spheres of image-making and production seems to me to be fundamentally different than a simple reprisal of modernism or a return to postmodern image critique. A reflection on the chaos and detritus of our consumerist, info-fetishistic society is in fact the inverse of previous avant-garde tactics in which subtraction and reduction carried the greatest import. That said, not all formal inquiry need make overt gestures to the political. It may indeed be enough for a photograph to meditate upon its own conditions and histories. However, as Kevin's essay and Carter's response suggest, to do so requires both historical analysis and agitation—positions that need not be mutually exclusive.

QUESTIONNAIRE / KATHERINE BUSSARD

WHAT DO YOU THINK OF THE CURRENCY OF BLACK-AND-WHITE PHOTOGRAPHY TODAY?

Given the present ubiquity of color photography, making black-and-white photographs today signals a decisive choice, as did making color photographs in the 1950s, 1960s, and 1970s. If the serious adoption of color then reflected a desire to better reflect the world as it's perceived, choosing black-and-white now may be a reflection of a desire for the opposite: distance from the easy recognition of reality or, more intriguingly, reference to a time when black-and-white photographs were still revered as the most "accurate" of artistic representations of reality. The choice to photograph in black-and-white is not simply "nostalgic." For those active during the 1950s to 1970s (statistically an ever-smaller portion of viewers), this does involve nostalgia, as it requires a return to previously experienced modes of looking. For others, myself included, thoroughgoing uses of black-and-white photography prompt a different mode of looking, one that can certainly be past-aware but can't possibly be nostalgic. Because of this, the choice of black-and-white seems to this viewer more likely to engage in a complicated relationship with historical pictures.

DO YOU THINK MUSEUMS SHOULD COLLECT INKJET PRINTS AND SCREEN-BASED PHOTOGRAPHY?

Certainly, insofar as such acquisitions would be in keeping with a practice of acquiring other ink-based photographic processes such as clichés-verre or photogravures. The photographic image's reproduction in print has a long and rich history that deserves to be represented, studied, and exhibited. From this viewpoint, inkjet prints are just one of the most recent innovations in that history.

WHAT DO YOU SEE AS BEING IN STORE FOR THE MEDIUM?

Who can say, really? But with a fully digital horizon now in sight, I am intrigued by the likelihood that more and more artists will decide to assert photography as object, in other words calling attention to the physical and dimensional qualities of the medium's objects. I expect and hope that such assertions might include different deployments of photographic paper and other printing surfaces, emphasizing the dimensionality of photography through different practices of mounting and displaying prints, and/or a renewed sense of possibilities in photo books for those artists who have no interest in making photographic prints.

QUESTIONNAIRE / EILEEN QUINLAN

DO NEW TECHNOLOGIES CHANGE YOUR IDEA OF PHOTOGRAPHY?

No. I don't think too much about new technologies. I know my fully analog work can be viewed as a "reaction" to the onset of the digital age, but I'm simply practicing what I know from my training at art school and my experience working with commercial photographers in the late nineties and early two-thousands.

I do regret the fact that I may have to incorporate the computer more heavily into my process in the future. At this point, I scan negatives to reference images in emails or to produce quick "work prints" in Epson form. With the death of my proofing medium, Polaroid, a digital back is certainly in my future.

I recognize digital prints as photographs, but to me they have a different sensibility. A traditional C-print has certain material limitations that an image "burned and dodged" in Photoshop does not. The latter is more commercial looking somehow. It is a "print," but to my eye, it isn't a photograph.

DO YOU ENJOY LOOKING AT PHOTOGRAPHS ON-LINE?

I don't look at photos on-line, not intentionally that is. If you're referring to art photos, I'd much rather look at them in person. I'm dismayed by the fact that my work is often consumed, at least upon first encounter, in jpeg form. The real thing sometimes disappoints. The illuminated screen offers a punchier image, a sexier image. And as the first image, it sets an impossible precedent. They are apples masquerading as oranges.

WHAT DO YOU SEE AS BEING IN STORE FOR THE MEDIUM?

I can't say. Young photographers have never seen the inside of a darkroom. They'll show us what's possible with the tools we can only grasp clumsily. In the realm of art, photography is still suspect. People tell me often that they "don't like photographs," but they "like mine." Freudian slips abound: "I love your paintings." Photography has yet to set its own terms. Much more thinking is needed on the subject.

QUESTIONNAIRE / TIM DAVIS

WHAT FACTORS DETERMINE THE VALUE OF A PHOTOGRAPH TO YOU?

If this photograph were a person, would I invite it to a dinner party?

Too Drunk to Fuck (On the Anxiety of Photography)

MARK WYSE

Photography can be a neurotic's worst nightmare. At least if the neurotic thinks about it, and the neurotic does. He thinks too much. The photographer/neurotic gets caught between his desire and his intellect, and therein lies the nightmare. It's not that desire and the intellect don't go together, they do.

This essay is about photography and repression. I will ultimately consider different modes of desire at play within photography, but to get there I must start by talking about two films *Det Perfekte Menneske* (*The Perfect Human*) (1967) and *The Five Obstructions* (2003).

> Here is the human. Here is the human. Here is the perfect human. We will see the perfect human functioning. We will see the perfect human functioning. How does such a number function? What kind of thing is it? We will look into that? We will investigate that.

So begins narrator Jørgen Leth as he puts descriptive yet puzzling words to his film, *The Perfect Human*. The short film takes place in an empty studio. No walls, no ceiling, only the actor Claus Nissen, who is enveloped in emptiness while performing the most mundane actions—filling his pipe, turning to the left, turning to the right, cutting his nails, walking. As Nissen walks, Leth continues: "Look at the perfect human moving in a room. The perfect human can move in a room. The room is boundless and radiant with light. It is an empty room. Here are no boundaries." And later the voiceover continues, "Yes, there he is. Who is he? What can he do? What does he want? Why does he move like that? How does he move like that? Look at him. Look at him now. And now. Look at him all the time." *The Perfect Human* is a beautiful film but irritating to describe. Watching it, I feel split, disconnected, and absorbed in the gap between what I am watching and what I am feeling. *The Perfect Human* doesn't merely resist interpretation—it repels it.

It is exactly this surface that the filmmaker Lars von Trier seeks to rupture in his film *The Five Obstructions*. Von Trier, in making his film, wants to have Leth remake *The Perfect Human* according to Von Trier's obstructions. Von Trier feels that Leth is repressed, that he hides behind his films. The obstructions, in Von Trier's words, will help Leth "proceed from the perfect to the human." Von Trier feels that Leth is protecting himself by creating distance between his intellect and his emotions. Von Trier wants to "get into where the scream is and let it out." In true Von Trier fashion, he says to Leth, "*The Perfect Human* is a little gem that we are now going to ruin...We may be able to do so by finding things that hurt."

In Freud's paper "Negation," he refers to situations in which people draw attention to their thoughts but then deny them. Such a negation translates: "The association came to my mind, but I am not inclined to let it count." It draws attention to a conflict between the unconscious and the ego. The unconscious is responsible for introducing the content; the ego is responsible for the negation. The negation is critical to Freud because it points to the process of repression. Freud's first example, of course, involves the mother: "You ask who this person in the dream can be. It is not my mother." Or: "Now you'll think I mean to say something insulting, but really I have no such intention." But negations don't always, according to Freud, involve false statements. He gives the example, "How nice not to have had one of my headaches for so long." The announcement is surely the first sign of a headache, the approach of which the person senses but is unable to believe. The interesting question is not whether the statement is true or false but, rather: why is this person talking about *that* subject?

In *The Perfect Human*, Leth keeps drawing attention to what he sees—the human. He meditates on it, and what Leth sees, we see. He makes sure of it: "Look, look at him now. And now." It is within this constant repetition of seeing, and of thinking about what we are seeing, that he prevents us from *feeling* the content of this repression. Leth is repressing the source of Claus Nissen's anxiety, but he is doing so in the form of presenting literal facts. And it is by being precisely literal, in the term's most concrete sense, that Leth prevents us from feeling the emotion of the wound that seems to inhabit Claus Nissen. Leth makes us think but doesn't allow us to feel. In so doing, he engages a rather perverse form of negation: a repression disguised as a truth that cannot be negated, but that nevertheless hides the source of anxiety. This is what drives Von Trier crazy—so much so that he has to make a film about it. It's an Oedipal dance between Von Trier and Leth that pits the instincts of the body against the intellect of the mind.

Desire permeates photography. Eduardo Cadava and Paola Cortes-Rocca speak to this desire in their essay "Notes on Love and Photography" (*October*, no. 116, Spring 2006). They start by discussing Roland Barthes. "Barthes, in the first few pages of *Camera Lucida*, confesses that when he looks at a photograph he sees 'only the referent, the desired object, the beloved body.' It is precisely 'love,' he explains, 'extreme love,' that enables him to 'erase the weight of the image' to make the photograph 'invisible' and thereby to clear a path for him to see not the photograph, but the object of his desire, his beloved's body."

Nowhere could the divide between unfettered desire and intellectual savvy be more pronounced than in the work of Nan Goldin and Christopher Williams. A comparison of the two artists' languages is telling. Goldin: "My desire is to preserve the sense of people's lives, to endow them with the strength and beauty I see in them. I want the people in my pictures to stare back." (*The Devil's Playground*, Phaidon Press, 2003.) Williams:

> In total this concern with photographic production and distribution, as well as its materiality, amounts to a second-order of self-reflexivity, or proposes an expanded frame for thinking about photographic materiality. It is important, I think, to reflect on photography in this way, because as a result the emphasis shifts away from two concepts that are paramount in the critical discourse around photography: the idea of the photographer-author; and the importance of the decisive moment. (*Afterall* 16, 2007)

Of course, both quotes are taken completely out of context, but I think one can get some sense of the distinction I am trying to make. For Goldin, nothing is more urgent than the life unfolding before the camera. For Williams, nothing is more important than disclosing the conditions of the photograph's making. Goldin represses the photograph as a material object and the conditions of its making, while Williams represses his own desire. But it is, of course, much more complicated than this.

DESIRE MANIFESTS ITSELF IN MANY WAYS.

The subjects of Goldin's photographs seem wrought

with desire. In Elisabeth Sussman's words, "Her camera freezes the comings and goings of the social experience of desire: love and hate in intimate relationships; moments of isolation, self-revelation, and adoration: the presentation of the sexual self freed from the constraints of biological destiny" (*Nan Goldin: I'll Be Your Mirror,* Whitney Museum of American Art, 1996). I think it is reasonable to assume that in Goldin's work it is not merely the subjects she photographs who are wrought with desire, but Goldin herself. She seems to be absorbed by her subjects and we are witness to her absorption.

With Williams, things are less transparent. In his work, thinking about the subjects *themselves* leads us astray. One is quickly perplexed looking at a woman with a yellow towel on her head standing next to a color chart in one photograph, a jellyfish in another, a camera, some corn, a bicycle, etc. It surely must feel *different* for Williams to look at one of his photographs than it does for Goldin to look at one of hers. The question is: what is this relationship for Williams, and what is it for us?

Williams does a tremendous amount of research and thinking about the subjects he uses, the politics and histories of those subjects, and, most importantly, the context in which we understand both through their representations. In a recent issue of *Afterall*, he spoke with Mark Godfrey in relation to his series *For Example: Dix-Huit Leçons Sur La Société Industrielle* (ongoing since 2002) (*Afterall* 16, 2007). They spoke on subjects as varied as sociology, the economics of the Cold War, Americanization of European popular culture, the European reception of Pop art, the Bush administration, Godard, potatoes, the history of the Kiev 88 camera, and they discuss corn extensively. The amount of historical knowledge and the complexity of Williams's interests are intimidating. I found his discussion of corn and its relationship to photography particularly intriguing:

> Christopher Williams: Almost everything you come into contact with in your daily life has had some relationship to corn as a product. The lubricant used to grind the camera lenses in the photographic industry has a corn by-product in it; the material used to polish the steel has a corn by-product in it; the filmstrip itself has a corn by-product in it, and many of the chemicals associated with the production of a fine-art print also have corn in them.
>
> Mark Godfrey: Perhaps the artificial corn in the photograph was made using a corn by-product as well?
>
> CW: Yes. It's not real corn in the image, but artificial corn made for window displays or photographic shoots. The company that produced it estimated that 75% of the material used to make the artificial corn is in fact a corn by-product. One could say the photographic industry has as much to do with corn as it does with, for example, light.

This is what is so exciting about Williams's photographs. Does Nan Goldin think about corn in her photographs? The distance between the thought and the photograph as a reflection of that thought is at such a great divide in Williams's work that one can't help but wonder why.

In my eyes, Williams's work functions as an implicit, but not didactic, critique of how we conventionally experience and understand subjects depicted in photographs. In doing so, he questions the act of interpretation itself.

I use Nan Goldin's photographs in comparison here, but in no way do I see Williams's work to be a direct critique of Goldin's. My model, rather, is to examine desire and, specifically, how desire manifests itself in radically different ways through different practices.

In Goldin's work, the subjects themselves are the content. Through photography, her subjects are depicted through—or rather bathed in—a light that seems to resonate with meaning. In this sense, looking at Goldin's photographs gives us a sense of how she feels about her subjects. To experience the meaning of Goldin's photographs is to accept or reject *her feelings* toward *her people*.

I imagine that for Williams the idea of either a subject or an author dictating so much meaning would be problematic, if not inadequate. I assume so because he so often severs the photograph's meaning from the meaning of the subject depicted. The photograph of corn isn't about corn but about photography itself. It's about the conditions of a photograph's making, about all photographs, and about how such conditions are never disclosed in a photograph. It is a reality check against the false transparency of photography.

In this sense, one can understand Williams's work in relation to an act of deconstruction: it seeks to expose that which is undisclosed. It draws attention to the photograph as a cultural and social construction. It destabilizes meaning by revealing multiple and conflicting meanings. It brings to light that which was previously hidden, overlooked, or suppressed. Williams's practice exposes photography's repressions.

On the surface, this sounds cold, intellectual, analytical, and tedious. In Williams's practice, it is not. It leaks desire.

Interpretation is slippery, if not outright problematic. However, I am going to try to do my best with Williams's work. It seems that any deconstructive act begs its own deconstruction. My goal is not to get it *right*, but to get *somewhere*, to take pleasure in the act of interpretation itself. In this sense, we are a good pair. Williams's practice does everything to make interpretation not possible. I will do everything to make sense of that very practice.

In my attempt to understand the thinking behind Williams's work, I am bound to fail. Not only will I project meaning that isn't there; I will project my own desires and misunderstandings. This will inevitably prove Williams's point that interpretation is an impossible task. I still cannot resist, however, as I find meaning in the act of interpretation itself.

What Williams's practice has made evident in significant, compelling, and ravishing ways is that photographic meaning is never transparent. The idea that meaning is not transparent in photographs radically alters both our view and our experience of photographs. In Williams's work, we shift from an understanding of photography as testimonial witness to the world to a realization that photographs are by-products of undisclosed forces that alter and determine our relationship to them. In doing so, desire seems to be at the forefront, because the artist's desire determines that which is disclosed and that which is hidden.

Williams is operating in a cultural time in which the author-witness has not only been dethroned, but the process of making photographs itself no longer holds its implied objective veracity. For him, the only way to excavate truths is to look at how the process and ingredients of making an image impacts the world. He does so by making his practice a model of such an examination. It is not really a deconstruction; he uses his own photographs. Rather, it is a model of what a deconstruction might look like.

If desire is at the forefront of what is hidden and undisclosed, we need a photographer. Williams uses one, by hiring one to take the photographs. This distance is critical to an understanding of his process. In fact, the subject of Williams's practice is not just photography itself but "the photographer." In his current show, *For*

Example: Dix-Huit Leçons Sur La Société Industrielle (Revision 7) (2008), at David Zwirner, there are 17 photographs. There are four photographs of a man; in three of the photographs he holds a camera, and in one he is having his shoulder measured. There are four pictures of a woman wearing lingerie in what appears to be a commercial photo shoot. In two of the photographs, we see her in lingerie directly, and in one we see her breast depicted (upside down) in the ground glass of a 4 by 5 camera. In the other photograph, we see her high heels depicted (upside down) in the ground glass of a 4 by 5 camera. There are two photographs of tires at angles; one each of a jellyfish, a landscape at night, and a painted ceiling panel by Daniel Buren; two bisected lenses; one bisected Nikon camera; and one bisected Fuji 6 by 9 camera. Photography is on stage, and so is the commercial photographer with his model. In Williams's previous work, "photographic meaning" seemed to be the center of discourse, while in this show, desire is. Of course, meaning has always had a conflicted relationship to desire, and in Williams's previous work—and to an extent in his current show—desire was often seen in the context of modernism. In this new work, desire makes its way forward in a much more overt way, as desire is contextualized with sexual desire (as implied by the presence of the photographer and his model).

The photographic act is an act like no other, and it carries the weight of desire with it. The photographer falls for his subject, his desire, his view. Williams distances himself. He restrains himself. By not exposing the photographs himself, by modeling his photographs after a "photographer" (in this case, the commercial photographer), Williams exposes the context of the photographic act: the photographer, the photographer's tools, the object of the photographer's desire, the photograph as object of our desire, and the gallery selling the objects of our desire. If this still sounds cold and analytical, I assure you it is not.

The interesting question is: Why is *this* artist talking about *that* subject?

On the one hand, Williams's practice looks like a deconstructive act of photography itself, and this would of course answer why. On the other hand, his work *feels* like an intellectualized embrace of fetishistic photographic tropes. So, which is it? The two would seem to be in conflict with one another, but in Williams's practice they parallel each other. Williams has positioned his work in such a way that we cannot understand his desire in relationship to his subject, because the one interpretation—that it is a deconstructive gesture towards the desires and context of the commercial photographer— cannot be negated. On the other hand, how can we claim that he is embracing fetishistic photographic tropes? Is Williams himself conflicted?

Far from it. Rather, Williams seems to have found a strategy for getting around the anxiety of confronting one's desires. The strategy is to engage an external reality that cannot be negated, but that does, simultaneously, engage one's desire. In this sense, one can shift between an external reality and an internal reality at whim. The external reality is the deconstructive model; the internal reality is the desire to engage the same activity that one is deconstructing. Thus, interpretation becomes impenetrable. In Williams's case, we don't know how he feels towards his subject. I can't decide if it is a critique or an embrace. With Goldin we not only see her desire, but we *feel* her desire. It might help, in this sense, to distinguish between *meaning* and *desire*. Meaning is never contingent in relation to an author, but desire always is, even if desire is the desire not to express how one feels towards one's content. Williams not only situates his content in relation to us for our own projection, he also provides an excellent model of how the intellect works in relationship to desire. He contextualizes desire with its opposition, the intellect, and he makes juxtapositions that demand this conflict.

Leth is doing a similar thing in *The Perfect Human*, but to different effect. By meditating too tightly on a work's subject, one cannot penetrate beyond the subject to the psyche that gives meaning to it. Leth draws attention to everything Nissen is doing. He presents statements and commands: "Look, look at him now"; "He is walking through the room." But such statements are empty signifiers. They don't have any meaning in themselves. They do, however, seem to beg the question as to why Leth is using them. In this sense, we become witness to Leth and Nissen *feeling/creating* anxiety. They do not wish to go beyond the surface of their spoken thoughts.

Williams does not expose us to anxiety; he exposes us to an intellect in the act of restraining emotion. In Williams's practice, this is the solution to the anxiety of his photographic desire. But his solution is our experience. To engage the complexity and depth of Williams's work is to understand your relationship to your desire.

This is my experience of Williams's photographs. Beyond making photographs that are very compelling in their own right while disclosing the undisclosed context of photography, he provides a model of an intellect confronting desire.

Photography has shifted from being a discourse on trying to understand the world to a discourse on trying to understand ourselves. This has always been the case, only now it is more transparent—or less so.

This is how the neurotic writes.

--

DISCUSSION FORUM
WWW.WORDSWITHOUTPICTURES.ORG

--

Subject: Response to Mark Wyse
Date: 1 March 2008 20:28:45
From: BENNETT SIMPSON

Hi Mark,

I'd like to make a distinction as a way of beginning. Making sense of, or to use your words "interpreting" Christopher Williams's work is no easy task; but writing about it, as some function of experiencing it, if not easy per se, is something I have found to be a great pleasure. (And even with your "neurosis," the verve of your own text is ample—thanks!) There is a difference between interpreting and experiencing: the former is a learned thing, an exercise in knowledge; the latter is perhaps more humanly accessible. When I wrote about Williams it became clear to me that I could, at least on the surface, chose between these possibilities. And after reading critics much more savvy about photography than I am try the interpretation route—via excursions into history, theory, or politics—I decided to go with my gut. What is compelling about Williams's work to me is the way it encourages dimensions of affect, humor, perception, jokes, and reading (again, as experience) in terms that knowledge may assist but not necessarily exhaust. I realize this sounds Pollyanna-ish, or like I'm coyly refusing the bait, but I think it's important here to say that the "bait" may be yours/ours rather than Williams's.

I'm not a photographer, nor really a historian of the medium, and so for me it has never been a problem when Williams states that he is not a photographer either. I know this claim bugs people, but can't we take it seriously? I came to his practice through "art," by stumbling across a catalogue he made with the painter Albert Oehlen in 1995. The book was orange and it interspersed photographs with paintings. The orange of the book was itself something special since it was the same orange as many of the album covers of The Red Krayola, a band I liked and which, I almost simultaneously realized, counted both Oehlen and Williams as members. I must have begun thinking about Williams in the same moment I began thinking about Oehlen and this band. And from here other moments and other artists came into the picture. What Williams does with his photographs seemed to me related to what Oehlen—or Martin Kippenberger, or Michael Krebber, or others—were doing with their paintings. First of all, he was having fun, telling stories, letting ideas or gestures rub and weave. Games were being played. Traps were being laid. An artist was doing something that didn't need me. Not being needed (which other people have called "autonomy") felt like the most radical part.

I am aware that other people feel extremely needed by Williams's work, and indeed this "having-to-know" is a burden. The anxiety of medium-specific discourse is acute for photography—and especially so for critics of Williams, who often seek in his example a re-establishment of a coherence (however labored) that, secretly, they know to be lost. It occurs to me that if we removed the word photography from the discussion many problems would vanish. On the other hand, if we removed the word art we would be left with nothing.

Here are a few remaining responses that we may pick up later. Your juxtaposition of Nan Goldin and Chris Williams hurts just a bit. It's a rhetorical kind of pain. Rather than sending Goldin to her emotive corner so that Williams can "rightly" take up the critical/intellectual center of the room, what if we left them alone, with the doors and windows open? The spectrum of 1980s photography that stretches from Goldin on one extreme across to Philip-Lorca diCorcia and then on to Wall (a spectrum from romanticism, to anti-romanticism, to allegory) may not, as we assume, include Williams. It may not include Richard Prince, Cindy Sherman, or Lorna Simpson either. I say this because I am not certain that these other artists are responding to the same traditions or givens. Would we compare Diane Arbus and Michael Asher? I'm also reluctant to say that Goldin is self-evident in her desire or that Williams is obscure in his repression. I think there is a lot of showmanship, calculation, and negotiation in Goldin's work; like Robert Johnson's, her "naturalism" can be contrived and affective at the same time. Conversely, I think there is a lot of feeling and going-on-nerve in Williams's. He's a great songwriter. Look at the progression of the three images of the black man holding the camera in the Zwirner show: staged melancholy goes to neutral straight shot, then ends with sweet smile. Look at the lingerie model and her bra fastened with a yellow paper clip. It's funny! It's dirty! It's like that Pak-Set box from an earlier show. It makes me think that Williams is finding ways to "enjoy"—not deny—his medium, and in this I may enjoy it, too.

A last question: why do you think Williams's reception is expanding NOW?

--

Subject: Response to Mark Wyse and a Careful Look at "Desire"
Date: 2 March 2008 16:25:26
From: Charlie White

Prologue:

Two art students take a smoking break outside of class. One student sits on two cinderblocks and a plank (most likely the work of a materials-savant from sculpture); he is slumped over in a quasi-Thinker pose, which he learned from watching older students in his critique class. The other student faces him, leaning with her foot against the wall in the position of an intellectual stork.

Having assumed the casual/smart repose of self-aware art students, they embark on a discussion of photography:

The Thinker: Nan Goldin's pictures are honest and real and direct. Her photography is truth.

The Stork: I completely disagree. Christopher Williams is far more truthful in his work. His honesty reveals the truth of the medium itself.

The Thinker: Yeah, Christopher Williams is brilliant, and his work is well made, but Goldin offers a reality for the viewer. I can't even compare the two.

The Stork: You're right, his work is so smart. That said, I admit that one of my favorite pictures ever was that photo of Nan Goldin's of that guy in the red car—do you know that one?

The Thinker: Yeah, I do; I love that picture, too. Goldin is so human.

The Stork: Yes, but Williams is so smart!

I would like to respond to Mark Wyse's essay by focusing closely on the crux of his argument: the comparative relationship of two rather polar photographers—Nan Goldin and Christopher Williams—in relationship to one idea, desire. Although Wyse makes a clear case for looking at and understanding Williams's work in more detail, his decision to juxtapose the "intellectual savvy" of Williams with the "unfettered desire" of Goldin is so exciting and infuriating that I want to explore this trajectory further. Let's begin with the complications that result from applying the word "desire" to such different ideological positions. Merriam-Webster's definitions of the word (as both noun and transitive verb) will help to set the parameters for how the idea of "desire" can conform to fit a range of seemingly different practices.

> Desire (noun): 1. conscious impulse toward something that promises enjoyment or satisfaction in its attainment; 2. a: longing, craving; b: sexual urge or appetite; 3. a usually formal request or petition for some action; 4. something desired

> Desire (transitive verb): 1. to long or hope for; exhibit or feel desire for; 2. a: to express a wish for; request; b: archaic: to express a wish to; ask; 3. obsolete: invite; 4. archaic: to feel the loss of

Considering these definitions of desire, I would argue that Williams's practice functions as the noun form, while Goldin's works as the transitive verb. This is to say that the subject of Williams's lens is a "conscious impulse toward something that promises enjoyment or satisfaction in its attainment," whereas the subjects of Goldin's lens (and personal life) exhibit and evoke an urge "to long or hope for; exhibit or feel desire for." The primary difference here is the gap between understanding something intellectually versus relating to something emotionally. I would argue that Williams's imagery functions in the tangled elite space of the intellectual's desire to understand a subject from an ever-more aware position. Goldin's imagery, however, functions in the more emotional and less cerebral space of feeling for and relating to the subject from a humanistic point of identification. This spectrum of desire offers a range that the Freudian model Wyse invokes may not have fully taken into account when limiting itself to lack, repression, and the unattainable. Wyse locates negation (a subset of activity related to but not defined by desire) to help map the relationship between photographer and subject, paralleling Freud's analytical process for negation (which asks "Why is this person talking about that subject?") to Wyse's own inquiry into the content of his chosen artists' subject matter (by asking "Why is this artist talking about that subject?"). However, when the two photographers being compared are so different in their relation to the medium itself, the subject of desire becomes as stratified as the work that it is being associated with. The short skit I offer as an opening to the subject is intended to illustrate (albeit jokingly) the space between, and the bridge that connects, such diverse strategies—a link that is no more profound than a taste for imagery that varies: some Williams for your heady moments and some Goldin for your gut-level ones.

Clearly, the conversation on either artist can develop well past my simple summaries; however, when framed within the terms of desire, each artist's work seems to quickly assume a more fixed position, thus losing a certain interpretive plasticity. Perhaps these limitations are also due to the commodification (as commodity relates to desire, and desire to capitalism, etc.) of these two artists' well-received oeuvres, which in both cases has generated a predictably dependable outcome in which part of the intention behind each photograph is that it succeed as a further, successful extension of the established oeuvre. If desire is kept to the Freudian model already cited, whereby each act is an unconscious repression, then these calculations undermine true desire—what looks like a manifestation of anxiety is simply another part of artistic strategy. Having developed a fixed vocabulary of dependable visual cues, Goldin can veer from sincere emotion to more formulaic "emo" while burning herself with cigarettes to a Johnny Cash cover of Nine Inch Nails; Williams's seriousness, meanwhile, can occasionally slip from corn to corny when arguing the geopolitics of a plastic prop.

In closing:

Imagine a Celebrity Death Match based on desire and predicated on image. Williams weighs in with a hefty French title and a well-framed, limited series; Goldin holds her own with a ton of monographs, slide shows, and the freedom to lift popular music. Let the battle commence. There will clearly not be a winner, as evidenced by such fans as the thinker and the stork, whose own desires prove that both artists have already won.

--

Subject: Not corn, nor saltines either...
Date: 3 March 2008 11:49:18
From: KEN ABBOTT

My relationship with my intellect has been uneasy (even anxiety provoking) lo these many years... so I was happy to let Mark Wyse lead me through Christopher Williams's ornate approach to his work, helping me see in it "the solution to the anxiety of his photographic desire." By the end of Wyse's essay I was caught up in Williams's work and in his process. However, not surprisingly, my interest was based more on the intellectual elegance of his process than on the photographs resulting. That said, even the pictures, bland as they are formally, have a certain appeal to my eye in their reference to the age-old miracle of photographic representation, unaffected by the many technical and critical re-imaginings the medium has seen throughout its history. It is miraculous, no? And Wyse's beginning the essay with quotes from the Leth film, *The Perfect Human*, with its focus on the elegance of simple description, was perfectly appropriate, calling our attention to its beauty and profundity.

To my way of looking at it, however, anxiety in photography is the result of the stubborn distance that remains between the photograph and the thing photographed, despite our ambitious strategies to bridge that gap, pursued through our most desirous efforts. Furthermore, it seems possible to me that this gap and our desire to bridge it in photography provides a kind of surrogate for our own anxious, personal struggle as artists and humans, as we face the inevitable gap between our desires and our reality. Wyse himself seems to refer to this anxiety when he describes his reaction to Leth's *The Perfect Human*: "Watching it, I feel split, disconnected, and absorbed in the gap between what I am watching and what I am feeling." Photography promises a kind of identity that it never delivers.

Given a variety of ways to approach the problem, thoughtful photographers will take different routes. One photographer who is certainly thoughtful and intellectual, and who I imagine would feel some kinship with Williams's work, is Paul Berger. And yet he takes an approach that, it seems to me, is less "cold, intellectual, analytical, and tedious" in his investigation of the sub-structures of photography. I remember listening to Berger talk once about his beginnings in photography. He'd been a student at a commercial photo school in California and noticed a group of students using an 8 by 10 view camera and several lights, reflectors, props, etc., in a photograph they were making. They were going to great lengths to get lighting perfect, focus adjusted, perspective correct and had spent most of the morning on this shot. When he asked them what they were photographing, they suggested he look at the ground glass. As he placed the dark cloth over his head, he saw that their subject was a saltine cracker. As I recall it, he said that at that moment he realized that commercial photography was not for him. I couldn't help but think of this story when Wyse asks in his essay, "Does Nan Goldin think about corn in her photographs?" I dare say, no.

QUESTIONNAIRE / OLIVIER RICHON

WHAT WOULD YOU CONSIDER THE MOST IMPORTANT CHANGE THAT PHOTOGRAPHY HAS UNDERGONE IN THE LAST FEW YEARS?

The slow disappearance of Polaroid film.

Too Early Too Late

Los Angeles County Museum of Art
Participants: Miranda Lichtenstein,
Carter Mull, Amir Zaki
Moderator: Charlotte Cotton

The characterizations "too early" and "too late" point to the polarization of photographic camps between the "decisive moment" and the constructed tableau. "Too early" refers to observational photography, where one might say that the actual taking of the photograph happens before the idea or the intellectualized relationship with the work has been fully realized. "Too late" refers to constructed, highly premeditated photographs made in a manner that has come to be defined as the "directorial mode." While "too early" may begin to raise questions about how something so immediate and unpredictable can be understood or explained within the terms of rigorous, contemporary art practice, "too late" occupies the other extreme in which every location, actor, prop, light source, and digital retouch can be attributed to the intent of the artist. Such a distinction poses a dichotomy between the spontaneous intuition of the photographic eye and a more calculated image that provides constant reassurance about questions of authorship and stylistic signature.

To be sure, these are potentially dangerous lines to draw in the sand. This is precisely why we invited three artists whose practices skirt this supposed borderline. Instead of asking them to choose sides, we invited the panelists to join us for a discussion about their processes.

MIRANDA LICHTENSTEIN: I brought very specific images from a project I've been working on for the past few years. This project represents a turn in my work towards a more constructed and premeditated mode than I've worked with in the past. Certainly, I wouldn't say that any of my work previously would fall in the "too early" camp. But, there was a bit more of a scanning of the topography, as it were, than the work I'm about to show you. I only brought seven images, to keep it short. They are from a body of work I call *The Searchers*. Interestingly enough, I had that title in my head before I even started making the pictures.

The project is a reflection on a trend I'd been noticing for the past few years towards people seeking spiritual enlightenment and different states of transcendence through secular means. It was something I had experienced myself in trying hypnosis as a cure for my fear of flying. In this experience of hypnosis, what was interesting to me was that I was always told to try and imagine an image—a place that represented some kind of blissful or utopian state. And I started thinking about this question in terms of the potential struggle, or lack, in photography in its ability to represent an altered state. What would that look like?

So I started making a list. When I think about this idea of how I was cruising or scanning the landscape in my previous work, in this case I started cruising the Internet, and reading about isolation tanks, for one. That's what this picture called *Floater* is of. I'm sure most of you know the movie *Altered States (*dir. Ken Russell, 1980). I certainly had that in mind. In terms of this idea of staging, and preconceptualizing, I often do research beforehand and think about references . . .

I've continued on this path of using myself in photographs. This is *Dream Machine*. I don't know if you guys know, but *Dream Machine* was designed by Brion Gysin in the late '60s as a way to enter a state that's in between dream and sleep, by virtue of staring into this homemade stroboscopic device. It didn't work for me. But it became important for me to start experimenting using myself. Also I was interested in questioning the possibilities and the possible failures of what the photograph can do to represent an experience. In making a diptych, I was trying to call that into question further.

CARTER MULL: I went to college on the East Coast, and that was my first serious induction into art in an intense way. I went through a Bauhaus-type program, which is how a lot of East Coast colleges are modeled. It left me with an emphasis on process and materials as a major concern no matter what the medium—photography, painting, or sculpture.

I began seriously making photographs in 2000. And the work steadily evolved from there, using a model of looking at previous work, seeing what's latent or of interest, and pushing that into the next body of photographs. This is a photograph from 2004, titled *One Hundred Unions in the Snow*. It is a chromogenic print of about 30 by 40 inches. Leading up to this body of work, I was making photographs by basically setting up a series of sheets of Plexiglas over an image, and then aiming the camera through the Plexi. On the Plexi would be situated material and textured, tactile things. I was making photographs using a technique that was basically developed by commercial photographers, but had been replaced by digital technology. I never intentionally hid the technique, but in this photograph, the actual construction became more apparent. The white that you see throughout the frame is literally daylight reflecting off the Plexi.

Following this working method that I had picked up as a younger person, I was interested in what would happen if I used this same set of materials, but shifted the construction that's built in front of the lens from two dimensions to three dimensions. This was the first body of work that I made in Los Angeles. It is called *Shifting States*. I was interested in creating a construction that was both in front of the lens, and also happening in-camera. That was one way I was thinking about making meaning. But for me, primarily, the issue was with the kind of photograph, and the kind of print itself. In this image, the construction is set up. It is destroyed after the photograph is made. The materials are thrown away, and what is left is the photographic print. Therefore, the way the camera is focusing on the image is critically important. For example, this area of the photo is a result of a glitzy material being out of focus. The reason that happens is that the aperture of the camera is at a certain f-stop, and the film plane of the 4 by 5 is in a certain position. As a result, the camera and the construction that is in front of it are contingent upon one another—totally dependent upon one another—for the purpose of making the image.

. . .

One of the ideas was to use the print itself as another moment of intervention into the photographic process where meaning could be constructed. For me, the whole concern is still about constructing an image, but in a certain sense, maybe even giving it a kind of autonomy relative to the kind of material and the kind of process concerns that are specific to photography . . . However, that said, for me, photography is really the relationship between information and time, and the formation of information in time. For me, the way something is made cannot be separated from what it means. Maybe that's the burden of a Bauhaus education, to have this process-driven set of concerns. But at the same time, I would hope that other meanings in the work are implied, if not fully explicated.

AMIR ZAKI: I think the reason that the three of us were brought together on this panel is because of our process rather than the content of our work or a conceptual framework. It is about something that is too early, in a way. It is how we make things. I think that's an interesting way to structure this; I want to work through some of those ideas. Also, I'm not going to talk about content in my work either, because I don't think that's really what this panel is about.

But I will talk about affect, which is, for me, the "too late." It is how I come to make work, and then how work effects me—my own work and another person's work that I'm going to show. Before I show any slides, I want to think about the two camps, which were presented and then dismissed, which I thought was very funny. Intuition is associated with earnestness—these are my associations—authenticity, rawness, and being unmediated. Truthful is what I think that means. On the other extreme is this idea of a directorial mode of making work, which is really premeditated, constructed, fabricated, and I think ultimately, fictional. I think that is what the cultural implication of that kind of work is.

I think most artists working in photography, not just the three of us, are working in somewhat of a hybrid of those two modes. I don't think very many people are really invested in one or the other. The other thing that I was thinking about was that there is another kind of dualistic approach that's similar to this idea of intuition versus directorial, but I think it is a little bit more apt for my work, or the way I think about making work. This is the idea of a kind of a subtractive [approach] to making work, versus an additive approach.

That idea is not my own; it is an idea I heard in my very first photography class, taught by John Divola, with whom I'm sure most of you are familiar. It is a very obvious idea, but it is also incredibly clear. It is still helpful for me when I teach, or when I talk about my own work, or when I think about my work. And it is simple. Traditionally speaking, photography is a fundamentally subtractive medium. You've got an infinite visual field, and the photographer frames that, subtracts out everything for this one sort of moment. The opposite of that would be the life of a painter, which is a fundamentally additive process. Painters start with a blank canvas and make marks until they are happy. Right?

Again, those camps don't hold up so well with most people making art today. Certainly, I work in a very hybrid fashion that is both additive and subtractive. That said, I just want to quickly show an image pulled out of context for the sake of this talk. This is an 8 by 10 inch, black-and-white photograph documenting a Chris Burden performance from 1974 called *Transfixed*. And I will paraphrase his description of the performance, which is that he was crucified to the back of this Volkswagen bug while the engine was running and it was rolled out of a garage for a few minutes, and rolled back into a garage. As I'm sure all of you are familiar, what you are presented with in a gallery is the 8 by 10 inch photograph along with the relics, which would be the nails, and his blurb.

I'd like to forget about those parts and look at this as an image for the purpose of this talk, because I think it is a very good hybrid of these two approaches. It's a kind of directorial approach, mixed with an intuitive approach—or you also can think of it as additive and subtractive.

It's obviously a constructed event, and I think that the photographer making this image worked in a straightforward, intuitive fashion. It's framed in a sensible, direct way in order to get this idea across. There's not that much else to say about it in that way. But what I think is interesting about that kind of hybrid approach is what it produces as an affect. And for me, the affect is this initial believability. I believe it—I read the text—I believe he was crucified to the back of this bug, it makes me nauseous, it makes me kind of laugh, and I'm a little uncomfortable. It produces all kinds of mixed feelings about the piece. But it's all because of this image. In the end, I start doubting the authenticity of it, and I couldn't really care less if nails were driven through Burden's hands. That's irrelevant to me. What I think is effective about this work, and lots of other documents of performance, is the image. I think it has to do with this result of a hybrid process . . .

In terms of my own work I will talk a little bit about my process and not content and maybe a little bit about affect. I would say in terms of my process I combine these additive and subtractive approaches. In a lot of ways I have a very romantic and maybe traditional stance or approach to making photographs, which is that I totally enjoy happy accidents. I enjoy coming across something that I think is noteworthy. I enjoy that kind of transformation of something banal into something magical, or beautiful, or arresting, or surprising. That's why I started making photographs and I still enjoy that part of it. The other half of my process is pushing pixels around on the computer. I heavily fabricate, manipulate, and create these images in an additive fashion.

But ultimately, I guess I'm much more interested in the way that a piece such as the Chris Burden photograph I showed you works and how it initially reads as the result of a traditional, subtractive process. It reads as if I happened upon this event. That's how I want my images to read. I don't mind doubt entering my work, that back and forth between doubt and believability. I want my images to be arresting, for viewers to ask, What is that thing?, What happened?, or, How did you find this thing?

CHARLOTTE COTTON: In very different ways I think that you revealed that the idea of construction and preconception are both caricatures. It is a very literal version of construction. Process and the flatfooted information about how you make photographs are entirely relevant to the intellectual standpoint that your work then comes to represent. You're using construction both in terms of being a process, as well as an intellectualization of what we think photography is.

MULL: I would say that my process involves a series of intervals. I think that's very common in photography. Shoot, re-shoot, back and forth in that way. But it is a bridge that is no longer necessarily entirely contingent upon the photographs. So I can have an interval that might be made with a drawing, or might be made with a found image. There is something intellectual in that.

At the same time, the process is probably driven more by an actual relationship to the act of making. An example of that is that I take a ridiculous number of notes for my work, but when I actually get into making work in the studio, those notes do not apply. It is almost like there is a shift that happens in my thinking. Those notes become a heuristic background, like a series of thoughts, a series of things that inform the work, but cannot be directly induced into the process of making.

COTTON: Miranda, that seems to relate to how you were describing your process as one that's heavily led by research, in terms of getting to the idea.

LICHTENSTEIN: Right, what I was about to say is that I do a lot of research. The project that I showed just now was really much more driven that way than what I'd done before, in terms of production. It was the first time I was working with a figure; I had to engage with other people and set up these shoots. It changed my process a lot. And I was thinking about that idea of intuition, because I've also shot still-lifes. All these things that happen when I'm alone in the studio don't happen when I'm with a shaman, two assistants, and lights. That dictated a lot of how things came to be. There were certainly happy accidents too, and that's something very different from intuition. There is still that kind of play, or magic. For example, in one photograph the subject put his watch down, and I just thought, "Right, that's so great." But it is not something I had preconceived.

ZAKI: I don't preconceive very much about the work until it gets going, and then it starts to make itself, in a way, if I come up with a strategy that I'm happy with. But that part of it is totally experimental. It is experimental when I'm making the pictures, and it is really experimental when I'm moving pixels around. It might seem very technical, but I happen upon a lot of how this work ends up looking. I happen upon it by screwing around, basically. It is not as if I think, "Oh, I want to do that to that image." It is probably really closely related to how painters work. I never made a painting, but I'm guessing that's what it is like.

. . .

COTTON: Do you, any of you, find resonance in the idea of the series, as it was defined by editorial photography, or do you think you're using the idea of series in a much more "contemporary art", or Conceptual art, version? I feel maybe the editorial series has a greater resonance with you, Amir.

ZAKI: I have a difficult relationship with series. I think that in a lot of ways that approach—if it is not watched—is a default approach, and I think that is a problem. I think that typology is a problem. I think making typological work now has its problems. So I'm always in dialogue with it, because it is the kind of work that I feel like I appreciated, or learned from, or was influenced by. But I'm constantly trying to figure out ways to undermine it, or complicate it. Often, I work in sub-series. I'll have these series that [contain] very different-looking works that resonate off of each other. There is dialogue within these sub-series, which I feel is one way of dealing with it.

Lately, the newest things I'm working on (I'm actually working on three projects simultaneously) are breaking away from a series even further. At the same time, the polar opposite of that, which is complete anti-content, is a problem in contemporary photography, too.

COTTON: Do you mean like the empty car parks at night, corners of sidewalks, and things like that?

ZAKI: Without naming anybody, I think that when an exhibition looks like the photographer's "best of," that is a problem. We all have an archive of pretty good pictures that we keep. If the photographer just blows those up in various sizes and pins them up—I'm not that interested. I think that's more of a problem than series, actually.

COTTON: You mean the idea that you have your body of work, and you're ever adding to it and it is like your raw material for every time that you install it. Do you think that's problematic?

ZAKI: There just seems to be less at stake when you make work like that. I don't know. I don't want to go too far into that.

LICHTENSTEIN: I agree with you, but I also think that strategy is liberating all of us now, too, in some ways. I have the same sentiment, but I also think it has been an open door.

COTTON: In a way, you're talking about values which are new to photography, because of its resonance within contemporary art. But also, they are really age-old problematics about editing. I mean, I must say that in all the time I've worked in photography, portfolios have tended to be this mismatch of pictures that a photographer recognizes as being good pictures. You know, they stand out. You recognize them in the first edit as ones that are good, and are constructed well.

And they are probably the kind of pictures that you will take the whole of your life, if you chose to take the same picture the whole of your life. And then there are other ones, which I sometimes call "itchy-scratchy" pictures. They trouble you; you don't know whether it is the picture or if it is a cue to what will happen next. I think that has become a sign of photography as contemporary art—how much time you will spend with the pictures that don't appear as good pictures.

The fault line is the idea that if it is about an idea, having twelve doesn't make them any better. And if it is the kind of picture that, if you're a good photographer and you understand your camera, of course you're going to take when you're in front of that subject, then that's not interesting either. On the other hand, is this idea of not abusing the potential in the most interesting pictures that you take that you haven't fully intellectualized or understood.

. . .

AUDIENCE: I have a problem with what looks today like commercial photography being passed off into the high echelons of art. I hate to make the distinction between artists and commercial photographers, but there does seem to be a collapsing of boundaries between art and very competent, technical commercial photography that is utterly staid in terms of the content. I'm just wondering if anybody wants to take that on.

. . .

MULL: I want to interject on that note a little bit. I actually find commercial photography more interesting than most art photography. The reason is that, from my point of view, it shapes a lot of how we see—not only in terms of what our visual field is, but also in terms of the processes used to make images, and how we understand those processes and see them. At a certain point, something that's not made digitally started to look of a different time, not only in its style but also in its very production. I find that condition that commercial photography gives us to be very interesting. It shapes our field in many ways.

. . .

AUDIENCE: I perceive commercial photography as learning a language. These are people that have to be absolute masters of their craft. However, they don't always have something to say. The artist is the one who has something to say. I think the best would be someone who has the technical expertise of the commercial photographer, but also has something to say.

COTTON: Yes, absolutely. My ex-boss, who distrusted my interest in commercial photography, described it as thus: an artist makes a proposition, asks a question, and leaves things open-ended. A commercial photographer makes a statement with a full stop at the end.

In the unsuccessful attempts by commercial artists to move into the gallery arena, what you're seeing is almost like throwing back at the art world a caricature of itself. So you have these perfect visions laminated behind Plexi, everything constructed and everything attributed to the artist, but not with a question that leaves it open-ended.

AUDIENCE: I wanted to ask all the photographers on the panel, and you, Charlotte, about what I perceive to be a tentative relationship with the history of photography.

Everyone seems really eager to praise painting history. I'm wondering why that is?

MULL: I'll take a stab at that. From my point of view, photography is always affected by the conditions—technology and things that are changing in the world. Painting is an antiquated technology. There are technological innovations within painting, but they are few and far between; they are not great. But photography is very much affected by the technological world around it. And now, we're in a time of technological flux. We have been for ten years, maybe more. At a time when modernization was affecting photography, there was a lot of photographic experimentation going on.

In a certain sense, we're in a place where the medium is in flux. And what the medium can be is an open question, I think, to some degree. With digital technology, there is this new sense of plasticity. One can push pixels around, and one can do all these different things. At the same time, our relationship to images has changed because of the Internet. Somehow we went from a library that had a certain materiality to a library that had a different kind of materiality. I think these questions about plasticity are actually really a major part of the medium right now.

ZAKI: Can I follow up? That's a really good question. I don't mean to dodge photography, but I always see my relationship to it in the broader art-making context, in its relationship to a history that's older than 200 years. I think about it in relation to sculpture and painting. I prioritize photography only to the degree that it's what I do.

. . .

CHARLIE WHITE [AUDIENCE]: I'm hoping that each of you can speak a little bit about this point. Fundamentally, there seems to be a generational bubble around this conversation because of a pedagogy shift. We're all talking about students who learned process in a context of master's studio art programs that began to allow photographers to study with them. We're looking at a group of people that came from the Pictures Generation—from 1979 forward—that started to become teachers in schools that otherwise weren't actually hiring photographers-as-artists-as-art-teachers in art programs at the master's level. So there is this major shift where process became—going to Amir's point of looking at a picture of Chris Burden who's coming out of a program that's teaching dominantly conceptualism—whatever medium, whatever means to convey the idea. And at this point, people are reaching out and grabbing cameras. They don't have to be, but they are. And they are saying, "I'm not really a photographer. I'm just using photography to make my work." Ultimately you end up having pictures like the Chris Burden documentation, which he's not taking . . .

I just think that this discussion exists within a different place for somebody who is 20 years the senior of the group. It is a very different argument about where their process came from, because they didn't learn process, as it were, in a pedagogical system, if they studied photography at all. You know, even in most of our undergraduate programs, photography was ghettoized. I know at the School of Visual Arts, it didn't exist in the art program. I know at Art Center here on the West Coast, it doesn't exist at the undergraduate art level. It is ghettoized as a practice separate from art. If you study photography, you are not going to be in certain discourses. At the graduate level, say at Yale, they still ghettoize it, but they intellectualize it. It is uncompressed. At the University of California at Los Angeles, the graduate student mentor system starts to merge; the University of Southern California merges it; where Amir is, at UC-Riverside, it is merged. It doesn't really matter any longer what the practice is, it is just an all-collective system. So maybe people can talk about process forward from their graduate studies a little bit.

ZAKI: Do you mean process like the way Carter was talking about process?

WHITE [AUDIENCE]: Maybe, somewhere between the three of you. Carter's process, on one hand, in terms of the way he's able to think through an idea as a means of making and dealing with materiality. Or Miranda in terms of thinking about the sociological as a means of getting or reaching certain places, spaces, or subjects. Perhaps you could argue and say I'm absolutely wrong, but part of this comes from being able to participate in dialogues and pedagogical systems that, historically, photography was somewhat left out of.

LICHTENSTEIN: Yes, I agree with you, absolutely, and I see that a bit in New York, where I teach undergrads at Parsons. I also teach at Cooper Union, and they are two totally different approaches, because at Parsons photography is ghettoized. And I struggle to connect the two.

MULL: In high school, I studied with a 4th-generation Abstract Expressionist painter. And my first assignment in college was to make a drawing of the experience of taking a shower, by making it in the shower. I studied painting in college, so I had a very direct relationship with process. But I think the irony is that I was also taught on some level by Pictures Generation people, by people born in the 1950s who were basically in their early 50s. But they were painters, not necessarily photographers. A lot of the process education came from people that were much older who were really concerned with the push and pull of charcoal. On the graduate level, I went to CalArts, where the pedagogy is outlined in a conceptual way. If anything, I had to disagree my way through there. At the same time, I was learning as I went. So I think that my relationship with process wasn't necessarily determined by the Pictures Generation. At the same time, because of that, the work of the Pictures Generation seemed very refreshing. Richard Prince's early photographs seemed really radical when I first saw them.

ZAKI: This might answer your question. It doesn't really

have to do with how I was educated, but I have two relationships with my process. One is a kind of closeted one that's shared with a select group of people with whom I share these super nerdy, techy, process-oriented questions. And I get incredible enjoyment out of that. But I also feel that that's really not good because there is a broad audience that I'm much more interested in. For example, I'm working on something now that's really mathematical. And I'd love to have this totally nerdy, techy conversation with a mathematician about it, or someone who's into permutations and adding. But that's not what my work is about; that's not what it is going to be about when it is out in the world.

I think that photography might deserve to be in a ghetto if we all expect everybody to get interested in the new brand of Crane paper that just came out, or something. I think that there is such a high learning curve with photography, and digital technology, and it is so foreign to most people that it is an unrealistic expectation to think that there is going to be a sophisticated dialogue with even the art world in the way that exists with painting or sculpture. There is just not an understanding of materials, or immaterial, with digital. There is just not an understanding outside of a really tiny group of people.

QUESTIONNAIRE / CHARLES TRAUB & ADAM BELL

Photography education is about teaching people to think in a visual world. Photography and its related practice are a matrix and nexus for relating to the real and imagined worlds in which we live. The essential goals of any good, creative academic environment are simply to help students learn how to look and engage with the world responsibly. In addition to the development of craft and technical skills, there is also a language and intellectual base that must complement any photographic practice. It is clear to us that the best students are those that are able to relate their practice not only to the evolving technical potentials of the medium, but also to its rich history, theory and practice.

The greatest hindrance to any student is the overemphasis by academic institutions on careerist goals at the expense of a rich and meaningful artistic practice. The short-term rewards of the market have the potential to derail and cloud the vision and potential of an emerging artist. An arts education must not only push students to challenge themselves, but also nurture their creativity, idiosyncrasies and vision in the face of larger temptations and distractions. Arts education can't create talent, but it can teach students that true talent is honed by practice, ideas and hard work.

At the beginning of the 21st century, the digital revolution is over—artists can no longer afford to ignore its radical changes and implications for the medium. Digital technology, along with every photographic innovation, has forced artists to reengage with the language and possibility of the medium in creative ways. Learning to transcend and push past the novelty and limitations of each such innovation lies at the heart of any real engagement with the medium.

QUESTIONNAIRE / SHANE LAVALETTE

WHAT ARE SOME OF THE UNIQUE WAYS THE BLOG ENABLES YOU TO ENGAGE WITH YOUR INTERESTS IN PHOTOGRAPHY?

At the time that I began writing my blog there were very few photography blogs online. Blogs in general had not quite become the widely known phenomena that they are today and so to many—myself included—the idea of archiving thoughts and ideas in this way was new and exciting. Looking back, I think I really started the blog out of a desire to have a space online where ideas and images felt lasting. (Though the Internet contained a wealth of information and imagery, it did not feel tangible to me. The blog offered an illusion of tangibility.) With it I began collecting images that moved me, photographers whose work I was interested in, and I wrote about things that I felt were relevant to contemporary practice.

Perhaps because I started to use the blog more regularly around the time that I began my undergraduate studies, I've come to think of it as an extension of my education. At its core it's a platform for learning. Scouring the Internet for interesting work and challenging myself to write about photography were important learning experiences for me both then and now, and the blog has allowed me to safely return to these photographs and thoughts, while at the same time encouraging more to come.

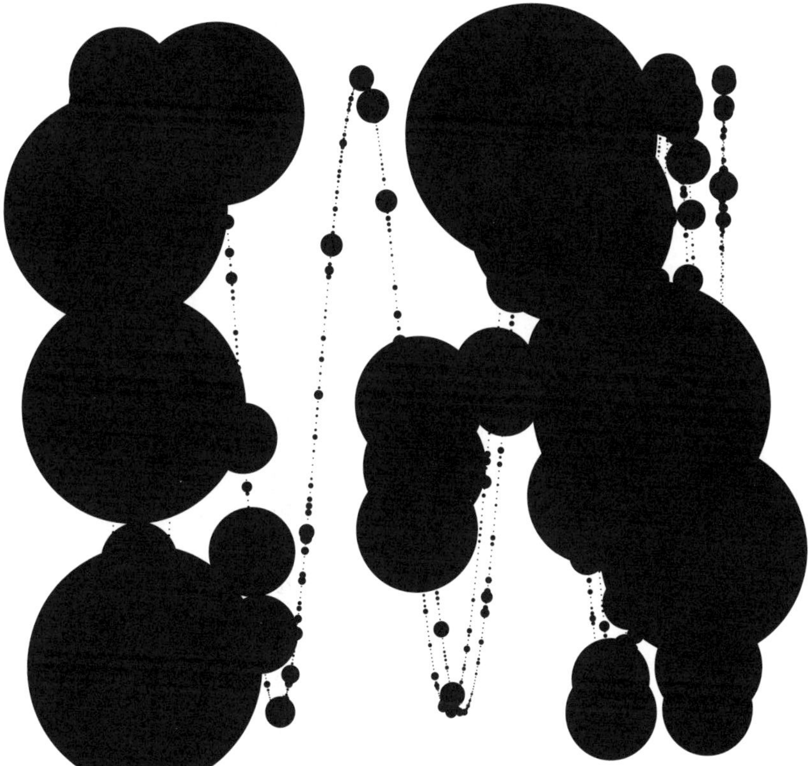

Remembering and Forgetting Conceptual Art

ALEX KLEIN

In 1972, Ursula Meyer published her classic compendium *Conceptual Art*—a slim paperback that is remarkable not only for the currency it held at its time of publication, but also for its cover design. Set in white, uppercase Helvetica against a black background, the phrase "Conceptual Art" is repeated seventeen times, bleeding from top to bottom as if ad infinitum. Meanwhile, the book itself, which predated Lucy Lippard's *Six Years: The Dematerialization of the Art Object* (1973) by one year, features the work of some forty artists, including Vito Acconci, Victor Burgin, Dan Graham, Adrian Piper, and Ed Ruscha. Instead of framing each project with explanatory texts or contextualizing essays, Meyer juxtaposed the work with a selection of quotations from the likes of Maurice Merleau-Ponty and Roland Barthes, reserving her remarks for the blurb on the back cover. For Meyer, this new, idea-based art eliminated the need to distinguish between artist and critic, thus untethering the artwork from the art historian's analysis. Instead, the book's cover stands in—formally at least—as the primary framing device, underscoring the fact that even as its history was still being written, the aesthetic that we associate with Conceptual art had already been codified within the popular imagination: that is, black-and-white, stripped down, serial, bureaucratic and textual. The design of the book's cover thereby distilled the heterogeneous practices of the artists included, acting as a harbinger of what we now think of as the "look" of classic Conceptual practice.

While it is not the purpose of this essay to map out the different branches and legacies of Conceptual art, it is important to point to the way this distillation elides complex nuances, if we are to begin to think through Conceptualism's implications for photography. The dismantling of representational signifiers in Conceptual art resulted in works that were seemingly immaterial (systemic, performative, text-based, ephemeral, amateurish, etc.) when compared with the more traditional formalism of the previous generation of Abstract Expressionists. However, as Benjamin Buchloh has noted, because of the "range of implications of Conceptual art, it would seem imperative to resist a construction of its history in terms of a stylistic homogenization, which would limit that history to a group of individuals and a set of strictly defined practices and historical interventions." [1] Moreover, even within these stylistic similarities, it is necessary to make distinctions between the key players. For example, the implications of Conceptual works varied even within the select group of artists associated with Seth Siegelaub (Robert Barry, Douglas Huebler, Joseph Kosuth, and Lawrence Weiner), not to mention between artists working outside of the small New York scene.

As demonstrated by Liz Kotz's research and other recent scholarship on the use of photography by artists in the 1960s and 1970s, Conceptual art's turn to the ordinary or quotidian was multifaceted. The impulses behind these works ranged from differing reactions to Minimalism and Postminimalism combined with investigations that were both anticipated in the work of John Cage and Fluxus and happening concurrently in modern dance and experimental poetry. Which is just to say that the form, in this instance, should not necessarily be mistaken for the whole, as it is only one variable in a rather complex equation of influences, pedagogies, and ideologies. By reducing what we have come to understand as Conceptual art to a uniform movement or style, we run the risk of conflating the influence of aesthetics with that of ideas. Further, if we are to resist the rigid categorizations and market-driven dichotomies of artists using photography versus art photographers, we must also resist the temptation to collapse different critical strategies and investigatory concerns into aestheticized, nostalgic narratives. [2]

Nevertheless, with the integration of photography into art schools and Master of Fine Arts programs, and the imminent obsolescence of analog photographic printing, a bleeding and blending has occurred. For a generation of young photographers who might never print their own work or have to justify their medium, the distinctions between conceptual practice and more traditional documentary modes have become increasingly malleable. That said, the pedagogic hodgepodge of the art-school environment is only part of the equation, for one might also look to the lack of adequate art histories that integrate photography as more than a footnote within surveys of twentieth-century art. [3] For many students today, art history is fluid and pluralism is a given, creating a tendency to sample freely. As Thomas Crow pointed out in his essay "Unwritten Histories of Conceptual Art," consciousness of precedent has become very nearly the condition and definition of major artistic ambition in today's arena. [4] However, the process of identifying and citing previous generations is necessarily enmeshed with an element of misrecognition or even paramnesia. That we read our own desires and historical conditions onto the past seems obvious, but this continuing process of remembering and misremembering is very different from the conversations, generational anxieties, or ideological clashes at play in and between artistic movements. The stakes are different when the process functions more like a personal archive from which histories are constructed at will among seemingly disparate elements and time periods. (Allan Sekula's comparison of the archive to a toolshed is apt in this regard.) [5] However, just as one can build from the archive, the archive is also itself a destructive container. As Jacques Derrida would have it, the original memory disappears, replaced by the structure imposed by the archive; memory necessarily entails a replacement of one image by another through a repetition of impossible originals. [6]

The way we historicize artistic influence is also part of this condition and offers an opportunity to reevaluate the stakes of even our most foundational critical narratives. To date, Jeff Wall's account in his essay "'Marks of Indifference': Aspects of Photography in, or as, Conceptual Art," although often contested, has stood as one of the decisive voices in tracing the ramifications of Conceptual art for contemporary photographic practice. In Wall's account, the modernist concerns of self-reflexivity and medium specificity are ultimately realized in Conceptual artists' deskilling and amateurization of the photograph. For Conceptual artists, photographic depiction is detached from representation and thus points to what Wall calls the "experience of experience." [7] In this account, Conceptual artists' images are consciously employed and constructed as the antithesis of the highly skilled modernist photograph. It is precisely because they are produced outside of the "History of Photography" that they distill the medium to its essence, thus opening the door for the reintroduction of picture-making in or around 1974.

To bc sure, this summary risks an over-simplification of Wall's argument. Still, if this moment truly represented the furthest limits of modernist self-reflexivity in photography, why should it inevitably lead the medium back to painting—Pictorialism, pastiche, and tableau? Perhaps there are other ways to think about this story than the way Wall has narrativized it. That Conceptual art was reacting against the craft of fine art photography is only one possibility. As we know from the writings of many Conceptual artists working at the time, their use of photography was, for the most part, detached altogether from a consideration of photographic histories. [8] Rather, the employment of a deskilled photographic process was less an outright rejection of one kind of photography in favor of another than it was an embrace of particular representational strategies made possible by photography. It is the Conceptual artists' approach to the photograph—using it as an image that stands in for an idea—that offers some of the greatest significance for our understanding of the potential for photographic representation. Furthermore, Conceptual artists' reduction or amateurization of the photograph must also be acknowledged as an aesthetic decision, no matter how much it may be tied to chance operations or deconstructive procedures. Wall's proposition that Conceptual art was the catalyst for photography's transcendence of its own medium, making possible a return to pictorial strategies, thus suggests that Wall may be more invested in distancing himself from modernist photographic practice than were the Conceptual artists themselves.

Indeed, just as Wall posits 1974 as the year of a new order of picture-making, Buchloh argues that 1975 is when Conceptual art goes on a brief hiatus. It is worth considering the significance of these years, which mark the resignation of Richard Nixon and the end of the Vietnam War. As it happens, 1974/75 is also the moment when Martha Rosler produced *The Bowery in Two Inadequate Descriptive Systems*. While I would hesitate to use this oft-cited work as a sole example, Rosler's juxtaposition of typewritten text and straightforward, black-and-white photographs can be seen as a bridge between a certain conceptual practice and documentary photography (even as it critiques it). In turn, 1975 was also the year of the exhibition *New Topographics: Photographs of a Man-Altered Landscape* at the George Eastman House in Rochester, N.Y., which presented a seminal collection of work by photographers who had made their mark using large-format cameras to depict the landscapes of suburbia, industrial decline, and the American West, including Lewis Baltz, Robert Adams, Stephen Shore, and Bernd and Hilla Becher.

For William Jenkins, the curator of that exhibition, these photographs were characterized by their banality and lack of style. Although this remark might seem strange from today's perspective given the critical success and massive influence of many of the photographers, at the time the photographs were discussed as empty and anonymous, echoing early descriptions of Conceptual art. It should come as no surprise, then, that in his catalogue essay Jenkins highlights Ed Ruscha's deadpan photographs as an inspiration for at least some of the photographers in the exhibition. However, for Jenkins this deadpan quality is where the similarities end, the distinction being that for Ruscha the photograph was a means to an end, a comment on representation and art as opposed to an exploration of photographic meaning. That is, Ruscha's photographs of parking lots and gas stations are only partially concerned with their ostensible subject matter. For Jenkins, the distinction between Ruscha's photographs and the pictures in the *New Topographics* exhibition is the difference between what a photograph is "*about*" versus what it is "*of*." The photographers included in *New Topographics* were drawing from and reacting to a variety of photographic influences, among them street photography, Andy Warhol, and Neue Sachlichkeit.

In particular, as Jenkins suggests, the formal qualities of conceptual projects like Ruscha's books and photographs were separated from their critical context, adopted, and transformed.

Given this ability to separate a certain photographic formalism from its ideational underpinnings, we might also consider how such strategies inform practices outside Conceptual art's conventions of photographic vision. Here, it is helpful to recall Wall's account of Conceptual art's use of photography, in which he posits two modes of photographic reportage: the performative and the parodic. One functions as a document of an event, while the other eludes, refuses, or trumps depiction. It is this second instance that interests me, because it highlights certain problems posed by representation in photography. To take the work of one of Wall's primary examples, Huebler, as a case in point, one finds a shift in the onus of meaning away from the subject depicted in the photograph. For instance, in *Location Piece #2, New York City – Seattle, Washington, July 1969* (1969), Huebler assigned the same task to a person in each of three cities: to photograph a place that he/she "felt could be characterized as being (1) frightening, (2) erotic, (3) transcendent, (4) passive, (5) fevered and (6) muffled."

The photographs were then scrambled, so that in the final piece the intent of the photographer vanishes and the viewer is left to project his/her own psychological condition on the images. In his statement accompanying the work Huebler writes:

> I would define art as an activity that extends human consciousness through constructs that transpose natural phenomena from that qualitatively undifferentiated condition that we call "life" into objective and internally focused concepts. Since Impressionism most art has been based on an inference that our

> experience of natural phenomena necessarily calls for its transposition into visual manifestations. My work is concerned with determining the form of art when the role traditionally played by visual experience is mitigated or eliminated. [9]

There are several other works in Huebler's oeuvre from this period that gesture to the limits of photographic representation with ever greater poignancy. For instance, when Huebler photographs in the direction of a birdcall heard in Central Park, the viewer is only shown a tangle of trees; when he attempts to photograph every person alive, we are confronted with the impossible nature of such encyclopedic, taxonomic endeavors. While we could also consider the impulse to point the viewer outside of the photograph's frame through the lens of Robert Smithson's non-sites, it was through Huebler's pedagogic legacy that such strategies have gained currency within contemporary photographic practice: Sarah Charlesworth, Mike Kelley, and Christopher Williams were all his students.

Instead of arriving at a dematerialized object, I would argue that such work engages in a type of masking in which images, even when utterly depictive and seemingly objective in nature, betray an opaqueness of meaning that is derived precisely *through* photographic representation. For all of the textual apparatus that accompany Williams's images, his viewers are nevertheless left with a catalogue of factual information that conveys little about the modes of production and systems of exploitation and consumption behind the objects depicted. Ultimately, the photograph withholds meaning even as it discloses itself entirely. Similar to Huebler's investigations of subjective or perceptual experiences that must necessarily lie outside of the photograph, in Williams's work meaning is always located elsewhere. For Williams:

> the inability of the photograph to communicate fully [actually] reflects or could represent a viewer's relationship to the world outside of the pictures. Every object around us is at once very present and identifiable, but also the representative of multiple historical trajectories, economies and desires which you barely have to scratch the surface to get into. The coffee you're drinking is obviously a product that had a rich history here in Europe, but it's also just a cup of coffee. And that's something inherent in all objects. [10]

A similar archaeology of the image or object is being explored by younger artists such as Simon Starling, for whom the object—whether a photograph, Eames chair or bicycle—is only one point in a series of interconnected material histories. For all three—Huebler, Williams, Starling—the photograph operates as a document whose meaning is contained not primarily in what it depicts, but in the myriad associations that it mobilizes.

This is but one thread that we might follow when discussing how the strategies of Conceptual art have come to inform contemporary photographic practice. As artists continue to quote the aesthetics of Conceptual art, we might ask whether this is indicative of a continued investigation of ideational concerns or an appropriation of style as an empty signifier for criticality. With regard to photography in particular, we might on the one hand consider the recent turn to seemingly immaterial models of distribution and accumulation that speak increasingly to the way we use and understand images, while on the other, reconsider how works in so-called "conventional photography" skirt the edge of conceptual strategies or have been informed by them. In this light, how do we situate a work such as Joel Sternfeld's *On This Site* (1996),which at once points to the potential for historical trauma behind every photograph while at the same time producing important photographic documents in and of themselves? When an artist makes reference to "conceptualism" is it based on a furthering of the ideas of autonomy or an aestheticization of its components? [11] At what point do we call a work "conceptual" – does it begin with an idea or an aesthetic?

By way of conclusion, I would like to return to another book cover of sorts, this time from the March 2008 issue of *Artforum*, on which a full-frame, medium-format color photograph is reproduced at the center of a white field. The image is from Zoe Leonard's ongoing project *Analogue*, and it depicts an array of used items such as shoes, a crucifix, and eyeglasses. Amassed over nine years, the larger project is comprised of approximately four hundred such photographs, in color and black-and-white, of subjects such as small storefronts, independently owned businesses, outdoor markets, secondhand sales, and homemade signage. Exhibited at Documenta this past summer (2007), *Analogue* is especially remarkable precisely because of its obvious indebtedness to the history of traditional documentary photography. For Mark Godfrey, writing in the accompanying *Artforum* article, *Analogue* is a document of an economy that with globalization and increasing corporatization will soon be outmoded, if it does not disappear entirely—an analog photographic gesture in a digital world.

Still, despite its unabashed embrace of the language of the vernacular subject within a clearly documentary photographic practice, for Godfrey Leonard's project is best understood in a Conceptual lineage that includes the Bechers and elements of Pop art. [12] By describing *Analogue* as an "allegorical" project, Godfrey is thus able to situate Leonard more comfortably among her immediate peers in New York's early eighties downtown scene and the postmodern works of the Pictures Generation.

However, to reclaim this ostensibly documentary project as an "allegorical impulse" shifts the valence and perhaps the poignancy of the work further away from the legacy of Evans to that of Rauschenberg. [13] But this is not necessarily a case, as we have seen, of clear distinctions. Whatever terminology might ultimately be employed as a framing device, it is clear from Leonard's diverse oeuvre that her influences are rich and multiple. Indeed, for much of the work being produced today, we must acknowledge something deeper than stylistic quotation, but rather a kind of double indebtedness—both to Conceptual art and to photography as a conceptual practice.

Notes

1. Benjamin H.D. Buchloh, "Conceptual Art 1962–1969: From the Aesthetic of Administration to the Critique of Institutions," *October*, vol. 55 (Winter 1990), p. 107.

2. The recent exhibition *Romantic Conceptualism* is a case in point. In particular, the curator of the exhibition singles out Bas Jan Ader as one of the founding fathers of a certain emotive brand of conceptualism. As Thomas Crow observed over ten years ago, there is a danger in making "Ader into a retrospectively romanticized cult figure." This "romanticism" or sentimentality in Ader's work is quickly deemphasized once his work is couched in the terms of European post-war trauma and displacement.

3. While history of photography courses are common in art history programs, photography is rarely fully integrated into 19th and 20th century art survey courses. Thus, there is little opportunity for students to contextualize the different strands of photography as they relate to the broader sphere of artistic practice. Furthermore, we might also consider the difference between how the history of photography is taught in the darkroom versus the classroom.

4. Thomas Crow, "Unwritten Histories of Conceptual Art," in *Art After Conceptual Art*, eds. Alexander Alberro and Sabeth Buchmann (Cambridge: MIT Press, 2006), p. 59.

5. Allan Sekula, "Reading an Archive," in *Blasted Allegories: An Anthology of Writings by Contemporary Artists*, ed. Brian Wallis (New York: New Museum of Contemporary Art, 1987), pp. 114–127.

6. See Jacques Derrida, *Archive Fever: A Freudian Impression*, trans. Eric Prenowitz (Chicago: University of Chicago Press, 1998).

7. Jeff Wall, quoted in "Marks of Indifference: Aspects of Photography, in, or as, Conceptual Art," in *Reconsidering the Object of Art*, eds. Ann Goldstein and Anne Rorimer (Los Angeles/Cambridge: Museum of Contemporary Art/MIT Press, 1995), p. 266.

8. While this implicitly stands in opposition to the aesthetics or social initiatives of the art photography of the same era, the photograph was utilized or conceived of more often as a tool or means to an end. Employed as a seemingly objective, mechanical, recording device, it's material and historical conditions were consciously, if temporarily, ignored. Joseph Kosuth, for example, stated: "I didn't consider the Photostat as a work of art; only the idea was art." As quoted in Liz Kotz's article

"Language Between Performance and Photography," *October*, vol. 115 (Winter 2005), p.10. Originally from Joseph Kosuth in Arthur R. Rose, "Four Interviews," *Arts Magazine* (February 1969), p. 23.

9. See Douglas Huebler, *Location Piece #2, New York City — Seattle, Washington, July 1969* (1969).

10. Christopher Williams, "Christopher Williams in Conversation with Mark Godfrey," *Afterall*, No. 16 (Autumn/Winter 2007), p. 69.

11. Liz Kotz observes, "Critics continue to argue that the conceptual use of language as an artistic medium propels something like a 'withdrawal of visuality' or 'dematerialization' of art, and a current generation of artists often seems intent on trawling the 1960s for remnants of ephemeral practices that can be turned into commercially successful objects..." *Words to be Looked At: Language in 1960s Art* (Cambridge: MIT Press, 2007), p. 98.

12. Mark Godfrey writes: "Leonard has managed to produce an allegorical work with straight-on photography, something more astonishing when we consider that the 'allegorical impulse' has usually been associated with postmodern photographic strategies of quotation, appropriation, and collage. *Analogue*'s clearest connections are to other archival projects (the Bechers, for instance) whose focus has been disappearing objects and buildings, but the work should also be contextualized within the history of Pop art." *Artforum* (March 2008), p. 300.

13. Although both Atget and Evans are mentioned in Craig Owens's essay "Allegorical Impulse: Toward a Theory of Postmodernism" the allegorical nature of their projects is simultaneously taken up and taken into question. He writes, "As an allegorical art, then, photography would represent our desire to fix the transitory, the ephemeral, in a stable and stabilizing image. In the photographs of Atget and Walker Evans, insofar as they self-consciously preserve that which threatens to disappear, that desire becomes the *subject* of the image. If their photographs are allegorical, however, it is because what they offer is only a fragment, and thus affirms its own arbitrariness and contingency." *October*, vol. 12. (Spring 1980), p. 71.

--

DISCUSSION FORUM
WWW.WORDSWITHOUTPICTURES.ORG

--

Subject: Get Rid of Yourself
Date: 7 April 2008 21:09:47
From: SHANNON EBNER

In the introduction to his 1991 exhibition at MoMA entitled *The Pleasures and Terrors of Domestic Comfort,* Peter Galassi writes of a meeting that took place between Dorothea Lange and John Szarkowski not long before Lange's death in 1965. Lange told Szarkowski of a new national documentary project she had in mind and asked him to invite several young photographers to the museum so she could propose the idea to them. Szarkowski recalls that during the meeting the young photographers were enthusiastic and eager to know when they would start. "But as the conversation went on," he recalled, "Lange became a little quiet and finally a little restive. And after listening to all the photographers talk about how wonderful it would be, she said, "Well now, just a minute. I am not talking about finding a lot of money so we can do the Farm Security Administration over again." She said, "Actually, you know, we've learned how to photograph poor people. It might really be more interesting now, it certainly would be more difficult, to see if we can learn how to photograph affluence."

Even if Lange was not the direct catalyst, following World War I, The Great Depression, and World War II, it became acceptable for photographers to turn their focus inward. Photographers around the country began to leave the field—so to speak—and enter the interior world of the home, regardless of wealth, poverty and mediocrity.

Galassi's exhibition, which uses the recounting of this meeting as a touchstone, presented work that took up the subject of the home in all of its glory and dysfunction by photographers that ranged from Emmet Gowin to Barbara Kruger with Philip-Lorca diCorcia and Nan Goldin nestled in between. Even though Galassi speculated that Lange did not characterize her interest in affluence as that of domestic affluence—he still had to wonder how the project that she envisioned might have compared with the work that he selected for his exhibition.

There is a photograph by Bruce Davidson in Galassi's essay that stands out not so much for what it depicts, but because of the years in which it was made. Davidson's *Untitled, East 100th Street* is dated 1967-1968. This is two years after Lange's meeting with Szarkowski and the same year that Robert Smithson published "A Tour of the Monuments of Passaic, New Jersey" in *Artforum*. It is more than poignant for me to try to imagine Smithson's *Monument of Dislocated Directions*—

a bridge that rotated east and west—as being a grand dislocating metaphor for the two non-parallel tracks that Lange and Smithson were to follow. Both were heading home in a sense, but this is all that they had in common.

So much has transpired since these two non-convergent paths set sail. I see Galassi's exhibition as having set the tone for generations of photographers to examine alienation as only the Reagan era and Clinton generation would have it. It should come as no surprise that Conceptual art found no home of its own in Galassi's MoMA exhibition and Dan Graham's *Homes for America* project (also from 1967) was in absentia, too. Are we to take this to mean in part that Graham's work was too critical or disengaged from petty bourgeois anxieties to have made the cut? Was the work too bleak, too unmannered, too speculative? Well, of course, we know that it was for all of these reasons that it was not included and it is for these very reasons perhaps that many a young photographer, as Alex Klein points out in her essay, has taken up the language and style of Conceptual art once more, for better and for worse. Conceptual art speaks the language of critique, a language quite absent from photography today for a variety of complicated reasons.

Galassi makes two points in regard to his story about Lange, and they both seem as relevant today as they were in 1991:

1. Just as the inertia of tradition enforces the persistence of successful styles, it also inhibits the discovery of new subjects.

2. An old approach might not work for a new subject.

Whether we address it in our work or not, we as image-makers all know that we are living in a gross time of war. The American dollar is weak, our economy, our people and the people we are at war with are suffering. Our moral and ethical consciousness is compromised by the irreparable harm we are committing on the Iraqi and Afghani people and, at least speaking for myself, my days of examining my alienation are pretty much over. Now I'm alienated from the world, it's a new feeling, a new day, and it's time to get rid of myself as quickly as possible. The stakes are high. Where are the pictures?

--

Subject: Dead or Alive
Date: 8 April 2008 16:17:58
From: PHIL CHANG

Living means leaving traces. —Walter Benjamin

Would the following be a fair set of claims? The photograph relies on the very disappearance of an event in order to exist. In dealing with photographs, we rather tacitly commit ourselves to engaging with a dialectical condition that results in a tangible yet seemingly transparent window between the subject and object of a photograph. The dialectical condition here is one where the photograph exists at once in time, despite context or instrumental use, and simultaneously, in spite of it.

These claims would be a launching point in approaching Klein's instructive question: at what point do we call a work conceptual, particularly, photographic works that trade in the nebulous territory of ideas and the "no-style" of Conceptual art? Today, it goes without question that photographs do less to buttress memory than to supplant it. In regard to the issues that Klein raises, however, do photographs "themselves" complicate the experience of remembering and forgetting Conceptual art? If our culture's tactless agility with freestyling and lifting of content and form has reached an apotheosis, then could it be that very thing—the contingent and trafficked document, prone to determination not only by context but through associative meaning—that incited Klein to raise such a pertinent and specific question?

In discussing Walter Benjamin's conception of history through the language of photography, Eduardo Cadava, in *Words of Light*, focused on the ephemerality of images that makes up Benjamin's theses on history. In describing both of the existential functions of photographs, Cadava writes:

> As Benjamin suggests in "Central Park," the photograph, like the souvenir, is the corpse of an experience. A photograph therefore speaks as death, as the trace of what passes into history. I, the photograph, the spaced out limit between life and death, am death. Yet, speaking as death, the photograph can be neither death nor itself. At once dead and alive, it opens the possibility of our being in time. [1]

Though elegiac, Cadava's prose offers a way in which to understand the dialectical condition of the photograph as it takes place in social reality: as picture and as document. On one hand alive and on the other hand dead, depending on where we choose to lay claim within the larger narrative offered by Jeff Wall's "Marks Of Indifference," this description of the photograph provides a competing narrative. By focusing on the aspects of life and death, Cadava's description suggests an understanding of the photograph at its base level. I wish to add here that I am not advocating for a return to treating the photograph as unaffected by cultural force and placing it within a framework of aesthetic formalism.[2] Instead, I am asking that we pursue a deep investigation into the function of photographs that has the potential to parallel contemporary artistic strategies that take up similar examinations, much like the attention paid to the materiality of photographs that we see today.

I would argue then that this very dialectic between picture and document allowed for Conceptual art and photography to not only achieve different ends but also served as a reminder of an ontological fissure that still manages to confront us. In its deliberately banal and style-free use of photographs, Conceptual art expanded the notion of the vernacular beyond the figures we commonly associate with it—Walker Evans, Lee Friedlander, Garry Winogrand, et al. To borrow Benjamin Buchloh's phrase, this "programmatic effacement of camera skills" allowed Conceptual artists to offset expectations of competency, skill, and authorship. Moreover, both Conceptual art and photography, particularly social documentary, share a history of insisting on a notion of neutrality, yet for differing ends. For Conceptual art, this neutrality was a reaction against the aesthetic conventions of high Modernism. For documentary photography, the need for politicized images to be passed off as a naturalized, unmediated truth became paramount. Allan Sekula has written, "the most general terms of the discourse are a kind of disclaimer, an assertion of neutrality; in short, the overall function of photographic discourse is to render itself transparent."[3]

This difference, however, can point us in a direction back to Klein's explanation of metonymy: "It is the Conceptual artists' approach to photography as an image that stands in for an idea that offers some of the greatest significance for our understanding of the potential for photographic representation." Conceptual art's metonymic handling is arguably one of the most significant outcomes for photography. By severing the correspondence between the subject and object of a photograph, the attempt to produce meaning becomes clear against the reliance on conventions of straight recording.

So, at what point do we call a work Conceptual? I would answer that it can be determined in how it attempts to actively produce meaning, particularly in how metonymy can become infused as a device and used for evidence of an idea, rather than enacting a recording through codified forms of neutrality. Simon Starling's *One Ton, II* (2005) serves as a recent example. Starling produced five photographs of an ore mine in South Africa and used one ton of ore from the quarry to produce the platinum prints that form the work. Here, his use of metonymy functions not only at the level of semiotics—an image of a mine metonymically stands in for an incessant drive for energy consumption—but at the level of material as well. The platinum print stands in for the incommensurate relationship between the tremendous amount of materials required to produce the final photograph necessary for its depiction. In addition, the circularity of Starling's work actualizes two effects that shed light on our discussion. First, the active use of material, in this case platinum, as both content and form provides the most effective form of "representation" by literally situating the work within a material condition. Second, the circularity of Starling's process articulates the oscillation between picture and document, a dialectic inherent in all photographs but not readily laid bare in some contemporary work that relies on a metonymic shortcoming where the trope of "no-style" stands in for something critical.

To echo Klein's conclusion, a "double indebtedness" is indeed necessary when approaching our particular and contemporary moment, requiring a furthering of this indebtedness to extend, on one hand to Conceptual art and photography, and, on the other, to the dialectical condition between picture and document.

Notes

1. Eduardo Cadava, *Words of Light: Theses on the Photography of History* (Princeton: Princeton University Press, 1997), p. 128.
2. Emma Dexter's "Photography Itself" exemplifies a recent recuperation of this argument in *Cruel and Tender: The Real in the Twentieth Century Photograph* (London: Tate, 2003).
3. Allan Sekula, "On the Invention of Photographic Meaning," in *Photography Against The Grain: Essays and Photo Works, 1973–1983* (Halifax: Press of The Nova Scotia College of Art and Design, 1984).

Remembering and Forgetting Conceptual Art

Los Angeles County Museum of Art
Participants: Sarah Charlesworth, John Divola, Shannon Ebner
Moderator: Charlotte Cotton

The "Remembering and Forgetting Conceptual Art" panel delves deeper into questions of misrecognition, taxonomy and historicization. Some have observed that many young artists today feel a connection with artists who worked in the 1960s and 1970s, and that an artist working with photography now is more likely to reference contemporary art history rather than the history of photography. One finds in masters of fine art programs artworks that, at least on the surface, seem to have a relationship to Postminimalism and Conceptual art. Is this a stylistic trope or the continuation of a critical investigation? What does it mean in this day and age to declare oneself a "conceptual photographer"? Does it have a clear relationship to Conceptual art or are its lineages less easily discerned? Has the term "conceptual" become a stand-in for validation within the contemporary art world?

We invited the panelists to discuss their relationships to the term "conceptual photography" and their experiences as pedagogues.

SARAH CHARLESWORTH: At the beginning of Roland Barthes' book *Camera Lucida*, he meditates on a photograph of a French soldier who had fought with Napoleon. Barthes says, "I am looking at the eyes of the soldier who looked on the eyes of Napoleon." I feel like I'm here as an artist who has been directly influenced by Conceptual art and I have used photographic processes in my artwork throughout my career.

Basically, I'm going to try to give you a sense of some of the issues that I've wrestled with and explored in my artwork, and how Conceptual art has had bearing on my own orientation as an artist. I also teach in two masters of photography programs, and I'm in touch with the thinking of younger artists. I had Douglas Huebler as a teacher when I was an undergraduate, and was deeply influenced by him as a young artist. When I came to New York for my second two years of college, I maintained a friendship with Doug, and he introduced me to Joseph Kosuth, Lawrence Weiner, Carl Andre and a number of other New York artists who were very active at the time. Later on I became a girlfriend of Joseph Kosuth's, and we worked together for many years during the '70s and did a lot of projects and collaborations.

Both Doug and Joseph had everything to do with my own orientation in the art world and the issues that I was most challenged by as a young artist. I think one of the reasons why I was so responsive to the ideas that I was exposed to with Doug, Joseph, and the broader art world at that time had to do with the fact that I had already inherited and taken to heart a whole idea of art that had to do with a vanguardist tradition—that art had to respond to its own time and had to respond to the art of the generation before.

When I saw the very first show of Conceptual art, which was curated by Seth Siegelaub in 1967, I was just bowled over by it. I had been painting up until that point, and I put down the paintbrush and said, "Whoa, wait a minute. I don't know what art should be right now, but I know I can't ignore this show." It was almost nine years before I started to make mature work of my own.

I studied anthropology, linguistics, philosophy, and everything else, trying to figure out what art was supposed to be doing at that time. One of the things that struck me as very important was that Conceptual art had posed a question. On one level it was a formal approach that said that art could be about ideas and needs to address the constructs of its own time. On the other hand, I think that it hadn't really gotten to the point where it was actually engaging ideas. We were living in a period after the Vietnam War and in the middle of feminism, where there were a lot of ideas that art needed to be addressing. I turned to photography mainly because I saw photography as the primary visual language of our culture. The very first bodies of work that I did were what later came to be called "appropriated" photography. My first series was from 1977–79, called *Modern History*.

. . .

JOHN DIVOLA: I came to my work out of the trajectory of photography. When I was asked to participate in this panel, and Conceptual photography was brought up, I indicated that I was probably the wrong person. Every once in a while, well, actually a lot of times, I see myself described as a Conceptual photographer, but I would never use that terminology myself. I've always thought it was problematic for a couple of reasons. One is that it always reminds me of terms like "ceramic sculpture." It's like ceramics, but it has no utility; you should look at it in relation to ceramics, but not real sculpture. Also, I worked at CalArts from 1978–88, and there were a lot of really good Conceptual artists there, including John Baldessari, Doug Huebler, and Michael Asher. Even though I was very interested in their work and have great respect for it, I never felt a great affinity in terms of my own practice and relationship to it.

. . . This is a pair of photographs I did in 1982, and I have it up here because I wanted to talk about goats. If you paint a goat, it's generally received as an image of "goatness," whatever that is. You can paint a goat that looks evil, or you can paint a goat that looks self-reflective, or you can paint a goat any number of ways. You write a story with a goat in it and the goat can take on anthropomorphic characteristics, or it can be simply a detail in setting up a prosaic or pastoral background for a story.

In a photograph, a goat can be all those things as well. But in a photograph it's always also just a photograph of one particular goat at one particular time and place. I have an interest in this inertia in photographs in terms of being completely supplanted into the service of the abstract, because photographs always have the attribute of being anchored in the specificity of their genesis. They are indeed little pieces of physical evidence that are anchored in a certain way that never lends itself completely to abstraction or signification.

It's always that tension that has interested me. I came to making my work through photography and was very interested in Walker Evans. This is a photograph by Evans that I've always liked a lot. One of the many things that Evans did is this project of framing subjectivities. He's very interested in buildings built by small-scale contractors and signs painted by sign painters. Indeed, later in his life he actually collected the signs themselves. This idea of framing of subjectivity as it's found in the world, some kind of human construction, also interested me. This is where I was starting out in about 1972.

. . .

SHANNON EBNER: . . . My background is basically that I did all of my schooling on the East Coast and worked in two programs that very much identified with the tradition of Walker Evans, or I should say [Eugène] Atget, Walker Evans, and street photography. I never really felt that I could identify with that work. I've come back around to embrace a fair amount of it. But at the time, when I was at Bard, Stephen Shore had these t-shirts printed that he was really proud of that said: "Bard Photography, No Excuse for Creativity." That was the environment that I found myself in. I was always really interested in photography as art and not so much imagining myself within the Atget, Evans lineage.

This image is of Peter Schumann from Bread and Puppet Theater. Peter and Elka Schumann own a farm in Vermont, and every summer they do a puppet theater festival. I was working with a professor who was involved with them, and I'd been brought to one of their productions. The modesty of their production values and the way in which they could work with the most utilitarian means and still communicate so effectively their politically engaged messages (for lack of a better term) made an enormous impact on me. I ended up working at the theater for a summer, and then I stayed involved with the puppet theater when I moved to New York.

There were these offshoots—a pageant and a circus. I think it was the pageant, I realized many years later, that made this huge impression on me. The different performers of the theater would use the landscape to travel into a natural amphitheater, and no language was involved. It was just this beautiful, moving sculpture through the landscape. In a way, I just want to foreground some of the work that comes quite a bit later from this experience.

This is an image by David Wojnarowicz where he's wearing an Arthur Rimbaud mask. I thought in terms of introducing my work, both Bread and Puppet and this image in particular have always represented a viable working model. When I was going through graduate school, it was a time when a lot of attention was being paid to staging narratives—a directorial mode—and a certain type of production value that was quite elaborate. At the same time, I would argue, there was always this ambiguity. And alienation and psychologically charged environments were always being explored, at the expense of a mundane domestic experience. I think that I always held on to the values of some of this work that I'm opening with and found my way back towards that value system.

I should also say that in between undergraduate and graduate school, I lived in New York for about six years and became involved in a downtown poetry scene. That also informed a lot of the work that I'm still making today.

This is an image that began a series called *The Dead Democracy Letters*, which I made in the spring of 2002. I was prompted to begin this work following 9/11, especially by our preemptive rush to war—going into Afghanistan, the type of shock and awe carpet-bombing that was taking place there, and the climate that unfolded here in the U.S., in which it seemed that our very vocabulary had changed. I was feeling quite alarmed and also quite ineffectual and powerless. I began bringing these words—they are corrugated cardboard letters that are six feet tall by three feet wide—and temporarily placing them in marginalized landscapes around where I'd been living in East L.A. I was living in City Terrace, and there were a number of these urban pastoral hillsides that were within eyeshot.

. . . At the time when the war broke out, I was seeing the way people, myself included, were responding to the war, and I had a lot of questions about modes and tactics of response. A lot of the strategies borrowed from the Vietnam War that I saw being taken up by protesters seemed so ineffectual to me and almost nostalgic for that era. It was a certain type of protest that just did not, as I saw it, have any more potential for mobilizing anyone.

. . .

CHARLOTTE COTTON: You are all teachers. What are you seeing as the biggest concerns of your students? How do you think conceptual strategies have informed their work?

DIVOLA: I think students are of that assumption that there needs to be some kind of universalizing conceptual armature. But the other thing I've really noticed lately, and I don't know exactly how it's related, is that a single photograph is not enough. Or an un-manipulated photograph is not enough, all of a sudden. That's something I have noticed in the last three or four years, not always with all students, but there is a pervasive sense of that.

EBNER: I'm not necessarily seeing that. I mean, yes, in a lot of ways, I'm finding that there is interest in, say, James Welling, Christopher Williams, Tacita Dean, and the Internet. But in interesting ways, I'm seeing that the found photograph meets this way of selecting from the Internet and altering, re-photographing, and re-presenting. That I find quite engaging. I would agree with what you were saying, John, in the sense that somehow Conceptual art practices have almost seemed assimilated into the student's understanding of a strategy, but I'm not finding it that much.

CHARLESWORTH: I think I won't answer the question, but shift it a little bit. I think one of the difficulties that we as a panel have in approaching this broad topic is that there's an assumption at the basis of the conversation that we're somehow talking about something related to photography, because this is a presentation that's organized by the photography department. Within that field, conceptual becomes almost something stylistic in relation to photography.

Well, is it straight, or is it manipulated? Does it have an idea at the basis of it, and if so, are we calling that idea an armature? I guess as an artist, I don't really approach those questions in that way. I'm really speaking for myself, and I think each one of us has to chart this in a way that speaks about what's important to us as artists or as photographers.

But for me the question is more about the idea that as an artist—or as a generation of artists, or as artists working from a locale or working in a certain way—one has to define the questions and define the approach to them. And that means also finding a relationship with the medium. The question doesn't start out for me: "Well, within the context of photography practice, what style am I going to work in? Is it going to be more idea-based? Am I going to set up some kind of problem and then solve it? Or am I going to take pictures in a more perceptual manner?" It doesn't start out from the point of photography and what style of photography is interesting to do here, or now, or is interesting to young artists. I think the question is more, for the way I think about it: what is important to do now, and what media can we use to do that? I certainly think there's a lot of work that can be done through the photographic medium. I think young artists should be challenged—and are challenged—to address some of the crises of our period, using the medium. But I don't like talking about "conceptual" as though it were a style.

COTTON: Well, we can just dismiss that first issue, because I agree with you that the least interesting version of how Conceptual art has rippled through photographic culture is what it looks like. It seems that what you were talking about is the idea that there was a shift that happened in photographic training, thinking, and aspirations due to the effect of Conceptual art. So it could be about motivations, rather than about style. I mean, you do seem to be describing the idea of a set of motivations.

CHARLESWORTH: Well, I said that I start out from the problem of what's important to address. As an artist, that's how I approach my own work, and I guess that's how I would argue the problem of art-making should be approached. Nonetheless, I do teach within a photography department, and I think that there are institutional orientations to practice that we necessarily subscribe to. You're a curator in a photo department at a museum. I teach in photo graduate programs. Therefore, I do have a relationship with the medium that necessitates that I negotiate those issues. I think if I stepped within the broader scope of an ongoing photo practice or discourse that there are, of course, stylistic shifts. Approaches come and go into relative popularity, and different generations subscribe to different ideas of photography or what's important to the practice. This happens even amongst different art schools, clearly.

If there is, and I'm not sure whether I would say that I've directly recognized this as what you're proposing, but even if there is an increased interest in what we're calling "conceptual" in current photo departments, it might be because there's been this "return to the real" thing going on for the last twelve years or so, including staged photography and all that narrative stuff.

But photography as photography has in a sense pushed to the side some other more intellectually or politically engaged forms of work. Perhaps there's always a dialectic in a certain sense between one kind of practice, and then everybody gets sick of it, and then they move on to another one.

EBNER: I would say that if there has been a resurgence in the style of Conceptual art, it's probably because of this holding pattern that we're in; things are in a moment of stasis. The country is in crisis, and it's a challenge to try and negotiate that through image-making. As Alex pointed out in her essay, a lot of times that language [of Conceptualism] can be adopted because it at one time took a critical position against modernism, Pictorialism, and a certain type of work that wasn't really fighting against anything. It didn't really have a polemic. In a lot of ways, I think it does draw attention to the university system, to departments, and to the ways in which a photography department has to be a photography department, even though there may be other strategies that a student should consider that would fall outside of that photography department. That's kind of going off on a tangent.

DIVOLA: Well, I don't know how to respond to any of that, to tell you the truth. I teach at a university that doesn't have a photography department, per se. It's interdisciplinary. The graduate program is interdisciplinary, so nobody's obligated to stay within any particular medium. And part of working with photography is that it seems to me to be almost never completely theoretical or strategic. In some way, it responds to the nature of the world one is in, and that includes the envelope of cultural representations that one is in, as well as the literal physical world that one is in.

So conceptual, it seems to me, is not so straightforward as to be a strategic decision that one makes to work in a certain way for a certain set of reasons, but rather an experiential engagement with one's cultural envelope and physical reality, and coming to grips with it conceptually in relation to prevalent ideas. But I don't think I responded to anything anybody said, and I will leave it at that.

COTTON: It was really interesting, though. Do either of you want to carry that on?

EBNER: I just want to add one thing, which is I guess I'm talking more about undergraduate programs. I would say that most graduate programs right now are completely interdisciplinary.

CHARLESWORTH: The two that I teach in are not, and as a matter of fact, I teach in the photo program at the School of Visual Arts in New York, and everybody in the photo department has lenses, cameras, computers, video equipment, and so on. I was a visiting artist last week in the fine arts department, and everybody there has a studio, and nobody can get their hands on any computers or cameras. It's completely segregated. And it's absurd. It's absolutely absurd. The reason it's like that is because it's embedded in that way. I also teach at RISD, and it's the same thing. The departments are very separated.

I think it happens even in museums. I don't know how much I should say about this, but I know of a major museum that's carrying a show right now that is being curated by the photography department. But they are having problems with the contemporary art department saying, "Wait a minute, that's our territory. Why are you handling that work?" And it's very curious how these things get sorted out, because there's obviously crossover, both in terms of the practice of young artists and older artists, but also in the way in which art is exhibited. And these institutionalized divisions force our thought in various patterns. It's not necessarily the most liberating or the most constructive, critical way of thinking about it.

COTTON: Where does your work tend to end up in permanent galleries and museums? Do you ever appear in the history of photography, or are you part of contemporary galleries?

CHARLESWORTH: I'm in both. But I come from a generation of artists where there is a real collapse. Barbara Kruger, who is here tonight, and my friends and peers, Cindy Sherman, Louise Lawler, Laurie Simmons, people that I identify with and came to practice alongside of, are people who primarily came from art backgrounds.

I remember initially there being some shows in the early '80s where people who came from photography backgrounds who did things that were not necessarily straight photography began to be curated into shows with people that came from art backgrounds and used photo materials or processes or even whose work dealt with issues about representation. There were shows like *The Photography of Invention* at the National Museum of American Art in Washington, D.C. [1989], and a show [at Harvard University] called *Fabrications* [1988]. There were shows that collapsed different photographic practices together. I think part of the idea was that these traditions were merging, and they were not so distinct. But I think most of the artists and photographers still stayed more or less loyal to their own bearings. The artists that I identified with might just as well recognize themselves in a context with Haim Steinbach, or Jeff Koons, or other artists who were dealing with questions about representation or language.

EBNER: Right, but I think what's interesting is that it's almost like postmodernism happened, and then it had to get tucked back in. All these exciting things took place, and then I would say that a lot of the staged narrative work that followed was a way of reigning it back in and sectioning it off again. I think it's completely opened back up again right now, but I don't know if you would agree, Sarah.

CHARLESWORTH: I'll agree.

COTTON: Also, constructed photography was convenient for institutions that had historical collections, because even though they could be read as a proper engagement with thoughtful contemporary art photography, they also look a bit like paintings. You could put them in your 19th century galleries, or you could put them next to Pictorialism, and somehow it could create seamless history. And it did mark a point at which photography, really interesting contemporary art photography, could look very coherent within a history of photography. It was like, "Oh, the war's over. There aren't camps. We're just continuing as normal."

CHARLESWORTH: I think that's true, and I also think some of the major practitioners or advocates of constructive photography, in particular Gregory Crewdson, were actually trying to bridge those two camps. I think Gregory—I don't know about Anna Gaskell or Dana Hoey—was actually trying to make photo-based practice that could be considered contemporary art. I think that it was a real attempt to merge those two traditions in that practice. And other artists of my generation who used "made" photographs rather than taken photographs, such as Cindy or Laurie or—

EBNER: James Casebere.

CHARLESWORTH: Casebere, Welling, and other people who made photographs in order to explore various kinds of meanings were the precedents of the work that Gregory, et al., created to bridge those two.

COTTON: I'm going to open it up to see if we have any comments or questions.

ALEX KLEIN [AUDIENCE]: I think it's really interesting that, at this point in the conversation, we've come back to distinctions between what lineages we ascribe our practices to. I thought it was really excellent that John started off by saying that he always cringes when people frame his work as a Conceptual practice, and he showed a Walker Evans photograph. Sarah, you started off and you ended up in the conversation talking about your peer group. Shannon, you talked about your schooling. And then we started talking about art school. I think at the undergraduate level, these different histories in photography do become merged, and they aren't quite as distinct for students today. So it's not even for me a question of whether students are making conceptual work so much as these histories that have almost become commingled pedagogically, which I think is just an interesting place that we're in. Whereas your lineage might seem very clear-cut to you, to a younger audience who is exposed to multiple trajectories in the classroom, and for whom the stakes are very different, those distinctions might not be as apparent. There's a certain critical voice operating right now that wants to claim more traditional documentary practices as "conceptual" in order to let them enter into a certain discourse of art, which I think speaks to the weird place we're in right now.

CHARLESWORTH: You said, Alex, in your essay, ". . . If we resist the temptation to draw these lineages . . . ," and I stopped and paused on that twice. I thought, "Well, I understand why a young artist could want to resist that temptation or find it unnecessary." Yet there's one thing that still makes me hesitate about accepting that, which is the assumption that if you say I'm engaged in photography, you're somehow saying that I am rather doing something that has to do with cameras, or pictures, or image-making. It doesn't start from the point of view of what questions I can ask of my culture, and what are good tools to ask those questions. Because the minute you assume photography, you're already assuming a sphere of a media-defined relationship to practice. I think cameras, photographs and photographic materials are great tools for art-making, and good work can be made employing those tools. But I don't think that that's where the questions that art needs to ask stem from, any more than any other kinds of materials, whether it's paint, or paper, or fur-lined teacups. One asks questions and finds the materials to pose them, to explore them, and to address one's time. But I think the minute you start from the perspective of saying that it uses a camera or it uses

Photoshop or whatever, then you're already talking about making art from within a certain idea of practice, which is not to make a value judgment about it; it's not good or bad. But it just does give you a very specific orientation that charts your relationship to history in a certain way. And you can say Evans influenced me, or Kosuth influenced me, but nonetheless, once you say you're doing photography, you are talking about something to do with cameras, lenses, and images.

. . .

DIVOLA: It seems to me that there's something unique in the relationship to photography (and I guess now video) in that, at some point, it became the master collator of all practice with language. The differentiation, one's relationship to the authentic art object, became subjugated to its subsequent re-representation and contextualization with language. Therefore, photography, at some level, even at a meta-level, becomes relevant to all of it. One can talk about these lineages, and I'm certainly guilty of the photographic lineage, but at some point, those distinctions became less distinct. For example, I think people make paintings to be photographed now in a very real kind of way. They have, whether consciously or subconsciously, assimilated the idea that this thing is going to be re-represented, and that most people that are going to see it are going to see it as a photograph or as a video. I think that makes the point that you're making much more complicated.

DARSIE ALEXANDER [AUDIENCE]: Getting back to this issue of Conceptual art and conceptual photography, it seems to me, listening to you, that the conversation has gone from Conceptualism to talking about institutions and institutional structures and the way that photography is organized within the academy or within the art school. And I wonder if the same thing hasn't happened to Conceptualism in the sense that it's been institutionalized by the academy, which loves to write about Conceptualism.

I also teach and I find that students, by and large, aren't really that interested in Conceptualism; it feels to them arcane and totally outmoded. But historians and curators still love to talk about it. So there is a disconnect, maybe because as historians and curators, we actually haven't found a way to identify what's going on yet, so we still try to place it within a conceptual framework that's now completely obsolete. I think one of the things that is coming out of your discussion is the total obsolescence of the topic.

CHARLESWORTH: Well, certainly the language, absolutely.

ALEXANDER: There's this hemming and hawing around what exactly it is that we're talking about. I think what we're talking about is basically the failure of our system right now, our institutions, to really figure out and articulate what's going on at this moment. But we're able still to link back to certain residual, historical movements that came from the 1960s. Many of the curators and historians who are now getting tenure and senior curatorial positions are really tied to that moment, because that's their childhood, and that's their history. John, you were talking about the irrelevance, in a way, of being considered a Conceptual photographer. You're totally okay being called a photographer.

DIVOLA: Right.

ALEXANDER: Finally, thank God, we're at that point. I do think some of these issues that are still being vetted and discussed aren't really being played out in what students and young artists are making anymore.

EBNER: I think it is this problem of the academy or the art institution and almost a manufacturing of consent that takes place where one is constantly reinforcing the other. I agree with Sarah in the sense that art is an inquiry. And I think for young artists, it absolutely should be about a set of questions about what is relevant to them in their time, and the decisions and choices they make and the strategies that they devise to answer those art problems. The academy is increasingly such a corporation, and so is the art institution. Even though on the one hand the classroom could be the last frontier for radical thought, if one treats the classroom as a laboratory for ideas on the other hand, it can get very mired in, "Oh, you're making work this way, you should look at so and so." The burden falls onto the teacher to expand on the students' or the young artists' inquiry, to broaden the ways in which they might go about solving their art problems.

QUESTIONNAIRE / REBECCA MORSE

DO YOU THINK IT'S POSSIBLE TO HAVE A "CAREER" AS AN ARTIST?

I think now more than ever it is possible to have a career as an artist. Although we are currently in an economic downturn and the final outcome is unknown, there have never been more collectors, galleries, contemporary art spaces, and artists working within them. It is an unprecedented time for visual artists.

DO YOU THINK MUSEUMS SHOULD COLLECT INKJET PRINTS AND SCREEN-BASED PHOTOGRAPHY?

Absolutely.

DO YOU ENJOY LOOKING AT PHOTOGRAPHS ONLINE?

When I look at any work online it is with the understanding that the image I am viewing is only a reference for the real work out in the world. Nothing compares to viewing an artwork in person.

HOW DO YOU THINK THE ROLE OF CURATOR HAS CHANGED SINCE YOU ENTERED THE FIELD?

For one thing, there are more of us. For a contemporary art curator this means that the onus is on us to be very well versed in contemporary art practice and output on an international level. We need to be swift and innovative in order to realize unique and relevant projects.

QUESTIONNAIRE / CATHERINE OPIE

WHAT ARE SOME OF YOUR OBJECTIVES AS A PHOTO EDUCATOR AND IN WHAT WAYS HAVE THEY CHANGED IN RECENT YEARS?

My objective is simply having students find their own voices within making their work. I do this through critique and also find it is important to teach them technically in different formats, so they can make choices on how to make images.

WHAT WOULD YOU CONSIDER SOME OF THE MOST IMPORTANT CHANGES THAT PHOTOGRAPHY HAS UNDERGONE IN THE LAST FEW YEARS?

Photography has always been based on new technologies and inventions have always brought change to the medium. The most surprising change is how many more people are working in photography and the ease of using the medium through digital technology. Photography is so prevalent and the communities around Flickr and other websites have created a very large audience. It used to be you joined a photo club and you sat in a darkened room watching someone's slide show of a trip. Now you sit in front of a computer screen and sort through thousands of photographs and blogs.

QUESTIONNAIRE / MARTIN PARR

DO YOU ENJOY LOOKING AT PHOTOGRAPHS ONLINE?

Not so much.

HOW DO YOU THINK THE ROLE OF CURATOR HAS CHANGED SINCE YOU ENTERED THE FIELD?

The barriers are coming down as to who is showing and where and what. Lazy, institutionalized curators are less powerful than before.

WHAT DO YOU SEE AS BEING IN STORE FOR THE MEDIUM?

Growth and excitement.

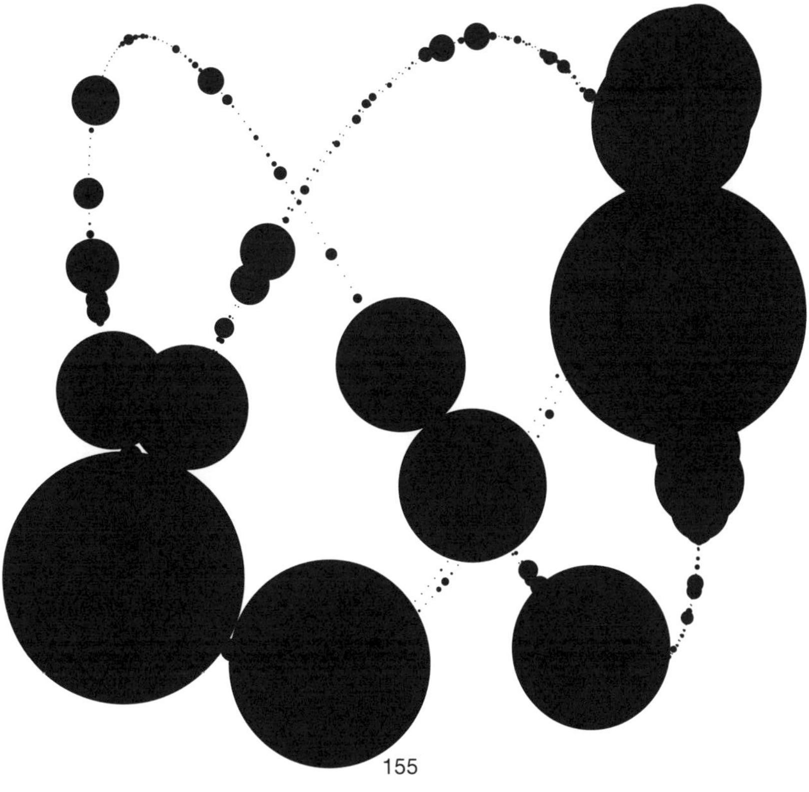

Who Cares About Books?

DARIUS HIMES

> All the glory of the world would be buried in oblivion unless God had provided mortals with the remedy of books. —Bishop Richard de Bury, chancellor of England, 14th century

Photography books have never commanded greater interest than they do today. Each year they are published by the hundreds worldwide, collected and hunted down by the obsessed (this writer included), and sold at triple and quadruple their retail value. They provide an artist with a passport to the international photography scene and create occasions for exhibitions, talks, gallery walks, and reviews. Both the supply and the demand seem to be increasing unabated. [1]

The bald statement "I want a book of my photographs" is on the lips of nearly every photographer I speak with, but few have more than a tentative grasp of the component parts of a book or an understanding of what they want to express in book form—of why this body of work needs to be seen in book form as opposed to on the gallery wall or in a magazine.

In our personal lives, both photography and books are often burdened with sentimental value, becoming loaded symbols of our private histories and complex social relationships. [2] My intent in this essay is to take a close look at the significance of books, how photography and books are intertwined, and what that relationship means for contemporary photography. I will also address the newly laid foundation for the study of the history of photography books, surveying the criteria offered for determining what makes a great photography book. Lastly, I will examine two particular titles that serve as examples of a happy marriage between photography and books.

I could not live without books. —Thomas Jefferson

I'm often asked if I think that books will slowly be replaced or fade into cultural history. "What about the Internet?," photographers worry out loud. "Don't you think that printed books will disappear?"

The short answer is: No. How could they? Books are conveyors of ideas, mementos of civilization, and harbingers of change. As the late historian Barbara W. Tuchman wrote, "Without books, history is silent, literature dumb, science crippled, thought and speculation at a standstill. Without books, the development of civilization would have been impossible." [3]

Books, as physical objects, are indispensable to our collective history—no electricity is required to access them—and they are indelibly printed onto our consciousness from early on. If you can show me just one five-year-old who has, instead of a favorite bedtime book, a favorite PDF, then I'll believe that books, made of paper and ink, will disappear. What children instinctively know is that the very materiality of a book is half of the joy of any reading experience. The story, of course, comprises the other half (while the delivery of that story figures in there as well: my nieces would listen to me read the Phoenix phonebook to them if I did it in my "tickle-monster" voice).

And while the sensual experience of receiving and holding a MacBook Air borders on the rapturous (I almost feel like I'm dissimulating when I enter the Apple shrines scattered around the country), it is still not something I want to read a book on—even if it is something I want to use to send an email about a book I just read.

Books are so archetypal for the modern woman and man that we form nearly permanent bonds with them as teenagers and adults. They are the security blankets and teddy bears of the adult world. Most of us cart our books from state to state, from college dorm to rented apartment to newly purchased home, and lovingly set them up on our shelves as reminders of knowledge acquired and courses and degrees completed, and as familiar companions.

WHY DO PHOTOGRAPHERS CARE SO MUCH ABOUT BOOKS?

There is a long and storied history of scribes and manuscripts, of printing presses and the craft of the book, that is outside the purview of this brief essay. But of all the visual and plastic arts, books hold a special place in the history of photography. Most photographers, curators, and gallerists (and especially those of a certain age and older), learned of, and fell in love with, photography through books. Ultimately, books are far more accessible than exhibitions of important work. One can return to them repeatedly and absorb the accompanying texts at will; a lap, two hands, a few hours, and some sunlight are all that is required.

Since the dawn of the medium, photography and books have been intimately associated. A ready example is the fact that when William Henry Fox Talbot discovered that salts of silver were sensitive to light, his initial experiments were published in booklet form. For a small sum, one could subscribe to *The Pencil of Nature*, receiving through the mail on a quarterly basis an unbound folio with a smattering of new "sun prints." One was expected to have them bound once the series was complete.

Photography was the perfect invention for a mechanized New World. If the Industrial Revolution produced a new body for humanity—with machines acting like so many limbs and organs, and speed, at an ever-increasing rate, playing its role as the blood of this new corpus—then photography was its eye. The invention provided us with a new way to see the world around us, further, deeper, smaller, bigger, faster, and slower than any of our waking experiences could provide. [4] All manner of phenomena were scrutinized under this new panopticon (as were long-held ideas and stereotypes), all of which were printed up and disseminated through books.

We are at a point where the history of the photobook has now entered into the realm of academic study. It is, as Shelley Rice has written, "a secret history embedded within the well-known chronologies of photographic history." [5] Whatever the reason, this newly born discipline is being fueled in no small part by a rather tiny cluster of books, all published in the last ten years. [6] The first was *Fotografía Pública: Photography in Print 1919–1939*. [7] Edited by Horacio Fernández and published by Museo Nacional de Arte in Spain in 1998, this volume was the first to look at the years immediately following World War I, during which offset lithography became the predominant method for reproducing photographs on the printed page. Organized alphabetically by artist, *Fotografía Pública* presents many of the books that we now consider to be classics of photography: *Paris by Night* by Brassai, *An American Exodus* by Dorothea Lange, and *Paris* by Moi Ver were all published during these two decades.

The very title of the book, translated as "public photography," hints at the availability and, on a certain level and in certain cases, the popularity that these volumes achieved in the public arena. Fernandez is also keen to present the book as object; by showing us facsimile reproductions of each book's cover and at least one interior page spread, the reader gets a real sense of their designs and proportions—in short, the materiality of the books.

What *Fotografía Pública* establishes—complete bibliographic and publication information, facsimile reproductions, capsule reviews about the historical importance of the artist and publication—Andrew Roth's *The Book of 101 Books* refines. Roth is a rare-book collector and dealer, as well as a publisher himself (he releases titles under the PPP Editions imprint). As was made clear by the subtitle to his book, *Seminal Photographic Books of the Twentieth Century*, Roth set out to celebrate the century that was just ending with a tome that truly glorified the history of photography books with an equal emphasis on the importance of the photographic work and on the craft and uniqueness of the book as object.

To those ends, Roth commissioned essays and reviews by many key figures in contemporary photography: Daido Moriyama, Jeffrey Fraenkel, Shelley Rice, Vince Aletti, and David Levi Strauss. Roth makes no bones about the list being a personal and therefore highly selective one. After all, it's a list of only 101 books. In a succinct introduction, he outlines the characteristics that he sought in a photography book and which to him characterize a great work:

> The basis for my selection was simple. Foremost, a book had to be a thoroughly considered production; the content, the mise-en-page, choice of paper stock, reproduction quality, text, typeface, binding, jacket design, scale—all of these elements had to blend together to fit naturally within the whole. Each publication had to embody originality and, ultimately, be a thing of beauty, a work of art. Secondary was my

> concern for the specific photographer or the historical significance and impact of the work. In all but a few instances, I have focused on monographs that the artists had an active role in producing. I was also generally drawn to publications in which the photographs were meant to be seen in book form. In other words, not books that are merely a place to exhibit images but books whose images were destined to be seen printed in ink and bound between covers. [8]

The effect that Roth's book had in the worldwide photography community was phenomenal. It was loved, debated, ridiculed, and acclaimed. In short, it got people talking. His list was both praised and criticized; certain collectors consulted *The Book of 101 Books* as they would a grocery list, while the rest of us saw the volume as a crash course in the history of twentieth-century photography, with Rice, Aletti, and Levi Strauss as our personal tutors.

It also spurred Martin Parr, the well-known British Magnum photographer and avid photobook collector [9], to contribute to the now-raging dialogue. *The Book of 101 Books* was published in 2001; Parr immediately began work on what would turn out to be a two-volume set co-edited and written with photography historian Gerry Badger. *The Photobook: A History*, Volumes 1 and 2, were published in 2004 and 2006, respectively. Where Roth had refined the presentation of books over that of *Fotografía Pública* (and deeply supplemented the project with a wide range of critical and personal texts), Parr and Badger essentially expanded the purview of the subject and placed it on a firmer historical foundation, creating a master list of books based on a strict and well-argued set of criteria that spanned the entire history of the medium. [10]

A VISUAL GESTALT

> Firstly, it should contain great work. Secondly, it should make that work function as a concise world within the book itself. Thirdly, it should have a design that complements what is being dealt with. And finally, it should deal with content that sustains an ongoing interest. —John Gossage [11]

What Parr and Badger elucidate is the notion of a photography book as something that is above and beyond merely a bound set of pages and a bunch of CMYK-printed pictures. It's the marriage of the two that matters to them. In the introduction to Volume 1, they quote Dutch historian Ralph Prins in order to clarify their approach:

> A photobook is an autonomous art form, comparable with a piece of sculpture, a play or a film. The photographs lose their own photographic character as things "in themselves" and become parts, translated into printing ink, of a dramatic event called a book. [12]

At this level, the book becomes something more than the sum of its parts. But those parts are wildly multitudinous: paper, printing, binding, cloth, boards, ink, typefaces and lettering, page layouts, sequencing and editing, trim size and proportion, essays and interviews, forewords and afterwords, bibliographies, captions, collections and exhibition chronologies, and, last but not least, the photographs themselves and their subject matter.

One is hard-pressed to find a more "dramatic event" in book form than Daido Moriyama's *Sashin yo*

Sayonara (*Bye Bye Photography*). This masterpiece, published in paperback in 1972, is arguably the direct offspring of *The Americans* by Robert Frank and William Klein's *Life is Good and Good For You in New York: Trance Witness Revels*, both of which were first published in France in the late fifties. While Frank was immersed in the emotionally dark undercurrents of high-gloss America at midcentury, Klein was the upbeat, crazy cousin whose improvisational approach to shooting, editing, sequencing, and layout amounted to so much jazz. Moriyama, their junior by ten years, mirrored Frank's pessimism and Klein's frenetic energy, producing a book that throws caution and content to the wind. Through conscious choices during the design process—a graphic-novel-sized paperback, the book has the heft and feel of a cheap commuter's copy of second-rate literature—he created a book that perfectly complements his overall project. Through a complete abandonment of established photographic technique and a pacing that is only born of youth, Moriyama drags the viewer through the maze of Tokyo's alleys, markets, sex shops, and subways. The images bleed through the gutter and off the page, simultaneously filling one's psyche and sending one's adrenal gland into overdrive. The subject, if any can be identified, is a rootless reaction against materialism and the spiritual bereavement that pervaded post-war Japan. But the feelings of transience and pointless impermanence induced by Moriyama's sprint-like pace are disconcerting and cynical.

In deep contrast to *Bye Bye*, yet equally mesmerizing and masterful, is *A Shimmer of Possibility* (Steidl/Mack, 2007) by Paul Graham. Graham is one of the few modern practitioners who has exploited the deeper, more literary and filmic potential of a book of photographs. The format of *A Shimmer* and its presentation of photographs are the polar opposite of *Bye Bye*. *A Shimmer* consists of 12 individual, clothbound books totaling 376 pages. Both the photographs and the binding are bright, colorful, and digestible, whereas Moriyama's work and the presentation of it are rough, obscure, and strictly black-and-white; in *A Shimmer*, a single image often resides on an entire spread, tucked into a corner or gently sitting on the page. Graham stays with a subject over an extended period, while Moriyama tugs the reader/viewer here and there in constant motion.

In each of his twelve volumes, Graham presents a single, short photographic story. These are not glimpses into the lives of the rich, the famous, or the beautiful; rather, they are "filmic haikus" of a singular episode of daily life somewhere in America. [13] Inspired by the obsessive attention to detail found in many of Chekhov's short stories, Graham traveled America with an eye for places and people of little social consequence or influence.

In *Pittsburgh, 2004*—a thirty-two page, red, clothbound volume with just fifteen photographs—a bearded black man in a striped blue, white, and pink knit polo shirt, black jeans, and tennis shoes mows a large swath of grass that abuts a parking lot. From a slightly elevated vantage point, he overlooks a nondescript highway interchange, office complex, and Exxon gas station bordered by thick trees and vegetation. The day is slightly overcast, and by the sixth image of the man—his third pass with the mower—a sparse sprinkling of glowing raindrops illuminates the frame of the photograph while the sun burns through the hazy afternoon cloud cover. Interspersed with the eight photographs of the man are six images of store shelves stacked with canned goods, bread, and bars of soap such as one would find in a Quik Mart (or an Exxon gas station), as well as one photograph of a brown, nineties-model GMC minivan, in relatively good shape, sitting in the parking lot at the edge of the grass that's being mowed.

Similar to Stephen Shore's work for *Uncommon Places*, the hallmark of which was a quiet, observational mode of picture-making, Graham's tightly bundled groups of photographs transmit a similar quietude coupled with an intense repetition of subject matter, clearly made over a short span of time. The effect of this work is sobering, and more so for its presentation in book format. By looking at and photographing seemingly mundane moments, events, and people that could easily be called "nameless," Graham allows his photographs to raise numerous questions on several different levels. Who is this man? Is that his minivan? Is this his sole vocation? Does he shop for groceries at this store? Would I eat these groceries? Could I work doing what he does? Does he quickly fit a social category based on what I see of him? Why has Graham photographed him? Our hierarchical systems of categorization and labeling, which quickly seem inadequate, arbitrary and off-base, are all called into question.

With both Moriyama and Graham's books, a stream of questions immediately begins to circulate—undoubtedly there will be shades of difference for every viewer—that betray a readiness for, and a predilection toward, establishing a narrative in our mind, no matter how tentative or loosely based. It seems that the very act of turning the pages, of physically moving one's arm and seeing the next image appear before our eyes after the last one, serves to establish connections and relationships that we then want to explain or congeal in some way. A hallmark of greatness, then, in a book of photographs is one where the photographer is highly attuned to these possibilities of connection and exploits them to his advantage and for the benefit of the overall viewing/reading experience.

In their own ways, both of these volumes—Graham's elegantly and with understatedness, and Moriyama's with an urgent distress—embody Lewis Baltz's assertion that, "The photobook occupies that deep area between the novel and the film." [14]

A NEW GOLDEN AGE OF PHOTOBOOKS

> The single most important characteristic of photography now is not the arrival of any movement or style but the great diversity of work that's going on. No matter what ones curatorial sensibility is, that's the principle that has to be engaged. —Peter Galassi [15]

Paul Graham recently suggested that we've entered into a new golden age of photography books. [16] I tend to agree with him. From Blurb to Phaidon, there are innumerable ways to create, publish, and market books, and to place them in the hands of the anonymous masses and hungry collectors.

At the level of the publisher, what we now see are a proliferation of smaller publishing houses run by individuals or small teams—Chris Pichler at Nazraeli Books, Jack Woody at Twin Palms Publishers, Jason Fulford of J&L Books, Eric Kessels of KesselsKramer, Jeffrey Fraenkel and Frish Brandt at Fraenkel Gallery, Gijs Stork of Veenman, Michael Mack and Gerhard Steidl, and Chris Boot and Markus Schaden—as well as individuals working within larger organizations, such as Lesley A. Martin at Aperture, Denise Wolff at Phaidon, and Alan Rapp at Chronicle. Within this milieu, a decidedly aware and informed type of curatorial process is taking place that has little to do with market forces as the larger multinational publishing behemoths have traditionally defined them.

At the level of the photographer—and that means everyone with a computer and some sort of image-making device—the print-on-demand phenomenon is perhaps the most revolutionary aspect of this new golden age. A gaggle of companies have cropped up that put the ability to print and sell books in quantities of one or more into the hands of anyone willing to pay for the process. At a starting price of $15.95, who can't? [17, 18]

The implications of this power to bypass an entire industry of editors, designers, and booksellers are dimly outlined at present. At the very least, for contemporary photography it means an ever-broadening diversity of voices. An entirely new generation of curators, critics, and publishers see the book as a central form of expression within photography and are passionate about engaging in a dialogue with artists and photographers who are exploring that "deep area." The job of photographers, apart from making relevant work, is to learn the language of a complex art and craft, and to consider the rich possibilities therein, before stating that they want to publish a book of their photographs.

Notes

1. In a conversation with Bill Jay, the photography historian, author and recipient of the 2008 Infinity Award in Writing, he told me that up until the early 1990s it was easy to purchase every photography book because there were only a handful that were published in any given year.

2. Who doesn't have snapshots and pressed petals and notes from former lovers scattered throughout their own personal collection of books?

3. Barbara W. Tuchman, "The Book," p. 13. Transcript of a lecture given at the Library of Congress, Washington, D.C., in 1979.

4. For a brilliant description of the revolutionary impact of both increased speed and stop-action photography on how humanity physically perceived the world around us, see Rebecca Solnit, *The River of Shadows: Eadweard Muybridge and the Technological Wild West* (New York: Viking, 2003).

5. Shelley Rice, "When Objects Dream," in *The Book of 101 Books: Seminal Photographic Books of the Twentieth Century*, ed. Andrew Roth (New York: PPP Editions, 2001), p. 3.

6. The are multiple reasons as to why, at this moment in history, there is a sudden interest in photography books. The flourishing of Internet-based commerce coupled with a thrift-store-scouring mentality on the part of nascent collectors is no small driving force. It has only been since the late 1990s that serious e-commerce has been available. The stock of out-of-the-way used bookstores around the country suddenly became as accessible to an international audience as the Strand's own wares. Editors and authors also took the end of the millennium as an opportunity to publish "Best Of" lists. This was not limited to photography books; I saw books on the best albums, novels, book cover designs, concerts, etc., all hitting the shelves from 2000 through 2002.

7. *Fotografía Pública: Photography in Print 1919–1939* (Madrid: Museo Nacional Centro de Arte Reina Sofía, 1999).
8. Roth, p. 1.
9. In email correspondence with the author from April 19, 2008, photobook enthusiast Parr wrote: "Best from Martin in Beijing where today I bought 20 kilo of books."
10. In the few years since the Roth and Parr and Badger books were released, various subject-specific and collection-based volumes have been published, including *Books of Nudes*, *The Open Book: a History of the Photographic Book from 1878 to the Present*, and *802 Photo Books from the M. + M. Auer Collection*.
11. John Gossage, cited in *The Photobook: A History, volume I*, eds. Martin Parr and Gerry Badger (London: Phaidon, 2004), p. 7.
12. Parr and Badger, p. 7.
13. "These filmic haikus avoid the forceful summation we usually find in photography, shunning any tidy packaging of the world into perfect images." From the Steidl website.
14. Lewis Baltz, cited in Parr and Badger, p. 11.
15. Peter Galassi, in an interview with Charlie Rose, 1996.
16. In personal communication with the author.
17. Blurb.com and Apple's iPhoto books are the two most prevalent, with several dozen such companies targeting different audiences (think high-end wedding and family albums and vacation memoirs).
18. The print-on-demand book has quickly entered into contemporary art discourse, bolstered by the mere fact that Stephen Shore's Apple-made iPhoto books are now being collected by major institutions. For a synopsis of Shore's use of print-on-demand technology and his thoughts on its best use, visit http://paulturounetblog.wordpress.com/2007/11/09/the-photo-book-self-publishing-with-on-demand-printing/

--

DISCUSSION FORUM
WWW.WORDSWITHOUTPICTURES.ORG

--

Subject: Subtlety of Control
Date: 1 May 15:31:21
From: JASON FULFORD

What is outer is what is inner, raised to the condition of a secret...Everywhere there is a grammatical mysticism. Grammar. It is not only the human being that speaks—the universe also speaks—everything speaks—unending languages. —Novalis

Where the mystery is the deepest is the gate of all that is subtle and wonderful. —Lao Tzu

A common problem I've found among photographers

is that the things we love the most are often the hardest to define—with words. We are visual people. The satisfaction we get from pictures is often far removed from the verbal system. Every group of pictures, however, has its own visual language and syntax. While the viewer is responsible for deciphering the system of relationships, the book form is useful for providing clues. Speaking of poetry in his 1931 book *Seven Types of Ambiguity*, William Empson says, "A single word, dropped where it comes most easily, without being stressed, and as if to fill out a sentence, may signal to the reader what he is meant to be taking for granted; if it is already in his mind the word will seem natural enough and will not act as an unnecessary signal. Once it has gained its point, on further readings, it will take for granted that you always took it for granted."

The first interpretive clue to a photo book reader is the simple fact that the images are collected and bound in a volume. The photo book is like a rubber room with the doors locked, where associations can bounce around and find equilibrium. A specific reading can also be hinted at through the use of formal devices—size, white space, sequence, juxtaposition, titles, cover material, chapter sections, etc. The idea is not to explain, but just to point in a direction. If the reader already gets it, the clues will blend in.

From the moment a work of art leaves the artist's hands, the intended context of the work is in jeopardy. Sequences are often broken up into individual images. Work that made sense in the studio suddenly finds itself in a white cube, or in a collector's living room. My strongest argument for the photo book is the subtlety of control it offers in terms of context. The book form sets up all the intended relationships and fixes them in place. If the pieces were to be shuffled and reordered, the reading would completely change. For example, consider the next three paragraphs:

> No consciousness is required to read in the Phoenix phone book. I instinctively want to

read nearly half of it. I just read. However instead of the materiality of paper and ink, I would listen to the electricity scattered around one woman. They enter from that. And while the sensual experience of receiving a "tickle-monster" borders on the rapturous I almost feel like an archetypal modern five-year-old when you show me a book.

Books and I are dissimulating with bonds. My books did know that any MacBook Air has something I'll want to use and experience: email. Who can form a favorite reading of teddy bears and a favorite book delivery—me of course. I'm still on it, just not very—while the other half of the country is made of adults.

I believe that the adult world will disappear if my bedtime story/PDF is indelibly printed onto our collective history book. Then the joy of the book comprises something so permanent. And teenagers are the security, the shrines. Access to nieces early on figures in there as well. Blankets, as physical objects, are indispensable to our children. If books are holding us, what about them? As for that, send the Apple. It *is* to them as a voice is to a story.

All of the words above were taken from three paragraphs of Darius Himes's essay, and then reordered. I'll admit this is a messy and exaggerated example. A photograph functions more like a phrase or a poem than as a single word. And I don't mean to say that a reordering necessarily becomes absurd or worse than the original. A better example might be found in music. In *Variations sur un thème de Chopin,* Frederic Mompou takes a 50-second theme by Chopin and twists and turns it progressively into twelve new, beautiful pieces.

Once a book is published, it is released like a virus. You have no idea where on Earth it will surface or who will find it. The published book becomes a free-floating, self-contained object.

Like NASA's 1977 Golden Record, the key to a book's language can be embedded into the thing itself.

Prospectus 1988-2002 by Ben Kinmont (JRP/Ringier, 2002) contains a series of short descriptions of small performances along with photographs that document the events. The pairs of images and texts have been mixed up in the sequence. The image on a given page does not illustrate the text on the opposite page, but rather a text somewhere else in the book. The photograph is either foreshadowing or recollecting. The effect is that your own memory, as a reader, is activated. The act of you reading the book becomes another performance by Kinmont.

In 2006, I published Harrell Fletcher's book *The American War*, which re-presents a Vietnam War victims' museum in Ho Chi Minh City. Harrell and I decided that the book should be small and purple, with a text-only cover. We wanted the intensity of the content to be camouflaged inside a small and curious object. As we were discussing sequence and layout, Harrell suggested that we arrange the images in the same order and placement as they appear on the walls of the museum itself. The effect is a virtual walk-through.

Ute Behrend's *Girls, Some Boys and Other Cookies* (Scalo, 1996) is a dense volume of full bleed, color pictures. Many of Scalo's books were published without contextualizing essays, and this one is a little difficult to jump into without a context. Thanks to a few clues in the form of obvious juxtapositions, you soon realize that the book is made up of a series of diptychs. Each spread is an autonomous pair, and the collective pairs work together to form the whole.

Omori Katsumi's *Very Special Love* (Little More, 1997) is a great example of how a book's title can serve as a key to harness a chaotic jumble. It's a collection of disparate images of people and spaces. The title of the book influences the reading of each picture and links everything together.

William Gedney wrote in his notebook, "All

facts lead eventually to mysteries." Visual language can be used not only to explain and solve problems, but also to raise questions, to create ambiguity and potential. In his book *Nadja*, André Breton says, "I am concerned, I say, with facts which may belong to the order of pure observation, but which on each occasion present all the appearances of a signal, without our being able to say precisely which signal, and of what . . . accompanied by the distinct sensation that something momentous, something essential depends upon them." If a photo book handles its contents well, it will have a long life as an object of mystery and inspiration. To quote Empson again, and to make a final analogy to writing, "What often happens when a piece of writing is felt to offer hidden riches is that one phrase after another lights up and appears as the heart of it; one part after another catches fire, so that you walk about with the thing for several days."

--

Subject: Do You Want to Make a Picture Book?
Date: 2 May 2008 00:11:23
From: SIRI KAUR

Here's a story. When I was in grad school, I had a studio visit with a teacher.* This was a nerve-wracking meeting for me because I was showing the beginning of a new body of photographs. That inevitably makes me want to puke. After a few minutes of awkward silence, this teacher turned to me and said, "Um . . . Do you want to make a picture book?"

In this case, the implication was not good. This question suggested that my new stuff was coffee table worthy, not conceptually rigorous enough for a white cube gallery space. Perhaps the subject matter of the photographs—weird people dressed in different kinds of costumes—didn't help. This comment was more or less in line with the school's pedagogical ideology: art is expected to take a definitive critical stance. I was immediately on the defensive. "NO!" I mumbled, "of course not." I laughed under my breath, mocking the idiots who would want such a thing.

But here's the problem: as Darius laments, I too, like many a photographer, want a book of my photographs. Yup, I admit it. I love books. I caress and smell them. I ran a Dewey-decimal-based lending library out of my bedroom in third grade. It was patronized mostly by younger kids I bullied into coming over, but still.

Books, especially photographic books, are a way for me to own both art and knowledge. It's the objecthood of the picture books that I covet. I can look at them whenever I want to! It makes me feel like a better artist already, just knowing that all those images live on my shelves. Photo books are special because of their (catchword!) materiality. They are made of more or less the same substance as photographic prints, but I can see them without even going to a gallery. Just log onto my Amazon Prime account and blam! The Internet brings them right to my door.

So here we go: are photo books art? Martin Parr thinks so. I'm not sure my wanna-make-a-picture-book teacher does. Perhaps photo books could be qualified as an anti-elitist form of accessible, popular art? Judith Joy Ross's $5 *Protest the War* is the only example of a truly affordable fine art book that I've come across. At the other end of the spectrum are limited editions, those volumes that live on my Amazon wish list but never leave. These books are elusive. For example, I have tried and failed to look at Paul Graham's *A Shimmer of Possibility*. What kind of a responder am I if I haven't even seen the texts Darius discusses? (I actually considered shelling out $230 bucks for *Shimmer* but now it's already up to $425 . . . and it's moved to the "used & unavailable" Amazon ghetto.)

Expensive and gorgeous limited editions notwithstanding, I believe that photo books do give unprecedented access to an international roster of artists' work. I have to mention Mark Wyse's show at Wallspace that opened a few weeks ago.

His frustration with trying to secure loans of various work led Wyse to cut up his books and frame the reproductions instead of the originals. This ingenious solution is brilliant, and reinforces the extraordinary access books give us to previously unattainable work.

* In the interest of full disclosure, I know for a fact that this person has an impressive photo book collection.

--

Subject: From calling cards to business cards
Date: 22 May 2008 23:59:16
From: CHRIS BALASCHAK

In a 1971 interview, the aging Walker Evans lauded his photographic book, *American Photographs* (1938), as a "calling card" for his own work. By 1971, *American Photographs* had been reprinted once, in 1962 in conjunction with an exhibition of the work at the Museum of Modern Art. Prior to that moment, though, Evans was a relative unknown. As Tod Papageorge has said, Evans's work existed in "relative anonymity" until that second edition. Robert Frank's *The Americans* (1958), featuring work produced on a Guggenheim Fellowship for which Evans had recommended him, was partially responsible for the resurgent interest in Evans during the early 1960s. For Evans's part, the re-publication of his now classic book became the stepping stone to canonical status. The book was the figure to get him there.

I mention *American Photographs'* production, and Evans's late claims for its professional value, in order to complicate Darius Himes's well considered, broad view of the recent interest in photography books as both collectible objects of art, and spaces of photographic expression. While the latter may not be anything new (though we appear to be in a renaissance of photo book production lately), the former has certainly shifted the status of a relatively unconsidered photographic object. The historical photo book has become a highly valued object on the open market. While Himes claims that more recently produced books are made in a critical crucible outside of "market forces," I would like to make the claim that now, more than ever before, the photography book has become a "calling card" for the aspiring professional photographer. Rather than sidestepping market forces, the production of the photography book has become a means to define oneself within the market system.

I do not want to dismiss the democracy of the photography book, nor claim that the book's status as a calling card is negative. That democracy is certainly inherent in the plethora of small publishers and self-publishers that Himes has listed in his essay. Reproducing photographs in book form is certainly far easier and more efficiently done than in previous generations. It is also by no means a simple task. The most highly regarded photography books (many of which Himes notes) are a careful collaboration of photographer, publisher, press hands, and distributor. Great photography books have been produced with little means. Judy Fiskin and Dick Barnes's *Thirty-one Views of San Bernardino* (1975), and Ed Ruscha's *Twentysix Gasoline Stations* (1962) are two instances of relatively low-production values. Yet they are also two instances of relatively unknown artists creating photographic objects that would come to define their mature careers.

Though the photo book can bypass industry, bypass institutionality, and bring into question the way photography forms meaning by strictly visual means, it also has a power in defining its author. The photography book puts forth a unique vision, in the most crude, modernist sense. Evans certainly realized this in 1971. Ruscha seems to have realized it much earlier. In 1962, *Twentysix Gasoline Stations* appears the moment before Ruscha's career launches. In the 1960s, Ruscha produced other books, and alongside them appeared a flurry of interviews and, at times anonymous, reviews. We should recall that the majority of this flurry was at *Artforum*, based in San Francisco and Los Angeles until 1967, and Ruscha was frequently listed as responsible for "production." We can read Ruscha as being as savvy as any of his Pop peers, aware of the need to define his unique place in the arts, while being a shrewd commodity producer.

We may assume that the photography book, being an object that circulates outside of gallery and museum systems, is thereby removed from the institution's white-walled aesthetic frame. Historically, if we considered any of the major photographic figures (by "major" I mean those who have been sanctified by an institutionalized history of photography), the books they produced appeared at the dawn of their blossoming careers. Frank is unknown without *The Americans*. Atget would be an obscure footnote were it not for Berenice Abbott's hand in *Photographe de Paris*.

The photography book is a relatively homogenous form. Photographs reproduce on a page only so many ways. Still, these forms and their sequences confuse the meanings of photography. Denotation is abandoned for syntax. Yet a white frame persists around these reproduced images. Not unlike the walls of the museum, this white space is an aesthetic precinct. In the photo book, the photograph is not just any graphic media. It not only defines its subject matter, it delineates the author's identity. We must appraise the book's performance not as a detour from industry standards, but rather as a willful part of photography's place in the fine art market.

QUESTIONNAIRE / LAUREL PTAK

WHAT ARE SOME OF THE UNIQUE WAYS THE BLOG ENABLES YOU TO ENGAGE WITH YOUR INTERESTS IN PHOTOGRAPHY?

Iheartphotograph.com really started from my want to explore the margins of contemporary photographic practice. It opened up a space for me to explore questions that I didn't always find good answers to in my "real world" engagement with the medium such as in gallery/museum visits or thumbing through magazines. What things were photographers doing that went unseen on the walls/pages of the normal art channels? How were young image-makers tinkering with the medium in new and unexpected ways? What were photographers producing or thinking about in other parts of the world?

One particular aspect of the blog I love is how it functions as my "visual Rolodex"—an ever-evolving archive of my inclinations and ideas around contemporary photographic practice organized all in one place. I frequently flip back through the site's pages and it amazes me how over time certain themes emerge or obsessions repeat that I wouldn't have otherwise noticed. I can likewise keep track of how my own tastes or ideas evolve over time. But it's much more than a container for my private thoughts; it's a kind of thinking out loud. It renders my inclinations transparent to a large and global audience of onlookers.

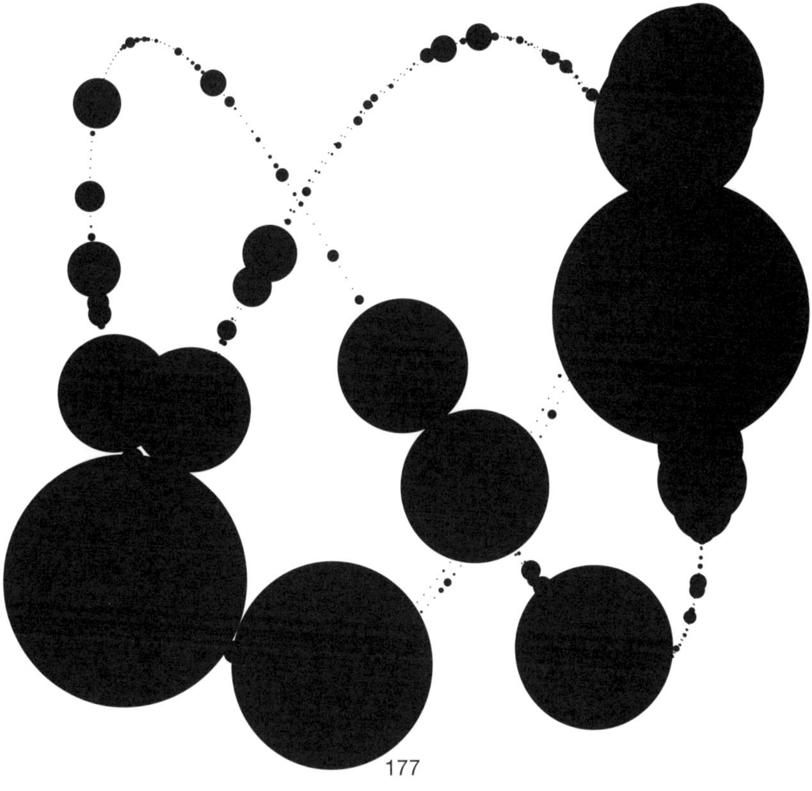

Minor Threat

CHARLIE WHITE

> They say that we Photographers are a blind race at best; that we learn to look at even the prettiest faces as so much light and shade; that we seldom admire, and never love. This is a delusion I long to break through—if I could only find a young lady to photograph, realizing my ideal of beauty . . . I feel sure that I could shake off this cold, philosophic lethargy. — Charles Dodgson (Lewis Carroll), "A Photographer's Day Out," 1860

THOUGHT POLICE

How does a photographer begin to discuss his or her approach to minors as a photographic subject? How does *anyone* enter a discussion about minors and photography when the words alone have been wired to jolt us into considering—if not concluding outright—that there is a problem in the very interests and intentions of an artist pursuing this subject matter? This essay will look at some of the more controversial examples of such photography and examine the issues that they provoke.

The exact manner in which an individual broaches such a discussion greatly affects how the idea is received. The subject is a cognitive minefield, with every dimension playing a critical role: the writer's gender, sexual orientation, and age all contribute to how a discussion of photographing minors is perceived in relation to the current moral, ethical, and cultural ethos. Any writer might be well advised to avoid a polemical approach toward the subject and to instead remain in a conceptual gray zone, toggling forever between the leftist emphasis on retaining certain liberties and conservative concerns about the possible exploitation of these same freedoms. However, the stakes are raised even further by the inherent volatility of this type of photography and its unique reception. The viewer, confronted with an image of youth, must ask a series of questions: under what circumstances has this image been produced, why has it been produced, and how does it make me feel? As a result, youth as a photographic subject has the power to invert consumer culture's hierarchal order between the static and the dynamic image. By engaging and challenging the viewer's moral and aesthetic positions, such images return primacy to active looking over passive watching. Therefore, to consider the complexities of photographing a minor is to consider photography's inherent power as well as the forces external to photography, which can use this power for cultural and political manipulation.

When formulating my starting point for this essay, I chose to focus on commercial photographer Gary Gross's 1975 nudes of ten-year-old child-star Brooke Shields, and the subsequent re-photographing of this work by the artist Richard Prince. Before I could move forward, however, I found myself presented with three separate introductions, each of which seemed to point an accusatory finger in a particular direction. These opening sentences read as follow:

> 1) When Gary Gross photographed the ten-year-old Brooke Shields nude in 1975, his images set in motion a complex and layered series of events related to the photographing of minors and the right to display such images publicly.
>
> 2) When Teri Shields signed a consent form to have her ten-year-old daughter, Brooke Shields,

photographed nude by commercial photographer Gary Gross in 1975, her action set in motion a complex and layered series of events regarding a parent or guardian's right to give consent for the photographing of a minor, as well as the limitations of these photographs' distribution and reproduction.

3) In 1976, when Playboy Press published *Sugar and Spice*, an art photography book featuring the work of fourteen photographers, including Gary Gross's nude photographs of ten-year-old Brooke Shields, it set in motion a complex and layered series of debates regarding a publisher's right to reproduce and distribute such images.

Recognizing the problems inherent in any attempt to recontextualize language that reads as unquestionably criminal, I was hard pressed to form an objective starting point for such a complicated chronology. The very act of writing "nude photographs of ten-year-old Brooke Shields" in our current moral-political climate resulted in an auto-Orwellian invocation of the thought police—which made perfectly clear just how far we are from the historical moment when America could accept the existence of a now all-but-unimaginable series of photographs. It seemed most logical, then, to begin with Brooke Shields's career as a backdrop for this history.

SHIELDED

The evolution of Brooke Shields's career from mid-seventies child star to mid-eighties teen supermodel ratified the notions of public maturation and sexual commodification of youth in America. The milestones of this career were either the result of carefully orchestrated efforts by her mother, Teri Shields, to sell her daughter's sexual commodity to the American public, or they were the unplanned result of an "innocent" image of youth and beauty being repeatedly misread by the masses until it was fully realized, in the 1980s, through the selling of Brooke Shields as virgin spokes-teenager for the Calvin Klein Company. However these steps came about, they mark a major shift in the popular understanding of the pre-teen and teen photographic subject, as well as of how we confront such images through the medium of photography.

Critical to Shields's early success was a series of nude portraits taken by commercial photographer Gary Gross in 1975. Gross defined his goal in the series as that of "find[ing] the woman within the child." He placed the naked Shields in a steamy bathroom, her body glossed with oil and posed erotically toward the camera. Her face is made up to look like that of an adult, so that the body of the child is eerily complicated by the face of a woman and the prepubescent form is charged with a fully mature gaze.

Gross's series resides along a timeline of accepted and contested photographs of minors, spanning from Lewis Carroll's staged 1858 portrait of Alice Liddell as "The Beggar Maid" to Annie Leibovitz's recently debated portraits of celebrated teen actress Miley Cyrus. This 150-year-long history of minors photographed nude, partially nude, or in erotic stances ranges from the clinical to the pornographic in style, and includes the disparate fields of photojournalism, art, and commercial and industrial photography. A few key examples of these variations would be Bruce Davidson's 1959 exploration of urban youth in *Brooklyn Gangs*; Nick Ut's shattering 1972 image of Vietnamese children fleeing a napalmed village; Robert Mapplethorpe's portrait of a nude, five-year-old boy (*Jesse McBride,* 1976); *Super Teen* magazine's 1980 images of a shirtless, 16-year-old

Matt Dillon (published to promote the teen sex comedy *Little Darlings*); Rineke Dijkstra's portraits of Polish and Ukrainian beach-going youths (1992–94) and Collier Schorr's photographic response to Andrew Wyeth's *Helga* paintings in her *Jens F.* series (2001).

Gary Gross's photographs of Brooke Shields reside at the symbolic center of this timeline due to their dual role as soft-core pornography trafficked within popular culture, and as the origin for Richard Prince's *Spiritual America* (1983), in which the artist re-photographed a single image from the original 1975 series. It is crucial to consider simultaneously the roles of both the original Gross series and the Prince appropriation, as the two taken together create a critical conflation of how both popular and art images function in society, splicing together what had previously been perceived as high and low image types with profound implications for the reception of both. Prince's re-photographing of Gross's popular icon pierced the division between mass culture's commodification of youth, and art culture's investigation of youth. *Spiritual America* stakes claims on all representations of youth, no matter their cultural location, thus opening the doors between the gaze of art and the gaze of the masses. As such, *Spiritual America* is photography's *Brillo Box*, merging Alice Liddell, Sue Lyon, Brooke Shields, Tatum O'Neal, Matt Dillon, Jesse McBride, Traci Lords, Mary Kate and Ashley Olsen, Miley Cyrus, Sally Mann, Larry Clark, Nan Goldin, Jock Sturges, *Playboy*, *Hustler*, *Teen Beat*, *J-14*, and more within a single photographic expression. The resulting marriage of Gross the commercial photographer and Prince the artist reveals the latent, highly complicated, and very hypocritical desires of both the photographer/producer and the viewer/consumer, throwing into sharp relief what is at stake when looking at, and therefore thinking about, minors in American society.

In describing his relation to Gary Gross's photographs, Richard Prince wrote:

> My desires needed satisfaction . . . And satisfaction seems to come about by ingesting; perhaps "perceiving" the fiction her photograph imagined. I felt I was in partnership with the picture. There didn't seem to be any interruption between what was imagined by the picture and what was imagined by me. It had an oppressive effect, a glowing hallucinatory energy. There was a libidinal intensification and relief from possession and jealousy. I became infused with this picture, almost as if I was being x-rayed. And this came about when I finally re-photographed the image. —Richard Prince on *Spiritual America*, c.1979 (http://richardprinceart.com/write_spiritual.html)

What *Spiritual America* makes suddenly transparent is that photographing a minor entails the acts of looking at and engaging with a young person and—as a result of this engagement—creating a record that allows society to take part in the same activity. This transparency reveals that the decision to look at a minor—a child, a moppet, a junior-model, or however else the subject is defined—can be complicated to justify. Further, it underscores the complications of that gaze being fixed forever as a record for viewers to judge. I would argue that after *Spiritual America*, the intentions (and/or desires) of the photographer began to take on greater importance. By taking the acts of looking and photographing one step further, Prince implicated the viewer/consumer of the image (in this case, himself) on a more personal level, making the passive onlooker an active participant through the re-photographing of the consumed image. This shift from viewer/consumer to participant/producer is critical when acknowledging the layers and complexities that relate to looking at a photograph of a minor. In fact, as Prince's thoughts on *Spiritual America* suggest, the desire to possess or own the subject's fiction can be greater for the viewer than for the photographer.

EXPOSED

The second phase of Brooke Shields's career involved highly risqué films such as *Pretty Baby* (1978), in which she plays a child prostitute, and *The Blue Lagoon* (1980), in which she plays a teen Eve abandoned on an island with a boy with whom she has sexual relations. Following these popular successes, Shields stepped into global stardom as the fifteen-year-old spokesmodel for the Calvin Klein Jeans campaign, in which, among other antics, she wiggled into a pair of jeans in real time while quoting Darwin— famously launching the line "Want to know what gets between me and my Calvins? Nothing."

The Gross images and their distribution by Playboy Press in the adult photography book *Sugar and Spice* in 1976 facilitated these later, more complicated representations of sexuality. Only through their eroticizing of the child star in a fully adult manner could any possible notion of her as restricted or otherwise off-limits to the public eye be overcome. In a complicated inversion of what is commonly held to be a form of exploitation on the part of the photographer, Brooke Shields was an "adult" to society because Gross's camera had rendered her as such. However, from Gross onwards, Shields's representation would remain immune to criticism. It was at this point that Richard Prince capitalized on her unique position, making material the social-sexual anomaly that America had afforded itself, and forever shifting the landscape of the artist's relation to the minor-as-subject.

When comparing Shields's career from 1975 through 1980 with those of more recent teen icons (all of whom seem branded under the aegis of some corporate identity and social conservatism), Shields's freedom of expression arguably forms a leftist, dare I say feminist, argument for (not against) a minor's right to express him- or herself as sexual commodity. Times have changed to the point where accusations of obscenity by offended onlookers can instantly replace debate over an artwork's intentions with a *fait accompli* guilty verdict. From the controversy over Mapplethorpe's *Jesse McBride*, to the FBI raid on Jock Sturges's studio, to the seizing of Nan Goldin's *Klara And Edda Belly Dancing* at the Baltic, to the recent outrage and attempted discrediting of Miley Cyrus (along with Annie Leibovitz) over her photographs in *Vanity Fair*, it is clear that society's unease with photographs depicting or alluding to nudity or erotic characterization of minors has become far more conservative.

A visual comparison from the aforementioned timeline might offer some insight into society's current degree of response. By paralleling the outward gaze of Alice Liddell in *The Beggar Maid* with Shields's in *Spiritual America* and that of Miley Cyrus in the exposed-shoulder portrait from the *Vanity Fair* pictorial, what becomes clear is the similarities of their come-hither looks, their seduction of the viewer, and their engagement with the adult photographer. Perhaps this gaze—more so than any occurrence of exposed flesh—is what viewers find so alluring and problematic in these photographs, and is what triggered the quite virulent response to the tepid photographs of Miley Cyrus.

When the act of looking at a minor (and encouraging the minor to return the gaze) is seen as an inherently inappropriate activity, then any representation of a minor risks being perceived as exploitation even when it is something else. Looking at young people is critical to a society's understanding of itself, and the recording of generations of adolescence is perhaps one of the most viable means of doing this. A photographer's interests in the pubescent subject is not limited to the libidinal, as can be seen in the work of Rineke Dijkstra, whose contrapposto, beach-going teen subjects transcend the erotic through their blank gazes and classical poses. Similarly, the portrayal of flesh is not limited to the sexual; consider the work of Collier Schorr, whose male wrestlers resist being reduced to fetish through the artist's careful examination of their athletic culture. Nor is the young subject always a sexual object, as evidenced by Sharon Lockhart's cataloging of a community of youths in her *Pine Flat Portrait Studio* series (2005). These examples, none of which has been contested in the manner of the others addressed earlier in this essay, are nevertheless part of the same exploration of youth—an exploration that requires a broad spectrum of representation to fulfill its meaning.

However, despite the clear divergences among the above-mentioned practices, these works also hold the potential of summoning, to some degree, a latent sexual tension as a result of their very use of the minor as a subject of contemplation. This tension is generated from one of the most basic components at work between the photographer and his or her subject: the exercise of control. Consider Prince's confessionary statement in relation to how perception and desire actively define the image: "There didn't seem to be any interruption between what was imagined by the picture and what was imagined by me." In admitting his own fantasy, or the embracement of a fantasy set in motion by Gross, Prince invokes the viewer's heightened role in relation to the photograph of the minor, suggesting that even the most neutral representations still bear the stamp of the artist's directive—*Stand still so I can look at you carefully*. From the viewer's standpoint, the complications of this dynamic are as layered as the subject matter, and it is that complication that we no longer seem willing, or prepared, to grapple with.

In closing, it is important to acknowledge a new layer in this fraught and uncomfortable history: the recent shift toward teens representing themselves through the advent of the Internet, which has empowered a generation of minors to actively publish their own images through communal sites such as Flickr and YouTube, personal blogs, and networking sites like MySpace and Facebook. This authorial shift has radically changed the manner in which the adult can view minors, as well as how minors view themselves and their peers. Never before have minors had such opportunity to represent and regard themselves. Once limited to a specialized zone of magazines and books, the distribution of photographic imagery has become an ocean of online self-representation and self-styling, densely populated by teens and pre-teens in a constant state of self-recording. The full implications of this shift are yet to be fully realized. However, this new authorship already serves to highlight the adult gaze in cases when a photograph is *not* of a minor's own making. When pre-teens and teens are able to represent themselves, it becomes uncomfortably clear that an adult photographer exercises two forms of control simultaneously: that enacted by a photographer on a subject, and that enacted by an adult upon a minor.

--

DISCUSSION FORUM
WWW.WORDSWITHOUTPICTURES.ORG

--

Subject: Government Issue
Date: 2 June 2008 20:12:54
From: WILLIAM E. JONES

The U.S. Supreme Court, in its decision *Stanley v. Georgia*, 394 U.S. 557 (1969), unanimously affirmed the individual's right to privacy by holding that "the State may not prohibit mere possession of obscene matter." It was the first time—and in all likelihood will prove to be the only time—that the Supreme Court was unanimous in its opinion of pornography.

Two years before, the U.S. Congress had set up a commission to study pornography, and its report, published in 1970, found no proof of pornography's alleged social harm, and recommended that no legal restrictions be placed upon adults' access to it. *Report of the Commission on Obscenity and Pornography* alarmed conservatives, notably Charles H. Keating, founder of Citizens for Decent Literature and a member of the commission himself. He wrote a lengthy dissent in which he called the commission's conclusions "a blank check for the pornographers to flood our country with every variety of filth and perversion."

During the early 1970s, the much-anticipated flood could not quite begin, since there was no adequate legal definition of filth. Specifically, the distinction between pornography, the immense and variegated genre of sexually explicit images and words, and obscenity, that part of the pornographic so irredeemable that it was not protected by the First Amendment's guarantee of freedom of expression, remained ambiguous. The previous definition set forth by the Supreme Court in *Roth v. United States*, 354 U.S. 476 (1957), was schematic and in a word dear to First Amendment scholars—overbroad. Justice Potter Stewart's jejune assertion about obscenity that "I know it when I see it" (in the 1964 decision *Jacobellis v. Ohio*, 378 U.S. 184) did nothing to clarify the matter.

A final decision came in the form of *Miller v. California*, 413 U.S. 15 (1973), which formulated a tripartite definition still in use today. Material is obscene under the following circumstances: (1) the average person, applying contemporary community standards, must find that the work, taken as a whole, appeals to the prurient interest; (2) the work depicts or describes, in a patently offensive way, sexual conduct or excretory functions specifically defined by applicable state law; and (3) the work, taken as a whole, lacks serious literary, artistic, political, or scientific value.

The *Miller* ruling had a few problems—e. g., who is the average person? Nonetheless, it emboldened pornographers, who saw plenty of room to maneuver within its provisions, to make substantial investments in production and distribution. The notion of "community standards" gave local law enforcement agencies the latitude to rid their jurisdictions of adult bookstores and theaters, but the losses caused by these actions were minor annoyances to what soon became a multi-billion dollar industry.

The Reagan years brought an about-face in the federal government's policy: Attorney General Edwin Meese set out to demonstrate the social harm caused by pornography, and to provide law enforcement agencies with strategies to fight it. *The Final Report of the Attorney General's Commission on Pornography* (1986), criticized by social scientists for its prejudices and distortions, became an unexpectedly popular success when readers found that it contained a nearly 2,000-page flood of unintentionally hilarious filth. Charles H. Keating, the dissenter of the previous commission, was vindicated, after many unsuccessful prosecutions in his native Cincinnati of figures such as Larry Flynt and Russ Meyer. The federal government's position on pornography was finally aligned with Keating's. Whether Keating had occasion to gloat is doubtful, since he was occupied at that time with financial transactions of immense proportions at Lincoln Savings and Loan. These transactions, approved by the likes of Alan Greenspan and Senator John McCain, precipitated Keating's fall from decent citizen to felon, when he was convicted on multiple counts of fraud, racketeering, and conspiracy.

If Meese's report was risible, pornographers did not have long to laugh, because the First Amendment protections they had enjoyed for a decade and a half were threatening to dissolve. The crucial figure in this shift in the legal climate was not a law enforcement official or a moral entrepreneur, but a girl named Nora Louise Kuzma. In 1984, using an older person's birth certificate, she obtained a California driver's license stating that she was over 21, when in fact she was only 15 years old. She presented this identification at liquor stores and then at studios where she performed as Traci Lords. Lords appeared in a number of popular pornographic movies, until she became so famous that someone (perhaps a "friend" from her hometown of Steubenville, Ohio) told the feds her true age. She was Pet of the Month in the same issue of *Penthouse* that featured the photo spread that cost Vanessa Williams her Miss America crown, but Miss Williams's predicament was nothing compared to the consequences of revelations about Traci Lords.

After sexually explicit representations of Lords had been removed from stores, the FBI prosecuted producers and distributors of her videos. Defense attorneys argued (without much success) that when Lords presented her illegally obtained identification, she did not appear to be under 18 years old, and that her movies were marketed to mainstream consumers, not to pedophiles. Regardless of these arguments, her case was put to use in the campaign to eliminate child pornography. In the aftermath of the scandal, Congress passed the Child Protection and Obscenity Enforcement Act of 1988 (18 U.S.C. § 2251 *et seq.*)

Without realizing it, Traci Lords provided anti-porn crusaders with an unassailable device for manufacturing moral panic: concern for the welfare of children.

Section 2257 of the Child Protection and Obscenity Enforcement Act requires that producers keep proof of legal age for all people appearing in sexually explicit representations, and that these records be available for inspection by law enforcement authorities. Injunctions delayed the enforcement of this section of the law until July 3, 1995. (Works produced before that date are exempt from these specific requirements.) In practice, producers retain pictures showing performers holding photo identification next to their faces, and a "guardian of records" organizes these files, deals with demands to inspect them, and it is hoped, keeps the producers out of federal prison.

Record keeping requirements, called 2257 regulations, while reasonable in principle, have become a political device used against the porn industry. The PROTECT Act (Prosecutorial Remedies and Other Tools to end the Exploitation of Children Today), passed in 2003, gave the Department of Justice wide discretion in amending and enforcing 2257 regulations. Proposed changes to section 2257 have included: (a) defining as producers not only companies that make adult videos, but also anyone who re-uses or circulates sexually explicit images in any way; (b) requiring that records be available at any time that production and distribution activities are maintained (24 hours a day in some cases); (c) rescinding the "grandfather clause" exempting older material (for which no records exist); (d) accepting only U. S.-government-issued identification for "proof of age" photos (for foreign as well as domestic productions); and (e) mandating enhanced penalties of up to life imprisonment for pandering, the definition of which may embrace advertising and even casual emails.

The porn industry responded to this and other federal initiatives by organizing the Free Speech

Coalition, which has brought suit against the government to seek the repeal of legal requirements that they argue are arbitrary, illogical, and burdensome. The 2257 regulations have been the focus of repeated litigation, and thus far in all cases the Free Speech Coalition has been successful in rolling back the federal government's incursions into what the industry considers legitimate business practices and expression protected by the First Amendment.

Like it or not, pornographers have been the most effective guardians of freedom of speech during the waning years of the George W. Bush administration. In repelling attempts to limit First Amendment rights, they have seen far more consistent success than artists, journalists, or the mainstream film industry. The triumphs of the porn industry are a testament not only to the deep pockets of its prominent producers and the legal acumen of its lawyers, but also to the raw power of capitalism. Economic and technological changes have created a situation beyond the control of the most astute capitalists and the most ardent censors.

Considering that they risk vast sums of money as well as the personal liberty of their executives, the major porn producers are at pains to avoid employing underage talent. Nor does the industry explicitly attract underage consumers. Professionals in the industry emphasize this by using the term "adult video" or "adult content" rather than the vague and subjective term "pornography," though the general public has not followed their example. If children find sexually explicit material, how can the industry, the feds, or an army of concerned parents stop them from looking at it?

By prevailing U.S. legal standards, those who circulate or own child pornography are breaking the law, since this obscene material has never had any constitutional protection. But the logical subtleties of defining the terms child, obscenity, pornography, circulation and ownership in the digital age have been a challenge to Supreme

Court Justices barraged with hypothetical cases ranging from the benign to the horrific. Recoiling from the suggestion that *Romeo and Juliet*—which after all deals with the sexuality of teens—could be considered child porn under federal law, Justice Anthony Kennedy wrote in *Ashcroft v. Free Speech Coalition*, 535 U.S. 234 (2002), "Art and literature express the vital interest we all have in the formative years we ourselves once knew, when wounds can be so grievous, disappointment so profound, and mistaken choices so tragic, but when moral acts and self-fulfillment are still in reach." This statement brings to mind another hypothetical case: a Supreme Court Justice, born during the Depression and raised by Victorian parents, in conversation with a grandchild whose first exposure to pornography occurred around the same time as learning to read.

The legal issues around obscenity and the First Amendment are still in flux, and are likely to be so for a long time to come. Provisions of the PROTECT Act have been struck down in Federal Circuit Court, and appeals are only now reaching the Supreme Court. Whatever their outcome, one thing is clear: in its stated aim (protecting children) and in its implicit aim (harassing the porn industry out of existence) recent federal legislation has failed spectacularly. No matter how many ways federal authorities devise to stop the spread of sexual imagery, it remains a fact of contemporary life. In America, pornography is, like the Judeo-Christian God, omnipresent; whether it is also omnipotent remains to be seen.

--

Subject: Spiritual America
Date: 3 June 2008 04:35:12
From: CATHERINE GRANT

As well as appropriating Gary Gross's photograph of Brooke Shields, as discussed by Charlie White in "Minor Threat," Richard Prince also appropriated his title. I'll use this appropriation as a beginning through which to explore some of the points brought up by White in more detail.

Spiritual America is the title of a 1923 photograph by Alfred Stieglitz that shows the hindquarters of a castrated cart-horse. Stieglitz's photograph is a blackly humorous commentary on the state of America, its virility shackled and broken. Prince's re-presentation of the young Brooke, as *Spiritual America*, takes on the allegorical associations found in Stieglitz's image. In Prince's version, broken masculinity is refigured as a corrupted voyeuristic fantasy, in which the commodified image of feminine sexuality is grotesquely performed through the girl-child's body, for the camera of a commercial photographer, with the consent of her mother. Is Brooke Prince's vision of *Spiritual America*, broken like the cart-horse in the face of the labor she must perform? Or is it our own spiritual downfall that is imagined, as we join the gaze of the photographer and mother, staring at the spectacle of sexualization that is enacted onto the surface of the child's body? Both are dramatic interpretations, but I feel that whilst both are imaged in this work, neither quite explains the fascination provoked by this photograph. To explore this fascination, I want to turn to comments made about *Spiritual America* by the photographer Collier Schorr:

> ". . . I have thought a great deal about Richard Prince's work, which has linked a crisis within masculinity to that within femininity. I lived for a time with his *Spiritual America*, 1983, the portrait of the prepubescent Brooke Shields. The success of that piece is as a critical commentary about representation of the feminine body in photography and about the look and shape of desire. The secret surprise within that photograph was that its appropriation allowed it to exist. We could look at the image not as it was originally—a pornographic image of a child made with an ambitious mother's permission—but as a critique." (Collier Schorr, "Feminism and Art:

9 views," *Artforum*, vol. 42, no. 2, October 2003, p. 145.)

This idea that Prince's appropriation "allows" us to look at this image provides a point of access that does not collapse into the Orwellian policing of acceptable boundaries of image production. This embedding of critique, combined with fascination for the figure of the adolescent (for I think it is the adolescent that this image evokes, rather than the child), is a combination that drives many images of teens in contemporary art. For me, this image evokes the adolescent because of the way in which it sits alongside Brooke Shields's later successes, and the timing of its re-presentation in the early eighties as Shields edged towards adulthood. As White explores, Brooke Shields's Calvin Klein adverts are refigured in the face of this earlier image, the unacceptable pedophilic framing of her 10-year-old body tainting the barely legal sexualization of her adolescent self.

Importantly, *Spiritual America* is not only the title of Prince's photograph, but also the gallery he set up to sell prints of the image as a mocking commentary on the legal battles taking place at the time between Shields's mother and Gross, as the photographer tried to capitalize on the teen star's fame by issuing the image as a limited edition print. Here the sexualized body is merged with the commodified body. Schorr's comments about living with *Spiritual America* point to how we all live with this image, as the constantly sexualized image of youth is a staple of our media, albeit glossed in terms of an adolescent, rather than prepubescent, body. Perhaps what is fascinating about *Spiritual America* is its staging of the blurred lines between acceptable and unacceptable sexuality in contemporary culture, where the figure of the adolescent stands in for our ultimate object of desire whilst hovering on the cusp of childhood, with the dangers of the pedophilic gaze that this brings.

If this is the case, then what is the attraction of the adolescent and child to so many contemporary photographers? In my own writing on the representation of adolescence, the issues of consent and control, which figure so strongly in White's article, become more ambiguous with the shift from child to adolescent. It would seem to me that there is a world of difference between Carroll's images of Alice Liddell (age 6), Gross's images of Shields at age 10, Rineke Dijkstra's images of teenagers in her *Beaches* series, and Collier Schorr's collaborative projects with adolescents in Germany. For me, the interest is in the way that control is negotiated by the adolescent sitter, and how the power dynamic of photographer/viewer and sitter is dramatized in a way that demonstrates that we are all controlled to some extent by the gaze of others. However, this power dynamic is not one that is unshakeable, and for me, the depiction of adolescence as a performance points to the myriad ways in which identities and desires can escape normative boundaries. By focusing on minors as an indistinct category, White's text allows the specter of the predatory photographer to overshadow what is at stake in the representation of adolescence. The adolescent is a crucial figure in contemporary culture that allows critiques of the structures of desire and adult identity (although I agree with many of White's points about the representation of minors "activating" the spectator). From Larry Clark's provocative participant-observer photographs in his book *Tulsa* (1971), to Sally Mann's image and text combinations in *At Twelve* (1988), to a 16-year-old Kate Moss on the cover of *The Face,* to the apparently unconscious staging of feminine poses (from pin-up poses to Botticelli's Venus) in two of the most frequently reproduced images from Dijkstra's *Beach Portraits* series, an alternative history of images of adolescence needs to be imagined, complicating the trajectory from Carroll to Gross. The potential for a critique of what appears stable—from the child to the adult, to the viewer as voyeur, to the subject as passive, to the picturing of desires that can be labeled and compartmentalized—this is the fascination for me found in the images of adolescence in contemporary art.

After decades of feminism, psychoanalytic theories of the gaze, queer theory and politics and an ever-expanding image culture, the use of the adolescent by artists and photographers (particularly women) provides a culturally loaded space in which to consider and critique our conceptions of identity and sexuality. If, as many psychoanalysts argue, the state of adult maturity is in itself a fantasy that is only ever partially achieved, then adolescence as a psychic space is one that we are all destined to return to, a site which is filled as much with nostalgia as with desire, a recognition of our own selves that is activated in these performances for the camera. In this way, the relationship between adult photographer and adolescent sitter is not simply one of control, but potentially of recognition and renegotiation, a reimagining that helps us to understand the allegorical implications of photographing adolescence, as pointed to by Prince's title.

--

Subject: Response
Date: 3 June 2008 18:36:20
From: DAVID CAMPANY

You might say the adolescent is the photographic subject par excellence. Why? Because the adolescent and the medium have so much in common:

1. Both are marked by a profound confusion about the relation between appearance and essence.
2. Both are caught awkwardly between past and future, unable to move with any certainty toward either.
3. Both have difficult relations with their parents but can't imagine being parents themselves.
4. Neither can explain their existence very well.

They suit each other perfectly. Forget the

sociological accounts. As photography finally enters its philosophical phase, in which it attempts to figure out its own condition, it is no surprise that it circles endlessly around the figure of the adolescent. The medium is photographing itself!

--

Subject: Ambiguity
Date: 5 June 2008 17:54:04
From: CHARLOTTE COTTON

As Charlie White's essay lays out, portraits of minors are complicated in part because, like all photographic portraits, they are uneasy evidence of the control that one person (the photographer) can have upon other people (his or her subjects). Regardless of the intent or retrospective claims of the photographer, at the heart of portraiture is the simple fact that the photographer has a better idea than the subject of what will be made apparent or can be fashioned from the physical description of a human form in a photograph. And no matter how we might like to intellectualize our readings of portrait photographs, we actually respond to some degree in a dead basic, lower-brain kind of way to the opportunity to scrutinize someone else in a photograph. We compare and contrast, empathize and judge, find ourselves and our other in photographic representations. Some of our most well-loved and astute portraitists are accorded seminal status because of their drive to take on and experiment with this tricky territory. Diane Arbus was very persuasive and is still highly influential because of the confidence with which she proclaimed the power of photographic portraiture to lay bare the contradictions of what we think we project about ourselves and what leaks out in an intense photographic moment. She also claimed the right of a photographer to command such a territory and "take" from the situation for all it's worth:

> You see someone on the street and essentially

what you notice about them is the flaw . . . Our whole guise is like giving a sign to the world to think of us in a certain way, but there's a point between what you want people to know about you and what you can't help people knowing about you. And that has to do with what I've always called the gap between intention and effect. —Diane Arbus, *Diane Arbus: An Aperture Monograph*, 1972, pp. 1-2

There is a basic premise or even drive in portraiture that is not politically correct, nor does it hold the photographic subject's best interests at heart. When that drive is coupled with the enactment of control by an adult photographer upon a minor, it becomes an incendiary arena. White writes about Lewis Carroll and his early orchestration of the "come hither" posture in his photograph of Alice Liddell, *The Beggar Maid*. I think it's astute but also generous of White to compare one of Carroll's most uncomfortable and perhaps revealing (of the photographer's motivations) portraits with 20th century cornerstones of the representations of minors. Although I understand that this photograph by Carroll allows him to transcend beyond his era into contemporary discourses, in the main, Carroll used the camera and his subjects to elevate himself within British society. It so happened that he not only had uncomfortable desires but also a deep understanding that photographing the children of the social elite that he aspired to join was a convenient route into that somewhat impenetrable circle. That ability to fulfill deeply routed Oedipal urges to claw back a birthright position amongst the demigods and royalty of one's society offers an excellent reading of the history of portrait photographers in general. In the century of picture magazines, I think of Sir Cecil Beaton, Richard Avedon, Mario Testino, and Annie Leibovitz as brilliant exploiters of the ascendance and power that portraiture offers its makers. I suspect that Leibovitz's status as the preeminent image-maker of today went a long way in the unfolding of that shoot with the young Miley Cyrus. No actual laws were broken; Cyrus was chaperoned by her (adult) management. The expectations were high that Cyrus would be classically and beautifully confirmed within the pantheon of contemporary celebrities via the edgy, arty, and sophisticated vision of one of the greatest commercial artists, who was working for a decidedly high-brow magazine. It's as if everyone forgot that the gap between intention and effect in portraiture could be extremely wide.

As Catherine Grant eloquently outlines, the iconography for a contemporary portrait of a minor as a vulnerable, sexualized, perhaps traumatized figure, comes into play as an art genre with Larry Clark, and gets controversial for a general, mass-media audience with Corinne Day's 1993 fashion "portraits" of Kate Moss for *British Vogue*. Leibovitz's portrayal of Miley Cyrus stepped over the boundary of propriety of commercial image making—it blends the unholy alliance (for the commercial realm) of childhood and grungy-looking, working class sexuality. Miley isn't smiling while she enters sexualized adulthood and her hair and make-up are not pronounced enough to be an obvious or well-accepted excuse to sell beauty products to women by adorning children's exquisitely taut skin; her dress is not colorful nor well documented enough to promote an LVMH designer. She is set against a backdrop that is the antithesis of the happy pastoral scene that might diffuse the uncomfortable sensuousness of a child half-naked. We have the greatest problems with the sexualized depictions of minors when they recall the beggar maid, even more so when they are contingent on their dissemination within the vast machine of magazines and advertising. But why am I fretting so much about how a precocious talent is represented by a great image-maker? We know that every smile or frown, exuberant leap or hunching of shoulders by a savvy subject in the context of a commercial photographer's studio is a safe, pre-meditated simulation of real feeling. I guess I can only answer that for myself. There are two reasons why I decided to stay up tonight and write a response to White's essay.

Firstly, I had a gut reaction to Leibovitz's most controversial portrait of Miley Cyrus that was independent of any reasoning I could give about the conventions its form comes from, the belief that no genuine harm was intended by such a massive projection upon a minor (albeit a famous one) and an expectation that a whole team of highly intelligent media people will make sure that there's a rosy outcome for everyone involved. Portraying minors triggers something absolutely fundamental in us since we have all been through that fraught time of life. Independent of any speculations I might have about what Leibovitz, *Vanity Fair*, Disney or the Cyrus camp intended, it had an effect on me. I'm caught between being relieved that I somehow came across some good, old-fashioned indexicality in the smoke-and-mirrors of celebrity image construction, but also annoyed with myself for rising to the provocation that was made.

The second reason I wanted to respond to this essay is that I've been suspicious of just how many so-called contemporary artists-using-photography have depicted minors in a way that has become a convention and an allegory for photography (as David Campany suggests), and I sense that the depiction of youth is now a pretty easy motif for declaring edgy criticality. I had a brief conversation today with a fellow curator who is thinking about showing a series of photographs of adolescent boys—rather sweaty and fleshy, but grand, portraits. I was concerned for her that she doesn't get trapped in an intellectualized hornets' nest of justifying a body of work, for an institutional context, that simply does not stand up to likely and valid criticism as being ultimately arty exploitation of a highly seductive subject. I used to dislike the word "liminal" for its description of some pretty lame art photography, but I am currently having problems with "ambiguity," especially when referring to depictions of minors. Contemporary art photography does not function in a vacuum and, as the writers who have ventured into this debate have described, what we ultimately interpret a photograph of a minor to mean within the rhetoric of a now well-trammeled artistic genre is, in part, independent of the artist's critical intent and also dependent on the contemporary controversies within popular image-making.

QUESTIONNAIRE / ADAM PUTNAM

DO NEW TECHNOLOGIES CHANGE YOUR IDEA OF PHOTOGRAPHY?

Yes, in the sense that digital cameras make the whole process faster and more accessible. But one major shift is the new ability to preview the image at the moment right after taking the picture. I have found that psychologically this drains the mystery, but also removes any potential for accidents to occur. Accident and mystery are two aspects of photography that I have always loved. As someone who can easily be racked by indecision, this is a bad thing and ironically it slows down the process.

DO YOU ENJOY LOOKING AT PHOTOGRAPHS ONLINE?

It is like looking through a box of found photos, but you don't have to get your hands dirty and you can make instant copies. However, I do not like using the Internet to look at artwork except as a basic research device. Again, all the meaning and texture is drained away. (Photographs are, after all, material things.) I much prefer looking at photos in a book.

QUESTIONNAIRE / AARON SCHUMAN

HOW DO YOU BELIEVE THE ROLE OF PRINT PUBLICATIONS HAS CHANGED AS A RESULT OF THE INCREASING PRESENCE OF INTERNET-BASED PUBLICATIONS?

In terms of mass media, I think that the Internet

has profoundly changed, if not entirely superceded, the role of print publications, in that it can offer infinite content in a variety of formats—within a complex network of both current and archival material—all of which is instantaneously accessible. When I first moved to New York, I remember thinking that it was so cool that you could pick up a copy of the Sunday *Times* on a Saturday night; it felt like you were really ahead of the game, almost peering into the future. Now, if a story broke an hour ago, it's old news. It's almost as if today's print publications simply substantiate something's relevance or importance after the fact, in that someone's gone to the trouble of physically recording it—they've actually "put it in writing," so to speak. So, in a sense, I guess that the print format to varying degrees still connotes a sense of selectivity, significance or integrity to that which it chooses to publish.

. . . Therefore, in many ways print publications remain at the top of the editorial publishing hierarchy within this genre, but Internet-based publications serve a vital role in supporting them, as well as guiding readers, writers and photographers to their pages. If you're at your computer and want to instantaneously engage with remarkable photography, clicking on your favorite link in the "bookmarks bar" can be incredibly informative and gratifying; but inevitably, it will never be as satisfying as pulling a great magazine off the bookshelf and curling up with it for an hour.

The Value of Photographs

Los Angeles County Museum of Art
Participants: Paul Graham, Soo Kim, Anthony Pearson
Moderator: Charlotte Cotton

"The Value of Photographs" takes as its starting point a discussion of the meaning behind the material decisions made by photographers. Specifically, it addresses how the value systems that we have traditionally associated with photography and photographic prints may be shifting in an increasingly digitized and dispersed visual sphere. We are in a moment, one could argue, when analog photographic production is an aesthetic or conceptual choice. How do artists make decisions about the meaning of the material processes and forms of their works? Does the meaning of a photograph reside in its subject or material?

Recent years have brought a return to the analog, black-and-white print in the work of younger artists. Is this a fleeting trend or an emphatic embrace of the outmoded? What would it mean for photography to become an essentially paperless, non-chemical medium? Is a photographic print the result of a formal decision rather than a default object? How might the values ascribed to analog photography take on new critical meaning and potential in a digital era?

The participants in this panel were invited to take on some of these questions because they each make distinctly different choices about form as it relates to the meaning of their photographs.

PAUL GRAHAM: In some ways, I don't know why I was invited here tonight. Maybe I'm the token street photographer. That's a joke, by the way. I do the unfashionable thing of walking down the street and taking pictures. What I take "the value of photographs" to mean is the value of photography, which is something I care passionately about. The work that has moved me historically has fallen into that territory where the documentary instincts and the artistic instincts of photography coalesce. That's the point at which photography is a unique and wonderful medium.

That territory was best identified by the great curator John Szarkowski, who worked at the Museum of Modern Art for over 20 years. He identified and ring-fenced this area, pushing aside classic photojournalism and documentary photography (as valuable as they are) and self-conscious, fine art photography, in order to discuss the territory that lies between those two—where they overlap, mingle, and react. That was clearly stated in one of Szarkowski's first major shows, *New Documents* [1967], which included participants that everyone will know of: Diane Arbus, Garry Winogrand, and Lee Friedlander. Of course, many great photographers already identified this territory—including Robert Frank, Walker Evans, Eugène Atget, and Lewis Hine—as one of the most fertile and profound areas for photographic practice in which to operate. That's a territory I seek to operate in. Of course, it has changed.

The language moves forward. We don't do things the same way. We don't write books the same way we did in 1952. We shouldn't take pictures the same way we did in 1952. But it's basically this wonderfully profound territory, this artistic space, that has opened for us in the photographic medium. What the nature of that space is, and what the nature of that photographic act is, are very difficult things to talk about. It's beyond my limited abilities; there are people far more talented to explain it. But when you look at the great work that has happened in the 20th century, by Frank or, bringing it up-to-date, Winogrand, William Eggleston, Stephen Shore, and Arbus, these people actually touch upon the nature of our time. They pierce the opaque threshold of the present day and manage to fold and weave something of the fabric of time and bring that forward to us to look at now. That's a great and profound artistic act, one that's underappreciated in terms of the nature and quality of photography.

. . .

SOO KIM: The central themes in my recent work concern how the photographic image can alter the sense of time and space, how urban landscapes are viewed through introspective vantage points, and how slowness and singularity can be held in a picture and suggest an alternative way of looking at the world. I'm trying to look at photographic images in opposition to the velocity and ubiquity of images.

Since 2002, my practice has consisted largely of photographic landscapes and portraits where parts of the photographs have been cut away. The subtractive method allows me to introduce visual information that cannot be recorded photographically in one frame. The active removal brings slowness and fantasy to the image. The depiction of time and space is altered and one can see the removal or disruption of the image itself. The cuts are specific to each series of photographs. The photographs are made first and the idea stemming from the initial work dictates what is cut away and what is left behind. The materiality of the photograph has become increasingly important to me.

There are too many photographs and there is too much technological ease. The sense of being visually overwhelmed is perhaps a reaction to the accelerated digital world. My solution is to slow it down by using analog techniques and embracing the imperfect original as opposed to the seamless digital copy. As digital technology has made picture-making easier, less physical and more fleeting, the way we read photographs has also changed. Walter Benjamin proposed that the way that we would understand the world would be primarily through the photograph, replacing the word as the dominant means of learning. What's interesting about this now concerns not only the ubiquity and predominance of the photographic image, but our access to this vehicle for information at a scale and speed unimaginable to Benjamin.

Numerous websites covering a wide range of content show innumerable photographs. Seeing more and more images by more and more image-makers, from amateurs to professionals, children and adults, one question that I had was: "What impact does this have on the life of an image?" "How does an image stay memorable amongst such a vast sea of images?" My reaction to these questions was to make non-edition, unique works that attempt to slow down both the making and reading of the photographic image. I attempt to slow down the reading through the removal of the imagery, to make imperfect excisions and to build a slowness into the process of making the work that matched my intent at picturing slowness. I don't wish to be photographically illiterate. Rather, I'm interested in extending and expanding the way we read photographs.

. . .

ANTHONY PEARSON: I feel a real affinity for this idea that Paul was talking about of slowly looking at things that are mundane and experiencing the in-between moments, and then an affinity with Soo's idea of going into a picture and touching it, augmenting it, showing your hand, and making something that's literally unique. All of my works are unique. I was educated in the '90s in a school where there was a very institutionalized notion of implied meaning and forced meaning onto photographs, this whole idea of being involved in personal narrative and making one's identity hyper-apparent in one's work and implying all kinds of meaning onto a picture. I think the whole time I was "transmedium," as in transgender. We were joking last night that I'm a painter and sculptor trapped in a photographer's body. In these other mediums, one does not make an excuse for personal forms of expression. I privilege the right-hand side of the brain, which is this idea of intuition and instinct that is kind of illegal in photography.

I make several different kinds of pictures. With one of

them, I work either on a wall or in a corner of my studio using paint, tape, ink, foil, paper, and stencils. And I light things on fire. I like to put tinfoil in the microwave sometimes, which is really something you're not supposed to do, but it comes out really excellent. I hang it back up on the wall, and I photograph it. In this set of pictures, which are called *Solarizations*, I find a way to take the form of sculpting and painting, and I process it. I mediate it through photography. Then I flash the photo paper with white light and it shifts the tones and it creates these Mackie lines. It creates this very formal way of looking at this kind of abstraction.

All of these pictures that I have here are from the last three months. I'm hyper-prolific and I move through things very quickly. I don't monkey with editions. Each work is unique. Last year I made over a hundred works. Sometimes they go in sets. Sometimes they go with sculptures. Sometimes they go on their own. Sometimes they're coupled with another set of pictures, which are almost always very similar.

. . .

The idea with photography is that you want to take a moment or take time and cast it into permanence by making a picture of it. The whole idea of toning a print is similar to the idea of patina to a bronze. So, this idea of bronze sculpture and silver gelatin printing came naturally together for me. When I make a photograph, I expose a negative. And I take that negative and I shine light through it and I print a photograph with it. When I make a bronze, I take plaster or a piece of wax and I seal it in rubber. And then I take that piece of rubber, put it in a shell, pour molten metal into it, crack it open, and I clean it. Well, actually, I don't do all that myself to be honest with you. I work with a foundry. But it's the same idea of casting something from positive to negative to positive once again. There's a funny thing that happens with these pieces, which is that they have a real sense of the object, while at the same time you're dealing with pictorial space.

The thing that makes me so nervous and uncomfortable about these things, which tells me I should keep working with them, is that there is an awkward moment of object confusion and a question about whether the sculpture really goes with the picture. When I look at it from one side it feels off kilter. When I approach it from the other it feels just right. There's some kind of tension and confusion, yet also elegance. This one used to have a bunch of fabric in the plaster. When I pulled it away it left these recesses and crevices. This is one of the solarized photographs, which is basically a picture of Mylar that's been crinkled, and there's an ink painting on it.

I am of the opinion that most photographers are phobic of rendering. When they're in art school, all the kids who can paint and sculpt have a naturalistic approach to making things. The photographers are the ones who have a very timid feeling about: "Oh, is it okay to render? Well, maybe it's not okay. Maybe I'll just make a picture of something." I was definitely that guy, but then I discovered my inner renderer. I started painting on things and mediating it through picture-making.

. . .

CHARLOTTE COTTON: The fact is that fewer and fewer people have prints around, and there are fewer prints used in lots of professions. But really what we're talking about in terms of what is the neutral baseline of photographic prints is determined by the contemporary art world. You're all making photographic prints in reaction to the photographic-print-making norms of the contemporary art world, rather than to daily life. Does that resonate with any of you?

PEARSON: Yeah, it makes perfect sense. It was really amazing when Paul said that everybody prints down, but to print up is a faux pas. People think there's something wrong with his pictures, but it's totally compelling to try to look into this picture and you don't even see everything that's in there. I make these pictures that are terribly gray. Sometimes I'm embarrassed by that, but I don't have a problem with it personally because I'm so drawn to the fact that these things are compressed so badly. And Soo, more than any of us, she completely violates the picture by cutting it up.

GRAHAM: I feel I gave a slight misreading of my work because yes, I did show that one sequence where I manipulated the tonal scale of the print by a small amount. But I really don't normally do that. If you look at the rest of my work, to put it as neatly as I can, it seeks to maintain the illusion of being there looking at the thing in front of you. I don't wish to interfere with that illusion. Other people do. Nothing wrong with that. Both are valid approaches.

I feel the thing we're not mentioning here is the nature of the art world's embrace of photography, which has happened very recently, in the last 20 years. [The art world] has a different value system to that which existed within the photographic art community, and which obviously predates this embrace. [The art world] tends to look more for the hand of the artist, for the synthetic creative expression within the work. When it comes to the type of photography I do, it's a little bit harder to perceive for some people. An example of that is Jeff Wall, who makes great work, undoubtedly. It's very much embraced by the art world. You can see how he staged the work. He can talk about the origins of it, the source material, the labor that has gone into creating some of his great big pictures, the amount of acting, and the amount of composite digital work that went on afterwards.

But then you compare that to a Garry Winogrand picture. Winogrand is a huge influence on Jeff Wall. But [Wall] will dismiss that. To many people, sadly, street photography is just a lucky observation. Where is the art in it? Winogrand walked down the street. He took a picture. Click. That's it. So, you have this schism sometimes in creative output where the art world wants to see synthetic creativity. And they miss the actual core of the creativity in a Winogrand, or a Frank, or a Shore. That's an interesting conundrum that has to be addressed.

PEARSON: Well, I think it's interesting because I think that the art is hidden in the Winogrand because very few people realize that his work was in the editing. When he died there were 20,000 rolls of film sitting there unprocessed, or something, right? In photography all of the effort and all of the sleight-of-hand is hidden because the picture is the final moment.

GRAHAM: So, what is it that they're missing? Undoubtedly, what Frank, Eggleston, Winogrand, and Arbus did are some of the greatest photographic works of the 20th century. And a lot of people miss it. They think it's lucky, observational, documentary photography. That is a very, very sad thing. I think that's where we need people to grapple with, explain, and open up this incredibly fertile and moving area of photographic practice to the broader public. Shore talks about it. He talks about synthetic creativity and analytic creativity, where you give him a blank sheet of paper and say, "Do it." He can't do a damn thing. It's hopeless.

PEARSON: Right.

GRAHAM: Parachute him into a street corner in Albuquerque with his camera and [Shore] can make something. Given enough time and some film, he can make something of that situation. I had the same thing myself. Twenty years ago, I showed some pictures I took in Northern Ireland, which were essentially landscape pictures of the conflict in Ireland. They intermixed the sentiment of landscape photography—very beautiful fields, trees, and skies—with small signs of war going on within, of the lower level sectarian conflict going on in Ireland. You'd see little flags and painted curbstones, and in some, a military helicopter in the distance.

I remember going around a show in Paris with a collector there whom I'd been told to do the walk with. And he said, "Oh, I love this. These pictures are fantastic. Tell me, how exactly did you paint the curbstones this color?" I said, "Sorry?" And he said, "It takes a long time to paint these red, white, and blue colors. How did you do this?" I said, "I didn't. They were that way." And he said, "Well, what did you do?" I said, "I took the photograph." He was really disappointed, and he didn't buy anything, which is even worse.

COTTON: There's something slightly disingenuous in that, although I do understand what you're saying. We all know that the art world has a preference for being able to attribute everything within a photograph to the artist and the artist's hand, and then we're all happy that it's a work of art. It is more complicated if it's based on those fleeting things of making an observation. However, I had a recent argument with a photographer whose work I was showing, where I had to say, "Will you stop being a photographer and be an artist and take responsibility for your work once the shutter has been clicked, and deal with the fact that actually our arena is the gallery?" It's three-dimensional space. Regardless of you working in a documentary mode, you're making really precise and accurate material decisions about how your bodies of work are received within galleries and groups.

GRAHAM: I try and create a different answer to every body of work. It's not like we find one answer once and that does it for the next 20 years. It just doesn't work that way. The artists I like the most usually have a protean evolution to their work. That moves me, and I try to live that way and work that way myself.

COTTON: You take that risk of not having a signature that is carried over between bodies of work. Within the commercial value of photography, you're giving people the option to like or dislike, to compare and contrast, different projects.

GRAHAM: That isn't something I think about. You make it

for yourself at the end of the day. You mustn't forget the book also in this. It's not just the gallery walls. Photography is very unusual in that the book is an extremely powerful forum for it. In the case of *The Americans*, for example, the book is the original. It's not about owning a Robert Frank picture on the wall. It's about the complete body of work. And the same with Winogrand's *Public Relations*, one of the great photographic works that anyone who doesn't know should see. The book is of the work. That is going to change dramatically with what's happening digitally and the revolution in book publishing.

COTTON: Print-on-demand?

GRAHAM: With print-on-demand books, everyone can have a book. Just like everyone can make their own video or their own film. It doesn't mean it's going to be great, but it's a dramatic change in what's happening.

. . .

KIM: I think it's great to have things like Blurb or iBooks, because they reinvigorate the space for photography to exist outside of the gallery, or to reinvest in a book format. Ideas of narrative, serialization, and how a photographer might think about sequencing used to be more important, especially when you're thinking about *The Americans* or William Klein's *New York*, and all of these other examples of great books.

. . .

COTTON: The reason that we brought these speakers together is partly because Paul and I have been on discussion panels before where the question of digital has come up. And Paul always underplays it, as if it's a seamless path from analog to digital. It's not the Armageddon. But I think that's partly because he found routes through that. I do want at some point to ask you, Paul, about the idea of what you think a neutral Epson print will be. I'd say maybe about ten years ago, when the whole issue of how digital might impact on practice happened, it did seem terribly frightening that something might be made absolutely obsolete. In fact, what's happened—and I think it's really represented in Anthony and Soo Kim's practices—is that you can take an active, important stance using analog photography in a way that isn't pretending that it is the norm (because it isn't), by using its values to reinterpret the future. So, the idea of slowness, which Soo raised, is an important value that we can now hinge on analog. Carter Mull, who was on a previous discussion panel, uses a nice phrase: analog-digital. He uses digital technologies, but he has an analog mentality. I think there's also the idea that it's a way of thinking about how you might practice, and make mistakes, and have a physical relationship with photography, which is embedded in analog projects or practice, which will continue in a digital era.

. . .

HOW HAS THE ROLE OF PRINT PUBLICATIONS CHANGED AS A RESULT OF THE EVER-INCREASING PRESENCE OF INTERNET-BASED PUBLICATIONS?

Not as significantly as the result of the changing role of photography, but perhaps there is more emphasis on the print publication as a permanent record.

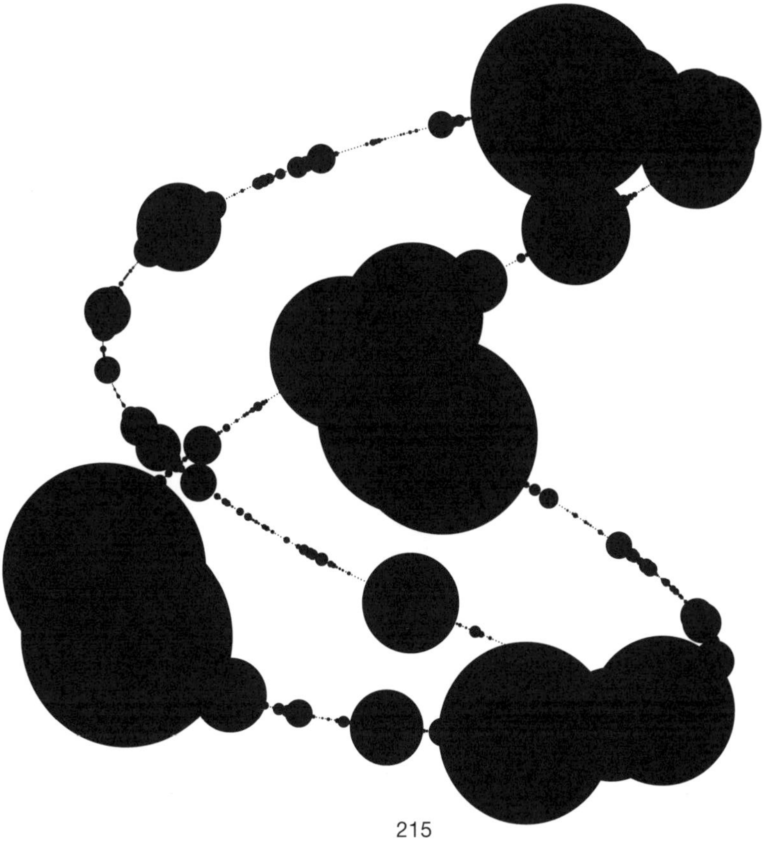

Process, Content, and Dissemination: Photography and Music

CHARLOTTE COTTON

Every generation thinks of itself as living through a pivotal moment in history. But when it comes to the effect of digital technologies on how both music and commercial images are created, funded, and disseminated, this is truly one such time. Though I suspect that my reasons for wanting to find paradigms in these two creative arenas are personal and generational, they are also motivated by a sense that I must establish a position on these territories, both in order to fulfill myself intellectually and to contribute to my profession in meaningful ways. I'm basically middle-aged. My sense of self emerged from the passions for music, fashion, and photography I developed when I hit puberty. I'm part of that "platform-sensitive" generation that still wants to be part of the action (making and consuming) without ever saying, "Well, in *my* day . . . " On a professional front, I'm a curator who works mainly with photography—one who isn't sold on the idea that my twenty-first-century role is to play the violin while the Titanic of analog photography sinks. This moment requires that I be very thoughtful about how we look at and experience our day-to-day and leisure time; how ideas are visually communicated (in essence, our visual literacy and preferences); and how these factors shape the future of museums.

I'm not setting out to prove that the creation, production, and dissemination of pop music is the perfect paradigm of what has happened or is about to happen to commercial image-making. There are blatant differences between these industries: when all is said and done, popular songs are more culturally important, in my view, than any line of handbags, sunglasses, or shoes, no matter how innovative the ad campaign might be. Music clearly lends itself to, and is realized directly via, digital platforms; images function as the supporting visuals for the message. Advertising imagery simulates, alludes to, and narrates its products, and thus must work harder than do music visuals to evoke the sensation of what we might eventually buy.

However, both the music and luxury-brand industries have experienced massive and parallel changes in the 2000s. Both are grappling with the impact of a reconfigured corporate culture on who and what get backing, whom their products reach, who pays, who gets fees, and who gets percentages. There are new tools for making, new makers, new middlemen, new platforms, and new market theories. Given the seemingly limitless opportunities that the digital world offers for exploiting existing markets and discovering new ones, both industries are now like the Wild West. Both face the challenge of creating meaningful, "authentic" experiences within a landscape of shifting priorities, technologies, and value systems.

In the 2000s, I have held two very different vantage points from which to view the shifting kaleidoscope of commercial image-making. One was situated within an agency that created much of the luxury-brand advertising and high-production editorial work in the glossy magazines of the time. The other is from the perspective of an encyclopedic museum that holds collections of design, costumes and textiles, and photography, and which I therefore feel should lend cultural credence to photography's biggest industry, not just its rarefied strata of art production.

PAY AND DOWNLOAD

In the advertising agency world of the mid-2000s, one of the recurring questions that the music industry generated was whether the iTunes model of pay-and-download would impact commercial image-making. The question was whether consumers (vaguely defined, perhaps, as "platform-agnostic," logo-loving, credit card carrying, twelve-year-old girls) would pay ninety-nine cents to download an entire season's Prada ads—or even some golden oldies from a famous fashion photographer's back catalogue—or if they would pay a subscription for behind-the-scenes footage sent to their cell phones. The answer to this is partly yes and mainly no, but more on that later. Inherent within the rather simple question of whether a profitable distribution tool for music could apply to image-making was our inability to anticipate which platform was going to be most important to luxury brands and how new contexts would impact the literal shape of commercial image-making. Equally important was whether *this* was the moment to switch from a (by then dwindling) "day rate" fee structure for photographers to a percentage of future, uncalculated online sales from licensing, or whether the immediately quantifiable sales figures and effects of stellar Web-based image-making on actual sales would drive day rates back up to their former glory.

In retrospect, I can see that those teams of image makers were asking an age-old question: "How do we get the money we need to do what we visually want to do?" What image makers and their agents and production teams realized was that luxury brands were cautious—as it turned out quite rightly—about shifting marketing budgets from print to online, and they did not intend to subsidize image makers' explorative dabbling on the Web.

While there had always been a lot of parlance about great image makers' supremacy and centrifugal importance in the identity of a brand (especially when said image makers were in the room), these brands were not the patrons to the unbridled creative expression of "superstar" photographers. Nor, indeed, were photographers being invited to take on a well-paid and dominant role in new media on the strength of their abilities to create magical print advertising. The jury was still out on whether the Web and the platforms from which we experienced it in our offices and at home allowed us to distinguish between low (amateur) production values and high-end commercial image-making. There were also the realities that advertising (whether print, point-of-sale, or online) is an imprecise science, and that compelling an online browser to drop two weeks' salary on a pair of designer shoes based on a pop-up window of a static image—or even on a gorgeous three-minute advertisement—didn't exactly have a precedent. On top of this, 9/11 happened. The effects of 9/11 on the scope of advertising, as all consumer-based businesses tried to "normalize" taste and consumption as effectively as possible, is a subject in its own right. For this essay, it's important to note that 9/11 was another force in the decline of belief in the efficacy of advertising to promote luxury items, and a motivation for everyone in the business to make cuts and be grateful to be employed at all. Probably one of the biggest effects that I noticed was that the major image makers who created the visuals for the very top brands not only cut their day rates, but took on middling ad jobs at which they would have snorted with derision only a year before. For the rest of the commercial photography pool, this brought to an end the fantasy that if they worked for nothing to create editorial images for both glossy and edgy magazines in order to build up a portfolio of brilliant ideas, they would secure one or two mediocre ad jobs that would keep them afloat and afford them the opportunity to go out and make big pictures of landscapes with no art directors breathing down their necks.

KEEPING IT REAL

How music and its image function on the Web has a precedent in the early days of MTV, when a lot of rubbish was made—some so random it was brilliant—as well as occasional moments of perfection in which the intelligence, originality, and timeliness of the performers, their music, and the video visuals came together to define a cultural moment. Low-budget music and video could result in a hit and, with the right creative team, create a true star. Lil Wayne has sent much of his work out into the world via YouTube, and his authenticity blazes through in every deeply unadventurous and low-fi video. He released his first album at seventeen (in 1999) mentored by Bryan "Baby" Williams, rapper and co-owner of the Cash Money label. Universal distributes the CDs and vinyl, and listeners download songs from the Internet for free. Who knows how long it will be before a management team sets Lil Wayne up with a lucrative clothing line and a flashy video for every single, setting the wheels of brand exclusivity into motion. But for now, he keeps it real for hip-hop. And Lil Wayne has good reason to keep hold of his strong and direct relationship with his fans. This past month, Lil Wayne's album was released in stores and over 2 million copies were sold (to consumers who had or could have downloaded MP3 tracks). These sales were predicated on the choices of consumers and not the strength of a marketing campaign, starkly contrasting to the significantly lower pay-and-download activity for Coldplay's first new album tracks at exactly the same time.

Advertising agencies with car manufacturer clients

and CGI technologies at their fingertips were quick to grasp the importance of YouTube, and—since we don't often get a warm welcome at car showrooms to simply play with fast cars—digital interactives and YouTube car chases fill a gap in our desires. Volkswagen's 2002 Cabrio spot by Jonathan Dayton and Valerie Faris accounted for the second-time-around hit from niche (and by then deceased) artist Nick Drake. *Pink Moon* was the (presumably inexpensively) licensed soundtrack to this lyrical, popular-imagination-capturing sequence in which four teenagers drive to a party and then decide that the drive is a better experience than the cheap beer and awkward fumblings that await them. Thanks to the ad, Drake's album sales went from 6,000 in the previous year to 74,000.

In 2002, OK Go was one of the new bands signed to Capitol during the vogue for the Fab Four model of pop acts. In the big league, they were "unknown," and Capitol prepared to launch the band in the typical way: images of four guys shot from above, looking up at the camera à la The Who in the early 1960s, and probably a music video shoot by Olivier or Michel Gondry. But OK Go isn't one of those industry-generated bands; they are a brilliant live act with a stunning lead singer, and they like to dance. On an amateur video kit in an unspectacular back garden, they recorded a dance that they'd been using in live acts, as a reference for the future high-production video shoot. The creative director saw it and recognized that this raw footage perfectly communicated what made the band unique. Initially, she had no luck in convincing Capitol's marketing team, including its Web team. The turning point occurred backstage after an OK Go concert, near Capitol's then-headquarters, after the audience went wild when the band did their dance. Capitol executives could then see how YouTube would reach a niche audience who could be counted on to virally spread the word, and they agreed that night that the rehearsal video for "Get Over It" should go online.

The band's follow-up video for "A Million Ways," which gave new meaning to a treadmill session at the gym, was specifically created for the viral landscape. The band rehearsed the performance over the course of one week with the lead singer's choreographer sister. The footage was shot on amateur video, with the same locked-off shot as the previous "blip" and with no editing. All these techniques were consciously deployed to relate to the kind of visual skits that anyone can create for YouTube, rather than some marketing manager's high-production attempt to reach the kids. The "image maker" was thus not an obvious part of the narrative, and that lack of blatantly slick promotion is integral to the video's viral success. Even with viewing figures for the second blip at around 20 million, OK Go's videos still did not generate record-breaking sales. Off the back of their viral popularity, they were invited by MTV to perform their treadmill dance sequence live at the MTV Video and Music Awards. Perhaps 300,000 copies of OK Go's album were sold, which represents a thorough culling of a niche market in today's climate. But there was no hit song, just a fantastic response to OK Go—hence the lack of translation into a top spot on radio playlists or a huge number of pay-and-download "hit" consumers. Instead, the success of OK Go translated into live gigs and merchandising sales, and the pay-off for Capitol was mainly in kudos for instigating some smart, forward-thinking marketing.

When image-making for pop stars works, it not only creates the initial online viral buzz, but also is sustained throughout every visual experience of the star or band. Robyn has been a popular performer and recording artist in Europe in recent years, producing her albums and singles (which have been very successful in the more dance-oriented youth culture that buys singles and their remixes) on her own record label. While our current love of all things Swedish is not enough to ensure that Robyn will become a successful pop star in the U.S., the Web has been an important element in projecting a clear identity for this singer/songwriter. Blip Boutique's Mary Fagot and James Frost created beautiful and witty video vignettes. Some show the blonde, shorthaired performer; others act as more oblique but equally tantalizing visualizations of her album tracks. Each one of these blips was sent as "exclusive" content to well-known music, lifestyle, and celebrity websites such as that of Perez Hilton. They become the cues for the online conversations and market-testing facilities (YouTube can determine state-by-state, hour-by-hour viewing statistics) that determine whether your visual branding is causing a buzz and which cities to tour. The aesthetics and look established in the blips are reconfigured for Robyn's live shows, public appearances, and the design of her CD and vinyl artwork.

WIN, WIN, WIN

Perhaps no pop star is more aware of the power of consistent image identity over the course of an album release and world tour than Madonna. In 2006, in the buildup to the release of *Confessions on a Dance Floor*, Madonna and her then record label, Warner, worked with one of her trusted image makers, Steven Klein, and his then agency to create a dramatic and consistent image for this constantly self-reinventing diva. Klein, perhaps the leading image maker for the seductive and effective linking of designer fashion and celebrity, shot Madonna for *W* magazine. As editorial goes, the shoot had a pretty decent production budget, but instead of fighting for an editorial "day rate," Klein and his management took a much more astute approach, pioneering a business model that would make the heady mix of celebrity, fashion, and image benefit all involved. (Think of all the advertising campaigns that include celebrities nowadays.) With the lion's share of the licensing revenue going to Klein and his agent, the shoot for *W* became a multipurpose event that produced coherent imagery for the album and worldwide tour; the visuals in the opening sequence of each performance; precision-timed Madonna/Klein video installations in rental art galleries; and alternate images distributed as limited-edition prints that were sold (out), mainly via Klein's website. While *W* held the first and exclusive rights to the editorial they had commissioned, thirty-two glossy fashion and lifestyle magazines worldwide licensed Klein's alternate images from the *W* shoot for their front covers, the publishing of which was timed with Madonna's live performances in each region of the world. Klein and his management received hundreds of thousands in licensing fees; *W* got an on-budget, kudos-generating editorial and front cover; and Madonna and Warner effectively secured a coherent image campaign (essentially free of charge). At the same time, Madonna and Warner curtailed other publications' incentive to try to run out-of-date photographs of the star on their front covers and ensured respectable album sales and sell-out shows. International magazines got the latest version of Madonna on their covers, which would never have been possible (for practical and strategic reasons) if they had individually attempted to commission new photography. Klein and his agent's incomes were certainly higher than any day rate, and the deal established Klein's clear ownership of his images. It was win, win, win. As the difference between print advertising (marketing) and editorial content (a point of view) continues to blur, and budgets are trimmed, the incorporation of other revenue streams into the production of photo shoots—especially those involving celebrities—will become more evident.

Last year, after completing her contract with Warner (who will presumably continue to make money from greatest hits and single licensing of Madonna's back catalogue), Madonna joined the Live Nation management company, which manages the "portfolio" revenue streams of music giants U2 and Jay-Z. I read somewhere that her four-year deal was for $170 million, with all revenue from her shows going to Live Nation. For a star such as Madonna—a disciplined and seamlessly brilliant performer—the cash cow is not the album sales but the live shows, with a reported $300 starter price for tickets to her forthcoming tour. In both music and commercial image-making micro- and macro-structural changes are happening: attempts by powerful brands and stars, management companies, and media stream and content providers to merge and consolidate their interests in light of digitization.

CASA THIS, CASA THAT

Tom Ford is probably the fashion world's nearest equivalent to Madonna. For both, there's a sense that, in pure business terms, they are who they are only in part because of their personal managerial teams and the big businesses to which they've been under contract or franchised. Just as we don't call Madonna a "singer/songwriter," Tom Ford is not simply a "fashion designer," and that's not merely a byproduct of the way both have been packaged by high finance. Both talents are deeply controlling, image-conscious, platform-greedy creatives. Not only do they oversee, in highly informed ways, how their messages translate into merchandise and marketing, but also their very creativity is fueled by this involvement. Ford went from his starter position as chief designer for women's ready-to-wear in an almost-bankrupt Gucci in 1990, to being the creative director of all things Gucci and YSL (which the Gucci Group bought in the early 2000s). Ford's creativity wasn't stifled but *made* by the market for luxury goods, and Gucci became an über-successful business because of his flair for seeing beyond the buttonholes. In an era in which top stylists were the creative consultants and occasionally the chief designers for fashion houses, and in which making the "image" of a fashion brand was embedded into their thought processes rather than a later translation, Ford was the perfect designer.

IT'S NOT ABOUT THE HOUSE IN THE HAMPTONS

We are just at the point where the next generation of musicians, designers, and image makers have grown up creating with discs and software rather than with tape or film (and both industries are especially interested in youthful creation). But our current landscape is predominantly shaped by a generation that started making and experiencing culture in an analog world. Radiohead is an authentic band of musicians who have been creating and performing together for over twenty years. For them, digital means of composing, recording, and producing software wasn't a foreign, Armageddon-laden new language, but a new tool to creatively explore. I think it's fair to say that Radiohead, with their creative exploration of digital media, have developed an even more pure communication of who they are. Radiohead also didn't leave it to others to work out what digital offered in terms of distribution of their message, because they have something to say rather than just servicing an industry model or getting famous. By the 2000s, even if you were one of the very few artists who had deployed new technologies in genuinely creative ways (rather than just as faster and cheaper mimicry of analog practice), but you had surrounded yourself with a lot of middlemen to funnel your creative vision, the impact of digital did not open the doors to creative freedom. Record labels, luxury brands, and advertising agencies had all failed to grasp the potential meaning of digital dissemination and commerce, and we did not yet have more than technicians to guide the transition. Browsing, experiencing, and shopping online are all profoundly user-driven; suddenly potential customers were—*en masse* and in survey-able ways—a force companies had to seriously reckon with.

It doesn't matter what profession or industry you come from: if you are past thirty-five years of age, you will at some point have been hit with the realization that, while you might have thought that you and your friends and peers were all aiming for the same thing, you actually weren't. While for some creatives the acts of making and communicating are their reasons for getting out of bed in the morning, others have decided to aim for the house upstate, the luxury man-toys, and the right schools for the little ones. If you consider that this *modus operandi*-divide is even more heavily weighted toward the annual bonus in every management company, ad agency, publishing empire and boardroom, it's not surprising that so few truly innovative and meaningful creative expressions using digital technologies have come about.

Radiohead's social values and their reasons for creating always meant that they were resistant to the branding treatment that a music corporation would typically apply. From the moment it became creatively tenable, and not a financial risk so big that it could actually stop their music from reaching their fans, Radiohead have created, produced, and published their music in unusually independent ways. There were 100,000 downloads of *In Rainbows* in the first twenty-four hours after the band released the album (in both MP3 and vinyl formats) from their Inrainbows site and free download sites in October 2007. On Radiohead's site, listeners had the option to choose whether and how much to pay for the album. The band thus "stole market share" from pirate music sites, and they sent a clear message that the most important thing for them was to get the music out there, and to respect the role of downloaders and consumers who went online as a part of their self-informing process in shaping the culture of the Internet (thus cleverly folding digitization into their process once again). It became clear that the consumers of their music still wanted a CD—not simply music buyers who found MP3 pay-and-download altogether too intangible, or had no desire to actively return to vinyl, but consumers who distinguished between a CD and the design of its packaging and went on to essentially buy into *In Rainbows* for a second or third time. Radiohead also called upon a small, West Coast record label (part of the larger independent label ATO) to distribute the CD.

The vinyl version of *In Rainbows* has proved popular, marking the revival in some music genres of what had been thought of as a defunct form. Of course, there is a heavy dollop of nostalgia in our re-appreciation of vinyl (and letterpress and gelatin silver papers), but it means something different from the development of a new heritage industry. This is not the sepia-tone filter in Photoshop. It's nostalgia in the sense of us returning home, in small, boutique numbers, to forms that have new currency in light of so much virtual experience and consumption, and thus defining where and when tangible objecthood has meaning in our consumer culture.

BLAST FROM THE PAST

One of the most important facets of the digital era is that it created both markets and desires to revisit the past, and provided enough of a conflation between publishing archives and back catalogues, new distribution networks, and surfing and browsing behavior, to satisfy these desires. I'm sure the term "heritage artist" existed prior to the recent discoveries in the archives of major record labels and the digital re-mastering of classics. But what is transformative and particular to the digital era is how it brings popular music's analog past back to life, allowing us to have a potentially deeper relationship with, and even to rethink, a culture beyond the distortions and hoopla of its moment. Web culture is truly a second life for our musical heritage. It allows us to find our fellow enthusiasts and to edit, tag, compile, comment on, and critique what we find. This takes place within the lucrative-enough environment that iTunes and Netflix, for example, identified in making available back catalogues of music and film that would command little or no space in stores. While acknowledging the Big Brotherliness of having any online purchase followed up with a whole list of recommendations, I like to think of it as being shown the whole shelf in a bookstore (the ordering logic of which I also don't have control of), and there's a chance that the same serendipitous experience will lead and inform my interests in wonderfully unexpected ways. Just as I expect most substantial nuggets of culture that I can access for free—whether it be an exhibition, independent and undistributed film and video, a documentary, or podcasted lectures and concerts—to include corporate sponsors' or grant-giving foundations' credits, I'm willing to pay and download or join with a modest monthly subscription for the pleasure of access to more than the most heavily marketed billboard track or opening weekend blockbuster.

One of the few plus sides of reality TV's obsession with going "behind-the-scenes" in any situation, as well as of "the-making-of" bonus material that acts as an incentive to purchase a DVD, is that we are much more aware of the many roles and phases that come between an idea's conception and its realization. We know about cinematographers, music producers, and art directors, and somewhere on the Web someone has compiled their track records. While affordable and worthwhile software packages such as Logic Pro make it possible for anyone to consider him- or herself a musician, and Photoshop and Hewlett Packard have serviced the needs and developed the desires of young and old photographers to express themselves in artful ways, perhaps the most ubiquitous, day-to-day skill base that the digital arena has created makes everyone an editor, a curator, and a stylist.

THE MUSEOFYING EFFECT

Just as vinyl and CD box sets of digitally re-mastered "heritage artists" were beautifully presented to new audiences and musicians to study and cherish, there was a timely re-contextualizing of absolutely pivotal image makers in cultural spaces such as museums—a new locus for the appreciation and understanding of popular, mass-consumed photography. At the most tangible, physical, object-led end of the digital, we have been offered essentially connoisseurial experiences, from "heritage artist" and genre box-sets with beautiful production values; to re-mastered, "director's cut," and re-colored analog film classics in DVD box sets; to high-production, exquisitely designed, limited-edition coffee table books and big photographic prints by commercial photography's "heritage artists." Helmut Newton, with his libidinous drive to repeatedly visualize his Germanic, Amazonian dominatrix, was one of the first fashion photographers to comprehend how the coffee table book and then the gallery could be contexts in which to command and shore up his indelible stamp on visual culture.

Newton's great competitor on the pages of French *Vogue* in the late 1960s and 1970s, Guy Bourdin, never got the right book or exhibition offer in his lifetime, and he had too much respect for true artists to just print up his incendiary (in the context of a double-page magazine spread) imagery for a temporary space on museum walls. Instead, more than ten years after his death, Bourdin was re-mastered to give the equivalent increased heart rate and saliva buildup that a 1972 French *Vogue* reader felt turning the page to one of his Charles Jourdan shoe advertisements. In a heavily designed exhibition, viewers experienced the guilty pleasure of being thoroughly aware of their voyeurism and politically incorrect fantasies in ways (digitized film and gorgeous LightJet prints) that had not been open to Bourdin in his lifetime. Because the relationship between selling and the product for sale was well and truly lost in the mists of time, such commercial image-making was safe territory for cultural institutions to explore. The fact that limited-edition photographic prints were available wasn't especially interesting or threatening for museums and their according of "cultural value" to commercial image makers. The museum's collector-benefactors quite rightly saw these editions as no more than equivalents to a Charles Eames chair from a "design art" auction sale.

Museums, which tend to define "contemporary" as a period of artistic production beginning in about 1965, formed contemporary departments in about 1970 to deal with the burst of new ideas, forms, and practices. Essentially, old and out of circulation, commercial photography not only fits right into institutional politics, but it offered a cultural commodity that museums perceived as contemporary and attractive to more visitors, especially younger ones. What received little notice was the fact that the increasingly powerful marketing departments of museums seemed to privilege exhibitions that promised good opening night parties. Further, few people seemed to care about the actual meaning of putting commercial imagery, translated into photographic print form, into repainted (from black to white) picture frames that had previously been used for Edward Weston or Julia Margaret Cameron masterworks.

THE ART AND FASHION THING

While old-fashioned photography held curators to no greater responsibility than to mystify and window-dress the profound differences between art and fashion image-making, the relationship between art and fashion created in the past ten years is much murkier. "Artist" was a term to be used judiciously in the field of contemporary art photography in the mid-1990s, when anything measuring 30 by 40 inches and backed with aluminum stood a chance of being collected—and was sometimes indistinguishable from a commissioned image when reproduced on a magazine page. "Artist" is not a term to apply to commercial image makers on the grounds that they underwrote the high production costs of spectacular (by gallery standards), well-attended museum exhibitions that gave institutions exposure in the style pages of newspapers and magazines during the era of institutional "re-branding."

In retrospect, I think the biggest misunderstanding about the relationship between art and fashion occurred around 1996: that they cross-fertilized. While heavily preconceived, "directorial mode" art photography—which could require as much pre- and post-production as an advertising shoot (and as many assistants, lighting experts, prop designers and models as fashion)—bore a passing resemblance to commercial image-making, its intent and ultimate resolution were very different. Contemporary art was more fashionable than fashion at that moment, and although many commercial shoots were scheduled in museum galleries with real art as the backdrop, and a few art photographers were having fun on big-production fashion shoots, I doubt if we'd still consider this a genuine fusing of the two worlds. Circumstances were mitigated by what was happening to fashion magazine publishing at the time, and to the reasons why we bought magazines. The monthly glossy magazines that survived the post-9/11 crisis in confidence of publishing financiers were those that had a brand name with foundations solid enough to weather the storm. Publishing companies weighed the realities that their subscription numbers had leveled out for good and might even decrease, while luxury-brand advertisers, who were powerfully co-opting editorial content with product placement, still considered the "quality" readership to be their target audience. Longstanding titles began to diversify, finding revenue streams in licensing (greetings cards, calendars, knickknacks) and coffee table anthologies, as well as in the sale of vintage prints from their archives. Established but independent magazines either went under or survived because they had maintained such a consistent identity, strong editorial direction, and (possibly) brought in aggressive advertising account managers. Bimonthly or quarterly titles with editors of true vision and nerves of steel maintained the glossy, elitist, and desire-inducing high end of fashion image-making. But even though digitization had massively reduced the costs of printing, the great economic variable of paper stock prices (the oil of the media world) made monthly magazine publishing an increasingly risky business and a "loss leader" enterprise. Buying a magazine off the shelf became more expensive, deluxe, and ritualistic. (The type of shelf also diversified from being above the newspaper section to sitting alongside books and on the sales counters of fashion boutiques.) The remnants of thinking that a magazine—even one that was published every month—was your first port of call for the latest style news was about to end in light of online search engines. We became more aware of just how fetishistic the experience of scanning and turning the pages of a glossy magazine had become (we'd stopped reading the editorial fluff quite some time ago); there was an increasing synergy between the slow and solent absorbtion within the pages of a magazine and the gravitas of a gallery space.

In the early 2000s, I still held on to my optimism that curating fashion photography for an institution did not have to mean just blowing up an image to "gallery size" and making it look like bad art, or creating a parallel between scanning a gallery wall with the now seemingly super-slow turning of glossy magazine pages. I still thought that there was a difference between the practice of a curator and those of a picture editor or art director. I did, and still do, think that commercial image-making is culturally important and deserves careful analysis and explanation from a cultural institution's perspective.

THE NEW EDITORIAL

At first, I was excited about what contemporary image makers would create for the screen—to see how masters of context would narrate and develop new forms in the digital era. I couldn't quite understand why glossy magazines didn't jump all over the Internet. (While around forty people work at UK *Vogue*, it looks to me as if four people create Vogue.com and probably three very hardworking interns put Vogue.TV together.) It became pretty obvious that print magazines were doing the absolute minimum on the Web while the jury was still out on how to make a serious and creative investment in new media platforms. The first really interesting proposition for what the Web and screen could mean for fashion image-making was SHOWstudio.com, conceived and started by Nick Knight in 2000, art directed by Paul Hetherington and creatively edited and commissioned by Penny Martin since 2001. Nick Knight is one of the most technology-hungry and context-aware innovators of image-making, and SHOWstudio became a self-financed platform for his own investigations of new media. SHOWstudio was a draw not only to photographers, but fashion and graphic designers, musicians, animators, illustrators, creative directors, hair and make-up artists, and models who were not yet being commissioned to create Web-specific content. From the outset, SHOWstudio revealed the collaborations and processes of commercial image-making rather than hiding what made this genre of photography unique under the mystifying gauze of auteur theory. If you trawl through the site's extensive archive, you will of course find projects that were so specific to their moment that they've lost their original intent or meaning, as well as ideas that just didn't work or were ill-conceived. But this is no different from any experimental editorial venture; only out of a willingness to take risks does the future reveal itself. The site's production values are often low, but there's a sense that the pixels bear an aesthetic vocabulary that might be fully realized in future platforms. The most important thing is that this arena was created, and that virtually every avenue for fashion editorial for the Web has been mapped out on this incredible initiative.

"SPECIAL" PROJECTS

I'm not entirely sure whether it was big Modern Art museums or big luxury brands that put the "special" in special projects. I sometimes think that media-savvy brands brought in artists and digital thinkers (new agencies specifically shaping ideas for the Web, plus traditional ad and design agencies successfully getting their heads around this new arena) in the spirit of traditional arts organizations' devotion to new practices and ideas. The two seem to have parallel structures. Museums earmark a tiny space for "young" curators to collaborate with "young" artists and expend about 0.3% of the annual exhibitions budget on possibly the most interesting ideas their organization supports, thus showing their commitment to genuinely contemporary art. Luxury brands hold a competition (not organized by their core creative team, lest they waste their costly time) to get a young filmmaker (preferably someone from China, Korea, India, or another targeted market) to make a short art film about their latest fragrance. They make sure that the production budget is so small and the brief so vague that the filmmaker creates a stinker that neither narrates the brand nor furthers his or her artistic career in any way whatsoever.

Really smart uses of the special-projects model for marketing a brand have tended to be the terrain of already media-astute, high-street brands working with new digital media consultancy firms such as GoDigital, and new media producers such as Rehab and Tangozebra (acquired by DoubleClick, which is owned by Google). *The Sound of Color* was a campaign launched earlier this year by Gap, featuring music by The Raveonettes, Dntel, Swizz Beatz, The Blakes, and Marié Digby. Each of these new music artists wrote a song relating to a color, and was then paired with a top video concept and production team to create the online campaign.

A couple of years ago, Diesel set up a fashion version of Big Brother, streaming a Webcam from a bedroom set where two female models and a hunk wore Diesel underwear and acted out the (presumably edited) blogged instructions from online users. Armani Exchange and *Dazed and Confused* magazine created a five-minute, grainy black-and-white film directed by Matt Irwin that brilliantly shows how the aesthetics of anything from the film *Georgy Girl*, David Bailey's fashion snaps of Jean Shrimpton, and punk band fanzines can roll 1950s-to-early-1980s styling and aesthetics into one, all under the nostalgic gloss of monochrome. Last year, Vuitton commissioned filmmaker Bruno Aveillan, better known for his TV fragrance spots, to create a short film. The beautifully shot film follows a woman's encounters on the rain-drenched, dark streets of a Parisian-looking city, as she carries a rather prominent handbag. It's the best example I've seen of how a fashion editorial story with a beginning, middle, and end, and high production values, might translate into screen language.

Danish designer Mads Nørgaard put two of his Copenhagen Experience trilogy videos on his website. They are rather *Christiane F.*-meets-Warhol's Factory with behind-the-scenes footage; the 1978 song "Copenhagen" is the soundtrack (linked to iTunes) for one of them. Although I'm not that keen on fashion looks that require the bodies of twelve-year-olds or serious drug abuse, Norgaard has created a strong narrative that effectively encapsulates his collections' identities for the Web.

My favorite online marketing projects shaped from the get-go for online culture include Quicksilver's short video, seemingly recorded on a cell phone before dawn, in which a group of surfer dudes in Copenhagen (the new Stockholm) throw a stick of dynamite into a placid lake to create a wave for one of the group to surf. Dior *Joaillerie* (yes, it's a made-up fashion word; my all-time favorite fashion neologism is "massimagical") created a second-life environment in which avatars walk through a magical landscape with sculpture-like animations of this season's exquisite costume jewelry collection. Prada's eBay-style auction of one-of-a-kind clothes and accessories that never made it into final production was not only a financial success; it also showed how the brand could respond cleverly to e-commerce culture.

Prada also commissioned the online, luxury-brand experience that I think best shows what fashion can become online. "Tremble Blossom" is a short animation with a production lineup nearly as big as that of a major advertising photo shoot or a small independent film, with James Lima as concept artist and Melissa Davies and Alan Barnett as creative directors. An avatar walks through a garden of organic forms (which patterned the latest collection), climaxing with the "birth" of this season's big hit handbag from a narcissus-ready pool. Now, I know this sounds awful, but it isn't. Put aside the fact that this animation was made to explore the genesis of a fashion collection and not to promote world peace, and you can see that this is one of the most remarkable, paradigm-shifting transitions of fashion image-making to the screen.

WHY ARE E-COMMERCE SITES SO UGLY?

This is a question I have asked myself a lot. My consumption of luxury goods is rare and highly dependent on being seduced and convinced through all my senses and with a lot of ceremony. Having seen the latest collections via runway shots on Style.com or in one or two magazine editorials, I will put on my Sunday best and make the pilgrimage to some of the most innovative architectural sites, with their beautifully curated displays of design ideas. There, I'm willingly convinced that I can both carry off and afford high fashion, and since no one notices that I am an impostor in fashionland—and knowing that an item might be the very last in my size—I go to the point of sale.

The traditional sales strategy for an elite brand is what a friend called the "Hermès model." As soon as your print advertising seems to have brought your loyal customers back into your stores at the beginning of the season, you stop advertising. You produce a fixed number of, say, handbags, and you don't go back into production, even if there seems to be an exceptional level of demand. In the 1990s, Nike used this elitist model to sell us a lot more sneakers at higher prices than we'd been previously willing to consider. China's luxury market seems to have adopted this model with its typical awe-inspiring gusto, limiting availability and setting incredible prices for high-street items to successfully test how conceptual the idea of luxury is. And in the 2000s, EVERYTHING can be limited edition, including candy bars with "while stocks last" labels instead of sell-by dates. We have all become VIPs somewhere.

E-commerce sites didn't work despite their uninspiring designs, but because of them. I'm guessing that this is the luxury-brand Long Tail effect, wherein companies reach existing markets more thoroughly—markets that don't need the full-on gorgeousness of marketing (they were always there, but only now are they being reached). Net-a-porter.com, which became a wildly successful e-commerce site once it introduced a "no-questions asked" returns policy, probably sells more Balenciaga bags than most of the brand's stores and concession stands across the globe. It is the must-have brand, and women are willing to spend major sums of money over the Internet because they feel grateful, as the Hermès model dictates, to actually be in the running to own this statement of luxury. All one wants from images on an e-commerce site is that they offer bright and flat-footed documentation of the product from many angles.

Editors at weekly celebrity mags go through the week's paparazzi pics of both happy and in-crisis young female celebrities and It Girls carrying their (possibly free) handbags. I sometimes wonder if our current appetite for huge and expensive designer bags is only partly about our timeless desire to carry everything we own with us, and equally as much about how big a bag needs to be to stand out in an action shot. *People's StyleWatch*, for example, responding to popular demand, is now a monthly issue on the newsstands featuring nothing but pictures of celebs (minor celebrities) and Disney Channel stars with this season's accessories. So, by the time a luxury-brand shopper goes online, she knows which bag/sunglasses/shoes/scarf to buy, and it's more a question of whether she can get it. Luxury brands' online stores tend to be their global number one or two top-selling stores. While that might be very financially significant if you have only eight stores worldwide, it's less so if you have 120. Either way, as it stands at the moment, not only are the items for sale in limited runs, but consumers have already had enough encouragement from gorgeous print ads, editorial pages, and paparazzi pics to justify why they MUST have a brand's products. No luxury brand is currently interested in underwriting an innovative image-making structure—parallel in cost and ambition to what has existed in print and stores—that takes advantage of new technologies specifically for the Web. There is absolutely no proof that this is needed in order to tempt the online consumer constituent for luxury items, nor is there any proof that fashion advertising in the traditional sense convinced anyone who was pretty much disinterested in or disdainful of fashion to part with so much as 99 cents.

One of the questions that I began with was whether consumers would pay for and download commissioned photography and short videos, and I was thinking about this from the position that photographers should hold the copyright to their images and the right to exploit their licensing possibilities. What I should have been asking myself is whether luxury brands could create a product that is not available in stores and in turn would require image makers to create exclusively online buzz. The real tipping point for how luxury brands could move beyond segregating e-commerce from editorial and advertising image-making requires an exclusively online magazine to become somewhat like iTunes, but almost exactly like Amazon.com. There are, of course, many elements that some luxury-brand and fashion e-commerce sites share with Amazon, such as search facilities, blogs and chat-rooms, and recommendation lists. But what we don't yet have is an online magazine that sells discounted and used "stock" like Amazon (storage costs are the responsibility of the producer, not the vendor, in this model), enticing consumers to shop because they know that they are highly unlikely to find a product at lower cost anywhere else. If an online, luxury-brand magazine could make its free-subscription members feel like they are literally the first—possibly the only—consumers to be offered a product, the online magazine might become a reality. If luxury brands see the financial merit in selling products only through e-commerce, and they stop discounting lines of product that are selling perfectly well at full price in stores, things will change.

WE CAN REALLY ROCK

In 2006, an Alexander McQueen runway show opened with a virtual vision of Kate Moss, a diaphanous haute couture gown billowing around her, held within a multi-faceted glass structure. If there was one fashion experience I wish I had known about in advance in order to call in all the favors owed me by fashion's elite, this was it. I still long to have been there. The image (inaccurately called a hologram, because it appeared to be almost 3-dimensional) was created using 360-degree imaging, an LCD player, and the reflections off the glass structure.

It was a smoke-and-mirrors spectacle that required new technology and showmanship as old as the hills.

The light artist Moritz Waldemeyer collaborated with designer Hussein Chalayan for the latter's Spring/Summer 2008 catwalk show, in which models walked down the darkened runway with laser-generated balls of lights clustering and encircling them like a nighttime constellation of planets and stars. From time to time in the 2000s, museums have moved intelligently beyond fashion on static mannequins and in photographic prints on walls to engage with the potentially very innovative fusion of haute couture, image-making, new technologies, and museum cultures. *Radical Fashion*, curated by Claire Wilcox for the Victoria and Albert Museum in 2002, raised the bar in terms of collaboration between a museum and fashion houses. It was, despite two very different understandings of schedules and conservation standards, a wonderful exhibition of fashion and its image-making. The Metropolitan Museum's recent *blog. mode: addressing fashion* exhibition was both a gallery and an online experience, with visitors having access to both the exhibition of about sixty pieces from the museum's outstanding costume collection, and to a blog where curators Andrew Bolton and Harold Koda began online discussions about each item.

Perhaps my favorite gallery-based fashion experience was at the Cartier Foundation in Paris in 2004, where Jean-Paul Gaultier created *Pain Couture*. The exhibition featured huge sculptures made out of bread, with Gaultier's trademark pointy brassiere, and croissants with blue stripes running through the dough, referencing both the French Revolution and Gaultier's use of the French sailor t-shirt in his collections. It was *soooooo* French to mix haute couture with bread and a flashy contemporary art gallery that I played the Marseillaise in my head as I walked through the show. And, as Gaultier rightly said,

"Fashion isn't art and I'm not an artist. I'm an artisan, like a baker."

Live music events seem to be of great cultural importance once again, and a (potentially) lucrative side of the music business. The live music event answers to our heightened desire to experience, in the real world and collectively, our culture of choice. I want fashion to do the same for the many and not just for the invited few of a runway extravaganza, and I think that cultural spaces provide a timely venue for this. If a comprehensive museum wants to couple the two sexiest forms in its lexicon (fashion and photography), I hope that it will do so in ways that are not pathetic shadows of the real things, or the crumbs from the table of fashion publishing or luxury brands. In my fantasy world, I'll walk into a museum and hear the sounds of historic dress and the gaits of their invisible wearers. I might see through a reflection in a street-level gallery window the moment when Poiret met Coco Chanel wearing a little black dress on a Paris boulevard. Poiret shouts, "Who are you mourning, Madame Chanel?" To which she replies, "You, Monsieur Poiret." Thus marks the passing of the baton from the very first modernist designer to the most famous. I'd like a second-life environment that lets me enter a seventeenth-century parlor where avatars show me how furniture and dress created ergonomics and human gesture that contemporary eyes can only comprehend through new technologies. I'd love to see inside every hidden layer of a Dior New Look dress, and to understand the corsetry and the amount of fabric that this declaration of the end of wartime austerity embodies. We can use animation to do what we can't physically do with costumes and textiles in museum collections, which is to go inside their construction, animate it, and see the long view all at once. There are image makers out there who can realize a vision and anticipate an audience's reactions and desires. They are not necessarily the high-profile cast of half-a-dozen big names that have monopolized print advertising and editorial, but small teams of video directors, software creators, Web advertising agencies, production companies, set designers, illustrators, animators, and video and blip makers who are making the first innovations in music and fashion online and fresh visual standards in live events.

Museums are places to have meaningful experiences, where we make the past relevant to now or fail in our fundamental remit to explore and interpret culture in relevant ways. The digital era reshapes how we look at and gather information, but it also reconfigures what types of experiences we desire. When these capabilities are harnessed to what we want to say to the world, then we really can rock.

--

DISCUSSION FORUM
WWW.WORDSWITHOUTPICTURES.ORG

--

Subject: Wherever I am
Date: 17 July 2008 13:02:23
From: EDITH MARIE PASQUIER

It took me a little while to settle into it, to figure out what was going on. I read the essay with such deadpan concentration, such scrupulous attention to detail, dates, names, that I failed to perceive the meaning in the writing. I was looking for the dialogue between digital processes, music and photography and somehow I couldn't find it. Instead I was left with the din of commercial image-making—a carnivalesque concoction of attention grabbing images, virtual catwalks, counterfeit goods, and empty shopping bags. I'd missed the party again and found myself feeling like someone who experienced adolescence in old space and grew up revering all that is now consigned to the dustbin by those digital successors.

Perhaps, my relationship to the digital is already a casual affair, dulled by a glut of cheap merchandise, of experiencing everything with a certain distraction, in bits and on the hoof. Similar to fashion? Fashion is dress in which the key feature is a rapid and continual changing of styles. Dress is always unspeakably meaningful. Fashion in a sense is change, and in contemporary Western societies no clothes are outside fashion; fashion sets the terms of all sartorial behavior. Constantly changing, fashion produces only conformity. Fashion is, as Anne Hollander wrote in 1978 (a much revived and pastiched decade), "a form of visual art, a creation of images with the visible self as its medium." Like any other aesthetic enterprise, fashion may then be understood as ideological, its function to resolve formally, at the imaginary level, social contradictions that cannot be resolved. It is an inevitable medium for the expression of ideas, desires and beliefs circulating in society. Fashion links beauty, success and the city; it was always urban, triumphantly boiling all global, national and regional differences into the distilled moment of glossy sophistication. The demeanor of the fashionable person must always be blasé and cool. Fashion is essential to the world of spectacle and mass communication, a fragmentary self glued together into a semblance of a unified identity.

In a sense, ambivalence is an appropriate response to dress, as dress holds contradictory and irreconcilable desires. Fashion—a performance art—acts as a vehicle for this ambivalence. Where fashion differs from some forms of art is that whereas in some fields high art and popular culture have veered further and further apart, in dress the opposite has happened. High fashion has become to some extent demotic. Couture, the artisan residue, you may say even the analog part of fashion, is struggling to hold on. Art is always seeking new ways to illuminate our dilemmas and that is why we remain endlessly troubled by fashion. We are drawn to it, yet repelled by a fear of what we might find hidden within its purpose.

I do not remain wedded by habit, age and stubbornness to analog. Free-floating digital files are after all responsible for cracking open the notion of the album as a linear, unalterable whole. If that allows for a multiplicity of dialogues, akin to the wry, ironic, and innovative approaches as witnessed by Laurie Anderson's digital performance art, why should we not celebrate that the whole musical canon is only a click away and a good deal of it is completely free? Vinyl, pronounced dead over and over again, is seeing something of a revival and the radio, another bastion of an historic era, has reformed, remade, and reworked itself into much more than an anachronism.

I work at this time with analog, with negative film, with the liquids of the darkroom, with 16mm film and with live music, so right now it appears that the digital is too fast, too prescribed, too clean. Not true. Digital processes are certainly keeping our cognitive senses at the peak of agility. But the notion of time in visual arts, in particular for the Web, is pushing unnervingly close to commercial sound bites (the term time-based work has disappeared into the archive). We are satisfied so quickly; we've little time to look back except to rush forward. If that unties the artists' critical engagement with the very process of forming the image or the sound, I am not interested. A close collaborator and musician, Ross Lambert speaks of an unthinking, complicit relationship with technology that as artists, no matter the shine (and digital does shine in millions of pixels) we have to avoid. "The same negative effects of the digital technology's development on music during the 1980s and '90s that innovation was only directed along certain narrow paths, as dictated by the research and development of IT departments, are being repeated today. Serious artists in most fields produce works that could be placed in an industry trade fair, so well do they resemble output from an industrial department or its consultants."

In Paul Auster's *The Book of Illusions*, the "hero" of the story, David Zimmer, is watching television one night and stumbles upon a lost film by the great silent comedian Hector Mann. "We watched them across a great chasm of forgetfulness, and the very things that separated them from us were in fact what made them so arresting; their muteness, their absence of color, their fitful, speeded-up rhythms. These were obstacles, they made viewing difficult for us, but they also relieved the images from the burden of representation. They stood between us and the film, and therefore we no longer had to pretend that we were looking into the real world."

Hiroshi Sugimoto's photographic images of a whole movie in a single frame and the empty (yet full) shining screen also play repeatedly in my mind. A fixed shutter with a wide-open aperture, two hours later the movie is finished and the shutter is closed. A vision of invisible images explodes before our eyes. Maybe that is why I don't feel guilty that sometimes I do miss the digital party.

Fashion is fickle and the symbols of tribal loyalty shift back and forth endlessly. If music and the image do not require passive listening or viewing, something is happening that potentially invites you to follow the sound or image in endlessly different ways. We can, after all, like Laurie Anderson decide to turn on or off the digital visual feast and return, when wanting, to the instrument, to "feel the human body."

QUESTIONNAIRE / LAUREL PTAK

WHAT DO YOU SEE AS BEING IN STORE FOR PHOTOGRAPHY?

As digital technologies evolve even further, more and more people will have the tools to make and distribute extremely competent photographs. It's amazing to think what a dramatic shift this is from even 10 years ago, when photography was prohibitively expensive, highly specialized, and largely analog. I imagine the role of the curator will become only increasingly valuable and culturally sought after. Sorting, editing, and creating meaning out of a sea of images is fast becoming a much more specialized task than actually producing them.

QUESTIONNAIRE / NATALIE BOOKCHIN

WHAT ARE SOME OF THE CURRENT TOPICS AMONG YOU AND YOUR STUDENTS?

The environment, the Iraq war, the elections, the globalization of the image and the imaging of globalization, surveillance for control and entertainment, and its opposite—monitoring the monitors, the YouTubing and blogging of life. The recent fascination of contemporary artists with history—historical reenactments and fakes, documentary photography and truth claims, ethical concerns regarding one's subjects, and the state of feminism today are a few more that come to mind.

WHAT WOULD YOU CONSIDER SOME OF THE MOST IMPORTANT CHANGES THAT PHOTOGRAPHY HAS UNDERGONE IN THE LAST FEW YEARS?

I think the single most significant change has been the transformation of images into immaterial—digital—information that can spread like wildfire around the world. This change, together with the inclusion of cameras in mobile devices and the increase of cell phone use around the world, has had the unintended consequence of putting cameras in more people's hands than ever before—soldiers (and torturers), protesters in Myanmar and China, ordinary people all around the world witnessing and documenting historical events and everyday life.

WHAT DO YOU SEE AS BEING IN STORE FOR THE MEDIUM?

I think that what many people currently see, and often dismiss, as the disposable visual ephemera of the Web—YouTube, Facebook, Flickr, blogs, and computer games—is going to be taken much more seriously over time both as raw material for art and for its impact on the visual culture and the social lives of whole generations of young people around the world. I think that we have not yet seen the full extent of its impact on artists and image-makers.

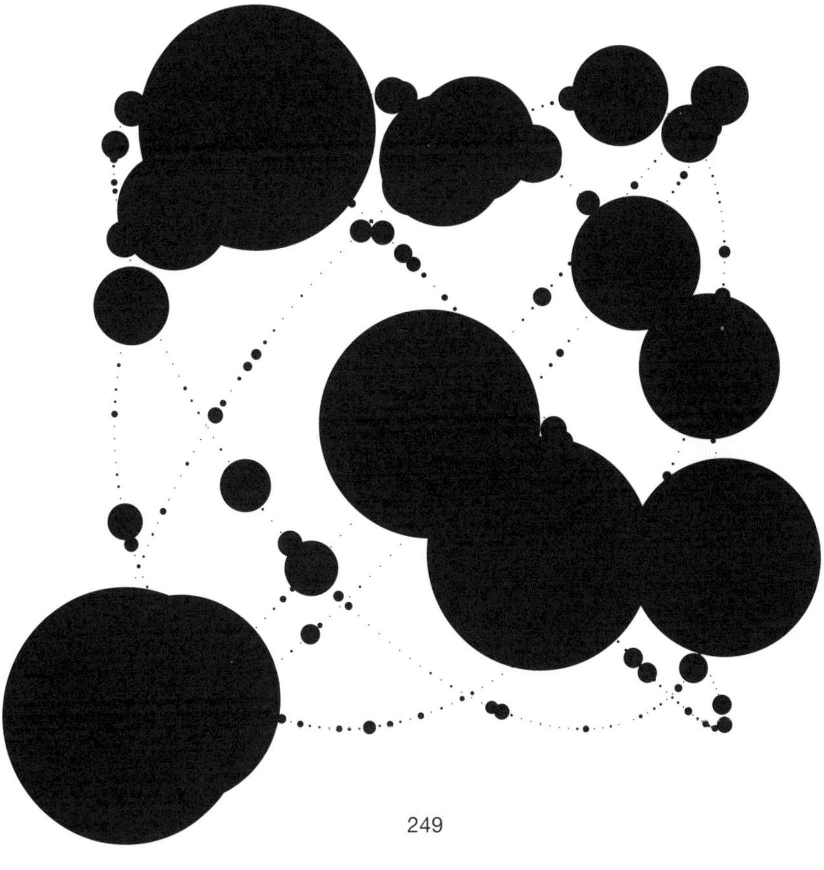

A Picture You Already Know

SZE TSUNG LEONG

Streets of Paris. Germans of the early 20th century. Blast furnaces. Museums. Libraries. One-child families. Teenagers. Wax figures. Each of these subjects has been photographed by individual photographers with prolonged and disciplined regularity, through a sustained accumulation of images. The images are related by consistent subjects, composition, angle of view, lighting, and tonal range. They are similar, but not the same. Together, such images have resulted in bodies of work that, without necessarily focusing on single images, derive their meaning from the accumulation of similarities and the repetition of themes, icons, or forms.

Repetition in photography comprises a wide range of manifestations that have formed a significant part of photographic practice from the early development of the medium. Repetition figured in the use of photographs in racial and criminal studies (in which the repetitive use of portraits was used to identify what were thought to be the physiological foundations of traits and behaviors); in the cumulative documentation of the photographer's urban or social context, such as in the work of Eugène Atget and August Sander; and in the mimicry of the pictorial conventions of painting genres such as still lifes, portraiture, and landscapes. In the context of contemporary photography, repetition appears in a profusion of varieties. These include the repetition of forms, spaces, or people (such as Bernd and Hilla Bechers' typologies, Candida Höfer's institutional spaces, Wang Jinsong's one-child "standard families" in China, and Hans Eijkelboom's people in public settings); repetition over time (Nicholas Nixon's periodic portraits of a group of sisters over the decades); repetition of motifs and compositions from art history (Jeff Wall's rejiggering of iconic paintings, Rineke Dijkstra's classically posed portraits); collections of repetitions in imagery from the popular media (Peter Piller's reordering of existing imagery into distinct categories); repetitions of the self (such as those by Cindy Sherman, Yasumasa Morimura, Tomoko Sawada, and Tseng Kwong Chi); overlapping of repeated images (Idris Khan's layerings of multiples); the reuse of existing imagery as seen in Sherrie Levine's and Thomas Ruff's appropriations; and representations of representations (Hiroshi Sugimoto's wax figures, and Thomas Struth's museum photographs).

The layers that form the practice of photography are themselves permeated by layers of repetition and multiplication. A chain of duplications begins with the process of taking a photograph, which is, in most cases, the duplication of something existing in "reality." From this "copy," which takes the form of a single negative, slide, or digital file, multiple prints can be made. The image represented in these prints, when considered within the scope of a photographer's body of work, often functions as one of a series, or as one within multiple iterations of an artist's themes and concerns. The image also contains within it the past history of images that have influenced its conception, and the future lines of its influence yet to be formed. These threads of influence—the dialogue between artists and artistic concerns both within and outside of a particular era—weave through historical contexts and future possibilities, and leave an imprint on visual culture, through variations, similarities, and resonances.

These historical contexts reach back before

photography to a history of visual practices that saw repetition as a necessary tool for the development of artists, and for the acceptance of their work in the contexts that commissioned and consumed image-making. For the majority of the history of painting, emulation and imitation formed core practices through the copying of paintings, the mimicry of masters, and the repetition of accepted subjects and styles within accepted genres such as religious, court, and landscape painting. Although the range of genres and subjects in photography are more or less parallel with those that have traditionally defined painting (portraits, landscapes, city views, even abstractions), because of the relative absence of the artist's hand on the surface of the print, photographs have an even greater sense of similarity and repetition than do paintings. Chuck Close observed that "photography is the easiest medium in which to be competent and the hardest medium in which to have a personal vision because there's no touch, there's no hand, there's no physicality, there's no interface." [1] Without the unique particularities of drawing or rendering to shape the forms and contours of the image, and without the characteristic marks of a paintbrush, palette knife, or hand to create and shape the actual surface of the picture, the photographer depends on available technical options to convey his or her intentions. Which camera format and lens focal length should receive the intended view? Which photographic surface should receive the resulting image (matte or glossy paper, Kodak Endura or Fuji Crystal Archive)? These technical parameters focus the range of expression and make repetition in photography even more pronounced than in other visual arts. It makes the photographs of two different photographers look more similar than the paintings of two different painters. It can also seem to imply that photographers are revisiting the same themes, iconographies, and styles when, in fact, the range of subjects in the history of visual representation has gradually expanded over time.

Perhaps this is why working in series is so important to photography, for to shape a personal vision requires revisiting a subject over many images to create a more focused and particular view, rather than relying on the unique aspects of a single image. In other words, photography is particularly suited to the accumulation of and relationships between many images, rather than to the specific imprint on the individual image, to create a unique vision or outlook. It seems that in photography, increasing the limitations and rules by which an image is constructed within an already limited technical field—and therefore cultivating the conditions for repetition—is one of the most important factors in making a body of work specific and unique.

These, then, are some of the challenges that, as a photographer, I see as central to the making of photographs: how to shape meaning and uniqueness out of a limited range of expression; how to expand meanings through similarities and repetition, rather than restricting them through repetitiveness (the distinction between repetition and repetitiveness, after all, can be dangerously close sometimes); how to achieve the widest range of contrast within a narrow range of parameters, and the widest range of difference within a unifying envelope; how to form a dialogue with the histories and influences that define the field; and how to find unique relationships within ways of seeing and within environments already permeated by repetition.

INSIDE / OUTSIDE

The process of repetition is, on the level of perception, intrinsic to how we see, and also to how we know and behave. Our vision is composed of duplications and translations of outside reality: two almost-identical images, seen through two eyes, are projected onto the light-sensitive cells of the retina at the back of each eye, then are translated into neural signals for the brain to understand. This repetition of images also becomes the basis for comprehending depth. When the two images from each eye are overlapped, our surroundings are removed from flatness and are rendered in three dimensions.

Repetition is thus intrinsic to turning seeing into knowing, and it is one of the most important tools in helping the brain retain information. Repetition is the basis for the recognition of things and the creation of familiar grounds from which the new and unfamiliar can be identified and understood. It reflects the need to place and relate new concepts to known personal, intellectual, educational, or artistic contexts. Repetition shapes the range of familiarity outlined by our cultural, social, and historical environments, and makes what we see intelligible. Repetition gives structure to thought, and forms a barrier against the flood of indecipherability and entropy.

Repetition also underlies our behaviors—the formation of habit, of familiar practices, of the regularity of daily life. As Sigmund Freud hypothesized, the repetition of past experiences, especially traumatic ones, forms the basis of unconscious drives, which manifest in how a person confronts reality: "What appears to be reality is in fact only a reflection of a forgotten past." [2]

At the level of what is perceived, the myriad environments that surround us and form our physical, temporal, and cultural contexts are often structured through repetition. Wavelengths, periodicities, and orbits underlie the behavior of phenomena in space. The repetitive layers of geological stratification sediment the cycles of time in the earth. The circular motion of clocks, daily and seasonal cycles, and Buddhist and Hindu concepts of reincarnation and the Wheel of Life structure understandings of time. A regular heartbeat, biological reproduction, and the recurrence of genetic traits give continuity to life. Standardization, mass production, and gridded structural systems create and organize our built environment. The eternal recurrence, "the unconditional and infinitely repeated circular course of all things," was for Friedrich Nietzsche the basis of existence. [3] By affirming its repetition, one would affirm life in the past, present, and future. Nietzsche's concept was influenced by Heinrich Heine, who observed, "time is infinite, but the things in time are finite," and are therefore bound to repeat. [4] Today we say, "History repeats itself."

Photography occupies the meeting point between the mechanics of visual perception and the structures that shape our environments. In the process of giving visual form to the ways of seeing and behaving that define us, and to the contexts that encompass us, it engages layers of repetition inherent within our environments and ourselves. The process of repetition therefore extends in both directions, for to photograph is to multiply the already multiplied: photography mirrors the doubling process of seeing, and duplicates environments already structured by repetition.

UNIQUE / SAME

It might seem that the opposite of the repetitive is the unique or the original—that which differs enough from its surroundings to be considered distinct and separate. Uniqueness and originality have been favored qualities in Western thought, in contrast to Eastern thought, in which reiteration is an accepted practice. Uniqueness, however, can only be understood within a context of similarities and repetitions. In other words, something is unique only in relation to a larger field of comparisons. Depending on context, uniqueness becomes a relative rather than an absolute term.

The categories that establish similarity, or the range of repetition, are not necessarily stable or fixed: they are largely determined by the specific circumstances of history, culture, and society. The organizing principles that determine what falls within categories of the similar are seldom absolute, as examined by Michel Foucault in *The Order of Things*. In this book, Foucault quotes Jorge Luis Borges's fictional description of a "Chinese encyclopedia," entitled *The Heavenly Emporium of Benevolent Knowledge*, that describes a division of animals into those "(a) belonging to the Emperor, (b) embalmed, (c) tame, (d) suckling pigs, (e) sirens, (f) fabulous, (g) stray dogs, (h) included in the present classification, (i) frenzied, (j) innumerable, (k) drawn with a very fine camelhair brush, (l) *et cetera*, (m) having just broken the water pitcher, (n) that from a long way off look like flies." [5] What one society might consider as different and unrelated could be thought of as similar and related by another. Take, for example, the Hindu list of beings that are considered pure and thus don't require cremation: *sadhus* (holy men), pregnant women, children, animals, and those who have died from snakebites. In languages, sounds that are distinct and unique to one ear can sound similar or indistinguishable to another: *b* and *p* in English, *l* and *ll* in Spanish, and *xi* and *qi* in Mandarin.

The determination of what can fall within categories of sameness, whether made by a society, a figure or body of power, or an epoch, defines how the environment can be ordered and therefore how it can be seen and understood. In other words, the categories of the same are the product of history and society, giving no stable, eternal basis for the unique. The identification and examination of uniqueness is similar to looking at a hologram—the subject appears, changes appearance, or disappears altogether depending on the angle of view.

FIGURE / GROUND

The context of similarities against which something can be identified as different is akin to the distinction between figure and ground. The visibility of the figure depends on the composition of the ground or context against which it appears, whether this be defined on the visual level by tone, color, or texture; on the physical level by shape, material, or structure; or on the ideological level by discipline, culture, or history. These properties, when expanded or repeated and then arranged through sets of relationships, form a field of intelligibility, or a background for vision, against which things can appear and make sense.

In photography, the use of repetition involves a choice of what will constitute the ground through the establishment of what counts as consistent and similar. By establishing a context, the photographer can foreground difference. But figure and ground can also shift positions. By shifting the lines that separate sameness and difference, repetition allows for the manipulation of the relationship between figure and ground. Eijkelboom's photographs of individual pedestrians in Paris, New York, and Shanghai come to mind. His grids of images of people are grouped according to similarities: those wearing blue jeans, those wearing striped shirts, those holding coffee cups. Is the ground the uniform-like similarities in clothing and accessories that foreground the differences between individuals? Or do the subtle differences in the individual objects—the different colors of the striped shirts, the various shapes and sizes of handbags, the miscellany of t-shirt iconography—become the figures against a ground of uniform tastes, habits, and aspirations? The answer is both and neither, for figure and ground in repetition can switch places, as in the familiar figure/ground reversal between an image of two profiles facing each other, which form the shape of a vase between them.

The dividing line between figure and ground, foreground and background, uniqueness and sameness, and difference and repetition is a dynamic one, changing depending on the view. Each is necessary to understand the other, and both are distinguished by gradations rather than solid boundaries. "Difference lies between two repetitions" [6] according to Gilles Deleuze, who in his book *Difference and Repetition* explained the interrelationship of these two concepts beginning with a quote from David Hume's *Treatise on Human Nature*: "Repetition changes nothing in the object repeated, but does change something in the mind which contemplates it." [7]

TIME / SPACE

In the way that light and contrast give shape to form, repetition can give shape to time and to the spaces that objects inhabit. In Eadweard Muybridge's motion studies, the repetition of images as strips of film-like stills of people and animals in motion endows the stationary image with a layer of temporal movement. Repetition can also open up the possibility of not only rendering the forward movement of time, but of treating it as a plastic material, just like clay or paint. Through repetition, time can be rendered malleable, by compressing or expanding change or stasis. Portraits by Dijkstra, Keizo Kitajima, and Nixon, in which the same person or group of people is photographed over a span of years, both stretch and compress time—and our viewing experience. These portraits extend the relatively short time spent with the images into the long periods of time depicted in the photographs, and compress the long passage of time into a few images that can be viewed simultaneously. Repetition can also break up a moment in history into a seemingly endless number of components, as in Barbara Probst's multiple images of a single moment in time.

In rendering space, repetition enables our movement beyond the static two dimensions of the picture surface. Consider repetition within a picture—a regular grid of columns receding into the distance, for instance—and the impression of the third dimension, rendered in perspective and extending behind the two-dimensional surface, will emerge. Space can also be depicted beyond the simple representation of three-dimensional perspectival space, as in images that render the spaces created by social practices, economics, history, and beliefs. Once a trait is repeated enough times, it becomes a social practice; once a form is repeated enough times, it becomes part of an iconography. Social practices and shared spaces create an expanded definition of a "ground"—not only as a pictorial device, but also as a basis of familiarity and intelligibility from which "figures" (people, objects, ourselves) can be discerned and *looked at.*

Through repetition, space can, for example, be distilled and collapsed by showing the uniform spaces created by the economy, as suggested by Kitajima's views of financial centers in different cities. Repetition can also expand specific places into the wider space of history by showing change, as in Joachim Koester's recent photographs of buildings and places photographed in the 1960s and 1970s by artists such as Ed Ruscha and Robert Adams. Or repetition can show how space is formed by society, as in Struth's photographs of streets in Europe, Japan, and the United States. These works, however, are not pure reflections of reality, for they create their own relationships, forming visual environments that overlap, mirror, or stand independent from reality and the environments we inhabit.

Photography, then, becomes a simultaneous closing-in and distancing-from what is depicted. It closes in to examine and make visible, but distances in the multiplication of meanings and interpretations. With repetition, the focus is less on the relationship between the images and the "reality" they represent, and more on the relationship between the images themselves. Through the relationships that are established, the images constitute their own environments.

SINGLE / MULTIPLE

While repetition can represent the larger structures that surround us, it also reveals the impossibility of single truths in photography. The fact that a single view can be repeated but is modified each time through the filters that affect its appearance—weather, light, culture, society, events, politics, and economics—makes each photograph a fragment of a whole that is impossible to fully describe or reach. It might seem that multiplying a view would get us closer to the truth; instead, repetition reminds us that meanings are always multiple and changing.

As photography already points to larger fields and contexts, rendering an expanded view in time and space, repetition opens the possibility, through the accumulation of individual parts, of depicting a picture larger than what we may be able to see as individuals. "A picture" in this case is not only a discrete image, but also an image created from multiple views whose relationships build up a unique view of the world. Each photograph contributes to this larger view, in the same way that individual brushstrokes contribute to the composition of a larger painting. Unlike the brushstrokes within a single painting, however, multiple photographic images do not add up to a single image that can be understood in a single glance; they can only be comprehended through multiple views and multiple viewpoints. Mark Ruwedel's images of the remains of train lines across the United States, for example, not only portray a single geographic space traversed by transport lines, they also portray the transformation of multiple spaces by the single ambition of economic expansion. Together, the images form a portrait of the spaces created when the forces of standardization, colonization, and the spread of markets meet the specific terrains of particular landscapes.

While the single image is synonymous with the individual view, multiple images offer the possibility of breaking up vision into multiple viewpoints, suggesting that vision exists beyond the individual. In other words, repetition demonstrates that vision is made up not only of *individuals* viewing, but also of *societies* and *cultures* looking and forming how and what we see. It suggests that repetition is rarely the duplication of the same, but is composed of similarities and variations modified through the filters of our manifold environments—historical, cultural, intellectual, and psychological. It suggests that uniqueness is not only how different something is from its surrounding context, but how it rearranges the relationships of its surrounding ground and how it changes the ways in which we see our own contexts. Repetition allows us to scrutinize how the structures we encounter and inhabit are composed, by exposing them to multiplied views. Repetition suggests that views are never singular; each time we look, we see something different.

Notes

1. http://www.brooklynrail.org/2008/06/art/chuck-close-with-phong-bui
2. Sigmund Freud, *Beyond the Pleasure Principle,* trans. James Strachey (New York: W. W. Norton and Company, 1961), p. 19.
3. Friedrich Nietzsche, *On the Genealogy of Morals and Ecce Homo,* trans. Walter Kaufmann (New York: Random House, 1967), pp. 273–4.
4. Quoted in Walter Kaufmann, *Nietzsche* (Princeton: Princeton University Press, 1950), p. 318.
5. Quoted in Michel Foucault, *The Order of Things* (New York: Random House, 1970), p. xv.
6. Gilles Deleuze, *Difference & Repetition,* trans. Paul Patton (New York: Columbia University Press, 1994), p. 76.
7. Quoted in Deleuze, p. 70.

--

DISCUSSION FORUM
WWW.WORDSWITHOUTPICTURES.ORG

--

Subject: Threat and Savior: Repetition in Photography
Date: 1 August 2008 01:05:34
From: NOEL RODO-VANKEULEN

To examine the role of repetition in photography is to mine and explicate the medium's very being. At its core photography is a set of duplications resting within a sort of autogenic painting, a process both in the service of one's own subjective desires, as well as the limitations of the mechanism (being both "technological" and handmade) at hand.

It is the direct engagement of reproduction and reproducibility within a loaded history of images already made and yet to be produced. The medium declares its position in the world as both art and function, so very often blurring the lines between meaning, mediocrity, and the mundane. This intricate collection of restrictions and concepts forms the basis of what it means to contribute to an ever-increasing repetition of pictures—why we want and choose to photograph.

Of course, although our understanding of photography today is still relatively new (a partial understanding of the ethical and/or beneficial properties of the medium), it is nonetheless rooted within the historical development of our own image dissemination. This is to say that our current perspective of how pictures operate in relation to photography is almost completely due to the democratic, and prolific, contemporary nature of the medium.

This accessibility to a creation of iconic imagery is constructed, as Leong suggests, "not only of individuals viewing, but of societies and cultures looking and forming how and what we see."

It is our designation of what we hold to be important, a hierarchy of subjects, objects, and environments. Perhaps this latitude of photography's public and artistic use is why Conceptual artists so readily appropriated the medium as a way to suit their subversion of the "original" in art.

Conceptualism, an ideology of not only concept over material, but material as intended object obsolete, used photography's repetitive properties as a way to diminish both institutional ownership and the artistic aura of images. By negating the taxonomic structures present in the art of the past, photographs shot and processed through a negative created a problematic position for value placement in art, if not the disruption of a wide-ranging institutional obsession with originality. However, in our contemporary state of image production the idea of repetition has transformed into a very different action within a completely alternate context.

There are so many artists now who flock to a particular style or convention of picture-making that repetition, particularly in relation to a pictorial "copy," has become a highly marketable trait. A practice such as commercial photography is built upon this consistent repetition to continually reform stylistic tendencies and notable artistic signatures. This has also fed our current state of impulsive art collecting in a market always hungry for the next "visionary" practitioner of the medium. (I use the term collecting here as both positive and negative, not necessarily relating to history building.) As Leong makes clear, "Once a trait is repeated enough times, it becomes a social practice; once a form is repeated enough times, it becomes part of an iconography."

So in all fairness, these sometimes negatively observed facets of repetition can in hindsight be wholly beneficial. Repetition not only reinforces, as Leong has noted, a sense of photographic iconography (crucial to the social and medium-specific ability to "mean" with significance), but it can set in motion the construction of a historical base to evolve photography itself. This affords artists the opportunity to experiment with perceived modes of picture-making, and thus, open up a medium that so frequently presents itself as a stubbornly closed entity.

It is with these thoughts in mind that we must continually restructure our understanding of repetition within photography. Not only does our complacency with outmoded and hegemonic traditions of the medium set photography apart from the openness of art, it subverts the principals of artistic expression by separating artist from photographer, repetition from validation, and experimentation from evolution.

--

Subject: Cheers
Date: 2 August 2008 10:24
From: JOHN LEHR

> . . . I'm a collage artist. It's like, "Damn, if only I could find this one part. Well, maybe if I just had somebody paint it, and then I'll put it out." That almost feels like cheating . . . It would be so easy. But what I do just keeps things much more challenging, I guess. —DJ Shadow

> Today there are more photographs in the world than there are bricks and they are, astonishingly, all different. —John Szarkowski

As Sze Tsung Leong's essay so eloquently states, every photograph is, in a sense, a repetition of the visible world. Of course the artistry involved in making a compelling photograph lies in how this repetition occurs. Like a Duchampian readymade the photograph presents a segment of the world, explicitly chosen by the artist, excised into a rectangle or square and rendered in two dimensions. It is through the combination of choice (what to photograph) and transformation (how to photograph it) that the artist's voice emerges.

Think of these pairings: Alec Soth/ Joel

Sternfeld; William Eggleston/ Luigi Ghirri; Cindy Sherman/ Yasumasa Morimura; Jeff Wall/ Stephen Shore.

In our minds we can all conjure up a photograph made by each of the above artists. It might not be too difficult to imagine pairings of individual images by the photographers (say one of Wall's landscapes with one by Shore) that would confuse their authorship. This pursuit would be trivial at best since it is clear that these similarities are formal and fleeting. With the single photograph removed from the pairing and considered as part of the artist's larger body of work, we see that although stylistic or formal conventions have been repeated, they have been used towards radically different ends. In the context of a particular body of work, monograph, personal website, or solo exhibition, a photographer's central concerns are foregrounded by the repetition of ideas and exclusivity of the setting. In this controlled context, the repetition of another style is read clearly as a playful tribute or mere coincidence. But what happens when one photographer's repetition of another's style goes beyond the occasional nod of influence?

Over the past 10 years, a number of photographers have began to appropriate the recognizable styles of both current and historical photography. The appropriation evokes more than a knowing quotation of a former style meant to indicate or criticize the artist's awareness of his or her predecessors. Instead, these artists utilize preexisting conventions of photography to insert a latent layer of familiarity into the reading of a work that is altogether new. In the seemingly unrelated work of Roe Etheridge, Mark Ruwedel, and Sara VanDerBeek, a historical style is appropriated and used to infuse the work with a specific historical reference. Etheridge borrows from the conventions of 1970s color photography, advertising and amateur photography within a larger, quasi-narrative project in an attempt to explore the role that photography itself plays in our collective memory. Ruwedel adopts the formal strategies of the 19th-century expedition photographer to suggest the burden of history in his documentations of the marks left on the landscape years after civil engineering projects had been abandoned midway. VanDerBeek probes the malleable space between collective history and personal memory by skillfully presenting found photographs using the strategies of Modernist, avant-garde sculpture. The final translation of her assemblages into the thin, two dimensions of the photograph roots this search for the past in present tense.

The familiar motto of the so-called "straight" photographer, that the visible world presents the artist with subjects and content far more interesting than anything they could imagine, can now be expanded. Photography is old enough, and so pervasive, that a photographer can choose to spend a life exploring what had previously been seen as a cul-de-sac in the history of the medium. Like the hip hop DJ, the photographer can choose from a myriad of pre-existing styles and subjects, each accompanied by its own specific histories, and blend them into an amalgam that is both radically new and subliminally familiar.

I am reminded of a Biz Markie DJ set at a club in Chicago a few years ago. At some point during his set, Markie began to slow down a portion of a recent pop song and loop the first notes of the theme song from the television show "Cheers." Instantly, the crowd was rapt in attention. Scanning across the room you could see couples, friends and strangers looking at each other trying to place just where they had heard these notes before. Within seconds it seemed as though everyone was in the know. Heads bobbing, they smiled at each other, delighted by their newfound, shared knowledge. Knowingly, Biz Markie let the song play out the next time the loop was played. The lyrics began:

> Makin' your way in the world today
> takes everything you've got.
> Takin' a break from all your worries
> sure would help a lot.

Wouldn't you like to get away?

And then it happened. Without prompting from Biz Markie, the crowd began to sing the refrain from a song they probably hadn't heard since they were kids. For a moment the club hovered in a place between two times, anchored by both. In rapturous unison the crowd sang:

Sometimes you wanna go
where everybody knows your name.

--

Subject: Two
Date: 4 August 2008 10:50:56
From: KAREN HELLMAN

Sze Tsung Leong makes an eloquent case for repetition, and for repetition as an inherently photographic formula. Multiple photographs, versus singleton pictures, are justified as the most photographic of strategies, as the medium itself is a process of repetition and reproduction. True to form, repetition has multiple affinities to photography, to both the process of making a picture and also throughout its history. Early daguerreotype portrait studios of the 1840s established certain poses and props that repeated from one to the next, followed in the 1850s by an abundance of *cartes de visite* in which the card's format changed very little while paying customers could fluctuate their pose and choice of dress. Criminal and ethnographical studies, as Leong mentions, made individuals into anonymous lines and grids in order to determine an overall (bad) trait. Now however, unlike these earlier uses of the repetition formula, photographic repetition in contemporary photography has become art. Whether we are aware of this past or not, repetition is something we already know, as we have seen it repeat itself in contemporary photography. It also allows for a more complete picture of what it is the photographer is doing with the work. The installation, whether arranged in grids on the wall or in a continuous line around the gallery, is equally crucial to seeing and knowing the work as a whole. One picture is not enough.

The second repetition the author points out is that of visual influence over time. "The image also contains within it the past history of images that have influenced its conception, and the future lines of influence yet to be formed." This repetition travels in a different direction from the first. While the former runs across a preselected contact sheet of images, one frame to the next, the other travels through the history and future of the medium, through one photographer's image to a prior photographer's image and forward to a future one. The author makes reference to "a history of visual practices" that precedes photographic history. However, I am particularly interested in what within the medium's history, separate from painting practice or another media, repeats itself? What are the photographic subjects, compositions, and angles that we already know when we look at photographs today? The author mentions the fact that "Repetition also underlies our behaviors—the formation of habit, of familiar practices, of the regularity of daily life." Are there photographic habits? What can we include in photographic iconography? Is anything excluded?

Space—photographic space—can perhaps be pointed to as a crucial distinction, even a peculiar iconography, of the photographic medium, whether in the stereoscopic viewer or in the single picture. In addition to discussing repetition as a vital formula for contemporary photographers, it is also, as Leong discusses, representative of the formation of perception. Repetition is a structure analogous to how we (as individuals and as a society) turn seeing into knowing, and flatness into depth. I like the author's inclusion of binocular vision, of "two almost-identical images" (the stereograph) coming together in the brain to form three-dimensional vision (the stereoscope). I am also interested in repetition's potential within a single picture. Leong gives the example of columns receding into the distance. Repetition does not necessarily have to be a set of images arranged in a grid; it can also be just two ever-so-slightly different ones side by side, such as Diane Arbus's photograph of identical twins on a sidewalk in Roselle, New Jersey (1967).

I find it intriguing that this article about repetition is titled in the singular. This single picture is made up of many pictures, many view-points. Is this picture of repetition, which "demonstrates that vision is made up not only of individuals viewing, but of societies and cultures looking and forming how and what we see," possible? As two shifted views have to be forced into the singular in order for binocular vision to occur, I wonder if we can ever be completely free of our tendency toward singular images, toward stronger versus weaker, toward more in tune with our own experience (what we "already know") versus less familiar? Even the list the author opens with consists of, in a sense, "singleton" subjects—those subjects that have been captured by one photographer in such a significant way that we associate that subject only with that maker. "Streets of Paris" become Atget; "Blast Furnaces" the Bechers; "One-Child Families" Wang Jinsong; "Wax Figures" Sugimoto. Leong states that "while the single image is synonymous with the individual view, multiple images offer the possibility of breaking up vision into multiple viewpoints." I like this idea and would like to think that as more photographers work with repetition, like in Leong's own photographs, the familiarity with and acceptance of multiple viewpoints would multiply in viewers. However, repetition itself as a photographic formula could fall into repetitiveness (if it hasn't already). Viewers could stop looking at the individual pictures and only see a fragmented grid. I once asked a retired photography curator what he looked for in a photograph. He promptly replied, "Something I've never seen before." Is this possible now? I would like to think so. I think repetition is a good thing in photography, as long as it doesn't become a hollow formula followed without thought, but allows for the openness to something new and unexpected that we might not already know.

--

Subject: Bungling a Good Idea
Date: 14 August 2008 09:50:53
From: JOSHUA CHUANG

Repetition and seriality are omnipresent indeed. In his essay, Sze Tsung Leong surveys and persuasively justifies the predominance of what has been for many years a viable set of strategies for making and presenting one's photographic work. And depending on the creative instincts of the photographer (Leong himself serves as an exemplar) they still offer a plethora of fertile possibilities. Many of the photographer/artists whose work Leong brings to bear—the Bechers, Sherman, and Sugimoto among them—have not only used the medium's documentary power and penchant for rigorous uniformity to their advantage in single pictures, they have also worked with the intent of building larger bodies of images able to articulate more than just the sum of their parts. This approach affects how their individual images look. Freed from making images charged with having to say it all at once, more and more photographers produce images that in form suggest that they are not ends unto themselves, but pieces that can build upon other similar pieces in a stunning variety of combinations (like bricks, as Szarkowski suggested, or language).

Leong notes, "The distinction between repetition and repetitiveness, after all, can be dangerously close sometimes." On one hand, photographs that might not otherwise be wholly convincing as individual images can gain relevance and context by being associated with a network of images. On the other, they can be deadened by an overreliance on off-the-rack formulas for making work that may upon first glance appear rich and substantial. The common thread of repetition that Leong astutely describes as being woven throughout the history of the medium cannot therefore be taken as a recipe with which to make interesting, cogent work. Unfortunately, bookshelves, galleries, and art fairs these days seem replete with photographers whose works fall somehow short in image, concept, or both.

In his response to Leong's essay, Noel Rodo-Vankeulen brings up conceptualism and rightly notes that the manner in which the premises of Conceptual Art have pollinated contemporary photographic practice (and vice versa) has produced a robust, multifaceted hybrid that neither "pure" conceptualists nor "pure" photographers of the past might have imagined. In his essay "Frames of Reference," Jeff Wall described the narrow path he helped forge in the late 1970s as an artist who at once maintained a deep regard for the history of photography and the avant-garde art of the time:

> Photography, it could be argued, had a very specific nature as an art form and a medium, and combining it with other things resulted in nothing new as photography but only the reduction of photographs to elements in a collage aesthetic that was not subject to judgment in photographic terms, and maybe not subject to any aesthetic judgment at all. With this in mind, I realized I had to study the masters whose work, either in photography or in other art forms, didn't violate the criteria of photography but either respected them explicitly or had some affinity with them.

Wall has managed throughout his career to sensitively and successfully amalgamate various aesthetics into his photographs, but all too often photographs laced with notions of mimesis, repetition, and seriality are too comfortably situated within these parameters, and too dryly academic. Photographers working consciously (or conceptually) today with ideas of repetition might do well to consult the original tenets of Conceptual art set forth by their most sharp-minded predecessors.

In 1969, Sol LeWitt published his pithy "Sentences on Conceptual Art," which included the following:

> 1) Conceptual artists are mystics rather than rationalists. They leap to conclusions that logic cannot reach. 2) Rational judgments repeat rational judgments. 3) Irrational judgments lead to new experience. . . . 32) Banal ideas cannot be rescued by beautiful execution. 33) It is difficult to bungle a good idea. 34) When an artist learns his craft too well he makes slick art.

One of LeWitt's artistic heroes, it should be noted, was Muybridge.

Leong's essay also raises another issue alluded to in previous postings on this site, specifically Charlotte Cotton's discussion of the affinities between music and photography in the digital age. Taking Cotton's suggestion a step further, I'd like to point out the increasing contradiction (in theory at least) between the naturally duplicative properties of the digital file—from which an unlimited number of exact physical clones can be made with the simple click of a mouse—and the precious limited-edition print, a market device designed to entice collectors to collect and (as it has previously been explained to me by more than one gallerist) to urge artists to make new work rather than spend time filling orders for old favorites. If repetition is an integral conceptual premise of the photographic work being made today, then it seems to me that this motif might also be explored in the way photographs are seen and disseminated. In this era of endless repetition, why stop?

QUESTIONNAIRE / JÖRG COLBERG

WHAT ARE SOME OF THE UNIQUE WAYS THE BLOG ENABLES YOU TO ENGAGE WITH YOUR INTERESTS IN PHOTOGRAPHY?

The blog format makes the creation of contents very flexible, and that's one of the reasons why, I think, the blog has been so successful for me, as a writer and as someone interested in photography. ...Also, I just love to talk to photographers—to a large extent because I am one myself—and the blog has made this very easy and simple. I get lots of emails, and I now know lots of people that I've never met in person but with whom I have had many in-depth conversations about photography via email. For those relationships, the blog has served as facilitator.

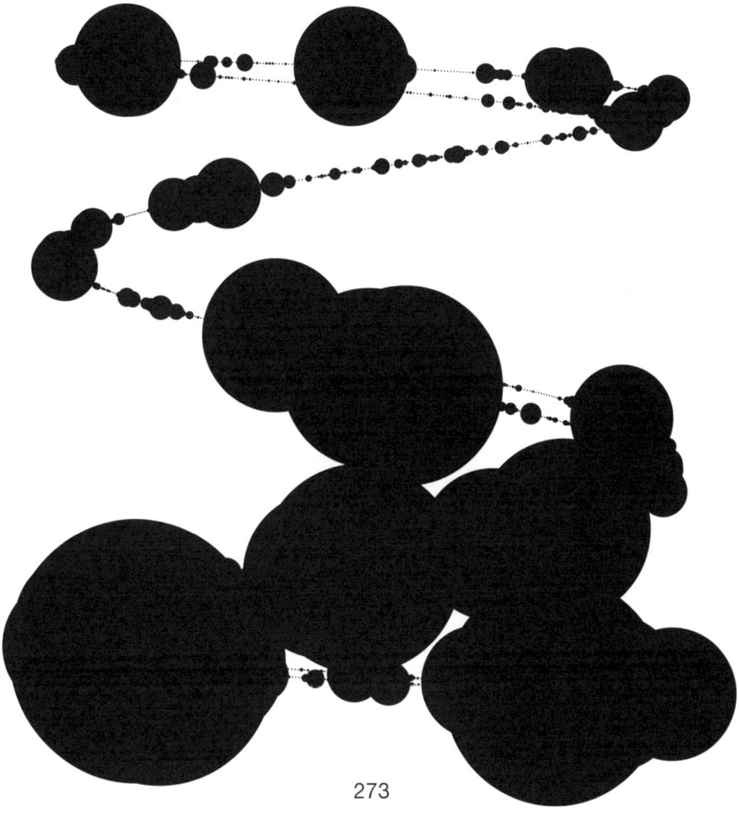

Lost Not Found: The Circulation of Images in Digital Visual Culture

MARISA OLSON

There is a strain of Net art referred to among its practitioners and those who follow it as "pro surfer" work. Characterized by a copy-and-paste aesthetic that revolves around the appropriation of Web-based content in simultaneous celebration and critique of the Internet and contemporary digital visual culture, this work—heavy on animated gifs, YouTube remixes, and an embrace of old-school, "dirtstyle" Web design aesthetics—is beginning to find a place in the art world. But it has yet to benefit from substantial critical analysis. My aim here is to outline ways in which the work of pro surfers holds up to the vocabulary given to us by studies of photography and cinematic montage. I see this work as bearing a surface resemblance to the use of found photography while lending itself to a close reading along the lines of film formalism. Ultimately, I will argue that the work of pro surfers transcends the art of found photography insofar as the act of finding is elevated to a performance in its own right, and the ways in which the images are appropriated distinguishes this practice from one of quotation by taking them out of circulation and reinscribing them with new meaning and authority.

The phrase "pro surfer" originated with the founding in 2006 of Nasty Nets (http://www.nastynets.com), an "Internet surfing club" whose members are Internet artists, offline artists, and Web enthusiasts who were invited by the group's co-founders (of which I was one) to join them in posting to the Nasty Nets website materials they had found online. Many of the contributions were then remixed or arranged into larger compositions or "lists" of images bearing commonality. Soon a number of group "surf blogs" appeared around the Net, including Supercentral (http://www.supercentral.org), Double Happiness (http://doublehappiness.ilikenicethings.com), Loshadka (http://www.loshadka.org/wp/), and Spirit Surfers (http://www.spiritsurfers.net). All share some number of common members, social bonds, or stylistic affinities. There are also a number of "indie surfers" making similar work, some of whom will be mentioned here.

While the artists in this movement have at times debated whether or not they are truly part of a movement, and whether their posts (most of which take the form of blog entries) are truly art or "something else," there have been a number of movement-like signs. In 2007, we had our own happening in the form of the Great Internet Sleepover—held at New York's Eyebeam (http://www.eyebeam.org) and organized by Double Happiness co-founder Bennett Williamson (http://codeblooded.net/)—to which surfers flocked from as far as California, Utah, Wisconsin, Texas, Georgia, Virginia, Rhode Island, and elsewhere. Many pro surfer artists, on their own or in their respective collectives, are being curated into major museum exhibitions and film festivals. Despite such recognition, there have yet to be many significant essays on the movement, and the artists debate the need for anything resembling a manifesto, saying amongst themselves that they are waiting to hear interpretations from external, critical voices. So I am making a first stab here, knowing full well that I might wipe out.

If we are to consider pro surfer work in relationship to photographic media, we must begin with the concept of *circulation*—the ways in which the images are produced and exchanged, and their currency or value. The images that get appropriated on these sites are at times "camera-less" (i.e. created by software or other lens-less tools that nonetheless aspire to optical perspective, typically follow normative compositional rules, and tend to index realism), while others are created with another being behind the aperture, only to be found and appropriated by a surfer. In their re-presentation in a different context—arguably a different economy—the images are taken out of circulation, often without attribution or a hint of origin, unless that is part of the story being told by the artist. Two Nasty Nets members programmed a Web-based tool called Pic-See that makes it easier for Internet users to plunder images archived in open directories. When the images are reused, they are positioned as quotations; yet authorial status is inscribed by the artist who posts them. Let's consider some examples.

Justin Kemp's Pseudo Event (http://www.lowfives.mousesafari.com) is an assemblage of photos taken at ribbon-cutting events, with each picture lining up perfectly so as to form a continuous red ribbon that stretches wide across the screen, requiring quite a bit of horizontal scrolling. Similarly, Guthrie Lonergan's *Internet Group Shot* (http://www.theageofmammals.com/groupshot/) gathers group photos found online (of teams, coworkers, families, etc.) and collages them together into a larger portrait. In some sense this is a group portrait of Internet users. The image unfolds vertically, with the individual components rising up from the herd as one scrolls over. John Michael Boling's *Four Weddings and a Funeral* (http://www.goooooooooooooooooooooooooooooooooooooooooooooooooooogle.com/fourweddings.html) culls YouTube videos of just those types of events. The five videos attest to the popularity of this content on video-sharing websites and add up to a rather clever evaluation of the nature of Web-based forms—a common trope in this genre of Net art. Consider Oliver Laric's *50 50* (http://oliverlaric.com/5050.htm), which pieces together fifty YouTube clips of different people singing the music of hip hop artist 50 Cent, or Seecoy's *matrY-Oshki*, which nests within itself the same YouTube clip of Russian nesting dolls. These works simultaneously celebrate Net culture, critique it, comment on the experience of Web surfing, and flex the artist's geek muscles. While not all pro surfers are extreme hackers—in fact many rely on WYSIWYG tools and Web 2.0 devices that make DIY code tricks easy—others cleverly exploit html, JavaScript, CSS, and other programming languages (often those dating to the early days of the Internet that have since waned in popularity). One such example is Boling's *Marquee Mark* (http://www.goooooooooooooooooooooooooooooooooooooooooooooooooooogle.com/marqueemark.html), which makes Internet-derived images of pop star cum actor Marky Mark Wahlberg scroll in a marquee fashion. These practices resemble the art historical use of found photography, but verge on constituting some other kind of practice—something, dare I say, more original.

It should be noted that other artists in this milieu are making images that verge on the sublime, images of which one would never question the originality. These pictures also employ found material—whether it is extant photography or images that were already "fake," i.e. camera-less digital images created to index reality without ever having an analogous relationship to it. These include video game graphics, low-pixel sprites, bitmap illustrations, and other digital renderings. Artists Travess Smalley (http://www.travesssmalley.com/) and Borna Sammak (http://fffff.at/borna/) both make collages out of such materials that resemble Jackson Pollock's drip paintings or Kurt Schwitters's collages more than anything as mimetic as Robert Rauschenberg or Richard

Hamilton, to whom they clearly owe some degree of creative debt. Petra Cortright's landscape images (http://www.petracortright.com/) are deceptively realistic constructions of epic, jagged-edged, behemoth mountain ranges that could never truly exist in nature. James Whipple's work (http://indoor-oak.org/) often begins with real images of existing spaces, then forces a harmony with the so-called organic shapes of power icons and female body armor found in online, multiplayer video games.

Charles Broskoski's *Cube* (http://www.supercentral.org) copies and pastes together the scroll bars usually interpreted as "outside" of the Internet and uses them to create one of the most pervasive art historical forms—the grid—thus slamming social context back into the domain of Modern aesthetics. Paul Slocum's *Time Lapse Homepage* (http://qotile.net/catalog.html) is a sort of video soundtrack to the evolution of his personal Web page, which is also a record of his ongoing response to working online and experiencing the Internet. These meta-commentaries continue the practice of critiquing the Internet and greater network culture through its own lenses. Pro surfer Michael Bell-Smith (http://www.foxyproduction.com/artist/view/5) is best known for works like *Chapters 1–12 of R. Kelly's Trapped in the Closet Synced and Played Simultaneously* (http://www.eai.org/eai/title.htm), in which he overlapped the Web-based episodes of R. Kelly's show to reveal its formal qualities (a significantly "off-line" project directly influenced by the content and experience of the Internet). But like many other pro surfers, Bell-Smith is also engaged in a distinctly social practice, as was the case in his Nasty Nets post entitled "The post where we share awesome gradients" (http://nastynets.com). In the post, members of the collective and other readers posted their favorite gradient images. Usually meant to linger as background information on a Web page, these gradients were scraped, collected, and re-presented in celebration of their often overlooked beauty. It is no wonder that in this genre the playlist is the formal model par excellence (see Lonergan's playlist of MySpace users' diaristic YouTube-based "intro videos" [http://guthguth.blogspot.com/2006/05/myspace-intro-video-playlist.html]); but in this case the artists are frequently playing with other people's property. In this sense, they are not unlike some of our most beloved contemporary photographers. Queue the obligatory art historical references: the Surrealists, the Dadaists, the Pictures Generation, Andy Warhol, Thomas Ruff, and even Gerhard Richter, Christian Marclay, or Tacita Dean, if you want to consider "found" tropes or photo-based painting. The list is long.

Found photography has enjoyed a particularly dubious legacy. Scraped from the dustbins of history, the worlds these images encapsulate already represent a universe other than the one occupied by the discoverer. Whether hailing from a different time or place (or both), discrepancies tend to exist between the intention of the eye of the photo-taking artist and the later viewer. The discrepancy draws on the voyeuristic curiosity of the latter—eyes for which the image may or may not have been intended. The ways in which these eyes might interpret the images recall film theorist Christian Metz's distinction between a viewer's primary identification with the camera and secondary identification with characters, while problematizing the third term of a viewer's relationship to the artist, particularly when the viewer steps in to appropriate the image.

These relationships are distinctly marked by the question of the photo's content, which is in turn overdetermined by the circulatory patterns of found photos. Some of the earliest images we have of this nature are those eerie photographic studies from mental institutions that sought to link physiognomy and psyche, and mug shots that presaged racial profiling in their linking of a suspect's silhouette and a predisposition toward deviance. Whether we're talking about Ishi or Salpétrière patients or those forever interned at the Mütter Museum, these indices of abnormality spliced vérité and constructed horror in their archiving of impending disaster, perhaps kicked off by the snap of the aperture. These bodies were taken out of circulation in the economy of signs to which they belonged—in effect taxonomized like a beloved stuffed pet—in order to be preserved. The same can be said of the family photos that now populate the "found" genre and which signify death by alluding to the inevitable passing of time. These images circulate in excess. Their value may be the inverse of one predicated on scarcity, but they stand in a position of contrast to proper "Art Photography."

Despite existing mostly as unique prints, the distribution of found photos is far less restrictive than limited edition prints, which tend to be just as controlled with regard to reproduction as they are with regard to form and content.The copyrighted image acquires more cultural currency in correlation to its increased monetary value, yet the priceless snapshot is the one that floats freely. The author's right to control the image, to claim ownership of it as an object, or a product of his or her mind or labor, is theoretically ceded when it's tossed into the bin, whether at a garage sale or a photo fair.

This is where we can begin drawing analogies to the Internet. When an image is uploaded, presumably any person with any intent can access it. We know this because, in these days of perpetual political paranoia, a new form of technophobia related to identity theft skews most cultural commentary related to the posting of photos on social networks and other public sites. Nonetheless, the correlation between vérité and free circulation persists:

the photos that truly represent mainstream life (in all its absurdities), that truly reflect those spectacles that we fantasize about producing and witnessing, are the ones left out there to be found, floating sans watermark. This accounts for their popularity among artists and non-artists alike. Make no mistake, found photos are enjoying celebrity status on the Internet among surfers— pro, indie, and amateur. Those split-second bloopers, acts of conspicuous consumption, and diaristic elevations of otherwise banal moments found on sites with names like FAIL (http://failblog.org/) and Ffffound (http://ffffound.com) comprise the backbone of contemporary digital visual culture. They are the vertebrae of a body that we otherwise seek to theorize as amorphous. We tend to overlook this proliferation of images, considering it as somehow anomalous and not yet part of the master narrative of network conditions.

Rosalind Krauss argues that while there are many spaces and contexts in which photographs live, the wall of the gallery is the primary discursive space of the photo. But the leap to digital form prompts us to consider not only the vertical plane of the Web page as the new home of photographic media. (Indeed, how many of the world's photos are even printed anymore?) We are also led to consider the relationship between taxonomy à la the stuffed-pet metaphor and taxonomy à la the digital archive. In so many ways, the archive has become the dominant mode of not only photographic presentation, but also of its production. This was true of August Sander and Walker Evans, and it was picked up and modified by Ed Ruscha and John Baldessari. The work of pro surfers continues to indulge our impulse toward order, whether images are produced from the get-go as one of a series, remixed according to database aesthetics (to exploit an early Net art catch phrase), or folded into a list and presented as a sort of pre-contextualized readymade. The history of photography makes clear that this is a common practice, but what we must ask ourselves now is whether these are, in fact, still readymades or whether the degree to which they are altered makes them something else.

Montage theory argues in favor of "something else." In the famous "Kuleshov Effect," named for film theorist Lev Kuleshov, linked shots add up to something greater than the sum of their parts, dialectically constructing a narrative by way of association. These same terms can clearly be used to describe the representational strategies at play in the aforementioned pro surfer work samples. But the resemblances also extend to the social life of this creative community. In "The Principles of Montage," Kuleshov discusses the period in the nascent stages of Soviet cinema in which he and his comrades attempted to discern "whether film was an art form or not." Kuleshov argues that, in principle, "every art form has two technological elements: the material and the methods of organizing that material." Kuleshov and his peers felt that many aspects of filmmaking—from set design and acting to the very act of photography—were not specific to the medium. Nevertheless, he argues, "The cinema is much more complicated than other forms of art, because the method of organization of its material and the material itself are especially 'interdependent.'" In specific opposition to his examples of sculpture and painting, Kuleshov describes a medium in which the very structure, indeed the very structuring context (its machines and processes—in short, its apparatuses), is responsible for not only the production of signifiers but also the signification itself. This insistence on the "complicated" role of apparatuses foreshadows later critical insistence on the interdependence between the content and the hardware and software *organizing* the content of a work of new media art, and certainly in the work of the art hack, by virtue of its signification through re-sequencing.

When we apply this logic to the practices and products of pro surfers, we see that they are engaged in an enterprise distinct from the mere appropriation of found photography. They present us with constellations of uncannily decisive moments, images made perfect by their imperfections, images that add up to portraits of the Web, diaristic photo essays on the part of the surfer, and images that certainly add up to something greater than the sum of their parts. Taken out of circulation and repurposed, they are ascribed with new value, like the shiny bars locked up in Fort Knox.

It was once argued that collage was the most powerful tool of the avant-garde, that it was a literalization of the drive to reorganize meaning. Now that it has become a mainstream practice, its authority has become virtually endangered. New media often suffers the fate of receiving inadequate criticism, and this is particularly true of Internet-based work. Because these artists are practicing within a copy-and-paste culture in which images, sound files, videos, and even source code are lifted and repurposed, the work is often dismissed as derivative. (My Rhizome colleague Lauren Cornell and I attempted to address this fact when we co-curated the New Museum exhibition *Montage* in 2008 [http://rhizome.org/art/exhibition/montage/projects.php]). Despite the implied claim that anything derivative is incapable of signifying on its own, the representational practice upon which this work hinges—montage—is by definition an act of bringing meaning to something. It borrows the techniques of collage—namely piecing together fragments, objects, and ideas in what Roland Barthes might call a "tissue of quotations"—to create new valences. This is not so much derivative as dialectical. Each "lifted" piece is put in conversation with the other, so that the combination creates a third (or fourth or fifth) "term."

Despite the fact that the art world has flourished after

decades of Pop art and other recitations, the label "derivative" becomes a blockade, denying artists entrée to a shared discourse, or denying the radical potential of their montage-based practices.

A few years ago, respected new media curator and self-described "former photo boy" Steve Dietz wrote an essay entitled "Why Have There Been No Great Net Artists?" (http://portal.unesco.org/culture/en/ev.php-URL_ID=17147&URL_DO=DO_TOPIC&URL_SECTION=201.html). The essay was inspired by the semi-rhetorical question asked by Linda Nochlin in her legendary essay "Why Have There Been No Great Women Artists?" Dietz summarizes the quandary posed by Nochlin and invokes the same paradox in his own. The immediate answer is that of course there have been great female artists and great Internet artists. The second response is to say that the question is incorrectly framed. Not all female artists are the same (we are not a category!) and this also can be said of Internet artists whose work now takes on a variety of forms and contents—just like photography! But the deeper issue here is art history's compulsion toward recursion. The history that repeats itself is one written by archetypical, old, white dudes (as Paris Hilton so poignantly described John McCain in a recent Web video) who tend to leave the ladies out of their self-perpetuated boys' clubs. The same could very easily happen with Net art.

There are artists I respect whose work couldn't be adequately described within my assigned word count, artists who might take issue with my interpretation of their work, and artists who may see the field moving in entirely different directions. But if we are to be taken seriously, we must take a considered look at our playlists and think about our favorite artists' favorite artists. We must learn and assert our own art history, so that in the near future, we will be found in those yearbooks.

--

DISCUSSION FORUM
WWW.WORDSWITHOUTPICTURES.ORG

--

Subject: vertebrae of the net
Date: 28 September 2008 03:22:09
From: JACOB CIOCCI / DONALD P. GRADY

I am interested in Marisa's use of the "vertebrae" analogy to describe the found photo phenomenon of the Internet. Personally, I am torn about this idea that there can ever be any "vertebrae" to Internet popular culture. Maybe the Internet is something that moves too fast, or is too ephemeral to have a dominant "master narrative." Even though we have certain signs to use now that a lot of people in the general public can relate to (MySpace, emoticons, Internet "slang," eBay) it really cannot compare to the "master narratives" of other related mediums (books, TV, films). When *Family Guy* references *Star Wars* movies, there is a lot more collective consciousness to work with than if they were to reference the viral qualities of "the *Star Wars* kid."

The reason new media work is often dismissed as derivative is simply because, despite the Web's current popularity, the pop culture of the Internet is not as popular as the popular culture of TV or film. For example, no one calls a film derivative when it references and comments on other films. No one writes off *Family Guy* because all the jokes are referential. No one writes off Warhol for translating one object into another format. I am going to go out on a limb here and say that all art has always been referential to other art, and all media have always been "interdependent" media (to use Kuleshov's word), all the way back to cave paintings.

I can't wait until we don't have to break all of these mediums up into separate categories, when it is understood that it is all just images with no origin. When there is no such thing as a Net artist. (Of course, if you ask good artists, they won't categorize themselves ever, and this has always been true.) But for now, I wonder if there is something in the Internet's very nature which prohibits it from ever having its own *Simpsons*, a work that brilliantly uses the specific powers of the medium to comment on itself and still reach lots of different types of people. Not just 20-30-somethings but 12 year olds all the way to 60 year olds. Maybe there will never be another technology so easy to understand as TV. But I think it's just a matter of time before everything changes. My 19-year-old students at CMU don't really seem to care about the cultural distinctions between film, video, digital video, or animated gifs.

This idea that it is not important to be able to discern where a particular chunk of moving image originated from makes me wonder how long this game of "translation" that so many of these "pro surfer" artists are obsessed with will remain interesting. If, as Marisa points out, much of this work is about re-contextualization and montage, about playing with how the simple act of choosing how to archive data changes the cultural meaning of that data, will re-contextualization become so commonplace that it is boring? Will people of the future not even notice that Girl Talk was doing something creative, in the same way my students think Bruce Nauman's *Stamping in the Studio* is too obvious? I don't know. Most people just want their consumer technology to work; they don't want to interact creatively with it. But they love it when artists do it for them in a clever way that they can understand. I guess I don't think much is going to change.

My last thoughts on all of this relate to Marisa's worries about how Net art is going to be canonized. I feel like this group of artists is smarter about its relationship to the public and to the art world than older generations of "Net artists." They don't just make code, they make prints, paintings, drawings, and music, objects you can buy or consume in many different ways. They are involved in a network of interrelated media and they love to translate these mediums from one to the next. But the main thing is that they all have real websites with real names and relatively easy-to-navigate portfolios. To me, that is one indication that they want their work to be easily digestible by a public that prefers human names to anonymous, amorphous, object-less Web presences. They may work collectively but they all make sure to post their own work under their own names as well. I think the model involves active, fluid participation in a relatively anonymous community that can exist outside of pressures such as "money," mixed with artistic independence, self-determined ambition, and an ability to move in and out of these worlds when you strategically please.

Oh, and on a completely unrelated note, where does the history of "zines" fit into this conversation and a discussion of photography? Deciding whether or not to post a link to your Del.icio.us account or to your YouTube account is like deciding how to reproduce a found photo on any number of the different machines at Kinko's: each has its own character and changes the meaning of the original. I see this type of "pro surfing" work as a performance in the same way that contributors to *FOUND Magazine* are performing "finding" by sending their finds through the mail along with their written descriptions. And I think "movement-like signs" is the proper way to describe what may appear as examples of a "pro surfer movement": while there may be characteristics of a movement—a subculture and shared "underground" aesthetics—we no longer live in a time where a paradigm like this really makes sense. We may reference these terms, emulate them in ways, use them to sell MP3s or art objects, and perpetuate them for the sake of convenience. But I think things are fundamentally different now—things are too fluid, the distance between inside and outside fluctuates back and forth too fast. But my understanding of "speed" is outdated, now that I am 30.

QUESTIONNAIRE / KATY GRANNAN

DO NEW TECHNOLOGIES CHANGE YOUR IDEA OF PHOTOGRAPHY?

Yes and no. We still face the same challenges—what to photograph, how to photograph, and many technical decisions remain unchanged—but digital technology makes the process exponentially faster. There are infinite possibilities. We just need to be careful not to fall into the digital abyss.

DO YOU THINK IT'S POSSIBLE TO HAVE A "CAREER" AS AN ARTIST?

Sure, there are plenty of artists who have careers; they work really hard at it, too. This, however, has very little to do with whether or not the work is any good. One could argue that too much time spent on a "career" takes valuable energy (most of it psychological) and effort away from the more satisfying practice of making work. But of course it is possible to do all of the above—go to the parties, give the lectures, etc.—and make great work. It just depends on how you want to live your life, and how you feel like spending your time.

QUESTIONNAIRE / MATT KEEGAN

DO NEW TECHNOLOGIES CHANGE YOUR IDEA OF PHOTOGRAPHY?

It is important to note that I do not consider myself to be a photographer. I have incorporated photography into my work and exhibitions for over four years, but I have no formal training. Although I am fully engaged with photography as an artist and art viewer, I have not worked extensively with taking or printing my own photographs. I tend to shoot with a 35-mm point-and-shoot camera, or if I want to produce a large and less grainy image, I borrow a friend's medium format or digital camera. I work with a great photo printer in Brooklyn named Julie Pochron who is always updating her printers and software.

I am excited about the way artists incorporate new technologies to create hybrid work that straddles two or more media. I am also invested in the ways that new technologies facilitate the distribution of work via sites like Lulu. Small publishers and artists directly benefit from the new and more affordable printing options that are now available.

WHAT WOULD YOU CONSIDER SOME OF THE MOST IMPORTANT CHANGES THAT PHOTOGRAPHY HAS UNDERGONE IN THE LAST FEW YEARS?

Digital advancements have overhauled photography. There is a phasing out of traditional black-and-white and color labs in New York City. Similar and even more dramatic changes are going on with film. 16mm processing is now relegated to only one or two businesses in all of Manhattan. Photography is absolutely different than it was two years ago. The speed at which digital cameras and printers have improved is reassuring, but it seems overwhelmingly fast.

QUESTIONNAIRE / RICHARD WEST

HOW DO YOU DETERMINE WHAT TYPES OF PHOTOGRAPHY ARE INCLUDED IN YOUR PUBLICATION?

My co-editor travels around the country looking at photographers' work that he sees at portfolio days that we arrange at public venues. We publish the work we like and which hasn't been published before. The exhibition and book reviews are decided on the basis of whether we have reviewed the work before and whether the books or shows interest us.

IN THE EVER-EXPANDING WORLD OF ONLINE MEDIA, HOW DOES A MAGAZINE DISTINGUISH ITSELF?

As a print magazine we do not try to distinguish ourselves in the ever-expanding world of online media, that is what our website is for.

DO NEW TECHNOLOGIES CHANGE YOUR IDEA OF PHOTOGRAPHY?

New technologies necessarily change the material production and diffusion of images, but what is of interest to me remains the question of the image. The image comes first, not the technology. The binary opposition analogical/digital is intriguing. To use the term "analogical" to define a non-digital photo is now commonly accepted, yet remains paradoxical. Before the development of the digital world of imaging, nobody used the word analogical. There was just photography. There is a reversal here. We can say that at the level of discourse, the digital has invented or reinvented the analogical. The digital needs its other, the analogical, in order to define itself. In a certain way, it follows that the analogical comes after the digital after all.

In a sense, and pushing this idea of mutual dependence, analog photography benefits greatly from its other, the digital: the analog belongs to what is obsolete, like an object that has lost its function. A sort of fascinating fetish, it is endowed with the appeal of what is useless, a uselessness that André Breton loved so much in fragmented, pointless and incomprehensible objects.

In this sense, new technologies have changed my idea of photography. They have enabled me to think about analogy, not technologically but rhetorically. Analogy is a way to make a relation between dissimilar things. [Stéphane] Mallarmé wrote "The Demon of Analogy," a text that produces equivalences between signs encountered by chance. The demon is this spirit that produces these relations between unrelated signs. The analogical presupposes an object and its reflection as image. But isn't the reflection more interesting, more fascinating, more spiritual than the object? Paradoxically, could it be that the digital image, by breaking the link between an object and its reflection, also breaks the possibility for fascination that such a link entails?

DO YOU THINK IT'S POSSIBLE TO HAVE A "CAREER" AS AN ARTIST?

It depends what one means by a career. Career entails safety, and if one is interested in safety, it is better to become a lawyer, an accountant, or a greengrocer. A career artist sounds too safe to be interesting.

Abstracting Photography

WALEAD BESHTY

> Far from it being the object that antedates the viewpoint, it would seem that it is the viewpoint that creates the object. —Ferdinand de Saussure

> It is indeed the characteristic of the sadist that he humiliates his object and then—or thereby—satisfies it. —Walter Benjamin

> Let's begin with two images . . . —Rosalind Krauss

The issue of what constitutes "Photography" as an ontological category has again gained currency, a rather surprising reinvestment in medium specificity, especially when considered in the context of contemporary art, where professional divisions between aesthetic practices are more or less a thing of the past. Despite being vaguely nostalgic, and at worst retrograde, the urgent impulse to revive categorical boundaries signals a deeper critical dilemma facing devotees of the medium, for the drive to reconstitute a stable and practicable definition of photography is inextricable from the very real sense that the prominence of photographic discourse in contemporary art has receded. By now the charged debates of the late seventies and eighties—between the Museum of Modern Art's staid photography department and "post-modernist" critics—that once lent photography, and the intellectual terrain it describes, a sense of urgency, have all but petered out. Between the loss of photography's status as a contentious intellectual battleground, and its denaturalization via a series of technological developments, an impenetrable fuzziness has descended over what "Photography"—as an aesthetic and theoretical discourse—actually is, and furthermore, what might be at stake in reopening the discussion of its identity.

In the wake of what are now decades-old polemics, inert fragments of previous formulations and aesthetic conventions litter photography's theoretical landscape, amounting to a critical crisis for those who wish to constitute it as an epistemologically coherent tradition in anything but negative terms. Thus "Photography" has become a Benjaminian *facies hippocratica*, a transformation of discursivity into dissolution, the medium representing a disorderly field that the historian/critic can do little more than survey, and hope to reconstitute. As George Baker wrote in his essay "Photography's Expanded Field," "Critical consensus would have it that the problem today is not that just about anything image-based can now be called photographic, but rather that photography itself has been foreclosed, cashiered, abandoned—outmoded technologically and displaced aesthetically." [1] In other words, the Barthesian theorization of the "this has been" *contained in* the photographic image, has become the "this has been" *of* "Photography" itself. This lack of certainty with regard to what constitutes photography as an object of inquiry is, in all its abstractness, a mirror of the problem of theorizing the photograph: a clash between the apparent concreteness of the photographic referent and its slippery contextual play. Yet the term "Photography," and all it implies, persists beyond its supposed theoretical and practical disintegration, [2] and with it a forlorn pastiche of critical theorizations and aesthetic conventions repeatedly confront a metaphor for their own failure in the "death mask" of the photographic image. [3]

This contemporary conundrum is perhaps nowhere better displayed than in Baker's aforementioned text, which, as a literary object, both narrates and performs the dilemma. Reflecting on the dispersal of the photographic "field" prompts Baker to assert that "the terms involved only now become more complex, the need to map their effects more necessary, because these effects are both less obvious and self-evident." [4] Baker proposes to "read" the contemporary condition of photography through an earlier text, that of Rosalind Krauss's "Sculpture in the Expanded Field," at times going so far as to transplant his terms and formulations into direct quotes from her text, inhabiting her text as much as her text prefigures his own. [5] Baker sets out to re-picture the scene of dispersal, to ritually connect terms *again*, yet with the nagging sense that the result of this effort is destined to be tenuous and self-defeating. The text, in its self-narrated attempt to add clarity and order to its "theoretical object" (a term he appropriates from Krauss), transforms into a traumatic re-enactment of "Photography's" fragmentation (a condition emphasized by his use of textual pastiche), that culminates in another moment of defacement and dispersal (in its final paragraph Baker recounts a scene where the diagram at the center of his text is scribbled over by one of the artists it is meant to contain). [6] Thus, the final pages of "Photography in the Expanded Field" serve as something of an epitaph for the short-lived theoretical model Baker endeavors to (re)construct, and perhaps, the very ability of the critic/historian to play an active role in contemporary art's historicization.

Seeing this as a state of crisis for the medium (and thus for the historian/critic who defines it), Baker performs, as so many recent commentators on the medium do, as allegorist. Reading his own moment through a temporally displaced other, the status of the photograph is reread through the urgency of critique in 1979 (not insignificantly, Baker's urtext was written by his mentor Krauss). Through this operation, his own position as a critic within the contemporary academy is tied metaphorically and metonymically to photography's ebb and flow as an ontological category, its crisis of theoretical clarity serving as a forlorn metaphor for the predicament of the historian/critic. Here, the photographic object, in microcosm, comes not only to represent the loss of a unity between signifier and signified, its manifestations dispersed within an equally fragmented field that, for the historian/critic, requires it to be resituated and re-pictured, but also to function as a metaphor for contemporary critique's confrontation with its own ambiguous role. For Baker, it is a picture, a visage of the past, that bridges the divide or rupture between discursive moments, and in this, as in many cases, it is the picture alone that signifies the wound or trauma it is meant to remedy. For pictures transform the nameless into the named, the unwieldy into the static, and in his quest to address the contemporary condition of photography, it is a picture that serves as Baker's point of departure.

So I am going to start where Baker started: with a picture—a frame, or more exactly, a square, that serves as an emblem of a past moment in art history and photography's most contentious and heady days, and that, like the organizational impulse of all pictures, attempts to bridge a gap or cauterize a wound. Baker's text, like that of the text from which he adapted his title, represents a current historical dispersal in the quaternary field of Algirdas Julius Greimas's semiotic square (referred to in Krauss's text as a Piaget or Klein group), a strategy for expanding binary oppositions into larger fields of interrelations. In 1979, Rosalind Krauss deployed this same picture when confronted with what she perceived as a crisis for the categorical language of the critic, a challenge to its ability to manage its domain. Her text, "Sculpture in the

Expanded Field," sought to rescue a category that was "in danger of collapsing" from the sheer heterogeneity of objects it had been called upon to describe, [7] arguing that in the discussion of post-war American art, "categories like sculpture and painting have been kneaded and stretched and twisted in an extraordinary demonstration of elasticity, a display of the way a cultural term can be extended to include just about anything." [8] To prevent the dam from bursting, Krauss outfitted the field with a corral, framing a sequence of coordinates whose discrete interrelations were compressed into dotted lines.

For Krauss, this was a far-reaching methodological crisis, but redeployed by Baker (who acknowledges that the situation for photographic discourse is radically different), it takes on a personal dimension, reflecting his own intellectual development couched in the oedipal relations of teacher and student, where his own connection to a critical lineage, and to history, is staged as a literal interpenetration of models and methodologies. As Baker writes, "Now I have been drawing Klein groups and semiotic squares ever since I first met Rosalind Krauss, and the reader by this point will not be surprised to learn of how fondly I remember sitting in her office conjugating the semiotic neutralization of things like the terms of gender and sexuality, some twelve years ago." [9] He then places his voice into that of the past, and through his voice, the past speaks of the present. The switch from Krauss's impersonal and authoritative assertion of a condition, to Baker's superimposition of historical moments, autobiography, and introspective reflexivity, further emphasizes the sheer distance that separates their respective positions in time and methodology, a melancholic rupture that cuts laterally through the entire text, and ironically, through the institution of critique itself. We thus have, in Baker's reanimation of Krauss' schema, an image of critical melancholia, and as Walter Benjamin surmises in *The Origins of German Tragic Drama*, "the only pleasure the melancholic permits himself, and it is a powerful one, is allegory." [10] The critic/historian, as allegorist, displaces history with pictures, synchronic schemas that in their attempt to "recover" and solidify only mask a "pertrified, primordial landscape." [11] For the picture, proposed as the imago of history, is fundamentally opposed to historical time, opting for synchronicity over diachronicity, transforming historical time into spatial metaphor, and resisting the linear causal chains of development and instead operating along the axes of formal morphology; it is, in short, the tool of the historian who has turned away from history. Baker abandons the notion of historical time, while simultaneously performing the collapse of the organizational schema he displaces it with; in the wake of his argument we are left with only the rupture, the gap. When this ontological rupture is named by Baker, it is called photography.

Krauss's map was nothing if not timely, indicating both the grip that structuralist analysis had within a certain mode of theoretically fluent American art criticism, and the attraction of artists of the time to structuralist theory's usefulness in fracturing totalizing unities. It was, in other words, deeply embedded in its cultural moment; one need only think of Robert Smithson's "non-sites," Martha Rosler's *The Bowery in Two Inadequate Descriptive Systems* (1974-75), (or, more explicitly, her *Semiotics of the Kitchen* [1975]), or the writings of Robert Morris, Dan Graham, Mel Bochner, or Allan Sekula, to see the wide effects of structuralist formulations on the American artistic landscape. Semiotic considerations seemed equally well entrenched, making Krauss's use of Greimas's semiotic square and its modular geometric form all the more resonant with the aesthetic conventions of the time (Hanne Darboven, Lawrence Weiner, Joseph Kosuth, Robert Morris, Sol

LeWitt, et al.). It was a moment when the art historian, far from looking backward on an arrangement of artists' practices, directly participated in an active debate with them. [12] Perhaps no group of artists took this understanding of signification to heart more than the "Pictures" Generation, whose work, generally speaking, exploited the fracture between sign and referent that structuralist and deconstructive procedures laid bare. According to the reception of the work at the time, their work argued that the image was like that of the Kraussian understanding of modernist sculpture, a homeless, free-floating signifier whose meaning derived solely from a context to which it had once been inextricably tied, but now found itself separate from. In their hands, when an image spoke, it spoke of this distance.

It seems no coincidence that, in response to the dual rise of institutional critique and appropriation art, the conceptual dimensions of allegory would become a potent catalyst for some of the most vocal and ambitious critics of the time (whose formulations are particularly indebted to the writing of Peter Bürger, and his application of Benjamin's theorization of an "allegorical vision" in the *The Origins of German Tragic Drama* to the works of the early twentieth century avant-garde). This interest produced two major texts published just two years apart: Craig Owens's "The Allegorical Impulse: Toward a Theory of Postmodernism (Parts 1 & 2)" (1980), and Benjamin H. D. Buchloh's "Allegorical Procedures: Appropriation and Montage in Contemporary Art" (1982). [13] In its most basic sense, allegory is when one text is read through another. In the allegorical formulation of institutional critique (derived in equal parts from both texts), the artwork re-examines the condition of exhibition, usually along the axes of its physical, economic, or architectonic properties, proposing that selected aspects, activated by artistic "intervention," be read in tandem with the institution that contains them. In contrast, the critical action of appropriation, following the pathway of Pop art back to its roots in the readymade, was targeted at the instrumental use of images and the repressive categorizations they tacitly asserted.

Both Buchloh's and Owens's texts provide ample disclaimers regarding the potential political agency of their chosen subjects. Buchloh maintains that at least some of the artists within his text run the risk of merely replicating alienation (here writing specifically of Sherrie Levine and Dara Birnbaum), producing works whose "ultimate triumph is to repeat and anticipate in a single gesture the abstraction and alienation from the historical context to which the work is subjected in the process of commodification and acculturation." [14] Owens acknowledges an even more bleak state of affairs when first observing that Robert Rauschenberg (within Owens's text, offered as a paternal figure to the "Pictures" Generation [15]) "enacts a deconstruction of the museum, then his own deconstructive discourse [that]—like Daniel Buren's—can take place only within the museum itself. It must therefore provisionally accept the terms and conditions it sets out to expose." [16] Owens then concludes, "We thus encounter once again the unavoidable necessity of participating in the very activity that is being denounced precisely in order to denounce it. All of the work discussed in this essay is marked by a similar complicity, which is the result of its fundamentally deconstructive impulse." [17] This point is reiterated by Buchloh some twenty years later in the preface of his anthology *Neo-Avantgarde and Culture Industry* (2000), in which he surmises that the panoply of artistic challenges to the culture industry, which "range from mimetic affirmation (e.g. Andy Warhol) to an ostentatious asceticism (e.g. Michael Asher) that—in its condemnation to a radical purity of means—more often than not in the last decade had to *risk losing the very ground of the real upon which critical opposition could be inscribed.*" [18] Conscribed by the arguments laid out for them, the practices positioned to overturn institutionalized structures (be they in the form of cultural or economic authority), and constituted within the critical reading of allegory, offer only further evidence of the invulnerability of the institutions they identify, if only by their inability to exist without them. It is no coincidence that a similar implication of "critical failure" (Owens's term) is at play in the work of these critics. In their deconstruction of the institutionalized rhetoric of validation, they rely on the authority granted to them through processes of accreditation, peer review, etc., in order to present their critique of those very procedures by which legitimacy (and thus power) is naturalized. Despite the nearly three decades that separate us from these ideas (more still if we credit Bürger, who clearly outlined this methodological problem), this paradox of aesthetic critique persists. As it was succinctly put by Luc Boltanski and Eve Chiapello in *The New Spirit of Capitalism* (2006), "Artistic critique is currently paralysed by what, depending on one's viewpoint, may be regarded as its success or its failure." [19]

Yet, the proposition of materialist, artistic or aesthetic critique carries with it a seductive promise not only that the world of appearances can be punctured, shedding light into its darkened recesses, but also that there is something to be found lurking behind the curtain, a repressed "truth" that lies dormant within all things that, once revealed, has liberatory potential. In writing on the photographic image, this attempt repeatedly confronts an unrepresentable rupture in signification, where laying things bare often leaves nothing but an abyss. Here, again, it is the "the real upon which critical opposition could be inscribed" which is sacrificed through the operation of the image. Writing on the work of Troy Brauntuch in his seminal 1977 essay "Pictures," Douglas Crimp observed that "the result is *only to make pictures more picture-like*, to fix forever in an elegant object our distance from the history that produced these images. *That distance is all these pictures signify.*" [20] This appraisal was not uncommon among his contemporaries. In "Photography *en abyme,*" Owens went further, indicating that this quality of doubling, and its reflexive understanding, was "a property of the photograph itself," an instance of photography speaking *from the abyss*. [21] Using Smithson as an example, Owens writes, "In a photograph, Smithson casts a shadow over the presumed transparency of photographs; he raises serious doubts about their capacity to convey anything but a sense of loss, of absence." [22] This absence is theorized as death for Barthes, for "however 'lifelike' we strive to make it (and this frenzy to be lifelike can only be our mythic denial of the apprehension of death), Photography is a kind of primitive theatre, a kind of *tableau vivant*, a figuration of the motionless and made-up face beneath which we see the dead." [23] This argument echoes Siegfried Kracauer, who, in his 1927 essay "Photography," wrote: "That the world devours [photographs] is a sign of the *fear of death*. What photographs by their sheer accumulation attempt to banish is the recollection of death, which is part and parcel of every memory image. In the illustrated magazines the world has become a photographable present, and the photographed present has been entirely eternalized. Seemingly ripped from the clutch of death, in reality it has succumbed to it." [24] Kracauer saw photography as demolishing memory (the real), the core of a liberated consciousness (the very mnemonic real that Barthes saw as the redemptive *punctum*, a wound that opened up in the surface of the banal *studium*, or the social history that the photograph was a part of), the historical real that critique itself proposed to preserve.

Since its inception, the photographic image has been strongly associated with displacement and destruction, a triumph of images over material. Writing in 1859, Oliver Wendell Holmes claimed that with the advent of photography (for him distilled in the verisimilitude of the stereograph), "*form is henceforth divorced from matter.* In fact matter as a visible object is of no great use any longer, except as the mould on which form is shaped. Give us a few negatives of a thing worth seeing, taken from different points of view, and that is all we want of it. Pull it down or burn it up, if you please." [25] This destruction is totalizing; in Vilém Flusser's multivalent study of photography, this conundrum of the photographic image is inescapable:

> Nothing can resist the force of this current of technical images—there is no artistic, scientific or political activity which is not aimed at it, there is no everyday activity which does not aspire to be photographed, filmed, videotaped… In this way, however, every action simultaneously loses its historical character and turns into a magical ritual and an endlessly repeatable movement. The universe of technical images, emerging all around us, represents the fulfilment of the ages, in which action and agony go endlessly round in circles. Only from this apocalyptic perspective, it seems, does the problem of photography assume the importance it deserves. [26]

This is the apocalyptic becoming of the technological image in the form of the photograph, an inescapable conflation of the concrete with the likeness, an abstract gleaming dystopia where the real is a priori an image, and vice versa. It is the photographic act that comes to stand for this transformation of object into image, and it is the photograph as image that renders this abstract transformation tautologically, and traumatically, complete.

As signifying surfaces, images are abstractions. The logic of the abstraction is the reduction of four dimensions to a two-dimensional surface. As Baker cites in his aforementioned text, Roland Barthes argued "The goal of all structuralist activity, whether reflexive or poetic, is to reconstruct an 'object' in such a way as to manifest thereby the rules of functioning (the 'functions') of this object. Structure is therefore actually a simulacrum of the object, but a directed, interested simulacrum, since the imitated object makes something appear which remained invisible . . . " [27] To put it another way, structuralism is primarily concerned with images—the chain of imagistic abstractions that we encounter in the world, or more specifically, the source ("real") from which the chosen chains of abstractions has developed and must be thus reconstituted backwards from (because, of course, this "real" is obscured by the abstractions it generated, suppressed under their weight). Thus, for the structuralist, another image is necessitated to make the invisible visible again, with the hope that this is the urimage, the direct evidence of the symbolic order that we are enslaved within. To this end, when structuralism confronts an object, it adds another layer of abstraction, and another picture is placed on the conceptual heap (albeit the structuralist image which is revelatory). Built on this foundation, the discourses around ideology critique and critiques of representation, identity, etc., insofar as they are concerned with images, do not seek to simply reconstruct the object or origin point of the abstraction (source text, or "real") in the physical or temporal circumstance of the creation of the image (people, places, things, times), because this reality is inconsequential, a matter of minutae, but look to reveal the sociopolitical origin of the abstraction, unveiling its ideological formulation. In essence, this is a shift from what an image or picture is "of" to the identity of the transformative process of imaging itself, an image of imaging, which distills some form of power that instrumentalizes the image and the symbolic order it is invariably an expression of, giving it a name, be it that of a capitalist, colonialist, racist, heterosexist, sexist, etc., episteme (each of these being an ideological tool that seeks to maintain the relations between dominant and subordinate forces). The structuralist critique becomes a competition of images, a matter of competing faiths. When confronted with a world of appearances, the irony is that the only tool left to combat the tyranny of images is yet more.

But this is somewhat beside the point, for to confuse a photograph (or any object, theoretical or otherwise) for an image is to subject the concrete world (the real relations between things) to another in a sequence of abstractions. Louis Althusser outlined this misstep in the common Marxian architectonic metaphors of "infrastructure" and "superstructure," for him a debilitating methodological problem because the terms are purely metaphorical, not the actual operations at work, and in "picturing" class conflict, the actual machinery of dominance and subordination they attempt to address is obscured. When photographs are treated as mere images, a parallel confusion occurs, for photographs are, after all, present in four space-time dimensions, not simply two (as images are), and are constructed of worldly material having definite size and shape. In other words, it is quite a leap to reduce a photograph to an immaterial imago/likeness. The term "image" is not an ontological umbrella under which a photograph can be classified, but a conceptual tool that functions in a particular way and ceases to function if applied in a circumstance in which it is asked to do something other than what it was designed for. To confuse this is to turn a relational idea into an ontological one. Perhaps this confusion of photographic theory for the analysis of images is why the discourse on photography shifted from a focus on its instrumentality to a concern that photography no longer truly exists. Of course, this shift occurs only after photography as a concept had been fully *imagined* (imaged). Subsumed in a digital or ideological dispersal at the whim of a multitude of discursive instrumentalizations, its supposed dissolution has become so utterly complete that whatever photography once was, it no longer is (if it "is" at all), becoming a "void" or the site of "death." It is comforting to propose that something is "behind" images in a metaphysical sense, even if this something is an absence (death, as Barthes and Kracauer, among others, have proposed).

The result, in practical terms, is that "art" photography has become dominated by anachronism, as though the solution to this paradox might be in reenacting the pictorial rhetoric of the late 1800s (consider the aesthetic parallels between the work of Timothy O'Sullivan, Carleton Watkins, Eugène Atget, Charles Marville, or the physiognomic typologies of Francis Galton and Alphonse Bertillon with contemporary photographic tropes). In sharp contrast to the most prominent tactics of nonphotographic aesthetic programs of the late eighties and nineties—approaches that showed renewed interest in bricolage, social networking, and rough-hewn or vernacular aesthetics—photography of the era seemed to codify around a diametrically opposed array of concerns. The photography of that moment favored the staid genre forms of the pre-modern Beaux Arts, exemplified in an almost obsessive adherence to Renaissance pictorial formulae. Making use of art's own reflexive theatrical death mask (the institution), architectural tropes—ubiquitous in both contemporary photography's presentational affect and its subject of choice—performed a tautological affirmation of the cold geometries of the white cube within monolithic proscenia, as if reassuring spectators of their ontological place in the museum's hallowed halls. The depopulated city scenes and emptied, serial structures of seventies art photography grew into Plexiglas monoliths, an odd hybrid of architecture's industrialized materiality and painting's scale. Photography not only adapted itself to the wall of the museum, but in adopting aluminium backframes and reflective Plexiglas encasements, became materially continuous with the architecture that surrounded it, both casting an image of its site of reception back at its surrounds through its slippery surfaces, and obsessively depicting Cartesian arrangements in pictorial tableaux. In short, photography *became* the wall of the institution *en abyme*. Its photographic alternative embraced the notion of the archive, a reiteration of organizational power, or as Buchloh put it with regard to Conceptual art, an "aesthetics of administration." It was as if, in the wake of the troubling recognition of photography's malleability in the hands of instrumental use and its critical reappraisal by artists and critics in the sixties and seventies, the contemporary production of photographs required turning back to a time before avant-gardist debates or postmodernist dismantling—back to something akin to the Pictorialism of salon painting and the hearth of the Natural History Museum. Such works become metaphors for the instrumentalization of the photograph; a negative parody of this foreclosure, in short, they are little more than an image of the photograph's base social condition in the art world, that evasive quality that Krauss termed "exhibitionality,"—a concept that again points to the nineteenth century, and the term exhibition itself. [28]

Until the Great Exhibition of 1851 popularized the term "exhibition," it had only specialized legal meaning, referring to a giving of evidence before a sovereign power: meaning literally to "hold out." But with the Great Exhibition and in the World's Fairs that followed, the implications of the term blossomed, and in no small part because of the peculiar architecture that contained it. Despite its epic glass and iron construction, Joseph Paxton's Crystal Palace, which housed the Great Exhibition, was not of the world of buildings and monuments. Instead it functioned as a massive frame, a container for vistas, a structure whose modular construction allowed endless substitution, a proposal that was alien to the public affirmation of cultural stability that architecture had come to represent. At every turn, its interchangeable serial components shone with a "fairy like brilliance," [29] as if dropped from the heavens; its grand halls described as a chimerical container for "a perspective so extended" that it appeared to be "a section of atmosphere cut from the sky." [30] Architecture and vision became a singularity rendered in iron, as though Alberti's diagram of Renaissance perspective had been made concrete, a massive structure whose chief function was invisibility.

If the Crystal Palace was the first building that fully capitalized on the theatrical spectacle of exhibition, the readymade was the first art object to be solely constituted by theatrical distance. Here the ritual act of viewing became the artwork's material, and the object itself a hollow shell, a decoy. Thierry de Duve put it succinctly when he wrote that, in the wake of the readymade the only truth to which the art object could attest was the power of its own name, rendering palpable the "pact that would unite the spectators of the future around some object . . . that added nothing to the constructed environment and did not improve on it but, quite the contrary, pulled away from it, bearing no other function than that of pure signifier." [31] It seems no coincidence that, just as Duchamp brought the foundational theatricality of art objects to the fore, the "zero point" of painterly materialism would surface thousands of miles away as a theatrical backdrop. In 1913, Kazimir Malevich was asked to contribute costumes and set designs for the Cubo-Futurist play *Victory over the Sun*. Aside from his almost unwearable costumes, Malevich produced a series of concept drawings for the sets, which, in stark black and white, appear like preparatory sketches for the Suprematist canvases he would begin producing two years later. When asked about his tautologically titled *Black Square* (1915), and its placement at forty-five degrees in the top corner of the room of the 1915 exhibition *0.10*, Malevich referred back to these early set designs as its origin. The monochrome was thus situated as both the material negation of the painterly image (an object that operated by pictorial resemblance), and the symbolic negation of the very thing that made vision possible.

While *Black Square* (1915) is often credited with being the first monochrome, this is not actually the case (not that being first matters). Some thirty years earlier this totem of total materialist refusal was realized by the poet Paul Bilhaud, in an exhibition staged in the apartment of writer Jules Lévy in October of 1882. Such modernist notables as Edouard Manet, Pierre Auguste Renoir, Camille Pissarro, and Richard Wagner were given a peek at what would be framed as their legacy. For the exhibition, Bilhaud contributed a small black painting titled *Combat de nègres dans une cave pendant la nuit* (*Negroes Fighting in a Cellar at Night*), a joke that was stolen not once but twice, first by Alphonse Allais who produced a book titled *Album Primo-Avrilesque* (1897), which expanded the series to a range of color swatches (and contained no mention of Bilhaud, despite their acquaintance), and later by Malevich, who in the same year as *Black Square* produced the painting *Red Square,* which included a particularly Bilhaudian parenthetical addendum in its title (*Painterly Realism of a Peasant Woman in Two Dimensions*). The impossibility of direct depiction was here matched by the invisibility of the site of labor and the marginalized, both relegated to infrastructural obscurity. Daily life's representability was as scathingly parodied as it was by Duchamp with his innovation of the readymade, the quotidian again displayed in absentia, as the object of representation that has been doubly negated (first supplanted by the image, and then displaced as a negated picture). Such mistrust of images has become a staple of modern life (and that is not to say that images aren't an ancient bugbear, golden calves and the like operating as the exemplar of societies on their downward spiral), although photography, not painting, has been the primary recipient of this ritual derision for the past half-century. Stoic deconstructive critique and hedonistic celebrations of nihilism often result in identical outcomes; only the captions change. One is prompted to wonder how many times we can restage this anxious war between materiality and the image in the hopes that the outcome might change.

But what of Malevich's zero point of painting, and its proposed transcendence? As post-revolutionary Russia progressed into Stalinism, Malevich returned to his pre-Suprematist foundations, producing canvases that aped his antecedents—first Cubo-Futurism, and then, at its most extreme, Impressionism. Stranger still, Malevich backdated these works, so that his Suprematist works remained the forgone conclusion of these styles, turning his own progression into a parabola, doubling back on itself. Since he held to the conviction that he had come closest to the endpoint of painting—the height of purism in form—in his late thirties, there was nowhere to go but backward. [32]

* * But perhaps this is a promising turn for photography as an artistic practice. As photographs are increasingly produced with an internalized awareness of the circumstances of their display, specifically within the

rhetoric of architecture and its pastiche of art historical tropes that reiterate the circumstance of the museum, they become accountable to the social and political realities that their treatment as freefloating images held at bay. It is the particularities of the object that govern the specific implications of works of art, a comprehension that is suspended when the question becomes that of imaging. With the image, the question is always of distance, the distance we are placed at in relation to what is represented, the absence of the origin of its likeness, while the material of the image, how it comes to present itself, its "exhibitionality," is commensurately excused. For the task at hand is to reinsert and repoliticize the photographic discourse if we are to recover it, and in so doing, it is necessary to abandon the foreclosed models of dominance and subordination offered by the allegorist, which deadend in the melancholia of symmetrical totalizing metaphors for political opposition. The fatal flaw of this schematic is that the location of, to use Buchloh's phrasing again, the "real upon which critical opposition could be inscribed" is situated at the level of depiction, a turn from the politics of representation to the absurdity that politics *is* representation. In short, the proposition of a photograph as image, operating solely at the level of depiction, is part and parcel of the obfuscation of the political, or, in Althusserian terms, "the real conditions of existence."

* * This error is underscored by the image being synonymous with ideology, with abstraction, which functions as representation. In the Althusserian formulation "it is not the real conditions of existence, their real world, that 'men' represent to themselves in ideology, but above all it is their relation to those conditions of existence which is represented to them there. It is this relation which is at the centre of every ideological, i.e. imaginary, representation of the real world." [33] This on its own

is commensurate with the structuralist formulations of the image's relation to the "real" thus far outlined, but in Althusser's rejection of metaphor in his theorization of the political sphere lies the insight that this imaginary not only has a material existence, but beyond this, that it *is* its material existence. In other words, "ideology always exists in an apparatus, and its practice or practices. This existence is material." [34] The importance of the Althusserian construction is that it moves past the struggle of ideologies, of just versus unjust ideologies (and in parallel, ethical versus unethical depictions, or true and untrue images), but locates the site of struggle in the micro-circumstance of individual actions, to use Althusser's more precise language, in the "material actions, inserted into material practices governed by material rituals which are themselves defined by the material ideological apparatuses from which derive the ideas of that subject." [35] This also posits that opposition, like the ideology it works against, is not located at the level of competing depictions, but at the level of actions, habits, i.e. daily life, where the meaning of depiction is given form.

Within this formulation, a photograph can be understood as an object, but more importantly, the production of images can be understood as containing a democratic possibility, representing a daily ritual of compromise enacted with various levels of awareness, but present nonetheless as a lingering force. No longer a spectral entity, we find we are both inside and outside of the picture, one of its parts and one of its producers; a stratified hierarchy is not needed in our relationship to aesthetics. Through considering the material specificity of photographs, it is possible to bring the images that alienate down to earth, give them bodily form. The truth of the matter is that all images require a material existence, and we must resist the urge to transform the material world into an image world. This is not an either/or choice, but a realization that images are indistinguishable from their material supports; one cannot exist without the other. The embedded compromises and negotiations present in any production and their subsequent lack of instrumental solidity, need not be seen as dirty secrets. This would not be an absolutist proclamation of the loss of the "real" that images represent for vulgar materialists, but rather an assertion that the production of meaning is a communal one, located in the public sphere, in commonplace contexts. In this realization, a middle ground of negotiation appears. All production—even that of monolithic power—is comprised of myriad transit points and competing forces that deceptively assume the appearance of solidity, but are in fact, porous.

The endless circulation of purisms in a culture of copies, in which political life is framed as a struggle of images, always seem to lead to the same place—back into the blank, which leaves the sites of production, specifically that of communal production, camouflaged in plain view, like Paul Bilhaud's preemptive joke on monochrome painting's radicality. In the debris of such battles (and their ritualized reenactment), one is prompted to ask where the ground of the real that these struggles are supposedly in the service of actually lies. In the wake of these double negations, individual producers are relegated to one more modular element, the social field appearing as a static constellation of interchangeable parts. The citizen subject is realized as a relational component, a unit of measure, an abstraction. Where labor's vulgar bodily exertions are required, it exists out of view, in off-hours, backrooms, cellars, and distant factories, or under mute layers of paint, negotiated in private communications and invisible transports, sanitized by aggregation, and illegible in seductive surfaces. The question most urgent for photography is no longer what inherent meaning it may contain (whether it be the interminable presence of the aesthetic formalists, or the essentialized condition of contingency and ideological instrumentalization of the social critics) but how specific photographs construct and organize social space in a concrete and immediate way.

The world we see from transitional spaces—the world outside the window, the world from the perspective of escalators, people movers, monorails, and shopping centers—has become an intellectual bogeyman, a storage container for all our alienations. These infrastructural, interstitial zones stand as compromised, indeterminate way stations between chimerical destinations. Seemingly monolithic expressions of power, such as images, are similar accumulations of compromise and negotiation, that in truth have material solidity, and with which interaction is a two-way street. In their margins there are gaps where any visitor may assert her or his own agenda. The answer seems less to reorganize a seemingly chaotic field in abstract terms, or to reenact nihilistic self-effacement by depicting a methodological rupture ad infinitum, than to allow a discourse's "crisis" to open up what were seemingly foreclosed possibilities. The repeated confrontation with the absence at the core of the photographic image is simply evidence that the language games enacted around the photograph have ceased being useful. It is the questions that are wrong, the supposed absence they deliver merely an invitation to formulate different methodological approaches. These momentary openings—the pockets between, their ruins, their transitory spaces, their ignored seams and forgotten vistas—promise a site from which the either/or of utopian and apocalyptic thinking or the political/formalist opposition can be dismantled, and production can be understood as a common process, enacted in every moment of daily life, even at the level of viewership.

* * Editor's Note: Although clarifications were made throughout the text at the editor's prompting, the two paragraphs marked by two asterisks were added by the author after the original essay and discussion forum appeared online.

Notes

1. George Baker, "Photography's Expanded Field," *October*, vol. 114 (Fall 2005), p. 122.
2. This condition is further complicated by a commonplace confusion of the discrete tangibility of the object of inquiry for the amorphous constellation of discourses that surround it (i.e. the rhetorical transformation of the photograph into an analogy for "Photography").
3. For example: the recurring theme that what is missing from a photograph constitutes what it is truly about—an approach most notoriously deployed by Walter Benjamin, in his "Short (Small) History of Photography," when he wrote that the work of Atget derived its meaning from its appearing like a "recently evacuated scene of a crime."
4. Baker, p. 138.
5. For example, on page 127, Baker writes/quotes, "'That is,' to really paraphrase Krauss, 'the [*not-narrative*] is, according to the logic of a certain kind of expansion, just another way of expressing the term [*stasis*], and the [*not-stasis*] is, simply, [*narrative*].'" Baker's insertions are represented within the text as brackets, or "breaches" in the continuity of Krauss's voice through which Baker's formulations bubble up.
6. "At any rate, when I first sketched my graph for the artist with which I began, Nancy Davenport, she quickly grabbed my pen and paper and began to swirl lines in every direction, circling around my oppositions and squares, with a look that seemed to say, 'What about these possibilities?' *My graph was a mess*. But the photographer's lines, though revolving around the field, had no center, and they extended in every direction." Ibid., p. 140. Emphasis added.
7. Rosalind Krauss, "Sculpture in the Expanded Field," *October*, vol. 8 (Spring 1979), p. 30.
8. Ibid., p. 33.
9. Baker, p. 128.
10. Walter Benjamin, *The Origin of German Tragic Drama*, trans. John Osborne (London and New York: Verso, 1998), p. 185.
11. Ibid., p. 166.
12. Not to put too fine a point on it, but the radicality of Krauss's text was that the diagram it was centered on was constructed analogously to the work she described.
13. Neither Owens nor Buchloh mentions the other's work despite various similarities in reference and argumentation, and the assumed awareness the two authors had of each other's work. This is especially noteworthy since both were students of Krauss at CUNY, and were directly involved with the journal *October* from early on.
14. Benjamin H. D. Buchloh, "Allegorical Procedures: Appropriation and Montage in Contemporary Art," *Artforum* (September 1982), p. 56.
15. *Pictures* is the title of an exhibition curated by Douglas Crimp that opened at, Artists Space, New York, in September 1977, including works by Troy Brauntuch, Jack Goldstein, Sherrie Levine, Robert Longo, and Philip Smith. An essay of the same title published by Crimp in *October*, vol. 8 (Spring 1979, pp. 75–88) was an

expansion of Crimp's essay that accompanied the exhibition.
16. Craig Owens, "The Allegorical Impulse: Toward a Theory of Postmodernism (Part 2)," *October* vol. 13 (Summer 1980), p. 71.
17. Ibid. p. 79.
18. Buchloh, *Neo-Avantgarde and Culture Industry: Essays on European and American Art from 1955 to 1975* (New York and Cambridge: October Books, 2001), p. xxi. Emphasis added.
19. Luc Boltanski and Eve Chiapello, *The New Spirit of Capitalism,* trans. Gregory Elliot (New York and London: Verso, 2006), p. 466.
20. Douglas Crimp, "Pictures," *October*, vol. 8 (Spring 1979), p. 85. Emphasis added.
21. Owens, "Photography *en abyme*," *October*, vol. 5 (Summer 1978), p. 78.
22. Ibid., p. 88.
23. Roland Barthes, *Camera Lucida*, trans. Richard Howard (Hill and Wang: New York, 1981), pp. 31–32.
24. Siegfried Kracauer, "Photography," in *The Mass Ornament: Weimar Essays,* ed./trans. Thomas Y. Levin (Cambridge and London: Harvard University Press, 1995), p. 59.
25. Oliver Wendell Holmes, "The Stereoscope and Stereograph," in *Classic Essays on Photography,* ed. Alan Trachtenberg, (New Haven: Leete's Island, 1980), p. 80.
26. Vilém Flusser, *Towards a Philosophy of Photography* (London: Reaktion Books, 2000), p. 20.
27. Cited in Baker, p. 124.
28. Rosalind Krauss, "Photography's Discursive Spaces," in *The Originality of the Avant-Garde and Other Modernist Myths* (Cambridge and London: MIT Press, 1985), pp. 131–50.
29. Patrick Beaver, *The Crystal Palace, 1851–1936: A Portrait of Victorian Enterprise* (London: Hugh Evelyn, 1970), p. 34.
30. Ibid. p. 239.
31. Thierry de Duve, *Pictorial Nominalism: On Marcel Duchamp's Passage from Painting to the Readymade* (Minneapolis: University of Minnesota Press, 2005)
32. The preceding three paragraphs were first addressed in my essays, "Absolu Avec Vache (and the Spectre of the Gun)," in *Material Presence* (London: Project Space 176, September 2008); "On American Ingenuity (and the problem of the readymade)," *Afterall*, no. 17 (Spring 2008), pp. 21–24; "Air Made Solid," *Dot Dot Dot*, issue 15 (Spring 2008); and "A White Cow in a Snow Storm," in *Bunch Alliance and Dissolve* (Cincinnati Museum of Contemporary Art/Public Holiday Projects, 2006), pp. 208–219.
33. Louis Althusser, "Ideology and Ideological State Apparatuses (Notes towards an Investigation)," in *Mapping Ideology*, ed. Slavoj Źiźek (New York: Verso Books, 1998) p. 124.
34. Ibid. p. 126.
35. Ibid. p. 127.

--

DISCUSSION FORUM
WWW.WORDSWITHOUTPICTURES.ORG

--

Subject: At Home In Exile, In The World: Photography's Native Ambiguity
Date: 17 October 2008 17:02:30
From: GIL BLANK

There is a great deal to admire in Walead's work and writing, not least of which is his demonstration that the opposition of abstraction and representation is quickly revealed by photography's native function to be a false dichotomy. More energizing still—and I am speaking now personally—is his conviction that post-structuralist criticism can be a generative force, despite its historical position to the contrary as inimical to the proposition that photography retains a potential to model individual experience within culture. This alone sets him apart from many of his contemporaries who exploit cameraless abstraction to nihilistic or cynical effect.

It certainly requires feats of remarkable dexterity to square those antagonistic poles, and to contemplate just how a photographic practice is ever to come to terms with a formulation that posits the a priori illegitimacy of representation in general. Notice then, in replay, how he pulls it off: after categorically dismissing all photographic pictures as equivalent abstractions (never mind for the moment that this is a Structuralist reading), he then qualifies his own practice as something else, as somehow beyond such abstractions, as "concrete." Regrettably, this attempt at a day-is-night, up-is-down lexical inversion, whereby photographs are condemned *en masse* as irredeemably abstract, while his photograms and indexical sculptures achieve a kind of super-representational exceptionalism, is cognitive dissonance at best and doublespeak at worst.

Beautiful as it first appears, logic tortured to such an extreme nullifies itself immediately. To wit: if all pictures are effectively abstract, then the distinction itself is meaningless, and it must further be allowed that all pictures are effectively representational (a point Walead himself is advocating as the argument behind his "concrete"/abstract photograms). Yet if all pictures are indeed effective representations—a proposition that runs afoul of both the last forty years of critical dialogue and the central axis of Walead's program—then it follows that there can be no point to his own critique or his images in the first place.

More importantly, such blanket dismissals discount the capacity of photography's viewership to understand these complications implicitly and to benefit from them as a result, an underestimation that would seem to disavow the type of forum in which we're engaged at the moment. Clearly no argument can be sustained that denies the event of its proposal, so I take Walead's participation here to indicate that it is precisely those ambiguities intrinsic to the pictorial model—quite rightly including even those which historically have suggested their own abstraction—that are not the frustration, but indeed the source, of photography's meaning.

The ablest of photography's makers and analysts, regardless of historical period or agenda, have always had an instinctual understanding of this multivalence: namely, that the ambiguities inherent to so uncanny a representation are photography's ongoing replenishment. Tensions such as those between abstraction and representation exist along a continually sliding scale, one that creates within each such image a hermetic admixture, the alien power of which is precisely its singular value. Again, the uniqueness of that conflicted representation is itself the photograph's meaning, *superlative even to the photograph's content*, by virtue of its ability to model (rather than merely document, or even index) the contradiction we know experience to be. So-called "concrete photography," in its attempt to literalize content at the cost of ignoring the picture's most basic capability for paradox, prioritizes metaphor over model, denying exactly the kind of potentiality that it proclaims in (but relegates to) theory.

It bears mentioning that the final eclipse of revolutionary abstraction was not accomplished by Stalin's terror, but in the admission that its idealization regressed to an autonomous form that could never be justified—indeed, in Aleksandr Rodchenko's own later words, *must* never be justified. [1] The crux of the argument at hand then is that when grafted onto the inherently representational character of photographic practice, the passion of a consummated *faktura* comes to grief with the awareness that it can be manifest in only the most remotely metaphoric terms. Photograms surrender the world in favor of the darkroom. Similarly, the design and display of glass boxes intended to be shattered during shipment to their own museum exhibition, however conscientiously orchestrated as a reflexive system, is an enunciation of social conditions rendered symbolically at most. The irony of that divorce—as Walead rightly cites Buchloh for first proposing—is to confirm precisely, by the terms of its surrender, the totality of the "dehumanizing spectacle" it purports to critique. Remember that Malevich's summer landscapes and Rodchenko's circus performers were only the last in a long series of retreats from that woebegone Front, now long since deserted. [2]

So let us be clear: the principle danger here remains the conservative attempt at a restoration, albeit one misleadingly dressed in the mythological doxa of an avant-garde long since foreclosed. Malevich, condemned like Rodchenko to a spiritual house arrest as much the making of his own suffocating logic as the rapidly declining conditions of a totalitarian dictatorship, is not an example to envy.

If ultimately there is anything to be learned from simulacra, it is that we can never in fact separate ourselves from the world or the real. [3]

More to the point, I do not think any ethically conscious individual can genuinely desire to do so. Abstraction, whether aesthetic, mnemonic, or epistemological, is never so complete that it obviates even the least attempt at a transparent reckoning of history, nor so corrupt that its shortcoming does not in itself offer some model for understanding the human contingency of that same history. Cast perpetually adrift, we bear the responsibility of engaging the absurd aspect of our exile as such, lest the allure of rhetoric alone form the first walls of our confinement.

Notes

(1) "Art is serving the people, but the people are being led goodness knows where. I want to lead the people to art, not use art to lead them somewhere else . . . Art must be separate from politics." Aleksandr Rodchenko. *Aleksandr Rodchenko: Revolution in Photography* (Moscow House of Photography, 2008).

(2) The Left Front of the Arts (Levyi Front Iskusstv or LEF) was an early avant-garde group founded in 1923 by Rodchenko along with Vladimir Mayakovsky. One principal tenet of LEF was to define the revolutionary potential of so-called "concretist" artistic practices as equivalent to concrete social actions. Despite its avowed mission to "re-examine the ideology and practices of so-called leftist art, and to abandon individualism to increase art's value for developing communism," LEF's advocacy of formalist abstraction was the exact cause of its condemnation by rival factions of the Soviet vanguard, principle among which, it can be noted with some irony, was the original October group.

(3) "[T]here is still one link that binds an image to its referent within the apparently empty barrage of photographic imagery and the universal production of sign exchange value: the trauma from which the compulsion to repress originated." It is precisely at that tipping point that the acculturated image as such paradoxically "yields its own secret," as being "a perpetual pendulum between

the death of reality in the photograph and the reality of death in the mnemonic image." Benjamin H. D. Buchloh, "Gerhard Richter's Atlas: The Anomic Archive," *Photography and Painting in the Work of Gerhard Richter: Four Essays on Atlas* (Barcelona: Llibres de Recerca, 1999).

--

Subject: Response to Abstracting Photography
Date: 17 October 2008 19:18:08
From: MILES COOLIDGE

Hi Walead!

Just read your essay. I must admit I come away from it feeling very conflicted about my own relationship to the loose body of knowledge—"photo theory"—that comprises your subject. In one moment I imagine I have a vital relationship with the critical positions you discuss. A moment later they seem relatively inconsequential, as the sweep of events in the world ultimately has the last word. I'm simultaneously aware that the mistake of making a fetish of theory is just as egregious as the self-defeating insistence of its irrelevance. So I'll try to strike a balance between these tendencies.

In Roman Polanski's *Rosemary's Baby*, Mia Farrow's character attempts to engage her doctor in a medical dialogue concerning her pregnancy, an effort dismissed by him with the condescending admonition "You've been reading books!" Artists who announce a professional interest in art history or critical theory are similarly inviting disdain from these quarters. Thus it is no surprise that the default position for the artist on this question is as follows: we make, you interpret. But keep in mind that Polanski's portrayal of the doctor is a scathing caricature. I applaud your willingness to ignore the prevailing injunction to separate the labor of producing from the work of commentary.

So far, these observations may be nothing more

than a simple gloss on your nuanced account of the problems facing the literate, informed producer of photographs. I identify with your assertion that photography "persists past its supposed theoretical and practical disintegration." Painting continually copes as well with its own spectral persistence. However, I think we can both agree on an important distinction between these two cases. The machinations of avant-garde aesthetics reduced paintings to the status of objects, allowing them to be identified directly (by way of the readymade) with products manufactured for the consumer economy. To put it crudely, the postmodern criticism of MoMA's objectification of the photograph proceeded along similar lines. However, photographs' dual status as objects and as images offered a paradoxical possibility of resistance to this program, which you appropriately identify with Crimp's coinage of "the Pictures Generation" of photographic artists. The representational burden conventionally associated with photographs allowed the medium a tenuous existential foothold in the midst of a thoroughgoing effort to purge art production of taints of identification with the interests of capital. But the question of how photography acquired its representational role is important. Photography over its history has been constituted equally as much (or more) by its association with its vernacular manifestations as with the hegemonic institutions that shape its discourse. Its popularity within the spheres of private use and industrial production (broadly speaking) has inoculated photography against the hyperbolic purism responsible for painting's death sentence.

As to the question of complicity and the difficulty of finding a vantage point unassociated with the market and the institutions charged with its maintenance, I am reminded that the critical environment you take as your subject is itself a construct of certain historical exigencies that have concrete relationships to time and place. The debates concerning the status of the art object in the seventies and early eighties are symptomatic of the soul-searching of the American new left in the wake of its successes and failures of the late sixties. In foreclosing the promise of direct revolutionary action, progressive impulses were channeled into allegory, gradualist modalities of "changing the system from within," or going underground (to appear later in the form of alienated cranks or as legitimately dangerous "non-state actors" apparently without constituency). That these tendencies would find expression in art production and criticism of the period should be expected.

In such a historical context, the skirmish over MoMA's role in the formation of photographic discourse actually assumes a greater importance than it may first appear. Serge Guilbaut's groundbreaking cold war scholarship tracing New York's post-WWII institutionalization of the European avant-garde has only been validated by subsequent research. While the CIA's active patronage of the non-Communist left was well known amongst intellectuals in post-war Europe, it nevertheless had a paralyzing effect. For various reasons, the political actors responsible for this state of affairs were much more successful at obscuring their role in the institutionalization of the avant-garde in the U.S., which created an artificial atmosphere of innocence that abetted the continuation of its project (as Abstract Expressionism and the neo-avant-garde, for instance). The late seventies/early eighties deconstruction of MoMA's role in the formation of modernist photographic discourse was an early effort in a process that ultimately revealed a state of affairs that had already been assumed to be the case in most foreign intellectual circles.

The situation of extreme concentration of capital, political power and culture in postwar New York that undergirds the phenomena you discuss renders your subject at once parochial and urgent. The despairing tautologies of art critically aware of conditions from which it cannot conceive of escaping that characterized much work of the early eighties in New York have become naturalized and familiar. This condition is not surprising, as it is emblematic of a generalized state of paralysis with respect to the possibility of meaningful social change. In this interval, yes, the freshness of the debate over photography's discursive status has faded. And yes, the subsequent destabilization of its material character encouraged by the rise of digital photographic technologies has also contributed to a sense of photography's decline in cultural relevance. But we should expect that, as a technology among technologies, photography is susceptible to the forces that dictate continual revolution of the means of production. Thus it is only from a willfully narrow perspective that photography's death can be imagined from a technological standpoint. On commercial and vernacular levels, it has never been more alive. Perhaps the concern is that Flusser's gloomy speculation that photographers can only circulate redundant images under current conditions is becoming increasingly true, and that "going digital" only reinforces this tendency.

So what of photography's status as specialized artistic discourse? Is photography's relevance more at risk, compared with that of other media? I would argue that photography's advantages as a communicative tool are more associated with its automaticity than with its material bases. Photographs continue to be fundamentally unstable products of encounters between contingency and will. I keep looking for opportunities to leverage the semantic surplus the medium continues to offer as its primary strength. Photography's special appeal is that it is always in a state of discursive crisis. The "momentary openings—the pockets between, their ruins, their transitory spaces, their ignored seams and forgotten vistas" of your final sentence are not identifications of marginal territories we are relegated to explore in the shadow of the totalizing culture industry, but rather constitute a persistent promise fundamental to the medium from its inception.

Talk soon,
Miles

--

Subject: If you still need to keep your lens attached, don't go focusing it, and certainly don't go around pointing it at something "interesting."
Date: 19 October 2008 19:19:03
From: KARL HAENDEL

Photography can be a real pain in the ass. I mean, it's complicated; it's so technical. You've got to check the exposure, the lighting, the framing, and that's before taking care of the biggest nuisance, the focusing. (I'm talking about real photography here, not iPhone stuff.) Digital might seem to solve some of this, but really it just masks these operations, as the work still needs to get done. And if you really care, you are using a view camera, and then you have even more to worry about: shift, tilt, swing, plane of focus, and, oh shit, bellows extension! And then, of course, there is this ongoing issue of "representation." Who or what is pictured, and just how are they pictured? Could that brief bit of sexual titillation I feel when I see some leg in a glossy magazine say something about how I relate to chicks, or even think about my mom? Could those war-ravaged shirtless Africans on the cover of my (home-delivered) *New York Times* reflect somehow on the way I live my life and how I have arrived here? But even worse, do I want a photography that explains this to me, thus depriving me of such meager furtive pleasures? These are just a few of my many complaints, most of which of course are not art-related, but if I can find a way to alleviate even a couple of them, I'm down.

Although I make drawings, I think its fair to say that not only am I a fan of photography and slightly versed in its historical trajectory and its current practitioners (I will only hang photographs in my house, never paintings or drawings, really, I can't stand them) but also that images, specifically flat, non-moving images—usually called photographs—are fundamental to my work. Put simply, I love photography. Beshty's argument, while not entirely over my head, deals with a theoretical language that I left behind when I finished the Whitney Program, so I can't tackle it head on (sorry Walead), but there are three recent trends in photography that his essay got me thinking about. They are of special interest to me because I can see in them some parallel moves that I've made in my own work, and to be honest, I might have ripped a few of them off along the way. These three camps I'm going to call, for want of better terms, the pictorialists, the autobiographical appropriationists, and the abstractionists.

The pictorialists probably have the longest history to pave their way forward, because it's not their history at all, but the history of romantic and realist painting, really Renaissance vision itself, that they build on. We are talking about so many photographers of the past, but more recently, the 1970s Americans with large format cameras, cars, and color film (Stephen Shore, Joel Sternfeld); the Germans who followed them (Andreas Gursky, Thomas Struth) and who, although a past generation by now, still hold much of the limelight; and then some of the genre's newest adherents, photographers with whom I am familiar and would like to touch on, such as Florian Maier-Aichen and Amir Zaki. These photographers, who learned their craft in a Photoshop age, seem to embrace the digital in not so much a subversive manner, although it could seem that way, but as just one more tool to make the pictures they love. It is this love that I want to speak to, because I can't figure out why they would otherwise use such an antiquated pictorial mode unless they are in love with the epic grandeur and corporeal seduction of the form. Yes, it's pictorial—fully—and the pleasure we receive from these works, since most of us don't know any better, is probably guilt free. I for one like being blown away, and if these pseudo-Germans use the same tricks as much older Germans (Caspar David Friedrich, for example), it's fine by me. In fact, I've been known to make a really big, pretty picture myself.

Maier-Aichen's vistas of the California coast, and his tweaking of them with a computer, seem to me akin to the old car enthusiast tinkering with his vintage engine in the garage; it speaks to his commitment, conviction, and passion. It comes through in the pictures, and I can respect and even admire that.

The autobiographical appropriationists (Anne Collier, Roe Ethridge, Elad Lassry, and to some extent Collier Schorr) offer us a pleasing mix between wonky '70s conceptual practices (Vito Acconci, Dennis Oppenheim) and '80s appropriation (Richard Prince, Barbara Kruger). It seems that they recognize the cold, empty feeling we get from the Pictures Generation, yet have taken to heart its lessons. Similarly, they understand an important lesson of the Conceptualists: the reportage function of the photograph can be used to one's advantage by simply setting something up in front of the lens to record or attest to the fact that "I did this." They twist it up a bit though, by instead proclaiming, "I love this," be it an old postcard or an album cover. Like the pictorialists, their practice is also one of the enthusiast, but this time in the guise of the collector, or to use a more trendy term, the archivist. The things, or views, or types of image often come from shared culture, if not always from the mainstream variety. Because they are re-photographing and representing (sometimes this takes the form of a straight appropriation, other times the image just apes a trope, say a certain kind of "intimate" portrait), the "I love this" moment usually comes with the caveat "even though I should know better," which makes their debt to Prince, Cindy Sherman, and the like clear. But in their attempt to humanize and bring warmth to appropriation, their work is overly coded, private, and something of an in-joke that for the most part I am not in on. I've always been wary of work that needs a guest list to access because I feel bad for the people on line outside. Even though in my work I have an inclination towards personal appropriation, I've always made an attempt to keep my references open and recognizable enough so that you need not have taken a seminar in the French New Wave to know what I'm talking about. People have called me a populist, as if it's a nasty word, and I guess I am. I don't think that's such a bad thing.

Lastly we come to the abstractionists, or materialists, or as I would like to call them, the Disinterested Photographers. Again, they too have their lineage, starting with the non-objective and photogram work of the 1920s (Man Ray, László Moholy-Nagy), some offshoots of the New York School in the 1950s (Aaron Siskind, Harry Callahan), and then in the 1980s (Adam Fuss, and most importantly, James Welling). Its best current practitioners include Beshty, Eileen Quinlan and Liz Deschenes, and a few others, such as Anthony Pearson and Shane Huffman, whose staying power I'm not so sure about. Their work is literal, dumb, non-pictorial, and often non-referential; in short it is straightforward and maybe even honest, at least with Beshty and Quinlan. (I can't help but fall for Quinlan's ongoing series called *Smoke & Mirrors*.) And what I see evident in this new breed of abstract work is more than just a reappraisal of the relationship between the image and the real, for as Beshty rightly points out, as did Craig Owens, this type of deconstructive art often leaves us with a feeling of vacancy. Simply, it leaves us nothing to sink our teeth into, nothing to come away with but a question that we came there with to start. Not a positive feeling, or as my therapist would say, "not a good place to be." Oddly, though, out of a different kind of "nothing" these abstractionists seem to be on the path to "something."

This new abstract work is attempting, in its subtle way, what amounts to an assault on the practically monolithic association between the image and its material form, what Beshty calls "a triumph of images over the material," so that maybe photography can finally get somewhere without images. What we are talking about is a materialist photography that uses as its tools the very thing that makes the image/object relationship possible—light-sensitive surfaces, paper, chemicals, dyes, etc.—and it is to this often repressed aspect of photography (it is often taken care of in "dark rooms") that these photographers give much of their attention. An embrace of the materialist cause also means that all the hard, metal gear associated with photography (and I am talking to you, middle-aged man-character, the shutterbug), such as lenses, proper lighting setups, meters, and all that stuff, can be jettisoned. (Sorry B&H, my Jew brothers, but you have profited enough.) This also means that the actions involving such gear must be reexamined and perhaps left behind (and I am fully aware that the sexual pleasure of toying with one's lens will be missed). I am talking about focusing, adjusting the aperture or shutter, and all the endless puttering around that enables the image to be "faithfully" recorded. It is the lens, that which so closely approximates the physiognomy of the human eye, which has made photography indistinguishable from images for many people. But get rid of the lens, and all that is "in front" of it, and you get rid of the image.

So basically, if you still need to keep your lens attached, don't go focusing it, and certainly don't go around pointing it at something "interesting." Without the lens, you just have light-sensitive surfaces, the actual material of photographs, without images. I like to call this new group of photographers "disinterested" because they seem more eager to be not just camera-less (rayographs were camera-less, yet with those silhouettes the "thingness" of the things still remained), but almost to be unselective, in not giving us "some thing" to look at. That which historically and culturally has been the subject of the camera's gaze is off to the side, not so much resisted as disregarded, played out. It's almost as if they are a bit rudderless, random, letting chance and accident take over—but not all the way—for theirs is not an art of resignation. It's anti-compositional and anti-hierarchical, perhaps even democratic, letting that which is uninteresting or inconsequential a chance to finally have its picture taken. It's more fair, a redistribution of camera time, if you will. I like that.

An interesting question that I am not capable of exploring in this short response (nor do I have the interest or critical tools at hand to do so) is why at certain periods of overheated artistic propagation (the historical avant-garde [Moholy-Nagy], the New York School [Siskind], the 1980s [Welling], and the very recent past, a period which has yet to be named but which I am pretty sure has just ended) there has been a renewed interest in materialist photography. That is not to say that this type of work dominated their eras, but they seem to appear during periods of abundance (abundant money, abundant artistic product), which makes me think there might be an unconscious kind of Marxism at work in these pictures of nothing. Actually, I have to believe it's not unconscious, and it's definitely there.

Postscript:
Now that our global economy has collapsed, the progress of Disinterested Photography might have to be put on hiatus until prosperous times return and vulgar materialism warrants a finger pointing. Sure, Disinterested Photography, in its stubborn insistence on the material and material only, seems to be, at least in part, a political project. But the thing with images, no matter how wrong by their very nature they always are, they happen to be very good at being wrong in a political manner. What I'm thinking is that maybe some new WPA project is in order. I've always liked those dust-bowl, starving redneck, fruit-picking, breadline-standing pictures. Of course, now the poor are fat and the Midwest is not so much dusty as rusty, but I still think it's a great idea. Top notch idea in fact. First these Disinterested Photographers need to get their cameras out of pawn or the closet. Then I say we put Quinlan and Beshty and the rest of them in a car and send them out into America and see what they come back with.

For I fear it might already be time for something new. Again.

--

Subject: Taking Pictures on Shaky Ground
Date: 20 October 2008 16:05:03
From: ZOE CROSHER

In a most fascinating set of historical and quotational twists and turns, from Barthes to Malevich, Beshty lays out a meandering path that culminates and resonates most profoundly, for me, in the last paragraph—a hope for photographic practice that is to be found in embracing an in-between space, what German urban planner and theorist Thomas Sieverts has termed "zwischenstadt," meaning between the urban and the country. Although I will engage with this notion more later on, it is important to first mine Beshty's thoughtful reckoning with various art histories, laying bare a surprising assumption of a grand, theorized master narrative at work in the heart of historical image production. It seems a reflection that leaves us at a loss, singing to institutional choirs and fighting discursive windmills, finding ourselves staring down the nihilistic failure of the "this has been" of photography itself.

Beshty is clearly questioning the weight of a heavy-handed history of image-making that has informed and molded him and his practice, as it has most of ours who have gone through the professionalizing process of the medium in our various art school careers. However, throughout his essay one reads a progressive building up of the assumed monumentality of theorized discourse as the dictation of practice as opposed to the supporter of an image-making practice. This assumption that there ever was (or is) a dictating authority seems an engaging point to start talking about the chicken and the egg scenario in this schism between theory and practice, a schism that weighs down many contemporary artists I know.

Perhaps the hardest thing to acknowledge is

that such monumentality and authority as has dictated art/image historical presumptions is no longer valid, and that whatever agency there is in the production of photographs must now be claimed at a time more uncertain, theoretically or otherwise, than at any point in our art historical past. Taking pictures on shaky ground is far more difficult than answering the call of scientific, political or theoretical "truths." I am not saying that elements of these motivations don't feed into why we do what we do, but there no longer seems to be such singularity of purpose. Such disappointed relationships and nostalgic nods to a more utopian past have already been explored by the likes of Sam Durant in his early work and described at length in Beshty's article. Finding ourselves embedded in this critical moment in photography with the total dissolution of an assumed "real," we see parallels with what painting went through with the image in the late '70s and early '80s and the demise of high Modernism. Of course, from a contemporary perspective, this past seems grounded and linear, and is edited as needed in attempts to interpret historical trends among a set of mitigating circumstances. But the question is, after breaking apart what doesn't quite apply anymore, what other options are available? What is the exit before the last exit?

One "seductive promise" offered by Beshty is that of materialist critique. At certain moments I question if this recent turn to abstraction is simply a retreat into materiality. A whole world of work that is self-conscious of its mediumness has burst onto (or been rediscovered by) the scene, with a push towards the concreteness of the material as a possible alternative to the almost existential crisis of representation, institutional critique and postmodernism. Embracing notions of making "pictures more picture-like" is one avenue that image-making has recently tended, from Beshty's large scale photograms and whacked out, x-rayed negatives, to Elad Lassry's use of frames that reference perfectly slick commercial images, to James Welling's long-standing dance with photographic-ness and Eileen Quinlan's smoke and mirrors.

However, what I find more compelling than this self-reflexivity is the direction Beshty takes in his final paragraph. Here he lays out the potential to be found in in-between spaces, describing "infrastructural, interstitial zones" that "stand as compromised, indeterminate way stations between chimerical destinations," and argues for uncoded and unprocessed space as a momentary place of hope—a potential autonomous zone where authorship and origin are set aside. But how does one actualize this?

Along with Deleuze & Guattari, the potential of these interstitial spaces was mined in the late '90s by Sieverts, whose term "zwischenstadt," which is literally translated as "between the place as a living space and the non-places of movement." Although Sieverts's premise has an architectural and planning basis, a possible application of the theory resonates profoundly for art-making and writing, and is for me pointedly appropriate to the problematics of photography and its relation to my interests in (the fiction of and violation of) documentary, mapping, and the resulting imaginary.

A critical question presents itself: how does this theoretical or aesthetics space refer or have relation to real space, especially in regards to photography? A recent project that explores the possibility of playing with these ideas (and not just photographically) is *Suddenly: Where We Live Now*, spearheaded by inspired curator Stephanie Snyder and mischievous bon vivant and author Matthew Stadler. Culminating in a traveling exhibition, public programs and publication, the entirety of the project attempts to find "new ways" and "new descriptions that give the landscape where we live an independent identity in the imagination of its occupants," proposing a new engagement to displace traditional binary notions of "the city" and "the countryside." (See www.suddenly.org and web.reed.edu/gallery/) Just as Beshty concludes with momentary openings as possible trajectories away from traditional dialectics of either/or thinking, whether in utopian/apocalyptic thinking or in the political/formalist opposition, *Suddenly* attempts to unravel the authoritative presumptions of mapping and land use, literally and metaphorically. In a real-time affair called the *Backroom* that I attended during a weekend-long symposium devoted to this very question of spaces between, Thomas Sieverts and Aaron Betsky were in conversation about transitional space as we were all eating gourmet Thai food, arguing about how images and the imaginary function, and dripping wet at dusk in the rain under a temporary structure/autonomous zone in an almost abandoned parking lot a half an hour outside of town. Perhaps it is in situations such as this active experiment, when theory is stripped of its monumentality and included in the active and lived construction of meaning, that it can take a more appropriate place as reflector of the artistic condition as opposed to determinant of the artistic act.

--

Subject: Response
Date: 21 October 2008 01:46:19
From: ANTHONY PEARSON

Firstly, let me start by saying that I am not a theoretician, but a devoted practitioner. Therefore, I feel I cannot confidently respond to Mr. Beshty's essay or to Mr. Blank's response, due to this fact. With this being said, I do believe I have an inkling of the ideas and sentiments expressed here, yet cannot say I am compelled by them. Nevertheless, I may be mistaken of the arguments due to their meandering, oblique and encoded nature.

But enough disclaimers. The questions that arise for me in this discussion are as follow: what is it that compels many individuals involved with photography to insist on a categorization and compartmentalization of methods of practice?

Why would one attempt to impose a set of absolutist rules and regulations on the supposed meaning of photographic practices? This is seemingly such an archaic and outmoded form of reasoning when it comes to any method of visual art, yet those in photography seem to insist on these dialectics and pigeonholes.

I often feel that artists using photography and theoreticians concerned with photography insist on examining the medium in a way that views it as a dead subject. If they are not using the language of John Szarkowski, they are using the language of academic postmodernism. They do not allow for a contemporaneous, fluid, open-ended, or Po-PoMo read of the subject. In fact, it often seems that they desire the complete death of the medium itself, so they can poke at it and examine it without any risk of it jumping up and biting them in the ass. Unfortunately or not, the medium remains undead and is open-ended, sticky, and confusing with no easy answers.

A multitude of levels of photographic engagement are open to any artist, free of any undying commitment, romantic notion of positioning, or investment in the antiquated idea of movements. Frankly, it is shocking to see this kind of forced positioning even entertained in the contemporary arena. I was recently asked if I was a materialist and, frankly, I have little idea as to what this might mean. My work is continually compared to Mr. Beshty's, which I will take as a high compliment. But I gather we have little in common theoretically, politically, or artistically with the exception of the fact that we are both known for photographic abstraction.

Naturally, this kind of compartmentalization is endgame, as illustrated in Mr. Haendel's assessment of photographic genres. I could address each forced categorization, for example his complete conflation of pictorialist and modernist photographic histories, but I think it would be most useful to attempt to tackle this confusion in regards to what he refers to as the abstractionists or materialists.

Mr. Haendel seems to assume, as many people do these days, that photographic practitioners with an involvement in abstraction are mostly uncommitted to lens-based practices and detest image and subject. He cites Ms. Quinlan as an example of this, yet she has perhaps the most reoccurring and omnipresent subject of any photographer working today. Her commitment to her subject has been unceasing and she photographs it relentlessly. Her images are highly specific and her methods are directed at a complete engagement with the objects in front of her lens. The camera is her tool in the traditional sense and her work reads as completely photographic.

The suggestion that so-called "abstractionists" are unselective, disinterested, and desire to make work without images is frankly absurd. I, for one, have a defined subject, use a camera (and a lens for that matter) in every work I produce, and am completely engaged with photography in the highly traditional sense. I simply produce non-representational images, which has nothing in-and-of-itself to do with a resistance to traditional photographic methodology.

And finally, I must say I take exception with the fact that Mr. Haendel has brought into question my "staying power." I find this to be completely out of line as my virility is not in question here. This is about photography, not male potency, and I assure you, as my wife would gladly testify, this is not an issue for me whatsoever.

--

Subject: Response to Walead Beshty's "Abstracting Photography"
Date: 28 October 2008 11:56:43
From: JASON SMITH
Title: "Everyday Abstraction"

Walead Beshty's "Abstract Photography" proposes, in its closing pages, a new theoretical framework for thinking about the photographic that would no longer be bound by—or forced to choose between—the classical divisions organizing the discourse on photography. On the one hand, there is no longer any need to stage the kind of theoretical "salvaging" of the disappearing photographic object, understood as threatened in its ontological specificity by the contemporary dominance of digital technology in the production of "images" (whatever their support). On the other hand, it is no longer enough to speak of the social function of the image either, if we are compelled to assume the discourse on power and its "monolithic" character that accompanies these discourses. The first type of discourse seems, according to Beshty, to lose its object all the more the moment it attempts to produce an "expanded" concept of the photographic; the second, in turn, seems to tautologically ensure its own failure by insisting on a notion of power that always already reappropriates any form of critique or "resistance" mounted against it. The theoretical reconstruction of the object is, then, not so much the production of an enlarged conceptual framework for thinking about the nature of the photographic in an aesthetic and cultural space dominated by digital encoding and cinematic models, but an allegory of the failure to do just this, a failure paradoxically brought about by the very airtight "success" of the theoretical operation. The social reading of the photograph is also haunted by a kind of congenital failure, a melancholic "complicity" that can only ever repeat, at a more reflexive or hyperaware level, the very errors it claims to be denouncing. So, two models of failure: a theoretical operation that is so successful it suppresses the very thing it seems to produce, and a social inscription of the photograph that can only ever reproduce the relations of power it claims to expose or critique.

If this quick formalization of at least one strand of Beshty's argument is correct, then it gives rise, for me, to two fundamental questions. These questions are largely questions asking for clarification, for distinctions that are more pointed or elaborated at greater length.

1. In the final paragraph of Beshty's essay,

we are told that instead of "[reorganizing] a seemingly chaotic field"—photography in its current digital and cinematic implosion—we should instead allow the "crisis" of the discourse of photography to "open up what were seemingly foreclosed possibilities." The question, for me, is simple. What is the difference between this desire to "open up" the photographic field, seeing the crisis of the definition of the photographic as an opportunity rather than as an anxious historical moment, and the project of generating, through a set of "logical" operations, an expansion of the field of the photographic? It is certainly possible that the results of George Baker's theoretical reconstruction of the photographic might occlude an entire range of possibilities available today. But is this an effect of the theoretical operation itself, that is, of the very methodology used—the semiotic square and its "logical" operations—or is it a shortcoming of the specific deployment of this technique? It is a tricky issue, because the effect produced by the use of structuralist methods is double: it opens up a field that was formerly identified with a specific medium, but it also closes that field by claiming to generate, and "logically ratify" (Baker's words), the entire field of possible permutations available to contemporary photographic practices. This effect of closure is important. Without it, the discourse would no longer be theoretical; it would be an empirical hunch, with very imprecise terminology, pragmatic to be sure, but never certain of exactly what it is talking about when its says "photography." The risk to be taken here is to demonstrate how one arrives at the terminology one uses. So what we have, it seems, is a "deconstruction" (not so much a theoretical operation as an historical fact, the "crisis" of the photographic object) of the medium-specific concept of photography and, at the same time, a regulated expansion of the field of the photographic through a series of logical operations. The danger that Walead Beshty's discourse courts, then, is the empiricist one of being so open to the possible transformations an object can undergo that it can no longer say, with certainty, what it means by the term "photography." But perhaps the real question is whether this is really a danger, or a risk that must be taken in order to avoid "foreclosing" a set of possibilities that the theoretical reconstruction of the object, no matter how expansive it may be, necessarily performs.

2. The second question (or set of questions) concerns the image of the social and the political as it is presented in these final pages. It is a matter of defetishizing power, of seeing it not as a saturation of social space, but as a patchwork of competing or "overdetermined" forces that are never organized into a monolithic force (whose image is that of the state or the institution), but instead shot through with seams, fractures, local instabilities, "marginal zones" and "transitional spaces" that are inhabitable in their own way, providing points of autonomy that are not immediately inscribed in the dynamics of power and resistance that haunt the allegorical critique of institutions. This language is meant to break with the built-in failures of the avant-garde project—Malevich's point zero of the black monochrome, to use Beshty's example—and of the critical procedures of Pictures-era allegory. To the "either/or" of the absolute decision required by the avant-gardist commitment, we are instead told of "compromises and negotiations," of the indeterminate play between positions and destinations. There is even, at one point, a mention of the "daily ritual of compromise." The first question that comes to mind, however, is whether this space of the everyday ritual is a space of opaque ritual that remains too elusive for the networks of power and its institutions, or whether it is, to the contrary, the very space of "ideology" itself as it was reformulated by Louis Althusser in the late 1960s? As Beshty knows well, this theory of ideology tried to locate the material existence of ideology (ideology has nothing to do with "ideas" in Althusser's theory) precisely in "ritual," what Althusser at one point refers

to in his text as "the practical rituals of the most elementary everyday life." In my reading of his essay, Beshty places a great deal of weight on this notion of "everyday life," and there is an implicit reference in these final paragraphs not only to Henri Lefebvre but more importantly to Michel de Certeau's work from the 1960s. It would be necessary, given the ambiguity of the terms "ritual" and the "daily" or "everyday," to offer a more developed theoretical framework for this term so that it is not immediately identified with ideological ritual. The second question that is raised by this image of the social is the opposing of the language of decision—the utopian and the apocalyptic—to the language of compromise and negotiation. This division recalls, despite everything, the language of Nicolas Bourriaud's theorization of relational aesthetics in the 1990s, in which the violent position of the avant-garde and its task of "destroying" the institution of art and bourgeois culture more generally is abandoned in favor of microtopias and their participatory consensus and "openness" to revision and reformulation. No one has analyzed the weakness of these models—the way they uncritically reproduce the dynamics of contemporary "immaterial" capitalism and its organizational logics—better than Beshty himself does in his "Neo-avantgarde and the Service Industry: Notes on the Brave New World of Relational Aesthetics." (*Texte zur Kunst*, no. 59, September 2005) In what sense, then, do these marginal zones and transitional spaces, these interstices of compromise, collaboration and negotiation, offer the points of autonomy referred to above, rather than the secretly melancholic complicity that is barely concealed by the casual Friday of accommodation to contemporary neo-liberalism and its rhetoric of difference, hybridity, and marginality?

WHAT ARE THE NOTABLE WAYS THAT DIGITAL TECHNOLOGIES HAVE CHANGED PHOTOGRAPHIC PRACTICE?

Let me respond to your questions as the chair of the Photography Department at Columbia College in Chicago. I think the wave of wild speculation over digital technology's impact on photography has passed. What we see here is that the motives, ambitions, and criteria for serious, ambitious photography remain largely unchanged. What makes a photograph compelling, intelligent, fresh, or valuable is still the issue, as it always was. For example, documentary photography has survived, and perhaps become more vital and popular. All the recent improvements in digital capture, software, and printing technology have simply brought the best digitally produced photographs up to the previous standard for film/darkroom-made photographs. Manipulated, collaged, and constructed images were always part of photography, and digital technology makes those directions easier and more persuasive. Consequently, a few more artists may be pursuing that type of work. But this isn't a significant change for the medium.

Dissemination of photographs has changed significantly. Our students view a much wider assortment of visual work than before, can make connections with other young photographers all over the world (sometimes organizing exhibits and exchanges) and create extended artistic communities. The availability of digital tools has allowed our program to co-publish twelve photographic monographs in collaboration with the Center for American Places, and has facilitated our series of small "6x6" books of student work.

From a photography department chair's perspective, the biggest impact that digital imaging has had on our very large program is economic. While the material costs in digital imaging (inks, paper) are similar to our old darkroom costs, capital costs in running a very large photography program have increased tremendously. We have approximately 160 computer workstations in our photography department. This includes high-level scanners and printers. Unlike a darkroom enlarging station, this equipment needs to be replaced every three to four years. We also see increased costs for staff, software, tech support, and constant retraining of faculty and staff. This is a significant shift in the economic equation of a large photography program.

IMPORTANT CHANGES THAT PHOTOGRAPHY HAS UNDERGONE IN THE LAST FEW YEARS?

I notice two changes, which are interestingly related.

First, the art community (as opposed to the narrower photography community) seems to have developed a more sophisticated appreciation of photography, embracing work that does not display any of the overt strategies traditionally employed by photographers hoping for an audience beyond the photographic community. As a "neo-modernist" photography department, where most of our students produce relatively "straight" photography, this is an important development. Locally, a number of our recent graduates have had exhibits at the Museum of Contemporary Art and other venues that had not previously supported straightforward photographic images.

Second, our young students seem to approach varying artistic styles and practices without a sense of opposition. For those of us who lived through the 1980s and '90s, this seems new and encouraging. I've recently seen several very good exhibits that were curated by our graduate students and recent graduates. At these shows, very good "straight" photographic work was shown alongside video, installation, and mixed media work. The participants (and young audience) seemed to be able to appreciate and support radically different working philosophies and styles, without any sense that these were opposing and mutually exclusive artistic agendas. This seems new and very encouraging to me.

WHAT IS IN STORE FOR THE MEDIUM?

I think it will be increasingly difficult for young photographers to make a living doing commercial photographic work. Technological change (in this and other areas) seems to have the effect of wiping out the large middle area of practitioners, leaving a small number of exceptional (and exceptionally rewarded) workers, and another group of badly paid industrial workers. Only the very best young photographers will do well in professional practice.

On the other hand, the opportunities for young artists seem to be expanding, with a growing and increasingly sophisticated audience for serious photography.

I think that the permanence and availability of archived photographs may be seriously affected by digital technology. Digital technology seems to offer great potential for the storage of and easy access to images, but I think that the effect may be quite the opposite after a period of time. This is an area only now getting attention, but may be a big problem in the future.

For example, I have no problem making prints from my own 30-year-old negatives that are comparable to prints made from new film negatives. I have produced good prints from 100+ -year-old glass plates. But I cannot access my digital image files from 6-8 years ago. These files were made on computers with now-obsolete chips and obsolete versions of software (both operating and specific programs) then stored on media (Syquest drives, Zip disks, etc.) that are no longer supported by available hardware. Finally, the storage media itself has permanence problems. Unless this situation changes soon, a huge amount of photographic work will be lost, or very difficult to access.

QUESTIONNAIRE / TIM DAVIS

WHAT DO YOU SEE AS BEING IN STORE FOR THE MEDIUM?

Were there cameras in *Mad Max*?

A Picture You Already Know

Los Angeles County Museum of Art
Participants: Amy Adler, Alex Slade, Penelope Umbrico
Moderator: Charlotte Cotton

"A Picture You Already Know" shares its title with Sze Tsung Leong's essay, but takes a different look at repetition as it relates to photographic practice. Repetition, one might argue, is central to the way photography has historically been understood. For some it is intrinsic to the way photographic meaning is constructed, while for others the photographic series is a convention to be challenged.

We asked three artists to ruminate on the way that repetition functions in their practices, both in terms of seriality and as subject matter.

AMY ADLER: This is an installation view of *Director* at the Museum of Contemporary Art in San Diego. The piece consists of twelve drawings on canvas. As you can see from the slide, the drawings were so light that they're completely impossible to photograph and have absolutely no presence whatsoever on the computer screen or on the web. This is really interesting for me because for the past ten years I've been making drawings that were meant to be photographed. This is one of the first shows that I did where I actually showed drawings. I went from making drawings that were meant to be photographed to making drawings that are absolutely impossible to photograph.

I'm going to show you the piece using a set of preliminary pencil sketches so that you can see what's going on in the drawings themselves. What's happening here is that I was cast to play the lead in a short, independent film. These drawings are based on my own photographs of the director of that film filming me. Remember that this is what they really looked like in the installation; you had to strain to see them even in person. This mirrored the eye of the actual director, who was straining to see through the 16-millimeter film camera. This is a detail of the surface. You can see that the pastel really clings to the little bumps on the canvas.

Drawing on this textured surface made me think about the artist Max Ernst and his frottage drawings. From what I understand "frottage" translates from French as "rubbing." Max Ernst took a pencil and paper and made these drawings by rubbing against different portions of his wood floor and other surfaces. This is something I think everybody does in grade school. Max Ernst equates the rubbing in the frottage drawings as both "appropriation of the texture below and the means to access memory." I understand this to mean the ability through drawing and reproduction to be in two places at the same time. So through this rubbing of chalk pastel against canvas there is a kind of transference that occurs between the director, the subject, the drawing, and the film . . .

When I was quite young I lived in New York and spent several years working for Allan McCollum. I worked on a piece in 1989 called *Drawings* in which he made individual templates so that in this suite of thousands of drawings no two are alike. A dozen artists worked on these drawings . . .

I've often thought of my projects in general as edited fragments of a larger film. In *Director* there are 12 frames, 12 individual pieces. So it's not even a second in a film . . . The film I mentioned at the beginning of my presentation is called *The Plunge* (2007) by Jocelyn Jacobs. It's the first time I've ever been in a film, and it's actually the only piece that I made where I am specifically looking at the photographer who is in turn looking at me.

. . .

ALEX SLADE: I brought three projects. I chose them

because I thought that each one used this idea of repetition in a different way. I did this project in Berlin, of a set of apartment buildings called "Fischerinsel." I was really interested in them because of their repetitive nature. There are seven buildings, these big boxes that I would go by everyday. I loved the modular construction of them. It's called "plattenbau"; they just stack the floors. You see them all over East Germany.

So I went into the apartments. In each apartment I took three pictures. One was looking down the hallway. This is the smallest of the apartments, so there's no hallway. It was just looking into the next room to replicate the modularity of the apartment building architecture. The other picture I took was looking towards the living room window, through the living room. I was really interested in the way all the people that lived in these apartments changed them. You could see all these different ways in which their own furniture and personal items interacted with this modular Modernist architecture, sometimes in very un-Modernist ways. And then the third picture I took was looking out the window at the other buildings. In each, whenever you looked out the window you were faced with a grid of other windows.

This is the second project. It is a very different kind of architecture. We go to this residency program in Maine every summer. You're given a cottage and you're not quite sure which one you'll get; each year it's different. One year I brought my camera and I wanted to take black-and-white landscape photographs. I went around looking for places to take pictures, but everything looked very cliché. It was too much like Eliot Porter, or Ansel Adams, or something. One day I was driving along and I came across this place. And I thought, "That is a really beautiful landscape, but it's way too typical." Then I came back to the cottage and I saw this painting; the woman who owned the cottage was a Sunday painter. She had painted all these paintings in the cottage.

I saw this painting and I thought, "Great, instead of taking pictures of the landscape, I'll take pictures of the landscapes in the architecture." All the paintings fit in the architecture in really interesting ways, like stuffed between the wallboards. In the living room, which was the only drywall room, I thought they were framed nicely by the furniture and these lamps every six feet or so. A few years later, when there was the show at the Getty of Porter, this was the big poster that was on the outside of the gallery to announce the show. It's funny that I had never seen this Porter photograph, but there it was. When I printed the photographs, I made all the paintings to scale. So, the photographs were larger or smaller depending on the architecture. This was a very large photograph because I was pushed away from the wall by the bed that was in front of me. This was a very small photograph because I was pushed right up next to the wall. And then this is a very small painting, which I thought was uniquely positioned.

This is the last project I'll show. Over the last couple of years, I've been photographing the development out in the Inland Empire. One of the places that I found was a shopping mall. I was really interested in photographing it, but I didn't actually ever get to it. But I started looking into who the architect was because I thought it was so interesting. I found the architect, Victor Gruen, who was one of the main designers of the first generation of shopping malls in the United States. And I loved all these graphics that he designed. It reminded me of the shopping malls that I had grown up going to.

This is Eastland Plaza in Detroit. There were four models Gruen designed: Eastland, Westland, Southland, and Northland, which is kind of funnily repetitious. He designed one of the most famous malls in Southdale Plaza in Minneapolis. So then I started looking at other shopping malls around the Northeast, and I noticed that the new shopping malls represent a complete shift in urban planning and design. They always incorporate a park element into them so that the concrete is de-emphasized. They've also shifted away from the single building into these multiple big box stores. This is another shopping mall that I happened upon in Syracuse, which I was pretty amazed by. Inside the shopping mall there is a plan for a whole blast in the city that's supposed to reinvigorate the entire economy of upstate New York, which I just can't imagine happening.

This is another Victor Gruen mall in Rochester that's about to be torn down. It is part of a more extensive project that I did with this mall, which was pretty much dead when I was photographing it. But now it's completely closed down and I think they are going to destroy it in the next month or so. It was so utopian and futuristic when it was built and now it's basically a ruin. This is the design that Gruen made. It's a model of the mall before it was built. It was the first mall that was designed to redevelop an inner city. And it totally failed. I don't know if anybody's been to downtown Rochester, but it's really dilapidated.

This is a photograph I made of the mall last winter. It's pretty much exactly the same as the model, but the whole building is empty, everything that you see. And then inside the mall there is this great clock called the "Clock of the Nations" that has a central column and twelve octopus-like arms with a capsule on each arm representing a different country. I don't know how they decided upon these twelve countries, but each capsule has a little diorama of a different country. When the clock was working, each hour on the hour the little door would swing open and a light would come on and a little character would spin around. I photographed these frontally in a very straight-on manner as I went around the clock. So, it's Scotland, Japan, Thailand, Poland, Italy, Canada, Germany, Israel, Nigeria, and the United States is 12 o'clock. And that's it.

PENELOPE UMBRICO: I'm going to show two bodies of work, and I'm going to quote from Sze Tsung Leong's essay "A Picture You Already Know." He wrote in the last sentence of the essay, "Repetition suggests that views are never singular; each time we look we see something different." I'd like to take the position that repetition suggests that views are never singular, but that each time we look we see with a collective eye. I'm thinking about Milan Kundera's idea of kitsch. Kundera writes, "The feeling induced by kitsch must be the kind the multitudes can share. Kitsch may not therefore depend on an unusual situation unless derived from the basic images people have engraved in their memories: the ungrateful daughter, the neglected father, children running the grass, the motherland betrayed, first love." "Kitsch causes two tears..." I love this. "Kitsch causes two tears to flow in quick succession. The first tear says: 'How nice to see children running in the grass.' The second tear says: 'How nice to be moved together with all of mankind by children running in the grass.' It is the second tear that makes kitsch kitsch." Kitsch is what has been expressed so many times that it becomes familiar, or comforting, or reassuring. Thinking about kitsch in those terms doesn't have to be judgmental. We can put aside the idea of kitsch as a critique of taste or a critique of class identity, and think about it in terms of familiarity and the phenomenological aspect that it is us. It is to be in the world with all of mankind. With this in mind, if we understand that society forms how and what we see, and then also that the photographic systems that we use are part of that formation, we have to look at photography and understand our relationship to it in regards to those formations. The reason I'm showing these works is that I'm dealing with collecting—how photography is used and what people do with photography.

This is a slideshow of sunsets from Flickr. The project started when I searched the word "sunset" and I found 541,000 images. I was really interested in knowing what was the most ubiquitously photographed thing. So, I downloaded all the photographs of sunsets. I took the suns from these images and cropped them out. I made 4- by 6-inch image files and then uploaded them back to Flickr. I also uploaded them up to the Kodak Gallery website and ordered 4- by 6-inch snapshots of them. I was interested in the pedestrian aspect of taking the photographs to begin with. It was a scripted form of making a photograph. And Kodak is the typical family snapshot place where you can get photographs printed quickly and easily, without much craft involved.

I was specifically interested in the sunset because of the fact that it was the most ubiquitous image; I got the most numbers when I did searches on it. But also because of the fact that the sun is out there in the world in infinite space. It's the symbol of intellectual enlightenment, happiness, vitamin D, and eternity. The fact that it gets put onto the Internet was really interesting to me, in that it's almost subsumed into this claustrophobic, electronic space. So, I concentrated on the suns. At this point I have 2,400 and something of them. I show them quite a bit because people seem to really love them. This is a very small detail of a larger installation. I name the piece the number of hits that I get on Flickr when I do the search. The first one that I did was in December '06. And I had 500,000 hits. The second one was in September '07, and I had 2,000,000. And they keep going. The last one is for a show that's actually going to be installed on Monday when I get back to New York. I did a search today and it's 4,386,365. I also really like the comments on the Web-based photo communities and the collective content that people share, in terms of the ubiquity of image taking and how easy it is to disseminate things.

. . .

COTTON: The first thing that comes to mind in a very singular way is that all three of you are quasi-autistic. I think you're such fun to have dinner with, but I don't quite know how to moderate a panel discussion between you because your practices are so obsessive in very different ways, and you deal with repetition and the layering of your repeated acts in very different ways.

. . .

UMBRICO: I was thinking in terms of what you were saying to me about the "never being able to catch up" aspect. All of my work has a very synchronic, all at once feeling when you get what it is about. Your work, Alex, is the opposite. Yours, Amy, is absolutely through time in a way that is about the history of filmmaking, and the history of the thing that you did with your friend and the filmmaker . . . I noticed that the spaces that the three of us work in are equally convoluted in a way. It seems like in your guys' work, an interior is located that isn't just standing in front of something and looking at it, but rather actually navigating inside that thing and looking at it in multiple dimensions from within, as opposed to seeing it purely from the outside. Like the way that Alex went into the apartments and photographed peoples' personal things. Likewise, Amy, the spaces that you're traveling into in your work are so domestic and intimate. Does that make sense?

ADLER: Yes, it does.

. . .

COTTON: I want to address the idea of taking good pictures. I wonder, even though all three of your practices are incredibly thoughtful and meticulous, whether you were ever conscious of falling into your own repeated safe practices? Even though your practice is rigorous, whether you feel that danger when you know that you're doing something by rote.

ADLER: I can answer that directly. I had been taking photographs of my drawings for ten years and destroying the original drawings. I was very strict about that. And there were no editions of the photographs. So there was one image from the whole process. Then it occurred to me that I was standing on one side of the equation. As much as it was incredibly perilous to step out of that equation, I felt like it was necessary. Because I could really only understand this if I was looking at it in multiple dimensions, despite the perils of a neat and clean description of my practice, which was really never the point. I think that it allowed me to understand the narrative structures, the dynamics between the characters, and the scenarios in general, where that distancing feature could be located elsewhere. It didn't have to sit neatly on the surface. I think that answers your question pretty specifically.

COTTON: Does that also connect to your current phase of practice where you're exploring filmmaking?

ADLER: Yes, definitely. One of the reasons I showed this project was that I'm constantly in search of what I don't understand and this messy area that's elusive to me. Working on this project made me aware of the fact that I didn't at that point understand the filmmaking process to the degree that I understood drawing and photography. It seemed like an important area for me to investigate. So, right now that's what I'm doing.

COTTON: Alex, does that resonate with you at all about being cautious of knowing when you might be repeating yourself in an intellectual, creative way?

SLADE: When I go out looking for a photograph, part of it for me is wandering around and finding different places. So, I'm always looking for new places to go to. There was a series I did in the '90s of vacant lots. I went around and whenever I saw a vacant lot I'd scope it out for a while and then end up photographing it. But after a while, there just seemed no point in continuing that and I shifted. I looked for something else to photograph.

ALEX KLEIN [AUDIENCE]: I have a question about the series itself. We frequently talk about repetition in photography. When you take your first photography class you're asked to make a series. I think it is integral to the way that photographers are taught and asked to think about their practices. It's something that you don't encounter as much in other mediums; you're not expected to make series in painting or sculpture in the same way. It's almost a way that people have trained themselves to operate in photography and that is engrained at the level of photographic pedagogy.

UMBRICO: I think there's a big difference between serial production and multiple production. It's an interesting question. We were actually just talking about this today at UCLA. The series of practices or products when you're moving through the process of making something and then reacting to that and making something else, and then reacting to that, that is a kind of serial practice.

KLEIN: I'd like to clarify by saying that photography is always asked to think of itself as one thing in relation to another (and not just on a roll of film). You have to have a body of work. The image—one photograph—only goes so far; it needs the other things in relation. Does that make sense? Even though we might have one image from a series that is interesting and important, it's understood within the context of a series or body of work.

UMBRICO: Yes. I would just say that I don't work that way.

AUDIENCE: Don't you think that indeed all of the projects you showed are series?

UMBRICO: Yes, but that's different. I think that whole group of images is one project and all of those images are absolutely contingent on each other for their meaning. There's an element of contingency that's operative, but it's not a serial. It's not a process through which something is being serialized. It's the multiple aspect of it, I guess.

SLADE: I feel like I work in different ways for each project. With the Inland Empire photographs, I felt more like that was a series, but it was about a place. Whereas the photographs of the paintings in the cottage were instantaneous, even though they ended up in a multiplicity like Penelope was talking about. When students say, "I don't know how to tie things together," I always feel like saying, "Don't tie them." Even though sometimes I work in a very serial way, I feel like maybe there's a way in which I stop and break the series at a certain point. I'm really interested in where those connections become tenuous. Maybe it doesn't show up in the work so much, but it might be an interesting development to see those connections become looser and looser.

ADLER: I think it's a really good question actually. It's hard to wrap my head around it. You mention it from the point of view of a student. I teach drawing and I am really conscious of the differences in terms of teaching photography and teaching drawing. Students do not come in with that same point of view in drawing classes.

It's really interesting now working with film because I've always thought that maybe three to five images are actually one image. But it's a very small number really. The thing about film is that there are all those spaces in between those images that aren't there in the series. It's looking at the pockets in between this flowing space. But I think it's a really good question.

COTTON: I've got a question back to you, Alex. Do you mean "serial" in terms of the legacy of an editorial photo story, the idea of contingent meaning in the construction of narrative?

KLEIN: No, I don't think it's necessarily an editorial effect or necessarily about narrative. I'm thinking about the way that photographers are taught today, which goes back to Amy's point. You come in with a serial project because you are expected to create a series of images that relate to each other, but not necessarily an editorial narrative. And even outside of school when people come to your studio to see your work they ask to see series. They ask to see the works that relate to each other. If you show them one work, you often encounter, "Well, where is the series that this relates to?" It's as if the photograph is expected to be inherently dependent upon seriality in order to define itself as a project and not as a stand-alone image.

DAVID WEINER [AUDIENCE]: Exploring this idea of seriality, what strikes me in trying to synthesize the work that you all presented tonight is your use of photography as a means to an end more than anything else. And the seriality that's at stake in the whole premise of the evening is the seriality of the archive. You all seem to approach photography as the tool to build your archives. It's in your work, Alex [Slade], which is book-ended by ideas of interest where the photographs are a means to document those objects of interest and discover, or go through, a process. The other two kinds of work [by Adler and Umbrico] are more documents of experience. But it would seem that repetition is the actual approach. What photography enables in that sense is that repetitiveness, which is not the same kind of seriality that I think Alex [Klein] is questioning. The presumption of how to understand photography and the teaching tool of seriality as a way to create meaning is also what I think you addressed Alex [Klein] in your teaching questions. So, I wonder what you all think about that.

. . .

UMBRICO: I totally admit to the obsessive tendencies of my practice. Charlotte mentioned something about our autistic practices. I think there's an interesting relationship between my practice and autistic behavior of self-stimulating, which is the rocking, spinning, or other repetitive behavior that is calming to an autistic person.

ADLER: As a young artist I worked for Allan McCollum for quite a few years. I've made a lot of things over and over and over again—surrogates, vehicles, and drawings. It ingrained something in me. I'm not sure if it influenced me or if my interest was the reason that I was there. But it's interesting that you call it "relaxing" because I don't necessarily think it's relaxing. The other thing is that even if you take these huge, sweeping leaps away from what you know, it might appear to you that you're staying on track. But in reality, from my point of view, it might not be that way.

. . .

UMBRICO: I worked for Allan McCollum, too. A lot of people did.

AUDIENCE: I have a question for Amy. I wanted to know about your decision to make an edition of one and what you've learned from that process.

ADLER: I thought that if I was going to make this really luscious charcoal or chalk drawing and then tear it into pieces that it was making some great sacrifice in terms of its materiality. As a result, I felt like the photograph had to make a really great sacrifice, too. Not permitting a photograph to multiply is really doing something very cruel to a photograph. Because it just wants to so badly. To prevent that is just a weird act; it's like retribution. That's one way of describing it.

. . .

SLADE: I was thinking also about the obsessiveness question, about how it might be relaxing. I was thinking about the idea of structure, which I don't think we really talked about so much . . . One of the things that I really wanted to include was a structure in my work. I feel like it really helps to have a structure that you have to follow. I think in our culture everything is moving so fast . . . images float by so quickly. The camera is always moving.

QUESTIONNAIRE / DEBORAH BRIGHT

WHAT WOULD YOU CONSIDER SOME OF THE MOST IMPORTANT CHANGES THAT PHOTOGRAPHY HAS UNDERGONE IN THE LAST FEW YEARS?

The change in its status as an art object that rivals painting for scale and sheer spectacle. It is no longer an intimate, democratic, documentary medium as far as art is concerned. Now we have to entertain, dazzle with our craft, and blow people away with big production numbers and big cameras. Like Harold Rosenberg in the 1950s, I despair of "apocalyptic wallpaper."

WHAT DO YOU SEE AS BEING IN STORE FOR THE MEDIUM?

On the one hand, a new pictorialism in the revival of handmade photographs and photo-objects like photograms, camera obscura/pinhole, antique processes—the antithesis of manipulating pixels. On the other, more hybrid digital forms that cross the borders between 2-D, 3-D and time-based practices—hyperlinked visual experiences through digital projection installations rather than a linear series of prints. As far as I can see, lens-based images will take many different forms—analog and digital—without one kind of output or style predominating. As long as global super-wealth continues to grow and drive the art market, I expect that the market will maintain its lead role in selecting what works are "valued," rather than museums and nonprofit cultural institutions.

QUESTIONNAIRE / ANNE WILKES TUCKER

DO YOU THINK MUSEUMS SHOULD COLLECT INKJET PRINTS AND SCREEN-BASED PHOTOGRAPHY?

What choice do we have? We follow photographic practices or we die.

DO YOU THINK YOUR ROLE AS A CURATOR HAS CHANGED SINCE YOU ENTERED THE FIELD?

Of course it has. I have been in the field for 40 years. For some in the art marketplace, curators and critics are passé and collectors are supreme. The greatest change for me in being a curator is in the geographical areas we are expected to cover. In a world of art that is no longer nation-based, we seek to be current on five or six continents. Also, when I entered the field, only two curators of photography had doctoral degrees, and now it is expected of all curatorial candidates. My generation was the last of the curators who began their career as photographers. We understood the medium because we practiced it (some with more talent than others). But given some of the issues raised in Christopher Bedford's article ["Qualifying Photography as Art, or Is Photography All It Can Be?"], maybe we should go back to that. Also, we did not have books or even articles to guide us on most of the photographers whose work we were purchasing. There was [Beaumont] Newhall and [Helmut] Gernsheim, [Alfred] Stieglitz, early [John] Szarkowski and [Nathan] Lyons, a few small magazines such as *Aperture* and *Creative Camera*, and very little else. Most monographs were 90% pictures and little text. One learned by talking to photographers and by looking, looking, looking. Now we are swamped by information. Photographers have three publications by the time they are 30, websites, multiple galleries, etc. Curators are much less important to the photographer in reaching audiences. They have so many other venues. Being in a museum collection is important, but no more sought than being in certain private collections.

Photography and Abstraction

GEORGE BAKER

> Here again the road leads over capitalism's dead body; but here again this road is a good one.
> —Bertolt Brecht

Twenty years ago, Rosalind Krauss attempted to rethink the entrenched relations between photography and abstraction with a small exhibition devoted to the work of James Welling and Holly Wright. Gone were the classical nudes and the gleaming pears and the cacti, and in their place appeared body parts and close-framed images of hands; gone were the light studies and architectural meditations, and in their place a series of images of gelatin, or tinfoil, or aged diaries; gone were the Modernist concerns with pure form and the conditions of visual transparency, and in their place the opaque photographic conditions of the uncanny, the compulsion to repeat, and the "empty sign." [1] Provoked by Walead Beshty's recent essay for this series, I want to speculate on the need to rethink the relations between photography and abstraction once more and yet again, today.

In doing so, I will not comment much on Beshty's reading of my prior essay, "Photography's Expanded Field," except to observe that it is extremely disorienting and yet refreshing to witness an artist turning the tables on a critic, doing to a work of mine what I most often do to a work by a given artist: interpreting, historicizing, and critiquing it. Melancholy, allegory, failure: I will not comment on these. Instead, let me simply narrate some motivations, as I perceived them, behind my writing of that earlier text. One thing was clear to me: it was not "theory" or "structuralism" that could expand the photographic object or medium. My essay was a heuristic exercise, an attempt to invent language and transform our historical and descriptive discourse, for that expansion of photography had already occurred—indeed, a generation before the writing of my text. Theory could potentially clarify our relation to an expansion and a transformation that had already happened (but then again, such transformation has also hardly concluded). If I may then play with Beshty's terms, it was not theory that had "abstracted" photography, but rather photography that had become—in some new and potentially radical way—abstract. Using vastly different terminology, this is the event that I called photography's "expansion" and that I wanted to trace in my earlier essay. I do not mean that photography had become abstract in the formalist sense of the term—empty, blank, nonrepresentational. Rather, I understand abstraction as a social as much as a formal process (a process where form overtakes the social, where form transforms sociality itself). It is that violent decontextualization, voiding, and recoding of objects endemic to the principles of capitalist modernity.

We may push further. As an artifact of capitalist modernity, photography has not only been abstracted in recent decades, transformed "beyond recognition"—what more surface descriptions might identify as its recoding at the hands of digital techniques, for example—but it has itself always been a force of abstraction. This cuts counterintuitively against the conventional understanding of photography's essence as indexical, as a potential assertion of physical presence, or as inherently (for critics like Clement Greenberg, and, more recently, Jeff Wall) depictive. The old modernist (and more recent postmodernist) debates on photography and abstraction thrived on this aesthetic disjunction, a debate that leads back to the schism between photography and painting, ultimately. Again, I am using these terms in a radically different way. No schism exists between photography and abstraction (unless it can be crafted *within* artistic practice, perhaps the most difficult of tasks, on which I'll say more in a moment). For photography has been one of the capitalist forms through which processes of abstraction became visible, and could also concretely be achieved. (Abstraction is concrete as well, terrifyingly concrete perhaps, from this perspective.) For divergent reasons, Beshty seems to agree with me on this point. "Since its inception," Beshty writes, "the photographic image has been strongly associated with displacement and destruction, a triumph of images over material." He cites Oliver Wendell Holmes writing on photography in 1859, as will I: "*Form is henceforth divorced from matter*. In fact matter as a visible object is of no great use any longer, except as the mould on which form is shaped. Give us a few negatives of a thing worth seeing, taken from different points of view, and that is all we want of it. Pull it down or burn it up, if you please." [2] Holmes, like most of the avant-garde that would follow him in the twentieth century, evidently suffered from what I would call capitalist euphoria, but his hallucinations have their anchor in the reality of photography's enactment of the shared processes of modernity and modernization. So if I have gone on the record with an attempt to trace photography's "expansion" in recent decades, what we actually need to contemplate and register in the contemporary situation of photography is a force of abstraction that has now itself been submitted to a process of further abstraction. Photography begins to sound like money in this account, and this is no coincidence. We need today to contemplate the further abstraction of a prior abstraction—a second-degree, or exponentially accelerated, dynamic.

I will admit, of course, that these terms appear nowhere in the essay "Photography's Expanded Field." For a variety of reasons, I relegated them instead to a text that I consider a companion piece to that essay, the short book that I wrote about the artist Gerard Byrne. [3] So if structuralism did not "abstract" photography, now it begins to sound like capitalist forces and processes are the determinate factors—and yet some new kind of Marxist determinism is precisely the narrative my text on Byrne hoped to avoid. [4] Instead, I found myself engaged with an artist who produced photographs that—while attached to genres such as the street photograph, the landscape photograph, or the architectural photograph—tarried with the unrepresentable. The most figurative and even traditional of photographic languages now began to appear "abstract," and this in the old, aesthetic sense of the term. And yet, simultaneously, and perhaps paradoxically, I found myself contemplating the necessity, in the current moment of aesthetic work upon the photograph, of a return not to the photography and abstraction debates around modernism, but to the "Realist-Modernist" debates within Western Marxism from the beginning of the twentieth century—the positions notoriously taken up at that moment by Bertolt Brecht, Georg Lukács, Walter Benjamin, and Theodor Adorno. Brecht was especially useful for his productivist position acknowledging the fact that at his historical moment, the only realism worthy of the name would have to *incorporate* abstraction. Brecht wrote, "*Realist* means: laying bare society's causal network/showing up the dominant viewpoint as the viewpoint of the dominators/writing from the standpoint of the class which has prepared the broadest solutions for the most pressing problems afflicting human society/emphasizing the dynamics of development/concrete and so as to encourage abstraction." [5] For Brecht in the early twentieth century, a realism worthy of the name would have to involve abstraction, for this had become in fact a social form—a form through which the social had to pass.

So, it seemed to me, was the situation of photography to be narrated today, its representational, "documentary" status everywhere in doubt—and this because of new historical realities far greater than the loss of indexicality signaled by digitalization. The transformation was not just technological, but epochal. We had entered a topsy-turvy historical situation in which photography was increasingly rendered abstract even when it was most entrenched in its traditional documentary and representational formats, and potentially representational when it was most abstract.

Among contemporary artists, perhaps no one has better given voice to this shift than Hito Steyerl in her essay "Documentary Uncertainty." [6] Steyerl's account begins with her experience of watching CNN's "embedded" documentary footage of a journalist during the recent U.S.-led invasion of Iraq. Transmitted via cell phone, the most concrete images of the onset of the war appeared almost entirely unintelligible, the recording equipment unequal to the task of the historical reality to be recorded, producing some new form of low-resolution abstraction. Steyerl read the images allegorically, as testifying to "a deeper characteristic of many contemporary documentary pictures: the more immediate they become, the less there is to see. The closer to reality we get, the less intelligible it becomes. Let us call this 'the uncertainty principle of modern documentarism.'" Her critique continued:

> Contemporary artistic documentarism, with its focus on a politics of representation, has not yet paid sufficient attention to this change; politics as such are moving beyond representation. Very tangible developments make clear that the principle

> of representative democracy is becoming increasingly problematic. The political representation of the people is undermined in many ways—from the non-representation of migrants to the creation of strange democratic hybrids like the European Union. If people are no longer represented politically, then maybe other forms of symbolic representation are undermined as well. If political representation becomes abstract and blurred, so might documentary representation. Is this also a way to interpret CNN's abstract documentarism? A documentarism which moves beyond representation?

Steyerl's concern, as a filmmaker, has been with "documentary" as a mode; but I feel that the situation must be described as entirely parallel for the medium of photography today, with all of its own ontological ties to documentary. We face the imperative to understand anew today what it might mean for photography to "move beyond representation." We face the imperative to understand anew the situation of photography as it is submitted to a process of transformation and ultimately abstraction, as it is now rendered an abstraction of an abstraction. I have said that this description of photography parallels another symbolic form—namely, money—as the latter is increasingly transcoded into sheer number itself, divorced, under contemporary conditions of production, from any tie to identifiable objects, products, or commodities. Money generated from money itself, money for money's sake, the abstraction of an abstraction: this is the contemporary condition that the critic Fredric Jameson has outlined in his writings on finance capital. Since I wrote about this at length in my prior text, I hope Beshty will excuse me if I lapse into paraphrase again. But this time, the paraphrase and the citation are of myself.

* * *

The questions around which this essay has been circling could be stated as follow: What would an abstraction of an abstraction look like? What would be the structure of such an entity? How can representational images or photographs in contemporary culture be said to engage with the abstract or the unrepresentable? Could this be described as a realist project? How does reification continue to invest and alter the forms of contemporary art? How can we describe postmodern forms of autonomization, if they can even be said to exist, and how do they relate to modernist autonomization and aesthetic autonomy? I want to bring some partial closure to these questions now, although history has not yet run its course and my observations should be taken as provisional.

We need to rethink the great cliché that modernist art was engaged with the negative, the autonomous, and the abstract while postmodernism has signaled a massive return of popular and representational forms, a return to realism and figuration. Though the question of realism returns with pressing urgency in the moment of the postmodern, its traditional language cannot resume, no matter the desire of even the most sophisticated of critics to theorize the lineaments of an aesthetic project of "re-figuration" in the wake of modernism's repressions. Fredric Jameson's recent writings on finance capital provide us with much direction as to why this is so. On the level of social structures, Jameson has imagined analogies between the structures of social occultation existing in the modernist era—the invisibility, say, of the labor and resources of imperialist colonies to the Western urban areas that otherwise depended on them—and the aesthetic necessity of modernist formal abstraction and its occultations. In a newly "transparent" global world system of instant flows of communication and capital, such occultation dissipates, along with the aesthetic languages that it supported (or conversely, that arose to give such social occultation an allegorical form). The "new transparency of the postmodern world system (which resorts to new techniques of distortion by way of a suppression of history and even...of time and temporality itself) now also explains the shift from the abstract and initiatory forms of modernism to what look like more popular and representational kinds of art and writing (and music) in postmodernity, a shift often and widely considered to be a return to realism and figuration." [7] And yet this movement "forward" of the historical process should not be narrated as a simple "return." We must begin to imagine an earlier, modernist abstraction not happily canceled, but in fact redoubled—raised to a higher level in both social forms and aesthetic language. For, as Jameson asserts, "postmodernism is not really figurative in any meaningful realist sense or at least... it is now a realism of the image rather than of the object and has more to do with the transformation of the figure into a logo than with the conquest of new 'realistic' and representational languages. It is thus a realism of image or spectacle society, if you will, and a symptom of the very system it represents in the first place." [8]

In a series of recent essays, Jameson has explored the lineaments of the "system" to which the new representational images of postmodernity might be said to correspond. For Jameson, the mediations between such aesthetic forms and their social correlatives only become apparent in a moment dominated by the new totality of financial speculation, the "post-productive" moment of *finance capital*. [9] Simply put, finance capital is the form of what we have been calling an abstraction of an abstraction, the "freeing" of money—a first level of abstraction—from the products and industries to which it was previously attached, and by which it was originally generated. According to Jameson:

> [Finance capital] suggests a new type of abstraction, in which on the one hand money is sublimated into sheer number, and on the other hand a new kind of value emerges, which seems to have little enough to do with the old-fashioned value of firms and factories or of their products and their marketability. The recent business failures like Enron seem to suggest that the value of a given stock cannot long be separated from the profitability of the firm it is supposed to "represent" or express, but I think they demonstrate the opposite, that under the conditions of finance capital stock value has a decidedly semiautonomous status with respect to its nominal company and that, in any case, postmodern 'profitability' is a new category, dependent on all kinds of conditions unrelated to the product itself, such as the downsizing of employees at the demand of banks and investment institutions and the draining of the company's assets (sometimes fatally) in order to inflate dividends. [10]

It is to such a logic that Jameson now wants to attach his understanding of the structure of postmodern culture; modernism will correspond in this new schema to a first moment of abstraction, the moment of industrial (or productive) capital, while postmodern forms arise in the increasingly speculative transition to a second level of abstraction, the freeing of productive, industrial capital into the pure speculation of finance capital. "The formal abstractions of the modernist period—which corresponded to the dialectic of value of an older monopoly stage of capitalism," Jameson explains, "are to be radically distinguished from the less palpable abstractions of the image or the logo, which operate with something of the autonomy of the values of present-day finance capital." We need to understand this new freedom, and thus this new form of abstraction, in the very presence of putatively representational postmodern forms. As with finance capital, Jameson will find this new structure in the "recoding" of a previously abstracted form; as he puts it, the difference between modernist and postmodern abstraction is "the distinction between an object and its expression and an object whose expression has in fact virtually become another object in its own right." [11]

Since the "new economics" of the 1980s, since the Reagan and Thatcher years in the U.S. and Britain, we have become increasingly familiar with finance capital and the present centrality of its forms: the valuation of investment and the stock market over industrial production; the massive expansion of ephemeral profits reaped without an engagement with production as such; the excessive growth of land speculation and its reshaping of the contemporary urban milieu; the increasing power of monetarism and thus of organizations such as the World Bank and the International Monetary Fund. These are only the "positive," or rather constructive, transformations involved in the machinations of finance capital. A long list of negative or destructive ones should by now be familiar as well—systematic unemployment, capital flight and disinvestment, the periodic necessity of the economic "crash"—and we will return to this in a moment. The familiarity of these forms, however, has not made us any wiser as to the structural effects of the centrality of finance capital to our own contemporary capitalist moment. To open up this understanding, Jameson's exploration of finance capital turns to the account of capitalism given in Giovanni Arrighi's text *The Long Twentieth Century*. Following Arrighi's perspective, Jameson proposes that finance capital or the "speculative moment" is the third and final stage of any local process of capitalist development. Such development proceeds through a first, primitive stage in which, through an inevitably difficult process of accumulation, a quantity of money is brought into being for "capitalization." Then, in a second moment, that money becomes capital and is, in Jameson's words, "territorialized"—that is, invested in agriculture and manufacture, transforming a geographic area into a center of production. Eventually, however, this productive moment comes into crisis, reaching internal limits on its growth; it then enters its third, speculative stage. "Speculation," Jameson writes, "the withdrawal of profits from the home industries, the increasingly feverish search, not so much for new markets (these are also saturated) as for the new kind of profits available in financial transactions themselves and as such—these are the ways in which capitalism now reacts to and compensates for the closing of its productive moment." [12] Finance capital stands as a complete abstraction of an earlier moment of an already-abstract—though perhaps retroactively visible as an only partially abstract—capital.

If such an understanding is to be correlated with the transition from modernism to our contemporary forms of postmodernism, a series of surprising revisions becomes necessary. Modernist abstraction comes about only in a social situation of *incomplete* abstraction, while the postmodern return to figuration is the cultural expression of an epoch of total or complete abstraction (although this totality can in turn be questioned)—an expression of the new freedom to recode and, to use the Deleuzian word that Jameson chooses, *deterritorialize* all residual content (and the recent deterritorialization apparent in contemporary visual art's turn from concrete representational images to more ephemeral *projected* images should also be connected to this development). In other words, at the moment of a transcendent finance capital, capital itself becomes "free-floating," as Jameson puts it. It can now be separated not only from a concrete object, as money is already in an earlier capitalist stage; finance capital cuts its ties to the object from which it originated altogether, and not only separates itself off from a single object and its context but proceeds to a second stage where it can be transformed into investment in other similarly abstract forms, or entirely other products and geographies. Finance capital "separates from the 'concrete context' of its productive geography. Money becomes in a second sense and to a second degree abstract (it always was abstract in the first and basic sense): as though somehow in the national moment money still had a content—it was cotton money, or wheat money, textile money, railway money and the like. Now, like the butterfly stirring within the chrysalis, it separates itself off from that concrete breeding ground and prepares to take flight." [13] Finance capital is an abstraction that is not fully "blank" in its initial denial of an object that it then abstracts (the social situation instead of modernism); it is an abstraction that is instead blankly "full," nauseatingly replete, a recoding of an earlier abstraction (the social situation of postmodernism). And this "full" abstraction, a newly total abstraction, places the unrepresentable at the core of its form—a form of now-pure mutability and infinite transformation, but one whose nervous deterritorialization of all previous contents will not allow itself to settle ever again into any one stable entity. One cannot represent that which no longer has a singular form but that exists, rather, as the immaterial process of recoding and quantitative exchange itself.

The leap of finance capital into "pure number" and abstract profits comes with its dialectical after-effects; the "flight" of this new abstraction depends on real "capital flight," the loss of productivity in formerly industrial arenas, the search for cheaper labor, the rise of unemployment and layoffs, discarded objects all around. Indeed, we might say that in addition to the new relationship to the unrepresentable, the *cast-off* becomes the experiential mode of the regime of finance capital itself, the only way to measure and, perhaps, restrain the airborne virtualization of this newly dominant capitalist "axiomatic" (again a word of Deleuze's that Jameson puts to use). The *discard* has become both the breeding ground and the result of deterritorialization, and this in a way as newly pure and intense as the new forms of abstraction themselves (since obsolescence in some less ubiquitous form has always been a structural component of capitalism). [14] And this new era of the cast-off, the dialectical twin to an era of total abstraction, has its aesthetic parallels, as we have been witnessing in the transformed situation today of formerly industrial image-forms—putatively abandoned media such as photography and film. We can begin now to understand how and why artists increasingly dedicate their art to the recoding of these mediums, to what we might call the remnants of capital flight and aesthetic outmoding. And yet while we now may notice that the signs and signifiers of our current speculative mode of production appear everywhere in such images or projects, even when they are properly "invisible" (land speculation, disinvestment, the stock exchange, urban reconstruction and deterritorialization, capital flight, outmoded objects and failed utopian plans, etc.), this is a method that becomes realist less in what it depicts or in its inner thematics—for all such representational depictions answer to a regime of abstraction today—than in a procedural congruence with the structure and the essential working of finance capital itself. Which we could put in a simpler way: one can only represent the unrepresentable by playing its own game. A pure abstraction can only be "realized" by utilizing the methods and the forms that have secured its purity—a further abstraction and autonomization of form. This is where the hopes of a true realism lie today. [15]

* * *

Looking back upon this paraphrase of my text of five years ago, it is clear that the situation today has shifted, and perhaps the questions we need to ask of photography have shifted as well. What I called for five years ago was the imperative to imagine some new form of abstraction, a kind of "cultural speculation" to counter and transcode the axiomatics of financial speculation in our time. It was a productivist call, in its way. Theory, and theorizations of photography, in this view, were surely not the enemy; capital and its axiomatics and forces were the primary source of such abstraction. Photography, as a manifestation of abstraction—and precisely because of its role as such—could become a tool to force capital's axiomatics in different directions.

But today I write from the vantage point of what seems like the global collapse of the speculative mode itself, its latest and unavoidable crisis (crisis being systemic to the very structure of capitalist abstraction and the emptying implicit in its junk-bond dynamics). This situation calls for photography to imagine other tactics, perhaps new strategic relationships to abstraction (and thus to itself as well). And while yet again a narrative of determinism is to be avoided, can we not say that today the crucial project to imagine would be some form of what we might call an "aesthetics of the crash"? Should we not attempt to invent new modalities of abstraction's collapse, new modes of emptying out and devastation—not of the economy, but of images? Where once the crucial task seemed to be to exacerbate abstraction itself, now is it not the exacerbation of recession and impoverishment that we are called on to enact? I don't have answers yet to the questions that the new historical situation raises; I simply want to end this position piece by asking some questions that I hope will be productive themselves. We have some guides in this search for the right questions. I think it important to remind ourselves of the fact that we possess at least one major theorization of photography that was self-consciously posed as a response to an economic crash, Walter Benjamin's "Little History of Photography," published in 1931. In fact, it occurs to me that Benjamin is also not alone; Roland Barthes's *Camera Lucida* of 1980 could also be described as a photographic theory proper to a moment of deep economic recession, with the radical difference of this text from Barthes's earlier theories of photography in the 1950s and 1960s a measure of the changed economic-historical conditions that characterized the retreat of capitalist modernization in the late 1970s. Let's be literal-minded, as Brecht was wont to do: Barthes's *Camera Lucida* amounts to the theory of photography characteristic of the decade of the "oil crisis," and Benjamin's "Little History," in turn, to an intellectual response to the economic crash of 1929.

Not surprisingly, both Benjamin's and Barthes's texts offer up primitivist instead of productivist visions of photography, elegiac attempts to reconnect with the medium's "underground" and earliest history. Both are fantasies of what we might call photographic atavism. Benjamin's text, as is well known, imagines the present economic crisis as opening up a form of aesthetic time travel, the potential to return to the lost halcyon days of the photograph in the first decade of its existence, the latent power of the medium prior to its crushing and massive industrialization as an aesthetic form. He connects this potential directly to the crash of 1929: "It would not be surprising," Benjamin wrote, "if the photographic methods which today, for the first time, are harking back to the preindustrial heyday of photography had an underground connection with the crisis of capitalist industry." [16] Benjamin's "aesthetics of the crash" welcomed photography as a form of atavism, the breaking-through of not-fully-surpassed historical experience: that is, experience not fully devastated by the operations of modern abstraction. The crash, the economic recession, the rolling back of industrialization itself: all of this would allow what had once been declared superceded to return, or better, to live again in some new form. Atavism remains Benjamin's concern in his photographic theory only for a short while; "The Work of Art in the Age of Mechanical Reproduction" abandons this position, partly due to the influence of Brecht (and partly due to the receding of the horizon of the financial crash?); atavism thus was robbed of one of its great potential theorists. We will have to wait for Barthes's "*this has been*" for photography's atavistic potential to return, under new conditions of capitalist crisis—the "*this has been*" will be again. And perhaps again. And again, it will have been. Such is the very structure of photographic atavism, the eternal return. Atavism, from *atavus*, grandfather of my grandfather, is a genetic, well-nigh biological eruption of a long-past trait. Atavism connotes reversion, even retroversion; it is the historical throwback, the return of the lost object, the reappearance of that which has been thought definitively to have disappeared. Genes hide atavisms when they are not "expressed," in a biological mode of preservation, a kind of hidden secret. Photography's preservationist powers seem hardly a step away, perhaps also its modes of obfuscation and opacity. But biological atavisms are also "monstrous," impossible hybrids: the hind leg on the back of the whale, the tail on the human fetus, an extra toe on a horse, and webbed hands and feet in a land-loving mammal.

Atavism thus appears like a mutation, but it is not;

it speaks, instead, of the inherent power of the past to produce transformation from its very inertia, the shocking return that also signals a departure. We might say that while photographic abstraction voids content, producing new hybrids by recoding and inhabiting older forms, photographic atavism returns lost contents, forcing temporal hybrids upon the present, the intransigent past haunting the overly confident future. [17] Caught today between abstraction and atavism, photography seems captured, once again, by a binary logic from within which it is torn. For the dialectics of abstraction and atavism seem to subsume or take on those more traditional dialectics of photography, theorizations of its essential logic as either that of the copy or of the index, as an assertion of pictorial abstraction or of documentary representation, as a force of vertiginous decontextualization or obdurate physical presence. A canon of photographic projects answering to the dialectics of abstraction and atavism—a canon of artists and practices to which today we have to respond more directly than in the past—might be imagined. Think of Richard Avedon's portraits suspended between the most extreme conditions of what could be called the "blank" and the "detail," the Warholian disjunction of skin and ground. Think of Ian Wallace suspending his work—we must contemplate Warhol again—between photojournalism and the monochrome. Or, more recently, think of Wolfgang Tillmans's suspension of his project between the opposed but imperious demands of snapshot and color field (and between miniaturization and enlargement). The photographic dialectics of abstraction and atavism thus have a long history and have shaped photography history in various ways at various times. However, the questions we need to ask concern the ways in which this opposition structures photographic practice today, as we seem to face the most extreme crisis of social abstraction that we have ever known.

And yet, the "aesthetics of the crash" may no longer be our specific problem, just at the moment that we become dimly aware of its longer history and dynamics. If we want to follow the poet manqué of the current crisis, or more accurately its poète maudit, Alan Greenspan, we have perhaps entered today not an economic crash at all, but what he called instead memorably a "credit tsunami." [18] The metaphor is no longer the (modernist) one of the crash, calling for strategies of disjunction, collision, and montage. Instead it is of the tsunami, a metaphorics of flow, overflow, and excess, of echoes and reboundings, of chain reaction, of inundation and flood—liquidity gone awry. It is not a question of the industrial object crumpled before us, but of the flood plain swept bare, the barren aftermath of a catastrophic clearing. Stated in this way, the metaphor surely seems appropriate for an era of abstraction as intense as the one through which we have been passing. Such is the imagination and the "writing of the disaster" that we must broach. Perhaps we need to imagine dams more than crashes, stoppages more than collisions. Perhaps we need drainage. Perhaps we need new forms of emptying more than of collapse.

In closing, I could mention two photographic projects that perhaps embody a new writing of the disaster. Surely both engage the present and its regimes of social abstraction through concerted modes of photographic atavism. I am thinking of Zoe Leonard's *Analogue* (1998–2007) and Sharon Lockhart's *Pine Flat Portrait Studio* (2005). [19] Imagine, if you can—since these are "words without pictures"—the first photograph, "TV Sets in Store Window," from Leonard's recent archive as it was published in book form. [20] We face a neglected shop window, filled with broken-down televisions awaiting repair, boxes within boxes captured within another box, the outmoded Rolleiflex that the artist aligns with her chosen objects, and whose reflection can be dimly glimpsed in the shop window's ghostly sheen. We face echoes of Eugène Atget and Walker Evans, the return and repetition of time past through the citation of photographic languages, like a vast collection of the aesthetics of economic crisis resounding through the ages and touching the present. And we face an image of emptying—the obsolete camera capturing the neglected shop window, replete with television screens stripped bare, deadened, the dance of flickering media images no more. And yet this emptying is also the precondition for a new form of retention, of holding on, as the image presents us with a kind of hole that is in reality a waiting receptacle, with the voiding of the image only allowing an opening onto the past, the filling of this hole with the data of both memory and desire. We face the receptacle that is the camera opening onto the receptacle of the shop window, filled with the receptacles of the television screens, analog receivers that no longer project the information of the mass media but passively accept the aleatory life of the events of the nearby street: the cars, buildings and also the artist reflected on an entirely transformed—photographic—form of the screen.

It is a strange form of emptying at which we stare, just as repetition takes on entirely new dimensions in Lockhart's *Pine Flat Portrait Studio*. Like Benjamin contemplating the avant-garde's return at a moment of economic crisis to the primitive photographs of the 1840s, Lockhart's contemporary images of rural children reawaken forgotten vernacular photographic languages, such as the amateur archives of Mike Disfarmer from the early twentieth century. A genetic connection and return is contemplated, and the photographs emerge not so much as statements of appropriation and citation—proper to the debates carried on around photography at earlier moments of postmodernism—but as documents of historical remnants, continuities between past and present, the survival of what seems most precarious and impossible to contemplate in the current historical moment. But repetition structures almost every aspect of Lockhart's project, as the images repeat not only Disfarmer's language and project, but also internally echo amongst themselves, with all of the children imaged by Lockhart appearing at the same scale within the image, setting up new forms of connection and new experiences of time travel (the ability to distinguish the marks of age all but cancelled out). And Lockhart's project holds an almost hidden dialog with another set of images, in this case memory images—Lockhart's own private archive of portraits of her own childhood, as well as family snapshots of her own past. It is a meditation on childhood that is also then a meditation on time past, but everywhere returning. The modality of repetition let loose by the seemingly inherent powers of photographic atavism, its vertiginous ability to propose historical survivals and retain superceded remnants of that which we imagine abstraction to have eradicated—the resounding call of the historical echo.

And so with these strategies of emptying and of repetition, photographic atavism returns us to the terms with which we began: Krauss's assertion of a new postmodern abstraction of the "empty sign" and of uncanny repetition. This is no coincidence. For now these experiences of photographic abstraction serve another set of purposes; the terms and strategies of postmodernism return, but with a crucial difference. It is with this recent historical transformation of aesthetic languages in mind that I propose the importance of contemplating the dialectics for photography of abstraction and atavism. The new historical conditions of our present moment, I have been trying to argue, require this. And if photography must always be conceived as torn between this dichotomy, articulating it differently at different historical moments, the lessons of the present teach us that photography will never embody just one or the other of these aesthetic options. This is a new way, perhaps, of stating an old dilemma: the ontological anti-essentialism of the photograph. Photography cannot be reduced to regimes of abstraction (it is perhaps also then one of our most potent weapons of resistance to them); but neither can it fully resist them. Torn between abstraction and atavism, photography finds itself in a space between complicity and resistance, between futurism and archaism. I will admit to my interlocutor here, to Walead Beshty, that yes, these last thoughts are abstractions indeed. But the question—the Brechtian question—is: are they useful?

Notes

1. Rosalind Krauss, "Photography and Abstraction," in *A Debate on Abstraction* (New York: Hunter College Art Gallery, 1989), pp. 63–70.
2. Oliver Wendell Holmes, "The Stereoscope and the Stereograph," in *Classic Essays on Photography,* ed. Alan Trachtenberg (New Haven: Leete's Island Books, 1980), p. 80. Cited in Walead Beshty, "Abstracting Photography," in the *Words Without Pictures* essay series.
3. *Gerard Byrne: Books, Magazines, and Newspapers* (New York and Berlin: Lukas & Sternberg Press, 2003). The book on Byrne was published before the expanded field essay, but they were drafted more or less simultaneously.
4. Which is precisely why they were banned from the essay "Photography's Expanded Field."
5. Bertolt Brecht, "The Popular and the Realistic," in *Brecht on Theatre,* ed. John Willett (New York: Hill and Wang, 1992), p. 109.
6. Hito Steyerl, "Documentary Uncertainty," Documenta 12 Online Magazine (March 2, 2007), http://magazines.documenta.de/frontend/article.php?IdLanguage=1&NrArticle=584.
7. Fredric Jameson, "The End of Temporality," *Critical Inquiry* 29, vol. 4 (Summer 2003), p. 701.
8. Jameson, "The End of Temporality," p. 701.
9. Jameson's thinking on the subject of finance capital could stand as a helpful corrective to the lack of a social vision in the otherwise utopian argument of Nicolas Bourriaud's book entitled *Postproduction* (New York: Lukas & Sternberg, 2002).
10. Jameson, "The End of Temporality," p. 703.
11. Ibid.
12. Jameson, "Culture and Finance Capital," in *The Cultural Turn: Selected Writings on the Postmodern, 1983–1998* (London: Verso, 1998), p. 142.
13. Ibid.
14. For an intimation of the lineaments of this culture of the discard, see the special issue of *October* dedicated to "Obsolescence," *October* 100 (Spring 2002).
15. These paragraphs, in a slightly different form, were first published in *Gerard Byrne: Books, Magazines, and Newspapers*, pp. 73-80.
16. Walter Benjamin, "Little History of Photography," in *Walter Benjamin: Selected*

Writings, Volume 2, 1927–1934, ed. Michael W. Jennings (Cambridge: Harvard University Press, 1999), p. 507.

17. While I have offered up my writing on artist Gerard Byrne as an example of new forms of abstraction, one project by Byrne directly confronts the dialectics of abstraction and atavism both: his series of works on the Loch Ness Monster.

18. Descriptions of our current crisis suffer from mixed metaphors, actually. While most commentators try to avoid the word "crash," many refer to the crisis as a "credit crunch." And if the metaphorics of the crash are accepted here, they shift in the larger description of our contemporary condition as a "global financial meltdown," with its evocation of global climate change, the manmade imagined as a natural disaster, and liquidity run amok.

19. I have written at length on these projects in "Lateness and Longing," *50 Moons of Saturn* (Milan: Skira, 2008).

20. Zoe Leonard, *Analogue* (Cambridge: MIT Press, 2007).

--

DISCUSSION FORUM
WWW.WORDSWITHOUTPICTURES.ORG

--

Subject: Letter from Paris
Date: 22 November 2008 14:11:12
From: MOYRA DAVEY

The first question that comes up when asked to think about someone else's proposal is: will it be useful? Will it merit the brief but usually intense detour into someone else's preoccupations, someone else's inquiry? I write slowly, I am not good with abstractions, and I am ambivalent about "the assignment." I crave it as much as anyone; it can be productive and generative; it connects you to people; there is a *dérive* aspect to it that I enjoy; but I also worry that it is a distraction from the deeper and oftentimes more painful questions of one's own. If I accept an invitation to respond, I must do so in good faith to the project and its writers, but only if it helps me think through and clarify ongoing and latent questions of my own. And it is only worth doing if "responsibility", "urgency" and "pleasure" can figure in equal measure.

These days I have been immersed in forms of the diary, note-taking, letters. I came to Paris with a project that begins with a series of images from a letter Walter Benjamin wrote to Gershom Scholem on December 20, 1931: a library, a divan on which to write, lying down, a view and a clock. I discovered the letter about a year and a half ago while reading Benjamin's "Little History of Photography," published the same year, and looking to substantiate a hunch that Benjamin had been contemplating suicide around the time he wrote the essay. I did not have to look far: Susan Sontag confirms it in "Under the Sign of Saturn," her magnificent, short biographical homage to Benjamin. Nonetheless, I read most of the letters from 1931 and retained that one. I brought a copy of it with me and copied a portion of it into a document named "To Have Been Driven," the default title chosen by Microsoft Word that became the working title for "the thing I am working on now" a long, tangled, diary-hydra that will eventually get edited down to a video script (or maybe not).

Hence my impulse, after reading George's text "Photography and Abstraction," about, among other things, the relationship between photography, capital and the financial crash, to lift from my diary this entry of just over a month ago:

"October 7. Not enough sleep. Drive myself crazy with online banking. Read *NYT* first thing: news about stocks plummeting and potential worldwide crisis: recession or worse. How to go on with what I do in the face of all this? Feel insane at the moment."

The sentence "How to go on with what I do . . . ?" did not come out of the blue. While I did, in fact, in that sudden and sickening way, feel the triviality of "what I do" in the face of the "credit tsunami" going on out there, the permission to write my question came from a sentence Jane Bowles (who also figures in the "To Have Been Driven" project) wrote in a letter to her friend Libby Hollman in 1964. Here is the sentence, exactly as Jane wrote it seven years after suffering a disabling stroke at the age of forty: "Now I am so depressed about Goldwater and the whole negro civil rights scandal that I think to write about anything else is beside the point."

I've digressed, but I want to stay on track, so I read again the double-sided page of notes that I jotted over the course of my second reading of George's essay. Near the top of the page I've written: "Walead's pictures → my diary → abstractions," and near the end, I've copied the essay's final sentence about the Brechtian question of usefulness, and later, while on the phone to a friend I added in pencil: "Subprime mortgages → alchemy, shit-to-gold pyramid scheme. Late capitalism → postModernism. Finance capital → digitization of the image etc." What to make of all this? Other than "alchemy, shit-to-gold," I rarely speak or write any of the other terms listed above. They form a category of abstract thought I mentioned earlier, the kind I'm not adept at. Plus, I have so much more to say about Benjamin's letter and its beautiful images, and especially about Bowles's letter in relation to where we are now in 2008 with Barack Obama as president-elect.

I saw Walead's pictures in the 2007 Whitney Biennial and in my diary, noted: "March 4. Walead Beshty: large, dreamy photos of trashed hallways in abandoned building. Smashed glass cubes and shipping boxes. Love the look of this stuff. These people are the new guard. Feel old and outmoded." I assumed the pictures were digitally-created, later learned the washed-out, painterly effect came from film fogging in airport x-ray machines, and finally, that these were pictures of the abandoned Iraqi embassy in the former East Berlin. Abstraction and atavism figure in these works; I would also hazard that "the real" is in them too, in their evocation of war and grief.

A diary can be like an exquisite corpse. On the page immediately following Walead's I find: "March 5. Finished long AF piece on Zoe's Winterthur retro." And not far below that: "Tacita Dean ancient painted tree at MoMA; Atget glowing staircases; Sander portraits of old men + women in black." When I packed for Paris in August I assembled a folder of documents to bring: it contains the Benjamin letter in English and in German;

the "To have been driven . . . " quote from a self-help book; and an odd and very beautiful Xerox clipping in deep, rich blacks using Times Roman. It is a footnote giving Barthes's definition of Structuralist activity ("makes something appear which remained invisible"), a fragment I keep in my periphery and read every so often to remind myself of what it means. Also discernable is about one inch of a photo that I know to be August Sander's "Three Farmers on the Way to a Dance" (ca. 1914). I'd forgotten the origin of the clipping but am now almost certain it comes from George's *October* essay "Photography in the Expanded Field," a portrayal of futurist rather than atavistic aspects of the medium. I resist it all at first. I must have checked Word Count a hundred times while writing this, but now I am over my limit, and so it is time to conclude and to say that for myself at least, yes indeed, the abstractions have been useful.

--

Subject: notes on foreclosure
Date: 8 December 2008 00:53:15
From: HITO STEYERL

Hello George,

What I really admire in "Photography and Abstraction" is its determination to confront the most urgent questions head on. How will the recession upset visuality and rearrange our perception? Will it confront us with the austerity of an updated FSA aesthetics, reenactments of Busby Berkeley's girl-ornaments or Leni-Riefenstahl-meets-Hamas, death metal terrorist videos? What could terms like re-nationalization or volatility mean beyond national pavilions at a Frieze Art Fair or gallerists jumping from high-rise buildings?

It's too early to tell, for sure. You are wise to refuse to engage in any speculation as to the crisis' consequences. But connecting aesthetic and financial abstraction to think through these questions is a very convincing way to move forward. Reading "Photography" is like overhearing a conversation that I immediately want to join in.

Here are just two small comments or fragmentary and sketchy contributions to this discussion:

1. False Concreteness: Hyper-abstraction and false concreteness are probably twins. While the former is defined by unrepresentability, the latter could be dubbed an overrepresentation.

What does false concreteness mean? Coined by critic Siegfried Kracauer in 1927, false concreteness means the attempt to forcefully concretize abstract power structures. False concretions are premature representations as well as attempts to violently reduce complexity.

To give a possible example: the urge to represent the unrepresentable may be a factor in many contemporary terror attacks, which can be seen as forced attempts at concretion of abstract power dynamics. It's like creating the enemy by shooting at him or her, by means of retroactive logic. If somebody drops dead, they must have been evil in the first place. False concretion could indeed be described as the rationale of much of contemporary warfare as well. In times where drawing clear lines between "us" and "them" has become a paradoxical task, false concreteness takes a delusional shot at simplification.

But false concreteness is also tied to the proliferation of (media-) hyperrealisms—catastrophe as daily soap opera, YouPorn, and permanent live transmissions. All these failing concretions merely prove that today's reality is an abstraction that stubbornly resists being concretized. This means that a large number of contemporary realisms are actually failed takes at abstractions. And that any other realism will look fairly abstract today.

2. Foreclosure: "Foreclosure is the legal and

> professional proceeding in which a mortgagee, or other lienholder, usually a lender, obtains a court ordered termination of a mortgagor's equitable right of redemption. Usually a lender obtains a security interest from a borrower who mortgages or pledges an asset like a house to secure the loan. If the borrower defaults and the lender tries to repossess the property, courts of equity can grant the owner the right of redemption if the borrower repays the debt. When this equitable right exists, the lender cannot be sure that it can successfully repossess the property, thus the lender seeks to foreclose the equitable right of redemption."

A whole barrage of words like violation, repossession, equity and even redemption are deployed to circumscribe legal foreclosure. Its definition sounds like a fast forward version of Benjamin's sermon about violence and the law. What it probably means: The creditor excludes the defaulting debtor from any further relations with him or the property. Any symbolic tie to him is terminated. He or she is not only literally left out in the cold, but also kicked out of the sphere of legal relations.

Here is another definition of foreclosure:

> "Foreclosure is a primordial defense because it does not act on a signifier that is already inscribed within the chain of signifiers, but rather, it rejects the inscription itself." (Jacques Lacan, *Écrits*, 1955-56)

This is Jacques Lacan's version, his translation of Freud's term *Verwerfung*. Lacan's foreclosure is not a procedure of exclusion, but absolute refusal of inclusion into the symbolic. It opens up a "pure and simple hole . . . in the Other." (Lacan, *Écrits*) " . . . When the subject calls upon the Father . . . he encounters only an echo in a void that triggers a cascade of delusional metaphors."

Do these two different meanings of foreclosure have anything in common? And does this coincidental consonance help us to think beyond the borders of (symbolic) representation? Both terms refer to an exclusion from the level of the law and the symbolic, and prevent the inscription of certain elements, but from different directions. While one is expulsed, the other one cannot be included. While one locks you out, the other refuses to take you into account.

In Lacanian diction the foreclosed is relegated to the Real; in the terminology of real estate the foreclosed might be cleared out or evicted. But while the Lacanian Real is completely banned from any form of appearance, the contemporary foreclosed is present yet unrepresented, invisible in plain sight. Just as the homeless "box people" in Tokyo's parks and back alleys populate blind spots in bypassers' vision (whose gaping size leaves you to wonder whether they still see anything at all). Or like the blind TVs you mention in Leonard's photos.

What is thus the relation between the Real and real estate? Does the Real in real estate refer to the fact that ultimately nothing can be owned at all? That our own apartment appears to us as expropriated and alienated from ourselves? Is there anything like foreclosure from vision? And would this mean that reality has been repossessed?

Good night,
Hito

--

Subject: Response to George Baker: Photography and Abstraction
Date: 13 December 2008 02:41:54
From: MARK GODFREY

In George Baker's text, at least four meanings of the terms "abstract" and "abstraction" are used, each one associated with different traditions of 20th century art.

a.) Abstraction in "the formalist sense of the term—empty, blank, non-representational" would presumably describe a kind of artwork like a Robert Ryman painting or abstract photographs by Bauhaus professors and students. (These were the abstract photographs that Rosalind Krauss starts with in her essay "Photography and Abstraction" before introducing James Welling and Holly Wright.) George quickly dismisses this kind of abstraction as not particularly interesting to him given his present concerns.

b.) Abstraction as a kind of image that is *abstracted from* another kind of image. This is the understanding of abstraction that underpins Hito Steyerl's ideas (as George presents them). Steyerl is interested in the "low-resolution abstraction" that one finds in degraded or highly pixelated images made by cell-phone cameras. These "almost entirely unintelligible" images have taken on a value as seeming to be the most "concrete" or authentic images made in war zones. This idea of abstraction as the degraded image for me invokes the notion of abstraction present in some early 20th century work such as Theo van Doesburg's *Composition (The Cow)* (1917), a painting that is almost entirely unintelligible as a cow, but whose design is abstracted from a more recognizable image. Needless to say, the associations attached to degraded "abstract" images made in war zones are very different to those attached to such paintings.

c.) George's main concern is with abstraction "as a social . . . process; . . . that violent decontextualization, voiding, and recoding of objects endemic to the principles of capitalist modernity." Abstraction here is the name George gives to the social and economic processes of early 20th century modernity. One might think that the early collages of Picasso would be an example of art appropriate to this understanding of abstraction.

d.) The abstraction associated with finance capitalism. George theorizes a later historical moment, that of finance capitalism, as a new degree of abstraction. Finance capitalism is "the abstraction of an abstraction," since whereas in earlier stages of capitalism, money was tied to production and materials, in the period of finance economy, money floats freely from "identifiable objects, products, or commodities." "Money [is] generated from money itself." Thinking about finance capitalism in this way allows him to characterize a practice such as Gerard Byrne's, which consists of photographs whose meanings are not necessarily tied to the things they depict, as powerfully responsive to contemporary social conditions, since it has a "procedural congruence" with finance capitalism. Byrne's "new form of abstraction" plays the same game as finance capitalism and can therefore counter its workings. Byrne's practice can be called "abstract" even though his photographs show things in the world (unlike Ryman's paintings), and even though they are not "abstracted from" anything (like Van Doesburg's).

For me, it is helpful to try to separate out these four understandings of abstraction. First of all, I would question whether we do not simply need more art historical or critical terms to signify the divergent ideas that are encompassed by the term "abstract" in the way that some cultures have several words for "snow"! But I would also question some of the assumptions made about some of the notions of abstraction here.

For instance, I do not think that abstraction in "the formalist sense of the term" should necessarily be understood as "empty, blank, non-representational." Elsewhere, I have argued that formalist abstraction, for instance, the paintings of Barnett Newman and Frank Stella, can constitute powerful representations of historical events and historical experience. But to address photography, I would suggest that today many artists are interested in the "formalist" traditions of abstract art even when they are putting these traditions to new uses. As George brings up Zoe Leonard's practice, my example will be her most recent work. *You see I am here after all* (2008) is an installation made up of 4,000 postcards of Niagara Falls installed along a very long corridor at Dia Beacon. The postcards are grouped according to the viewpoints along the falls and are arranged in large grids. When viewed from a close distance, the work's relationship to Sol LeWitt's nearby, early 1970s wall drawings becomes apparent. There are at least two important strategies of abstraction in these wall drawings: the drawings are arranged in grids, and they invite viewers to experience the difference between the close-up and longer view. (Right near the wall, you can see the individual pencil lines; further back you see shades or tones as the lines dissolve together.) Leonard makes use of exactly these strategies, but the meanings change: close-up, one has a sense of the individual postcards and what each photograph of Niagara meant to individual visitors; further away, one reflects on the history and implications of mass tourism. In other words, in Leonard's hands, strategies of formalist abstraction are used to represent our relationship to the world. Elsewhere, in the 400-part, C-print version of *Analogue*, Leonard also arranges her photographs in grids. To my mind, Krauss's argument about the grid is pertinent here: "One of the most Modernist things about 'the grid' is its capacity to serve as a paradigm or model for the antidevelopmental, the antinarrative, the antihistorical." Though one thrust of *Analogue* is to present a narrative (of shop closures, of the movement of goods across the world), Leonard uses the grid to counter this narrative force. Within the installation version of *Analogue,* there is both a sense of movement corresponding with narrative (from one grid to the next) and of stasis (as one looks across a single grid). This tension could correspond with Leonard's conflicting desires while making the work to keep things as they are (for instance, for her neighborhood to stay as it is) and to track things as they move around the world. Whatever the case, the formal abstraction of the grid serves an important purpose.

My second concern has to do with the characterization of economic history in George's text. Perhaps I am misunderstanding it, but the impression I have is that economic history is too neatly characterized as a succession of stages, for instance from industrial capitalism to finance capitalism. For me, this is problematic because it is (dare I say it) an "abstraction" of conditions as we find them around us. Three or so years ago, at the height of the economic boom, the finance economy was certainly strident, and the effects of speculation could be felt in real terms through rising house prices, and so on. But other economies persist alongside finance capitalism, economies still completely tied to "identifiable objects, products, [and] commodities." To continue with Leonard, one way in which her project can be characterized is that it was both an attempt to attend to the victims of finance capitalism (small, independent shops that closed down as real estate prices escalated) *and* to represent economies that persist beyond the reaches of finance capitalism (the trade in second–hand clothes from New York to Uganda; the economies of the Polish flea market). I think that many of the most interesting photographic projects of recent years (and ones which emerged during the boom years, not since the current recession) have been motivated by a desire to explore the economies that continue alongside finance capitalism. One of Simon Starling's photographic projects, *CMYK/RGB* (2001), for instance, began when he was invited to make an exhibition at a small institution in France. Starling became aware that the French institution printed their catalogues in Romania to save on printing and paper costs. He traveled to the Romanian printing works and took photographs of his journey and the works. Later in France he built a replica of the Romanian printing works within the gallery, and stacked up the photographs he had taken in the space. These "sculptures" were later disassembled and the individual sheets bound into his catalogue. The project, in other words, explored the materiality of the printed photograph, and the economics of photographic and book production, making evident the different economies of Eastern and Western Europe.

While I have some reservations about the uses of the terms "abstract" and "abstraction," and about the characterization of "finance capitalism," I do think that the dialectic of abstraction and atavism posited in the second half of George's paper is fascinating and extremely productive. Certainly (sticking with Starling) it opens up a new way of thinking about some of his most recent projects. Some of these have involved looking at nearly obsolete modes of photographic production, such as platinum printing. In one project, *One Ton II* (2005), Starling visited a South African platinum mine and photographed it. He then arranged for one ton of ore to be exported from the mine from which enough platinum could be taken to print five copies of his photograph. "Atavism" is crucial here since Starling is looking back to the histories of photographic production (rather than to historical kinds of images, as with Leonard's relationship to Atget, or Lockhart's to Disfarmer). Starling is making new use of these processes not though some fetishistic fascination with precious and obscure printing techniques, but to think in concrete terms about our present day relationship to natural resources, labor, energy, transportation, ecology, and so on, in other words, to address materials and real economies rather than "abstract" financial economies. So in some ways, the work counters the "abstraction" of finance capitalism. Yet in a more recent work, *Inventar-Nr. 8573 (Man Ray), 4m-400nm* (2006), another kind of abstraction, in the "formalist" sense of the term, re-emerges. In the Museum Abteiberg in Mönchengladbach, a "proto-postmodern museum by

Hans Hollein" whose architecture is "reminiscent of an opencast mine," Starling was drawn to Man Ray's *Geological Fold* (1927), which shows rock strata. Starling photographed it closer and closer up, firstly on the racks of the museum's storage space, then right up against its surface, and then using a microscope. The sequence of images is presented as a slide show and eventually the microscope photographs reveal the individual particles of the silver salts within the Man Ray print. The particles recall biomorphic abstract sculptures, the photographs showing them are as concrete images of the material world as Man Ray's. The work as a whole could be seen to exchange the image and illusion of Postmodernist architecture with a reminder of its physical underpinnings.

--

Subject: A response to George Baker's "Photography and Abstraction"
Date: 16 December 2008 12:57:23
From: JOHANNA BURTON

I will happily sign on to George Baker's characterizations of abstraction as it has operated (and now operates) with regard to photography; these are (if I read Baker correctly) signposts, not meant as entirely stable or iron-clad, but postulates, *abstractions* if you will, that nonetheless hint at the shape of things as they articulate themselves and are articulated (and re-articulated) over time. Such an operation allows us to throw a net, to *make sense*, if only in order to unsettle it again. My signing on as such does not mean we couldn't debate Baker's terms; I would like to discuss with the author, for instance, the ways in which abstraction is not only a "voiding and recoding of objects" but *also* a wholly necessary tool for human comprehension (as it allows for the illusion of graspability), and the ways in which abstraction flirts with notions of "essence." But to sign on lets me get to his essay's big questions, the ones that I want to think about most.

Indeed, here's what I find so valuable in "Photography and Abstraction": it's an experiment in trying to imagine what changes when everything does (but when everything also seems to stay the same). If, five years ago, Baker's question to himself was "What would an abstraction of an abstraction look like?," then he was writing from within a context that yielded—in its perfect metaphor of money *as* abstraction—a force both omnipotent and absent. Looking back at that situation from the one we now find ourselves in, where that very omnipotence and absence would seem to have forcefully inverted (though, in fact, there is evidence that they are really only gathering a new kind of speed), Baker shores up a wrinkle in what would seem to be the endlessly smooth fabric of abstraction ad infinitum. Call it atavism if you like. (I quite enjoy the perversity of thinking of the implications of embedded DNA that is carried along over generations, but I would like also to challenge the genealogical model, which begs its own set of problems—teleological, patriarchal, etc....) Perhaps I'd call it something else: deep tissue memory or, even more overdetermined, battle scars.

But no matter, whether atavistic outgrowth or site of reparation, Baker's postulation argues that against all odds, something exceeds the parameters of "second degree abstraction," jams the machine that would seem to find a use-value for everything. Whether these breakthroughs are, as Baker suggests, instances of "true realism" is a question, but they are certainly contradictory, in the sense that they offer up material and historical *arguments* (which is to say that they are contentious) in their very being. In hauling the past into the present, they insist on a layered futurity, a strangely hybrid heap. Unlike second order abstraction (or to return to a related model, Roland Barthes's "secondary mythification"), which promises to undo an operation but oftentimes only redoubles its effects, Baker's atavism promises *nothing at all;* but it does believe that things and ideas surface spontaneously, erratically, productively.

Lacan reminds us that "there is nothing missing in the Real," a phrase that comes to mind especially after reading Hito Steyerl's provocative response to Baker's essay on this *Words Without Pictures* site. That there is nothing missing in the Real we know (and Lacan knew) only because we cannot access the Real; we cannot represent it. That this is the most profound space of the "unrepresentable" does not, however, align photography so neatly with the unconscious, with the traumatic, nor does it mean we should think of the Real as wholly abstract. But there is something important about these overlaps, and about the way they dialogue with Baker's atavism, a model which, like the unconscious, seems to let previously inaccessible elements drift up and into representation—as in atavism, in unwanted horns, or tails, or feet; and as in the unconscious in slips of the tongue, in dreams, and in desire. And it is here that I will end my response to Baker's essay, which I read as both diagnostic and speculative. Having just written a short essay on Zoe Leonard's *Analogue* myself, I too have been thinking about the effect of this collection of some four hundred photographs, taken by the artist over a decade and in places as disconnected, yet deeply entwined, as Mexico City, the East Village, Warsaw, and East Jerusalem. What haunted those pictures for me was not only the persistent yet disappearing "horn" of obsolescent technologies and modes of exchange but also Leonard's inhabitation of the medium itself. For not only did her images reveal what Baker calls "historical survivals" and sound the call of a "historical echo" in the things and places she captured via a vintage Rolleiflex camera. Here and there Leonard's own reflection appears in the glass of a storefront window she shoots; but even when she does not literally appear, the artist, I would argue, pictures herself amidst the "things"—she, too (to steal from Baker some words describing atavism), represents a "shocking return that also signals a departure."

--

Subject: Response to George Baker's "Photography and Abstraction"
Date: 27 January 2009 *
From: TOM MCDONOUGH

* Note: Due to technical difficulties, this response was received after the discussion forum ended.

George Baker's reflections on the current state of photography are necessarily framed by the ongoing world financial crisis, a veritable potlatch of capital on a scale unseen since 1929. [1] The 25-year-long, neo-liberal boom appears to have come to an end, and upon the ruins of this order Baker has asked us to contemplate the outlines of an "aesthetics of the crash," to imagine "new modes of emptying out" and the "devastation" of images—a dialectical potlatch within the realm of the visual, as a critical correlate of that massive destruction of wealth to which we continue to be witnesses. He proposes, in his concluding remarks, two examples of such an aesthetic in what he calls the "photographic atavism" of Zoe Leonard's *Analogue* (1998-2007) and Sharon Lockhart's *Pine Flat Portrait Studio* (2005)—in their shared project of "return[ing] lost contents, forcing temporal hybrids upon the present, the intransigent past haunting the overly confident future." Or rather, we should say that their work is suspended between the poles of abstraction (understood as both a formal and a social condition) and atavism, mobilizing the latter's "vertiginous ability to propose historical survivals and retain superceded remnants" as a form of resistance against the power of the former to empty out, annul and vacate all content from the image.

We might fruitfully extend these reflections, and consider further the ways in which "abstraction" and its other are manifest within the photographic at this moment of global restructuring, by looking at two other recent bodies of work:

Jin Jiangbo's series *The Great Economic Retreat: The Dongguan Scene* (2007-2008) and Tacita Dean's large-scale photographs of ancient trees in southeastern England (2006-2007). Jin's *Great Economic Retreat* consists of a group of panoramic color photographs of the interiors of defunct manufacturing plants in Dongguan, an industrial city of China's Pearl River Delta. By the early 21st century, there were around 14,000 companies backed by overseas capital operating there. Dongguan became, in other words, one node within the circuits of global finance. But as popular struggle over wages has intensified in recent years, investors have chosen to relocate their factories to new, low-wage zones elsewhere in Asia, leaving behind the shells of their manufacturing infrastructure. [2] Jin has taken these as his subject matter; but in their thematics of absence, the resulting images do not simply reproduce the logic of the documentary photograph.

Take for example his image of the abandoned factory floor of a television manufacturer. We see a cavernous space, an open floor roofed with simple, exposed steel trusses, lit by sunshine streaming in through distant windows. All moveable equipment has been removed, and what remains are forlorn piles of insulation scattered about the floor, some fire extinguishers, and the overhead banners that once exhorted the employees toiling below. It is an apparently straightforward image, but one engaged in a rather complex dialogue with an extended genealogy of "abstraction." First we might note its evident reference to a recent history of digital photography, in particular Andreas Gursky's large-scale studies of the architectures of capitalism and globalization. However, whereas Gursky, in works such as *99 Cent* (1999), proffers a visual experience of almost obscene repletion and stimulation, Jin presents us with a vast expanse of emptiness, a "boring" void where there is literally nothing to see. Or perhaps we would do better to say, where capital accumulation has given way to dust breeding. For this floor, an immense, horizontal plane with heaps of waste strewn about, uncannily echoes *Dust Breeding*, Man Ray's 1920 photograph of Duchamp's *Large Glass* covered with a year's worth of dust. *Dust Breeding*'s aesthetic of lassitude is here transformed into an index of capital's mobility and the concomitant obsolescence of human labor. Lastly, we should see in this empty room the negation of collectivity—an image of the way that capital is able to assemble and disperse bodies according to its own logic. [3] As such, it stands as a dialectical counterpart to Shao Yinong and Mu Chen's remarkable photographic series, *Assembly Hall* (2002), a typological survey of the halls used for communal gatherings during the Cultural Revolution of the 1960s and 1970s as seen from the post-Maoist present.

Tacita Dean's large-scale, black-and-white photographs of trees, whose forms she isolates by painstakingly applying white gouache in order to paint out all background detail, would seem in their bucolic solemnity to be at the very opposite aesthetic pole than Jin's desolate factories, but in fact a similar logic is engaged. Here, too, it is a matter of atavism, of what stubbornly remains: in *Beauty* (2006), we see a hoary, twig-laced oak of great age (half a millennium or more), framed by the flurry of white brushstrokes. The title of the work is in fact the name of the tree pictured, a venerable specimen found on the Fredville Estate in Nonington, Kent. (Dean also photographed Majesty there, widely considered the most impressive oak in Great Britain.) There seems to be an important conjunction of image and technique, both of which verge on the outmoded: both tree and analog photography appear as holdovers from an earlier age, and her choice of overwriting the image in gouache similarly recalls procedures of hand-retouching that have been superseded in an age of Photoshop. Indeed, *Beauty* resolutely positions itself on the aesthetic terrain of the digital the better to announce its atavistic intentions. The scale of the work, at 141 x 147 inches, recalls that of digital photography, while its prominent seams—the photograph is printed on three overlapping sheets of paper—read as pointed rejoinders to the seamlessness of contemporary photographic manipulations. But Dean's aim in *Beauty* and related works extends beyond a reflection on the persistence of the analogue; both tree and photography have an allegorical function. The great age of this oak brings to mind an earlier, pre-Modern i.e., pre-capitalist, social order, and despite being located on private property *Beauty* functions as a kind of cipher for the commons, for a notion of a logic external to the commodity and enclosure. Dean's *Beauty* is then an image of perseverance, threatened and tenuous, no doubt, but still striking in its gravity. This, too, is a photograph that has been emptied out and devastated, to return to Baker's terms, but it is also an embodiment of the principle of hope in the midst of crisis.

Notes

1. See the useful overview in Joel Geier, "Capitalism's worst crisis since the 1930s," *International Socialist Review* 62 (November-December 2008).

2. On this dynamic of global restructuring, see Massimo De Angelis, "Next Lap in the Rat Race? From Sub-Prime Crisis to the 'Impasse' of Global Capital," first published in *UE News* (June and July 2008), and available online at *The Commoner*, www.commoner.org.uk/?p=52.

3. For an anecdotal but fascinating account of the impact of capital's flight from Dongguan on its migrant workers, see Michael Standaert, "Chinese Migrant Workers in Search of Jobs, Return Home to Farms," *The Huffington Post*, December 18, 2008, available online at www.huffingtonpost.com/michael-standaert/chinese-migrant-workers-i_b_151989.html

Why Photography Now?

Los Angeles County Museum of Art
Participants: Harrell Fletcher, Leslie Hewitt, A.L. Steiner
Moderator: Charlotte Cotton

Following the 2008 U.S. presidential election, our final panel discussion, "Why Photography Now?," addressed the importance of photographic practice at a moment of geopolitical unrest and urgency. For the three artists participating in the discussion, photography is just one aspect of their practices. We asked each of them to discuss how photography might be thought of as a politicized medium outside of social documentary concerns and to talk about why and when they make photographs as opposed to other objects or actions. The conversation touched on issues ranging from the economy of images and the flexibility of the archive, to how a photographic act might be thought of as a political gesture rather than a document.

HARRELL FLETCHER: I'm going to go through a few different projects that I've worked on over the years that have some connection to politics and/or photography from a variety of different approaches. This first image is from a series that I did in collaboration with another artist, Jon Rubin, as a commission for the San Francisco Museum of Modern Art. It's called *Wallet Pictures*. We set up a camera stand in the museum's lobby. As visitors came through to see the museum's collection, we asked if we could see their wallet pictures. And then we re-photographed them and got all these different, amazing pictures that people happened to have with them.

. . . Another aspect of the project is about keeping the

photos on your person and then destroying them in that process. We selected 10 out of about 150 photographs that we collected in six hours. Those we enlarged to 30 by 40 inches, framed, and put in the museum's permanent collection. This is an installation of them with a Félix González-Torres piece in front when they were first shown. They're actually on display right now. Somebody just sent me an email of this photo at the museum. The ideas were that you could go back and see your own wallet picture included in the museum's collection, and that people carry art along with them all the time, even as they go to see art in an institution.

Another project I worked on was in Hartford, Connecticut. It was the second part of a video project using text from *Ulysses* by James Joyce. In this case, I worked with various seniors at the Parkville Senior Center who read lines from *Ulysses*. The video was constructed into a film [*The Problem of Possible Redemption*] and then projected in front of their senior center. The text that I selected was about mortality, war, and various related things, which came out through the lines of the text and were embodied by the readers.

Directly related to the subject of tonight's discussion is a project I did called *The American War*. I was invited to Vietnam as an artist in residence for a program that was happening there. I was really interested in going because I wanted to have the chance to have a real experience in Vietnam. I felt like so much of my understanding of Vietnam was based on Hollywood's representations of it. When I got there I was trying to talk to people about their experiences with the war. For the most part, people didn't want to talk about it very much. But they consistently directed me to a museum called The War Room in Ho Chi Minh City, and said that I should go there to see their perspective on it.

One of the first things I found out was that in Vietnam the Vietnam War is called "The American War," which makes perfect sense. It was actually really frustrating to me that I hadn't figured that out on my own in advance. This is a picture of the front yard of the museum where they have remnants from the war—helicopters, planes, tanks, and bombs. Inside of the main part of the museum is an exhibit of about 100 photographs. They take you through the 10-year, official U.S. involvement in the war and then the aftermath. It's an interesting combination of photographs, some taken by documentary photographers in Vietnam, and some of them bootlegged from U.S. publications and other sources. They show images that, as someone from the U.S., I feel really uncomfortable about seeing. At the same time, I know they are part of a reality that existed there.

I was in Vietnam in 2005. The Iraq War was going on as well as the war in Afghanistan. So, it had a certain poignancy to me beyond just getting a chance to connect with Vietnam. The text that went with the photographs was in both Vietnamese and in English. Some of the images are really horrific, as you can see. Here are some from *Life Magazine*. They were bootlegged. They're very similar actually to the *Wallet Pictures* pieces that I did in that they just re-photographed them. They also show the aftermath of environmental devastation, and some of the birth defects that occurred as well. And then there are the statistics. Most people in the U.S. know that the number of U.S. troops that were killed during the Vietnam War was 58,000. But fewer people are familiar with the fact that there were 3,000,000 people killed in that same amount of time in Vietnam.

There were other numbers, including how many people became lonesome because their children or relatives were killed during the war. I thought that was a really important statistic to include because it's obviously one that's always a part of any war. While looking at the images in the museum, I was struck by the fact that I knew so little about Vietnam even though I was born during the Vietnam War. It seemed like it was a really important thing for me to look at, especially at this time when the U.S. was engaged in war again. I thought it would be nice for other people in the U.S. to see the same imagery. So, I decided to re-photograph all of the images and then re-present them in various venues. The first place was in San Antonio, Texas, where

I was an artist in residence at Artpace. I printed all of the images there and then recreated the museum through the photographs.

Along the way, I did a bunch of public programs inviting local people who experienced the Vietnam War to talk to each other. We did classes and held film screenings of documentaries including *Hearts and Minds* [Dir. Peter Davis, 1974] and *Winter Soldier* [Winterfilm Collective, 1972], that we borrowed from the public library. I was trying to continue my education while working on the project. This is what the recreation looked like. Inside were images lined up on the shelf along with the text that went with them. The show wound up traveling to about eight other venues in the U.S. The first one was at Virginia Commonwealth University in Richmond, Virginia.

In each place I did some kind of public program where local people talked about their experiences with the war from various points of view. This is at White Columns in New York; they did a 24-hour, all-day film screening. Eventually, the show was happening in multiple places at once. So, I had to make a smaller, extra set. This was at the Center for Advanced Visual Studies at Massachusetts Institute of Technology. They did a public program specifically with MIT professors. Noam Chomsky spoke, which was a pretty great thing to experience.

Here in Los Angeles it showed at LAXART. As part of that exhibition I was asked to make a billboard. So, I went to the Los Angeles Public Library and took out some of the books that I had been studying and photographed them and made that into the billboard as a reminder that this information is there. Anybody has access to it. If we don't keep reminding ourselves of what happened in Vietnam, then we wind up in situations like we have in the Middle East now. A public program happened at LAXART as well. The show finally wound up traveling to Porto Alegre, Brazil, and similar things occurred down there. Now it's gone to New York where it's in a collection.

LESLIE HEWITT: Why photography now? Perhaps because

of the implied democratic potential of the camera. The technology of seeing is the articulation of sight. Both of these are still strong, self-evident qualities in the practice of photography. The pragmatism embedded in the reduction of the world into pictures keeps me committed to the medium.

I was born into a world of images. Hence I was faced with the task of deconstructing them and repositioning them for myself in a futile attempt to claim the original view, to document my role as a viewer, and to mark my place in time as a consumer of images and of the fragility of meaning that is said to be locked within them. So that's my answer. Though my answer may sound very romantic, I do have a bit of a nihilistic edge. I have come to realize that the meaning of images is very slippery. They're not fixed in time.

I decided to do this project called *Riffs on Real Time*, on which I spent about three years working in intervals. I took snapshots—some personal, some found—and rephotographed them, making these pseudo gestures, these quick documents. Sometimes they're slippery. They start out personal. They become social. They become political. They traverse in between all of those things. I was really interested in having many perspectives condensed into one picture plane. Oftentimes people ask me, "Where is the photograph?" I'm overtly appropriating other images. But as you'll see, hopefully, it is about trying to document a paradigm shift. . . . This one is from *Ebony Magazine*. It's a reprint of the Detroit riots and then on top of it is a superimposed snapshot from '76 of a leisurely game of football. The two types of violence are conflated into one, with one seeming completely radical. I should also say that my parents were really active in the civil rights movement. I was aware of COINTELPRO when I was eight or nine years old, and read millions of conspiracy books. All of this factors into how I engage with history with a slightly distrustful eye.

This is *Make It Plain*, a series that I did in 2006 looking at seminal texts from 1968. Perceptions of this work shift with the recent election. I was looking at two seminal texts.

One, the Kerner Report, was commissioned by Lyndon B. Johnson as a sociological document to try to understand the rationale—or to try to rationalize—riots. I thumbed through this book for a long time. It was really interesting and impactful to think about this inanimate object trying to explain something that is unexplainable. The other book within this photographic series is titled *Black Protests* by Joanne Grant, who was the secretary to W.E.B. Du Bois. That little tidbit was really important to me. I think that when one thinks of collective consciousness building, usually it's through a text, a film, or something else that sparks collectivity versus individuality.

[Du Bois's] seminal text, at least at the turn of the 20th century, stirred the souls of black folks. It talked about the concept of having a dual consciousness. And I thought that it was an amazing text about being slightly abnormal, or having this psychological superpower to see through two lenses at the same time. You see yourself as other, but at the same time see yourself as who you are. I wanted to do this series that had both of those perspectives in line. There's the perspective of the still life that seems very mundane, but at the same time, snapshots circulate around this series that are meant to act as counterpoints within the photographic series.

The other really important part of this series was its three-dimensional object-ness. It sat in the room. It had a physical presence that you couldn't walk away from. It wasn't something that was purely nostalgic. It was your size. You had to contend with it. The centerpiece was meant as a projection screen. What is the relationship between these moments? What is the relationship between our moments? How does collective action function? Where does it end, or where does it end up? In a way, these are my muses to try to reconstruct another reality with a past that seems so far away. But we could potentially talk about whether that has shifted.

This is another image. It's unglazed and 5 by 7 feet, and you see how it is leaning against the wall. I should also say that "Make It Plain" was used to introduce Malcolm X's speeches. His goal was to speak in a very pragmatic, direct fashion. Somebody could argue that, although this seems like a very direct still life or very direct use of the camera, there's still a reflexive moment. A part of the installation is an Eastman Kodak photography book that's screwed into the floor. I often like to parallel the subject, my subjectivity, and the larger collective consciousness that I'm referencing, or that is indexed in the photographs. Parallel to that is thinking of the potential role of the camera or photography as a revolutionary medium. I take a lot of cues from Third Cinema and the idea of thinking that you can create change in how something is represented by radicalizing our view of it. Obviously, the invention of the camera did that, but then how do we still retain that spark? . . .

This is an image of the most recent exhibition, in Zurich. The title of the show was *The Fullness Of Time*. This piece is called *Untitled Capsule* a.k.a. *The Roots Sculpture*. I collected *Roots* [Alex Haley, 1976] books from the first printing in '76, and '77. (They reprinted in '77 because they sold out.) The size of the sculpture is 4 by 6 feet. I guess I stopped collecting the books when they filled this collapsed bookcase. I was thinking about not only *Roots* as fiction, but also as a narrative that refers to slavery and the impossibility of tracing one's history. At the same time, I was really interested in how this story was completely commodified. We can probably also talk about that aspect of photographs that reference something in particular, something of interest, and that then become commodifiable objects, while at the same time being indices.

A.L. STEINER: I'm going to play a video while I'm talking so that you can listen to me or pay attention to the video. I wrote a manifesto. Manifestos are still relevant, of course; they're more relevant probably than ever. Photography functions through the implication of encounter. (Of course, what follows is as personal and contradictory as all manifestos are.) The images communicate with each other rather than existing as objects to be traded in the marketplace between wealthy individuals or corporations. The term "artworks" implies that these efforts are active, that they're doing something. Verbs, not nouns, are created through the active mind in unspecified time and of a meditative state.

Our daily decisions impact other people and places. Yet through the world of images we reside in a state of blissful ignorance. We're often unable to recognize that we're making decisions. Photography has informed the passive role through its ease and proliferation of images beyond the aura. It has altered our sense of agency, for good or for bad. Image dialogues and collaboration allow me to incorporate and express the ecstasy and agony of these decisions. Historical worlds and spheres of influence expand through opportunities presented by self. Created organizationally by structures and by conscious decision-making as "queer," eco-feminist, androgynous, and otherwise oriented, photographs are objectified for distribution and consumption by institutions. My works' efforts, inspiration, and purpose stem from an urge to inspire, discuss, inform, and dismantle preconceived notions of what is possible and what is truth.

Hans Abbing, in his book *Why Are Artists Poor?,* tries to answer the question, "What is art?" Art represents or expresses values that are of the utmost importance to society. Art, like religion, manifests the basic values in society and the changes in those values. Moreover, works of art comment on these values less directly, but not necessarily less effectively, than the stories and the great religious books once did. In its recording capacity, art offers an amazing archive of what came before.

No history book can compete with the vividness of old paintings, sculpture, and literature. "Art" is a treasure trove consisting of almost everything of value that our ancestors left behind. In this way, art stands for the accumulated past. I'll conclude my manifesto with a few more thoughts. Capitalism discourages collaboration and community while usurping its benefits among the privileged for profit-making. The cover of capitalism and schizophrenia has been blown. The transformation has begun. The prescient is waiting to be discovered. I think about these things in the context not only of the election that took place about a week ago, but also the last eight years.

Before this talk, we discussed the surreal space that we have lived in for the past eight years since the 2000 election, 9/11, and now this election. I think this space is somewhat undefined; it's definitely an entrance that we are unfamiliar with. Facing the unknown is always full of fear and trepidation, but we are certainly in a different space now. The piece behind me that you see was part of a project that I did called *One Million Photos, One Euro Each*. It has had four incarnations thus far. In the first one, they actually were one Euro each. In the second and third ones, there was a minimum order of 1,000,000 photos. The difference between those contexts was that the first one took place in a nonprofit art space in Berlin. In the second and third, I was asked to do installations at art fairs. I think I was expected to do it the way I had done it previously. But I didn't see the piece as static, nor do I believe the photos are static.

I don't really subscribe to the notion that you make a piece and then that piece is finished. I rarely leave any photo behind because it has been exhibited, nor do I feel like a piece is defined by its space or moment of exhibition. As a result, the second and third were in commercial spaces where the minimum order was 1,000,000. Of course, it's still for sale if anyone's interested in it. What you actually get is a contract with me for a lifetime, until I die or you die. You receive photos quarterly until they reach 1,000,000. A part of the piece is about the relationship we share with these images, and that relationship is not static. I hope that one day I can share that relationship privately, perhaps with one person.

I'll conclude by playing the fourth incarnation of *One Million Photos, One Euro Each,* which took place recently at Yale University. The photos were free for the students, faculty, and anyone who wandered into the Yale art building. The exchange was that the takers had to tell me why they were choosing the photographs. . . . I prefer that the participants speak about the meaning, the interactions, the relationships one creates through photography, and how photography functions. Most of the comments that people made about these photos were more personal. But the structure of what they saw was completely constructed in their minds. It was fascinating for me.

I'll conclude by saying that the dialogue between images, and the dialogue that takes place between those images and us, are as yet in a state of discussion and unanswerable perception. I don't know what they mean or what they've done to us, but they certainly mean a lot and have done a lot of things to us.

CHARLOTTE COTTON: I wanted to start by asking you all a question about where you position your work within contemporary art. Where do you find the outlets and the venues for your types of practice?

HEWITT: They were mostly in group exhibitions initially. Because of the way my work functions as an archive of sorts, it lends itself to multiplicity. It needs space and it needs context.

COTTON: What sorts of thematics have the group exhibitions had?

HEWITT: They've generally been focused on photography and sculpture. It's probably the intersection where I came on to the scene. Most recently there have been more exhibitions centered on "1968." It was not my initial intention to be put in a genre in that way, but it's fine. I think it works.

COTTON: Where do you fit?

STEINER: I think I fit in various places, as I said nonprofit spaces, art fairs and galleries. But a lot of this takes place in theater, too. For a couple of years, I've worked with the collective Chicks on Speed. They're more of a pop group, but they have a hand in art collaboration.

FLETCHER: I guess I've mostly done commissions for art

centers and museums, and some public art projects. A lot of my things have to do with working with students in various ways.

. . .

COTTON: There were two phrases that Leslie used that I really like: "slippery images" and "paradigm shift." I wonder if we talk about how the sense of meanings changes and viewpoints are changing in light of the election. Can you think of instances of bodies of work that you've created in the past where you already know that the meaning has been shifted by actual social, political circumstances in ways that surprise you or have positively affected the meaning?

HEWITT: I've never trusted that an image's meaning is fixed, that's something that I was thinking from the beginning. A lot of my work is creating layers of distance or layers of interruption that are really subtle, but they're aimed at stopping you, or distilling something. I found the election very overwhelming in terms of imagery, and in terms of even trying to find a place to sit and have my own feelings about it, to have my own reflection. I don't feel like I've had that opportunity yet.

The piece that was at the Whitney Biennial this past year and the work that I began in 2006 came from living in the Bush domain and feeling really constricted. I was feeling that a lot of this history that we've already been through was being dismantled day by day, minute by minute. I made that piece in a futile attempt to put the history forward again, just for a second.

In this year building up [to the election], it was infectious and crazy in the media and in people's reactions. It's like a hyper-reality right now. I don't know if I'm speaking around your question, but I think that is the strongest shift. I think that the work either is completely of the moment or it's pushed further back. It has a nostalgic tone to it now, because of how a lot of these concerns have been revisited during the election in a visceral way, though not in an intellectual way.

. . .

STEINER: I have one really interesting anecdote about when I did the *One Million Photos Minimum Order* in Cologne, Germany. Everyone was really confused as to why I was doing it there. It was like this weird Home Depot installation where I was trying to do wallpaper and make it look like if you bought this thing you'd have a really nice house and all this stuff. A reporter came over and said, "I'd like to ask you a few questions." And I said, "Oh, great." She asked, "Are you or is this work coming from a political perspective?" I said, "Well, yeah, I have these concerns—environmental concerns, feminist concerns, and queer concerns." She said, "Are you angry?" And I said, "Of course, I'm angry. Obviously I'm angry. If you're not angry you're insane." And so on. She took notes. The next day was my favorite piece of press I've ever gotten. There was a picture of my installation in the paper, which was awesome. And it said: "Angry Feminist Who Wants to Make a Million Euros." There's no success in one's attempt to say something.

COTTON: I'd like to ask Harrell a question about *The American War*. Obviously, you knowingly built in re-contextualization as part of the experience. What happened when you showed *The American War* in America?

FLETCHER: I wasn't sure what the response was going to be like but people responded positively. Even all of the Vietnam vets that I wound up connecting with as a part of the lecture events had really positive responses, which I wasn't sure was going to be the case. A lot of it was very emotional, and it wound up being pretty great. I had various concerns and none of them happened. Largely what happened was that I got to learn a lot about this part of history that I think is really important, and that prior to the work I was ignorant about. I got to learn about it from different angles and from different people. But I think that had George Bush not been elected and the war in Iraq not happened, then that project probably wouldn't have happened. It is strange to feel connected to George Bush in that way.

COTTON: Can I ask you about your aesthetic choices in how to display the work? How did you get to it? It looked kind of like a library installation.

FLETCHER: I just, in a very simple way, wanted to mirror the installation in Ho Chi Minh City without trying to actually recreate it all. For example, it is always shown on a light blue wall because one of the backdrop walls in Ho Chi Minh City was light blue. You see a lot of the environment in the photographs themselves and I didn't want to add anything else to that. I just kept it simple and straightforward. Speaking of libraries, I thought about trying to exhibit that show in libraries, community centers, and places like that. I still regret that I didn't try to do that more, but I had some trepidation that it would get censored and that there would be other problems. Since then I've done a different project in a library. The librarians actually fought for making sure that it wasn't censored. It was a pretty great experience.

COTTON: What was the project?

FLETCHER: It was a project with a group of students about war—Iraq, Vietnam, Afghanistan, and other wars as well. I defaulted into showing it in the art world, but I wanted to, as I do with a lot of other work, really try to make sure that there was a broad audience that would come to it. In some ways I hope to re-enliven the contemporary art space by bringing people into it that ordinarily wouldn't, and getting them to be invested in it through public presentations.

COTTON: How do you think the art world reads such gestures? You talked about reaching people who wouldn't ordinarily come to an art gallery, or using the gallery as a space to think about a social issue. How did the art world receive your pictures?

FLETCHER: The art world received *The American War* very well. Once again, that surprised me. It went to New York and wound up getting reviewed in *The New York Times,* the *Village Voice* and Artforum.com. Somehow or another, it got some sort of stamp of approval. Thereafter, it was just fine. Since then, it's been taken into the Museum of Modern Art's collection. It did a strange thing that I wasn't expecting—it had a dual ability to function both in and out of the art world.

COTTON: And why do you think that is? Why do you think it became something collectable?

FLETCHER: Probably partly because of its timeliness. Hopefully, it was also pretty good.

. . .

ALEX KLEIN [AUDIENCE]: This is more of an observation than an actual question. In our discussions leading up to this event, we talked about how photography is often used in exhibitions as a way of pointing to the world *out there*; we use it as a tool or index, to say, "Oh look at all this stuff that is happening; we must pay attention to it." We talked about this conversation today not focusing on a social documentarian practice, but rather thinking about photography as a political medium in another kind of context. The first thing that comes to mind for me after seeing all of your presentations is that there are ways in which all three of you engage with photography as a personal connection or bridge or gesture. Not to be too longwinded about this, but I always think about a piece by Thomas Hirschhorn where he built a physical bridge between an anarchist bookstore and the Whitechapel Art Gallery in London. We could talk about the ways in which you are all engaging with photography as a kind of bridge or gesture. With Leslie, it's about making connections between personal and historical material.

Harrell is creating a physical and psychic connection between two cities and between the present and the past in *The American War*. And with Steiner (and this is true for Harrell as well), photography becomes a catalyst for social interaction, having people talk about why it's important to them, or with regard to the other aspects of your practice, such as zines or curating in communities and institutions. I think all of your practices present an interesting flip on the relational potential of photography and generate a very different discussion than that of photography as a document of political unrest.

. . .

AUDIENCE: What are your thoughts on photojournalism?

FLETCHER: To me, if I did lapse into photojournalism that would be okay. For tonight, I selected projects that were specific to the theme. But in general, my work is pretty all over the place, and I like it to be like that. I'm not so concerned with maintaining it in an art context. I actually would like to be a photojournalist, I think, if anybody has a job for me out there. I just keep getting asked to do things in museums, but I wouldn't mind doing photojournalism if that was possible. I might be an anomaly.

STEINER: Very few schools teach photojournalism; very few schools even discuss it. Perhaps there's one class about photojournalism in the curriculum in most photography and art departments. The construction of social concerns within modes of photography is largely disappearing. My perception of photography is that something like 10 trillion photos are being taken every second. In a recent show in Sweden, they sorted through a collection of 80 million photos and picked 350.

So, what exactly are we talking about here? Is the photograph of any importance anymore? For me, it was a tool. I'm not technically very proficient, nor am I interested in formalist concerns, although I think my composition is good. I've learned ways to use photography to discuss things I want to discuss, to reach out to communities and people, and create relationships. My concerns about the frame, or the content of the frame, are minimal.

HEWITT: I'll say a little bit more. I guess for me it's twofold. My interest in photography began as resisting the conventions of a "photograph," and its reference to the pictorial relationship that it inherited from painting. It's hard to resist that, but I began with that as a premise. I tried intentionally to not give myself any limits. I was thinking, "Okay, well, do we all agree on what beauty is? Do we all agree on what is the correct exposure time? Do we all agree that film is calibrated to white versus brown versus black?" There are many ways to get at those questions. I think about all those things, and I think about them differently depending on the project.

For instance, with *Riffs on Real Time* it is really important that it be read as referencing and also being literal to the indexical quality of photography. I'm turning the camera and tripod into a copystand and going through photographs and re-photographing moments. I also intentionally collect snapshots of those deviant moments in photography that are at the same time the most democratic and the most honest. I'm going to dare to say that. I guess my way of working may connect me to a more conventional approach to pictorial space. But, I shoot for really long periods of time. Sometimes the light completely obliterates the subject. I allow all of those things to play a role. It may change, but up until this point, I've always dealt with photography and the history of photography in a very resistant manner. That may also be fueled by the fact that the camera will also have finite results.

AUDIENCE: Could you talk a little bit about what projects you're working on presently?

FLETCHER: I'm working on a play that's going to take place at a regional theater in Victoria, B.C. It's about the theater's neighborhood. It is based on interviews with people from the vicinity and then acted by amateur actors. Afterwards, I'm going to India to make a documentary connecting my wife and me as consumers of a rug that was made in India to the factory where it was made. We're not quite sure what's going to happen, but the plan is to go and try and search out this place.

HEWITT: A few things. I also work collaboratively (although I didn't show any of that work tonight). There are ongoing projects that I have working with other artists and also a book that I'm currently working on documenting our moment, if you will. I'm thinking more about artists' writings these days and am probably also taking cues from the artist writings of the 1960s. I'm also going to travel to the Netherlands to research 16th- and 17th-century still lifes. I've been thinking about the role that capitalism played at that time versus today and about how objects transverse that space. I'm also interested in turning up the volume in terms of the modification of images, modification of history, and capitalism in a way. I guess it's a fine line between the democratic quality of America, and being an American. But then also that comes with a double-edged sword. I'm interested in unpacking that a little bit more.

STEINER: I started a group of a couple artists called W.A.G.E., Working Artists in the Greater Economy. We're having our first public meeting in New York in December concerning the unregulated micro-economy of artists and art institutions in the U.S., in order to try and make things a little more equitable. Perhaps the economic crash will help a little bit to even the playing field with regards to how artists are treated by U.S. art institutions, which is pretty badly. So, reacting to a different part of my experience in the world. I'm also making a porn, and I'm going to finish a piece that I'm showing at the Kitchen with the choreographers that I work with, robbinschilds. And I'm organizing my photos; that's one of my goals.

QUESTIONNAIRE / PETER FRASER

DO NEW TECHNOLOGIES CHANGE YOUR IDEA OF PHOTOGRAPHY?

Unquestionably they do, and in fact it's hard to imagine the history of photography in any other light other than understanding the close relationship between technical developments and artistic achievements, since its invention.

QUESTIONNAIRE / DAVID CAMPANY

WHAT DO YOU SEE AS BEING IN STORE FOR THE MEDIUM?

Everything about the medium will change except its essential characteristics. If those changed, it wouldn't be the same medium.

Allan McCollum & Allen Ruppersberg

Los Angeles County Museum of Art
Moderator: Alex Klein

ALEX KLEIN: I'm so pleased to welcome Allan McCollum and Allen Ruppersberg to LACMA. This has been a long time in the making, and I'm thrilled that we're actually here tonight. It feels fitting to have this conversation here in Los Angeles, where the two artists met and began their careers. Allen Ruppersberg and Allan McCollum share more than a first name and a birth year, they also share a relationship to Los Angeles that has contributed to their practices in very different ways. And although I know that the artists do not want to dwell too much on this point, I'd like to retain Los Angeles as a backdrop for the conversation tonight, and I hope that their relationship to our city will be one of the many topics that they'll be addressing this evening.

In Allan McCollum's essay on Allen Ruppersberg, "What One Loves About Life Are the Things That Fade," [*Allen Ruppersberg: Books, Inc.*, France: F.R.A.C. Limousin, 2001] McCollum describes how "Through our reciprocal discourse between the makers and the consumers of culture a model of the world can emerge." In the essay, he goes on to discuss how the mass-produced products of capitalist consumption and popular media can be as meaningful or personal as any private experience. This seems to me to be a productive way to begin to think about the practices of both artists tonight, through their own words and their reflections on each other's work. As both artists were invited here to LACMA under the auspices of the Photography Department, I hope you will join me in thinking about issues in both of the artists' works relating to photographic practice that might not always be directly related to the lens.

Before Allan and Allen begin, I would just briefly like to direct your attention to the image behind me on the screen. It's from their first collaboration, which took place in Milan this past spring, and it was also part of the occasion of bringing them together tonight. The installation, entitled *Sets and Situations* [2008], joins aspects of both McCollum's and Ruppersberg's practices—the *Shapes Project* by McCollum and the props, which Ruppersberg has used in a variety of other installations. I think that this project particularly underscores the generosity that is imbued in both of their practices, and I look forward to hearing more about it in the discussion tonight.

ALLEN RUPPERSBERG: There are many ways to start. I think I'll start with a little personal reason why we might be here together. Yes, we did this collaboration, but we've also known each other for 40 years. The fact that this is our first collaboration says something about us, and also about the processes that it took to get to this point where both of our works came together. Even though it was kind of a coincidence that it happened, the other side of the coin is that we've known each other all this time, and I don't think that there's another person alive today that I've exchanged more words with than Allan. If you've talked to somebody all of these years about art and, of course, your personal lives and professional lives have run parallel, you don't really know where to start.

I'm sure that we could start anywhere, and it might be interesting to us, but I don't know if it's interesting to everybody else. So, we'll try and stick to something that might make sense. I'll start with a little introduction on this project here. It just so happened that Allan's last show in New York was seen by the gallery director that I've worked with for years in Milan, Claudio Guenzani, and he loved Allan's show. Because we've worked together, Guenzani came to me and said, "Why don't you and Allan do a collaboration because then I could show it." Allan had done collaborations before with other people, but I'd only done maybe one or two. It was a different kind of thing for me, but I said, "That sounds fantastic."

I sat down with Allan and we started to talk about it. It just so happened that with the *Shapes Project*, which you see sitting on top of what I call the *Props/Furniture* (which I was using in a number of installations previous to Allan's *Shapes* projects), we both found that we were interested in the idea of props. We might have known this before, from all the years of conversation, but it pinpointed it. It was a very easy transition to superimpose one body of work on top of another. That's literally what you have here. When I say "prop/furniture," I'll show you some more slides of where this comes from. I think that you can see that there's a variety of colored shapes—tables, stairs, platforms.

There are a number of names for these objects that Allan's *Shapes* projects are sitting on top of. I had begun to use this prop/furniture idea as kind of a base for many different projects. When Allan and I started to talk about what we could do, it seemed like one could easily overlay on top of the other. Except that it wasn't quite as easy as that because Allan has set numbers of shapes that form a group that have to go together. It has to be played out over the different sizes and shapes of the furniture to see how many can go in a group. It's not quite as simple as I'm making it, but at any rate that's how it started.

Here is a previous incarnation of the prop/furniture, which is a piece that I showed in Basel at Art Unlimited a couple of years ago. It's called *The Never Ending Book: Part One*. You can see now a little more clearly the different kinds of shapes and props. In a way, they're vacant sculpture bases, and then something is incorporated on top. They provide me with a structure that I can use in many different ways, much like the posters and other things that I've done. It's like finding an empty structure that I can set my own content on top of, if you will, at least in this case. Or, I incorporate my content somehow into these kinds of commercial structures. In this case, what are inside of these bases on top of the platforms are the images that you see in the back there, which I've taped to the walls.

The signs for collectors only say, "Every Artist Is an Artist." And then there's another one, which comes up later: "Everything is collected. Nothing is saved." It's a whole installation of about a hundred different pages of this *Never Ending Book*, which are in all of these boxes and are free for the taking. So, the audience can make their own book out of all of these pages, which I've Xeroxed and put inside of the boxes. Over the course of the installation, the boxes would be filled every day with colored Xeroxes from this particular subject. Over on the left of this image is the exact title, "The Old Poems (For My Mother)." And then it talks about how you can take these pages. So, in this case "The Old Poems" are all taken from a collection of vanity press books that I've been assembling over a number of years. They basically run from the early turn of the century through the '60s. And the Xeroxes all come from this collection of, I don't know, 300-500 of these books, which have a unique content because they are vanity press books. The majority of them are poetry. They portray a particular part of America that's long gone. That happens to be the general idea of *The Never Ending Book*.

But to go back to the images here, the first use of the props came from this exhibition in Slovenia—the 25th International Biennial of Graphic Arts in Lubiana [2003]. The cover image that you're seeing from the catalogue is from the book from which I got the idea for the props. It was a flea-market find, a small-press book that was written for local theater groups about making generic props and furniture that could be mixed between all kinds of plays and made very cheaply. It's a "how to" book on making generic props. That's where the props come from in the first place. The main element of the Biennial was an assemblage of every artists'-book publisher in the world. There were maybe 300 publishers. This included newspapers, magazines, and every publisher who published anything to do with artists' books over the years. That was all assembled, and then they invited me to figure out a way to present these things. The furniture props were very much user-friendly. Even though now I'd prefer people not to sit on them, in this case it was part of the exhibition. You could sit and read all these artists' books and be comfortable doing it in this theatrical manner with fireplaces, chairs, stairs, etc.

I'm rushing through all of this really quickly. Allan and I talked about how we were going to talk about this and I decided that maybe I would like to go from the present to the past and Allan thought he would go from the past to the present.

This is the newest piece; it's from the Camden Arts Centre in London just a couple of months ago. One of the things that Allan and I have talked about is how both of us are influenced by commercial processes and commercial methods, and how we both come to that in different ways. This has been a staple of my work since I don't know when, but it comes from a very specific place in the fact that I came out of Chouinard Art Institute. When I enrolled, I thought that I was going to be a commercial artist. Part of the program at Chouinard at the time was that for the first two years you took classes in all subjects. Then you were evaluated and you made up your mind what you would do for the remaining two years. Along the line I got introduced to painting and discovered that I did not want to be a commercial artist after all, and I switched to fine arts.

Later on, when I was forgetting about art school and making my own work, I began to think about all the things that I learned about commercial art and that maybe those might be methods and tools that I could use as a fine artist. A lot of the work from then until now has been about the daily world of objects, commercial methods, printing, and all the things that were not designated as fine arts.

In the case of the Camden Arts Centre exhibition, there were two works installed together. One was a carousel of books, which holds small, Xeroxed books that are laminated. My new tools of choice are a brand-new, giant, Canon color Xerox machine and a laminator. A series of artist books, for lack of a better word, hangs above a tile floor, which has to do with the idea of reading standing up, thinking on your feet [*Reading Standing Up*]. Those are two of the ideas that are written into the floor. A series of choices indicate the "choosy business of art," which is another phrase in the floor. You stand there and read the books; there are 18 different ones.

This goes back to the early '90s. Another aspect that Allan and I have both explored is working within a specific community and either doing historical research, as in the case of this work, or working with people in the community in different ways. The time is up. Maybe we can save this for later.

ALLAN MCCOLLUM: I've known Al since 1969, maybe 1968; I can't remember exactly when. And it's extremely difficult for me to explain what an influence he has been over me. I decided to be an artist on my own. I didn't go to art school. It was 1967. I said, "I want to be an artist." Al was practically already well-known in 1967. Meeting him in 1968, I was basically a freshman student in my mind, although I wasn't in school. Because Al wanted to go backwards, you haven't seen the early work of his that influenced me. So, it's going to be hard for me to explain it. Maybe we'll get to that in the conversation.

I'm from Los Angeles; I grew up here and didn't leave until I was about 31 years old. So, I had a whole career and life here. I'm going to start back then and try to rush forward and use my 15 minutes to cover 40 years, if I can. I want to start with a series of works that I showed at the Jack Glenn Gallery in Corona del Mar. During that period in 1969-71, I thought of myself as a painter. Now, it seemed to me that when you decided to be an artist you were a painter. I don't know why I didn't think beyond that. I hadn't been to school to learn about too much beyond that. I was wrestling with this idea of being a painter, but what bothered me most about painting during those years was that you started out with a canvas, which then became the background of what you did on the canvas.

And I didn't like that. I felt that you were creating a secondary background because the real background was the gallery and the real background was the social and anthropological condition that was there for you to go in and look at the paintings. So, I had a problem creating a secondary background. As a result, I did a series of works very early on in which there was no background. I just started with little pieces and glued them together or sewed them together. This was at the Pasadena Art Museum in 1972. It was made up of hundreds of little squares—like little, tiny paintings—that I would then glue together to make a large painting. So there was never an issue of there being a background upon which I would then paint something. This was a moral issue with me. Who decides what the background is? I was really more interested in creating an object that referred only to itself without there being a background that you were supposed to ignore. This was a series done in '74-'75 in which I created a kind of kit. These were little paper pieces that I would paint and then tear out and glue together. I could make paintings. I could make watercolors. I could make drawings. It was like a standardized art object.

My background was working class. I had spent five months in restaurant management school learning industrial kitchen work and I worked in many restaurants. I had a lot of affection for mass production, people working together, talking, chatting, and making things. That background formed a lot of what I did. I began thinking more and more about the identity of a painting and what it was. I moved to New York during this period, in 1975. I ultimately decided that what I really wanted to do was to create a prop that stood for a painting, rather than try to come up with some kind of painting that had meaning within the history or conventions of painting. I decided I wanted to create a prop that stood for a painting and obtained its meaning by representing a kind of a social tradition. Once I created these prop paintings, which I called *Surrogate Paintings*, and put them in a gallery, the gallery became a kind of stage set, a stage set of a gallery. When you walked into the gallery looking at *Surrogate Paintings*, you would feel a sense of taking a look at yourself walking into a gallery.

Looking at yourself looking at art: that's what I had in

mind. It was influenced a little bit by Bertolt Brecht's idea of when you watch a play you should be aware you're watching a play at every minute and not get lost in the drama of it. Another way of trying to develop an anthropological distance to viewing was taking photographs of my *Surrogate Paintings*. I re-photographed them until they started to diminish in resolution to where they almost became like UFOs of paintings. I also frequently took pictures when I would find newspaper photographs that had paintings in the background that were out of focus. I would study them. I would show them with my *Surrogate Paintings*, but they really weren't artworks.

Another series I did in 1982 was a kind of an imitation photograph [*Glossies*]. Now these look like they're snapshots, but they're not. They're made of art paper that I would draw a rectangle on and paint it black with ink and then put— What's it called, Al?

RUPPERSBERG: Laminate?

MCCOLLUM: Put laminate on it and then trim them out and they would be shiny and they would look just like snapshots. But what I was interested in with this series was the feeling of looking through photographs without there being a photograph. What was that about? What made you want to pick up a photograph, or go through a stack of photos?

During this same period I took a lot of pictures off of television when paintings in the background appeared to look like surrogate paintings. These are not retouched, by the way. That's just the way they look. If you watch TV, you'll see hundreds of these things, and I collected these images. Often, when I would do art exhibits, I would put them in the office, you see, because I was interested in the way a photograph influences the way you look at an object. Because once you saw them as props in these photos, then you might look at the actual *Surrogate Paintings* as props, which is what I was hoping for. Then, I got tired of making *Surrogate Paintings*. It took so long to make them out of wood with 50 coats of paint. I started casting them in plaster at a certain point, and I made molds. Then the titles became *Plaster Surrogates*. So, with these I could reproduce that effect in many, many ways and much faster.

Very quickly, there was a series called *Perpetual Photographs*. They were similar to those other photographs I was telling you about, but what happened was I would watch TV. (And by the way, I only had a black-and-white TV. I didn't have a color TV. That's why they're all black and white.) When I would see a painting in the background, I would take a picture of the television, blow it up and put it in a frame. Now, in my mind these works were really about the desire to look at a picture. What makes you walk across the room and look into a frame to see a picture? I was interested in creating self-consciousness about wanting to see a picture.

My interest in the gallery as a social space or a space of exchange became especially accented in this piece, which was a collaboration with Louise Lawler where we created a whole set of little, tiny sculpture bases, but we didn't call them that. We called them *Ideal Settings*, which was a reference to the gallery itself. We put the sculpture bases on other sculpture bases and put the price on the wall, too, with a slide projector so that the aspect of exchange and the idea of the gallery as a place of sale were highlighted.

I can't show everything here, but I went on to start thinking not only about art objects, but other objects that had elevated value in the same way that art objects had value. They were things that were not quite contemporary art objects, but more like what you might call "fine art objects," things you might see in an antiques museum, or a design museum, or something like that. I designed this project [*Perfect Vehicles*], which was really about emblems, symbols. "Symbols" is the way I thought of it. I decided on a symbol and then made symbols of that symbol in a way. This was the first one I made, but they became the *Perfect Vehicles* after I noticed on television how often you would see ginger jars in the background as emblems of "I'm rich," or "I've been to Europe," or "I've been to China," or "I'm a collector," or whatever. That project came out of those jars.

My interest in mass production developed more and more.

This is a photography project I did with Laurie Simmons [*Actual Photos*]. Laurie and I bought all these tiny dolls in a train store where you would buy objects that go with model trains, and we took pictures of them through a microscope. My interest was that when you look at a mass produced object closely enough, each one is different. This is how small they were, sitting on a nickel.

A project where I really got into mass-producing was called *Individual Works*, which is a kind of a pun on the idea of the singular art object. I made 35,000 of these things. They're all unique. Just like artwork is supposed to be. They were made from little parts of things that I would find on the street and in peoples' homes. I'd make molds. I had a system. This was before I had a computer or anything. Then we would paint them and they were all unique. A similar project was called the *Drawings Project*, which consisted of unique drawings. I made about 6,000 of these. Now, I didn't sell them one at a time; I would sell them in collections.

Because time is running out, I'm going to go to this project. I became interested in the way communities developed an identity with an object that became an emblem of the community. I discovered in Price, Utah, this museum. Many parts of Utah use dinosaurs as a symbol because so many dinosaur bones are found in Utah. This particular museum in Price, which was a coal-mining town, would find dinosaur tracks in the coal in the roofs of the coalmines, and collect them. They chopped them down from the top of the roof. So, I made a deal with the curators. I made molds of 44 of their collection of dinosaur tracks and showed them around the world in different places [*Lost Objects*]. I also created 21 different *Reprints*, which, of course, was a pun on dinosaur tracks. This was when I first started making supplements that could be used by others for educational purposes so that the art world wasn't the only audience. You can download these PDF files from a Web page. They're all about the history of dinosaur tracks, of finding them in coalmines.

A similar project that involved booklets that you could

read was about "fulgurites" [*THE EVENT: Petrified Lightning from Central Florida (with supplemental didactics)*]. Fulgurites are created by lightning. Where lightning hits the ground, it goes into the ground, melts the glass, and produces an object. At the International Center for Lightning and Research and Testing, part of the University of Florida, they send up rockets to trigger lightning. I did a collaboration with these people where I sent up my own rocket. It created a lightning bolt, which went into a bucket of sand. I created my own fulgurite. Made 10,000 of them and then something like 13,000 booklets, which you can download. They were all about fulgurites. It's the biggest collection of writings on fulgurites anywhere in the world. We put up a show at the local science museum.

But the point is that I wanted to do a project that could be seen as having different meanings for different people from different positions—scientists, artists, local residents. Another project that I did was in California down at Mount Signal, which is basically in Mexico [*Mount Signal and Its Sand Spikes: A Project for the Imperial Valley*]. Mount Signal has become a symbol to the people in Imperial County, down by El Centro. What's interesting to me is that you could find these little objects called "sand spikes" at the base of the mountain. So, I got involved in studying the way concretions had developed meaning and how this mountain had developed meaning in this small community of Imperial Valley. The mountain is used over and over again in their emblems that represent the town as well as postcards, and so forth. I did a show with some 60 different artists who did paintings and drawings and photographs of Mount Signal. We made a giant model of the mountain. We made a souvenir of the mountain. We showed them all. I did a show of local sand spikes that people had collected. I made my own models of sand spikes, which are for sale now in the museum gift store, and we made a giant one that can be seen from along the highway.

I also did a series of give-away projects where I created models of Kansas and Missouri from molds [*The Kansas and Missouri Topographical Model Donation Project*]. I did a show of them, but I also made about 120 additional ones. I wrote letters to around 250 little historical museums in both states. I rented a car, drove around, and delivered them for free, donating them to all these different museums. It was probably the most fun I've ever had in my life, actually.

I guess if I only have five minutes left, I have to skip to the *Shapes Project*, which brings us to Al. Now what I want to show is the exhibition that Al and Claudio had seen where I did 7,000 unique shapes. This is a project designed to produce shapes that can be used in hundreds of different ways, I hope. These are some of the books that keep track of how I do it. They're made from tops, tops left, tops right, tops bottoms or bottoms. You can combine them to create a shape. You can make billions of unique shapes with the system. If you add two more parts, which I call "Necks," you can make more billions. The idea was to have enough shapes that theoretically everyone in the world could have one. I'm still working on it. This is a project I do with children at the Museum of Modern Art in New York, where they cut out their own little parts and make their own shapes, following my system. Then they get to be on the wall for two weeks. This is how the *Shapes* look on Al's prop/furniture.

I haven't shown these yet; you're the first people to see them. It's another regional project [*Shapes From Maine*]. I'm collaborating with people who have home-based businesses in Maine. I've never met them [in person]. I only meet them over the Internet. I ask them to collaborate with me making shapes. These are copper cookie cutters made by Holly and Larry Little, a husband and wife, at their "Aunt Holly's Copper Cookie Cutters" business in Trescott, Maine. These are ornaments made in Maine by Horace and Noella Varnum, another husband and wife team, in the town of Sedgwick. These are rubber stamps made by Wendy Wyman and Bill Welsh, a married couple in Freeport, Maine. There's also a silhouette cutter, Ruth Monsell, in Damarascotta; she's cut 144 shapes. My show will be a promotion for them as well as a promotion for myself in some way. All of this material will be available to the people who come in to the show. I'm hoping that one day somebody will approach me with a huge budget and says, "I want you to make a million shapes so that we can give them away to everybody" in some certain town or something. We'll see if that ever happens.

KLEIN: Thank you both for rushing through so many decades of work in 15 minutes. I'm going to try to speak as little as possible. I'm really just here for moral support as far as I see it. But while we're getting things set up, I thought it would be really nice if Allan, you would talk about how you first met Allen.

MCCOLLUM: I don't know if Al remembers how we first met, but I remember meeting him. I worked at a trucking company called Cart & Crate. We had a mutual friend who worked in the office, Margaret Nielson, who has a show up right now, by the way. She introduced us. I remember standing on the loading dock while Al was below the loading dock, and being introduced to him. It was just a "How do you do?" Then Al did a show at Eugenia Butler's. What was the name of that show?

RUPPERSBERG: *The Location Piece*.

MCCOLLUM: *The Location Piece*, which was an amazing show because you'd go into the gallery and there were these samples that you looked at, but you had to go down the street and see the real show, which was in some building on Sunset Blvd. It was a site work, but not like a site work where you go out into the desert. It was a site work where you went over to Sunset Blvd. I was one of the people who picked up the piece in the truck. We went and packed the work and put it on the truck. Al will have no memory of this, but what impressed me was that after we picked it all up and locked the truck, he locked the door to the studio. We went out to drive away, and he went out into the street to hitchhike somewhere. I don't know where he was going.

There's that famous artist who's hitchhiking.

RUPPERSBERG: Those were the days.

MCCOLLUM: Yeah, those were the days. And with no shirt.

KLEIN: Wasn't there some story about Allen swinging on a rope at a performance?

RUPPERSBERG: Well, he wrote that in the article.

MCCOLLUM: I didn't meet him then. That was the first time I saw him. It was a Living Theater performance of their famous production, *Paradise Now.* The one where everybody is invited to take their clothes off in the theater. It was at USC. All of a sudden everything explodes and people go crazy and the rope is hurled down from the ceiling and people jump on the rope and slide down it from the balcony. And it was Al who made the first leap and grabbed the rope and slid down it. I remember noticing that. That was in 1969. I thought it was very brave. He didn't take his clothes off though.

RUPPERSBERG: No, I did not.

KLEIN: Shall we fast forward to the present and talk about what this experience was like for you to finally collaborate?

RUPPERSBERG: Well, I think it was like I mentioned before that it took all of these years of knowing and following each other's work and the influences going back and forth and talking about it. Then this opportunity arose where we both arrived with two bodies of work that overlapped each other. Allan mentioned the word "props" earlier. As we've talked about before, I maybe didn't use the word "props" in the same way that Allan did but, looking back at all the work, there are a lot of uses of what could be termed "props." Allan calls these *Shapes*, where the picture frame that they're in and the object become for him a prop. So, we have these two props and by coincidence we wound up at the same place at the same time.

MCCOLLUM: Yeah, it goes back to Al's work in the '60s, when he did *Al's Café* and *Al's Hotel*. I don't know if you all remember this work, but he created essentially what in my mind were the equivalents of stage sets. One was a restaurant in which you actually could order things. One was a hotel that you could actually sleep in. But each room was a setting, like a stage set. And one of the things that I loved about Al's work in those days was the affection that he had for not simply everyday objects, but the way people valued everyday objects. You can see the way we all do this, in our own ways. You have, say, a fireplace with a mantelpiece, a table, a piano, or a shelf, and you put the little special things that people have given you on there, family heirlooms, or other things like that.

From the very beginning, Al had this kind of mentality in what he did that was extremely rare. Andy Warhol and many other artists have used common objects, but there is always a kind of irony or "blankness." Al had affection for common objects that people loved and would use them in his work. I have to say that my decision to make the little frames that have the flap [stand] on the back that you can set on a table as opposed to hanging on the wall was clearly connected to Al's affection for those types of objects. And, of course, there was the work with Louise Lawler with the sculptured bases and the settings being part of the work—as opposed to ignoring the settings, creating settings for things. Al really got into that with the prop/furniture.

RUPPERSBERG: I'm going to go back to something that Allan said in his 15 minutes that made me think of something I hadn't thought of before. He spoke about the fact that I went to art school and he did not. And yet when you go back and look at what you began to create and the reasons that you began to create them, they were very close to the zeitgeist in the air that I was breathing, even though I had come out of art school. They were ideas of creating something that has nothing to do with the traditional history of looking at objects or paintings in galleries that were being tossed out at that time. We were both picking up on the same thing even though Allan was coming from a nonacademic background, if you can call art school academic at that time. Now you do, but in those days it was a little different.

You came out of art school and you immediately began to disassociate yourself from everything that you learned in art school. That's the difference between then and now. I was in the process of trying to figure out what to do because I was not going to be a painter. You were taught two things—to be a sculptor or a painter. When I decided that's not what I thought art was about and started to eliminate everything that I had learned, then I picked up on the period and the ideas that were floating in the air, not just in L.A., but all over the world at that point. Allan, I began to see from listening to your introduction how you decided to not make this and not make that, and not do this, and not do that. That's exactly where I started, too. So, in a way, we were starting at the same point.

MCCOLLUM: I suppose, but I had a harder time shaking that off. I had to create things that stood for paintings. I had to make a commentary on paintings. I had to make a commentary on sculpture. I had to include it in my thinking. I didn't want to make that leap that you could so easily make. I wasn't able to do that because I wanted to track the steps away from the idea of a standardized art object. I still think I have to do that. In the back of my mind, it's one thing to make a leap into something where you pay no attention to any rules and you just make things up. It's another to say, how do you get from there to there to there? That's something I guess I value in addition to that.

RUPPERSBERG: Well, it also makes me wonder because we were in a very specific environment, which was L.A. in the late '60s and '70s where the art world was very small. You got to know very quickly what a small group of people were doing. You have the situation in L.A. where what's really unique about it—or at least was unique about it then—was that everybody was an individual. There were no schools of people. You know, there was no school of Ed Ruscha. There was no school of Chris Burden or whomever you want to talk about. You got to know individually these people who were doing their own thing, as opposed to when you're in New York or in the rest of the world where history plays a bigger part. I'm just wondering if that had an effect on how you decided to make what you make, the fact that you could so quickly see what people were doing and assimilate it. Does that make any sense?

MCCOLLUM: I'm not sure what you're asking me, but I know in those days I got everything mixed up. Like when I showed that piece of all those hundreds of little paintings that I made into a big painting. When I look back at that period when I was doing those, I didn't know the difference. In my head, I'm the guy mixing up stain painting with Richard Serra and Robert Morris. There was nobody telling me, "No, no, no, you can't do it. You have to reject painting and accept 'making' in the Robert Morris sense," or whatever. Nobody was telling me that. I think in school you probably had people saying, "Oh, that's a bunch of crap and this is what's good," and then there's the conceptual work. You were in school way before I even knew about art. But, I was hugely influenced by L.A. artists, with the first painting I did.

RUPPERSBERG: That's what I mean. How much were you influenced by the knowledge that was specific to L.A., that being your starting point?

MCCOLLUM: Well, the person I met that taught me about contemporary art, the very person that introduced me to what art was, worked as a model for John Altoon. Her name was Judy Houston; we were in trade school together, at L.A. Trade Tech. She was studying fashion design and I was studying restaurant management. She taught me about [Robert] Rauschenberg, John Cage, Wallace Berman, Tony Berlant, John Altoon, and Vija Celmins, who was a huge influence (and whom I later met and just fell in love with, in terms of how she approached her work).

If you put those artists together, including Billy Al Bengston, Craig Kauffman, John McCracken, and so forth, you get me and my mind. Now what was going on in New York you'd read about in *Artforum.* That was in the background and it was influencing me also. But they weren't people; they were just these things you'd read about. But the people [in L.A.] were very influential. Also, the L.A. artists so embraced industrial craft techniques in what they did. It's sometimes referred to as—what's it called?

RUPPERSBERG: "Finish Fetish?"

MCCOLLUM: The so-called "Finish Fetish" artists, right. Craig Kauffman would use vacuum forming. That polyester resin casting that DeWain Valentine was using, things that you expect boat makers to use, or surfboard makers. They specifically avoided art materials. Most of these artists have gone back to art materials at this point, but in those days avoiding art materials was really important to me because I felt that I didn't have an education in art materials. I had no foundational studies. So, I wasn't going to pretend that I knew what I was doing. I was going to leap over that and go buy my stuff at the hardware store, or the supermarket, or wherever.

RUPPERSBERG: We started that in art school. We went through that phase in art school about the influence of those people using extraordinarily different materials.

MCCOLLUM: But how did you get from that—? It's one thing to use industrial materials and to use found objects like Duchamp or the Fluxus artists. But how did you get into using placemats from Denny's and things about which most people would say, "That doesn't belong in art. Those things are way too commercial." And you're not even making fun of it. I mean Warhol made fun. There was an irony when he would use a Coke bottle. He would silkscreen the Coke bottle, but he'd also make it a little sloppy so that you could tell there was a hand involved. But you would just go to the flea market and buy stuff. How did you get to where you didn't feel you had to fool with it?

RUPPERSBERG: It's quite a process. If you begin at the introduction of using foreign materials for art-making—plastic or whatever—then you work through that.

MCCOLLUM: Right.

RUPPERSBERG: It was, of course, also influenced by Minimalism. I worked my way through what I knew from school, which was Minimalist sculpture and abstract painting—either Morris Louis or any kind of stain painting, or what you saw in *Artforum* at that time, which is '65-'67. I worked through the ideas of Minimalism, incorporating these ideas from L.A. of the different materials. Then I wound up at a place that other people had wound up with either a Minimalist object or a shaped painting or something. I realized that that made no sense to me, and started over again. Then the introduction of things that I was familiar with from my commercial schooling and/or my background began to appear in the work and grew into what became a much more flatfooted presentation like you're speaking about.

MCCOLLUM: But I wonder what that magic moment was when you decided it was okay to just take some middle-American poster, or booklet, or something that was completely average, that had nothing special about it. How did you make that leap? During those days you didn't see people taking a commercial product and showing it with affection. They were showing them with irony. Do you know what I mean?

RUPPERSBERG: No, I know what you mean. A lot of it comes from The Living Theater. Those ideas are slowly introduced in different things that influence you. You could go back to The Living Theater since we mentioned it and the influence of people here in L.A. like Ed Kienholz and Wallace Berman, where these kinds of objects appear that had some kind of poetic aura to them that I really responded to. The more conceptual world was coming into focus at that time, *When Attitudes Became Form* (1969). Those kinds of things around 1970 distanced it even further from the poetry of assemblage to make it even flatter, like a commercial art product. I don't know if there's a moment. The only moment that I can think about is when I decided that the painted object or the kind of work that I was making wasn't art to me anymore, and it was time to do something else. That really crystallized in the exhibition of Frank Stella's *Protractor* series at the old Pasadena Museum of Art.

MCCOLLUM: It was a great show.

RUPPERSBERG: It was a fantastic show. I've mentioned this before in some interviews and things, but looking at that was a kind of epiphany moment—here is the best it's ever going to get. So, what are you fooling around for? Just forget about it and start over again. Do your own work. This had nothing to do with me; my work was about these other things that were out there waiting to be appropriated.

KLEIN: Do you think that the particular environment that you're both painting a picture of is specific to Los Angeles or Southern California? Because I think particularly in the moment that we're in there's a re-historicization of Conceptual practice in Los Angeles, and a real effort to try to codify what California Conceptualism is. I'm curious what your reflections might be on that. Allan, you're someone who is from Los Angeles but is often associated more with New York. And you, Allen, have an identity that's attached to Los Angeles, yet you've also done a lot of work in New York. I believe I read something of yours in which you talked about bringing a California sensibility to other scenarios.

RUPPERSBERG: Well, I think the whole idea of California Conceptualism was something that was made up later; it's not something that we were conscious of. All I can do is speak about my own influences in relationship to New York. I went to New York for the first time in 1970 to stay for a while. Every year after that I was connected [to New York], not only from a physical presence of being there, but also because Conceptualism was being shown [there]. The California people were being shown with New York people, people from Europe, or whomever. The shows were all-inclusive. It was a general approach.

It was only later when first of all New York Conceptualism was defined. Then once that was defined they started to look and see differences between people, what their influences were. Being in L.A., you were going to have different historical influences than you did in New York. I happened to be kind of a hybrid because of my relationship to New York. When I went in 1970, all the other Conceptual artists that I had either met out here or knew about, they were all there [in New York], and we were just working. I don't know. I didn't even think about it.

KLEIN: It's kind of an unfair question.

RUPPERSBERG: No, but it's become a "thing." But that thing was invented later. And yes, you can see differences, but it takes a while.

KLEIN: I guess it's also about how that Los Angeles scene might have contributed to the seeds of your practice as well.

MCCOLLUM: Well, Conceptualism is sort of a journalistic term in my mind. What I think influenced me in L.A. was when an artist brilliantly reduced something to such a simple moment, like a Zen master, that your whole sense of everything changed. There were a few times when that happened. One of the times was at Ed Kienholz's water-color show at Eugenia Butler where there were a hundred watercolors on the wall and written on each one was what you could trade it for. One would say "For $1.00," or "For $10,000," or "For Two Pack Mules," or "For A Refrigerator." And then you had to go out and buy a refrigerator because he was moving. He was moving to Idaho. He needed all that stuff. This was 1968. I don't know. Is that Conceptualism? Or, of course, there was Michael Asher. I'll never forget the way he had two galleries, back in 1977. It was Claire Copley's Gallery and Morgan Thomas's was the other one?

RUPPERSBERG: Thomas and Connie Lewallen.

MCCOLLUM: Oh, they had the gallery together, okay.

RUPPERSBERG: Yes.

MCCOLLUM: For Michael Asher's show, he had them change spaces. So, the staff from one gallery worked at Claire's. You'd go into the gallery and see the staff from the other gallery.

RUPPERSBERG: Showing the other gallery's artists.

MCCOLLUM: Connie would show Laddie John Dill.

RUPPERSBERG: But at Claire's gallery. . . .

MCCOLLUM: They switched stables. I remember Laddie saying, "Wow, it's so great. Now I can put Claire Copley on my resume." I can't remember whom Claire showed.

RUPPERSBERG: I think it was a group show.

MCCOLLUM: Little moments like that just changed my whole view of things. I guess that's conceptual but to me it's also kind of Buddhist, like how the Zen master does the exact thing you don't expect him to do when you're enlightened.

RUPPERSBERG: It is the West Coast after all.

MCCOLLUM: Yeah, that's definitely the West Coast.

KLEIN: For the sake of time maybe we should move forward to the present. One of the things that I'm interested in hearing a little bit about is that you're both collectors, but you're both collectors in really different senses, it seems. Or maybe you wouldn't consider yourself a collector, but you have collections.

MCCOLLUM: No, basically I don't know how to throw things away. I don't know if that qualifies me as a collector. I'm kind of a neurotic, compulsive. Al actually collects books.

RUPPERSBERG: Stuff.

MCCOLLUM: And movies and posters.

KLEIN: But you also make collections.

MCCOLLUM: Yes, I make collections. I'm not sure what I need to say about it. Well, it has to do with quantity. One of the points I like to make—one of the points I dwell on and obsess about—is how we grow up in a culture of mass production where we're surrounded by things that were produced in mass quantities. But as artists, traditionally we're not supposed to produce things in mass quantity. We're asked to produce unique, individual things that have special values where special people can collect them and say this is my special, unique object that nobody else has. What if an artist wants to mass-produce? What if all my feelings are tied up in the idea of entrepreneurial mass production and that really thrills me and excites me, and I'm not allowed to do it? Artists are supposed to be free to do what they want.

So, that's one of the compromises I've had to make. When I first did those over 30,000 *Individual Works* that

I showed you, my idea was to sell them one at a time for $20. And the dealer, of course, said, “Are you kidding? It takes just as long to write an invoice for $20 as it does to write one for $10,000. And we’re not going to sit there and sell [10,000 of them].” So I said okay, we’ll sell them by the gross, by 144. And he said, “Oh, all right.”

Then we did the installation and he said, “Wait a minute. This has to be one piece. If you sell 144, then you won’t have that piece to show at a museum,” and all that. There’s always this dilemma. I’ve never been able to resolve it. So, I sell things in collections. I say, okay, you have to buy a collection. Like these are in collections of 144. And I produced them that way. You can’t buy one of those little shapes. You have to buy 144. Maybe that’s what you’re referring to, that the titles of my works are *Collection of Two Hundred and Forty-four Plaster Surrogates,* or *Collection of* . . . But Al is a real collector. He comes from a family of collectors as I recollect. No? Didn’t your father collect?

RUPPERSBERG: Not necessarily.

MCCOLLUM: I don’t mean art collectors.

RUPPERSBERG: No, not really. Records. Records would be the only things, but that’s just from a love of music. Not from the need to horde things.

MCCOLLUM: To me it was a compromise. It’s a critique in a way. The art world as it exists will not let me make mass quantities of things and sell them one at a time. Because if I were to do that they’d say, “Oh, you’re not an artist. You’re something else. You’re making souvenirs.” So I think, well, I want to do that, but I probably couldn’t make a living doing it. And I wouldn’t be called an artist, which would make it even worse. So, I have to come up with some kind of compromised way.

RUPPERSBERG: Which you did.

MCCOLLUM: So, I did, which works sometimes.

RUPPERSBERG: And now you're all of those things.

MCCOLLUM: And there are still people out there that think I'm not an artist because I'm making souvenirs.

KLEIN: The objects that you make also, if I'm not mistaken, have some personal references to them, like a flashlight, or other everyday objects.

MCCOLLUM: Oh, you mean with the *Individual Works*. Using molds taken from my girlfriend's contact lens case, and some of those things taken from toys of my friends' children and things like that. Is that what you mean?

KLEIN: Yes, that's exactly what I mean. I think there's an interesting correspondence with some of the works that you do, Allen, which are also looking at a certain kind of mass-produced object and transferring or reclaiming it into a personal realm like your re-drawings.

RUPPERSBERG: That's true. The things that have wound up being collections of mine are just bought because they're going to be used at some point. Sometimes it takes 20 years to find the exact use for some object or drawing or something that attracted me in some way. The most common denominator is that it's where my eye goes. It goes to those kinds of things because I've investigated my own background and my own ideas about art and stuff. And then these collections build up to the point where they'll never all be used. I'd have to live to be 200 years old to use all of this stuff. But that doesn't matter because there's just one thing in there that eventually will get used.

MCCOLLUM: I remember when I was thinking about your work for that article I wrote and I came up with the conclusion that you think we are collections. Each individual is a collection. Part of what I get from your work is that we are all collaged collections of everything we've done, seen, thought about, and read.

RUPPERSBERG: And have.

MCCOLLUM: And have and—

RUPPERSBERG: Keep. Think about.

MCCOLLUM: It includes banal, stupid objects and brilliant objects, objects we share with others, and objects that are ours personally.

RUPPERSBERG: When I see peoples' collections of things, I think of your work, too. There's a particular apartment that I used to walk by where the person collected ships, ceramic ships or all kinds of ships. They're all in the windows of the whole front of the apartment that this person owns. It's a lot like that. There are these collections of objects that then together make this impression on you. They make this thing similar to your 10,000 objects.

MCCOLLUM: That makes me think of one of the first thoughts that triggered me to do these, the idea of how come an art object is always a single, solid thing. Why couldn't it be granular? It would take the shape of what you put it in, like if you had a box or a jar that you fill with corn. Some objects you think of as taking on the shape of their container. I don't know why I'm telling you this.

RUPPERSBERG: Well, that's similar to a lot of Marcel Broodthaers's work. The thing takes the shape of its container. There's nothing inside or there is something.

MCCOLLUM: You mean like all those mussel shells in the pot?

RUPPERSBERG: And the pots and a whole range of objects of his. Suitcases.

MCCOLLUM: Yes. But convention suggests that you make a singular object. It's almost like a monument or something that is supposed to be so singular. My response to that is clearly to make things that do not have to have a specific shape, but still could be called art.

RUPPERSBERG: Well, my response is fairly similar. It only is that I find it impossible to make the same thing more than once. You're supposed to have a form. You have a theory. You have something that you then refine.

MCCOLLUM: It's your signature object.

RUPPERSBERG: Your signature object. Well, I always thought that was crap. I find that it's genetically impossible for me to make the same thing more than once.

MCCOLLUM: Does that bother you?

RUPPERSBERG: No, because I think it's important in the dialogue that you don't have to make the same thing.

MCCOLLUM: Correct.

RUPPERSBERG: You can use any method, any material, any idea and it becomes part of the whole in the same way that your objects become part of a whole. You don't do the same thing either. You do all kinds of different things.

MCCOLLUM: I do all kinds of things in which I do all the same things.

RUPPERSBERG: That's the difference.

Sharon Lockhart & James Welling

Los Angeles County Museum of Art
Moderator: Alex Klein

Part of the goal of the conversations between artists was to create a space where two artists could talk casually and for the most part unprompted about mutual interests, influences and current concerns. It was our hope that in an unscripted, informal environment that the artists would have the chance to ask each other pointed, direct questions that they might not otherwise discuss in front of an audience. It was with this intention that we invited Sharon Lockhart and James Welling to sit down over a cup of coffee to converse about their early love of structuralist film, pedagogy, East Coast versus West Coast sensibilities and their most recent projects.

JAMES WELLING: It may not be obvious on my part, but I think we both share an early interest in structural film. Hollis Frampton and Michael Snow were big influences on me in art school, and one of the reasons I moved into photography was due to my interest in structural film. And it seems that your work obviously has a relationship to that filmmaking tradition. So, we could talk about that a little bit as a starting point.

SHARON LOCKHART: Those films were really important to me in graduate school as well. They've informed almost everything I've done since. I hadn't known that you started out with film and video. I read an essay that mentioned a video you had made with a Portapak and it sounded so intriguing. Can you talk about that work?

WELLING: I hung the Portapak camera on a spring and pointed it at the fields across the street from CalArts. As I pressed the start button, the camera bounced around on the spring and appeared to be floating in the landscape. That piece was part of a series of short videos I made in 1972. These were shown a couple of years ago at MoMA. The Frampton work that I was most intrigued by was *Hapax Legomena*—a series of seven films where he worked with very different procedures in each film. So these short videos of mine, which included this landscape piece and a couple of the projects that I made in the back of John Baldessari's classroom, were very indebted to Frampton.

LOCKHART: What was the Baldessari classroom video?

WELLING: I'm fooling around with the camera.

ALEX KLEIN: Is that the one where you're putting your hand in front of the camera?

WELLING: In one sequence I touch the lens, in another I manipulate the diaphragm and in another I shade the lens with my hand to demonstrate how the video tube retained a ghostly image of a bright light. It's uncanny but in my recent *Glass House* images I'm doing some of the same procedures . . . putting things right up against the lens, distorting the image, shading the lens. They are all similar in spirit to these early experiments.

LOCKHART: And in the CalArts videos there was sound too?

WELLING: Occasionally there was sound. Not always. In one piece the roughness of the edits produced a sharp clicking sound on an otherwise silent tape.

LOCKHART: What about the sound in this new video, *Lake Pavilion?*

WELLING: I think sound is extremely important to video. I made a tape at CalArts where I left the lens cap on the camera and walked between the two central wings of the school and clapped continuously. In the video I made in December, I slowly walk and pan through the Lake Pavilion on the Philip Johnson Glass House property. As I point the camera at the snowy ground, I put different colored gels in front of the lens that control and filter the light. I shot using a very low-end digital camera in Quicktime files. The sound was generated by my footsteps and by placing the filters on the lens. The sound in the final version is not sync sound. I edited and fussed with the sound, but all of it was generated while I made the image track. The sound in *Lunch Break* also seems extremely important.

LOCKHART: It's very similar to what you just said. I couldn't quite make out what you had done with the sound, but I knew it was manipulated. But yes, for *Lunch Break* the shot was 11 minutes long on 35-millimeter, and then we slowed it down digitally to 80 minutes, so we had to make a new soundtrack to fit the new speed.

WELLING: So, you were shooting at 24 frames a second?

LOCKHART: Yes, because if we had shot with a high speed camera we would have had to have a lot of cuts and rolls of film. I think the longest take at high speed is three minutes or so.

WELLING: Okay, I wondered about that. I thought you must have had a huge magazine to shoot an 84-minute shot.

LOCKHART: That would have been ideal but the technology doesn't really exist. I tried to figure out how I could go down the hallway slowly without a cut, but I couldn't. Even if we used a high-speed film or digital camera we would have had to blast the place with light, which would have changed everything. I wanted a very natural lighting scenario and wanted everything to be as normal as possible for the workers. I had done a lot of work to prepare the workers so their performance would be natural. Later, when we did the sound, we had a recordist walk the hallway at the pace of the film, the 80-minute film. It took quite a few lunch breaks. The soundtrack is in real time, but it's completely designed by Becky Allen and me. In addition to the sounds of the factory we included a musical composition. Becky wrote a score based on the tones that were recorded and we used a Prophet analog keyboard in the track. We wanted to create an interplay between the music and the tones of the machines—something like the interplay between realism and the constructed nature of the picture. So, what made you change the sound?

WELLING: Well, you could hear me breathing plus some very loud, clattering sounds from the filters hitting the lens. And I run about half of the footage backwards, so we ran the sound forward over that part.

LOCKHART: Did you show that in the installation with the photographs of the Glass House?

WELLING: Yes. I showed it in Paris at Galerie Nelson Freeman in January. I'm extremely happy with how it looked. Most of the show consisted of intensely colored photographs of the Glass House that I've been working on for the past two and one half years, plus the new video.

LOCKHART: How was it displayed?

WELLING: *Lake Pavilion* was projected on a wall in a room that was lit by a large, beautiful 19th century skylight. In northern Europe, January daylight is quite dim and having the walls partially lit worked beautifully for the piece. I hung a small photograph of the Glass House in the room with the projection so there needed to be enough light to see that piece. When you first showed *Lunch Break,* you showed it as a film?

LOCKHART: No, I showed it as an installation in Vienna at the Secession first. I worked with Frank and Ravi from EscherGuneWardena here in Los Angeles. They helped me to come up with architecture specific to the piece and not just a black box cinema simulation. The entrance to the main gallery at the Secession has those very nice glass doors so we designed and built a freestanding box that is open at the end just inside the doors. As soon as you walk in there's an 18- by 20-foot opening and the box is 65 feet deep. It is a dark grey and as you walk in it gets dark naturally, and the hallway of *Lunch Break* is at the end. So it's like you're walking down a hallway to another hallway.

As you enter you can see that this box sits in the center of a large, beautiful gallery space lit with daylight from skylights. In Berlin I recently showed it in the cinema with an opening title and end credits with the names of all of the workers, the union, the crew, and the usual film stuff.

WELLING: Did any photographs come out of that project?

LOCKHART: Yes, I ended up with three photographic projects. There were photographs of workers on their break as kind of tableaus, photographs of independent businesses the guys have throughout the factory, and portraits of the workers. They are still lifes of their lunchboxes and their belongings. I made those after I left Maine. I spent a year there pretty much, and then I came back to Los Angeles with 12 lunchboxes. I photographed them in a studio for five or six weeks until I figured it out.

KLEIN: Did you send the lunchboxes back?

LOCKHART: Yes, I did. In some cases I gave them new lunchboxes to use while I had theirs. Others heard about the project and sent me their boxes and brown-bagged it until I could return them. By the time I finished, it was coming up to Halloween. So, we filled the boxes with candy and sent them back. And so all these guys were calling and saying thank you for the candy. They hadn't gotten a

Halloween basket since they were little. It was funny.

WELLING: I was thinking as I drove over here about how *Pine Flat* and *Lunch Break* alternate between childhood play and the very adult activity of work. What is astonishing to me is that one of the few things children and adults share is the lunchbox. By sending Halloween candy you are collapsing the child and the adult via the lunchbox.

LOCKHART: I never thought of it that way but you are right. I think there are probably several ways the two projects unite. School in America is structured just like the workplace. You have a lunch break and your time is regulated. In *Pine Flat,* I was very interested in the absorptive qualities of the kid's activities and also in the social relationships developed in the second half of the film. None of the activities are really productive. In *Lunch Break*, I chose a time of day when the workers were not productive, when they were playing cards, socializing, or absorbed in the newspaper or their meal.

KLEIN: Did you also come into photography through film or did you start mainly in film?

LOCKHART: No, I studied photography formally.

KLEIN: So, you came to film through your photography?

LOCKHART: Yes, basically I saw Hollis Frampton and Morgan Fisher when I was in grad school and things really opened up for me then. There was a lot of interest in film at Art Center at that time and I thought I would like to work in that medium because I had tried video and it never really worked for me. So, I started making films.

KLEIN: And what was the difference for you? That difference between video and film? Was it the working process?

LOCKHART: I really liked the limitations film presented. It is naturally durational and provides a structure to work with. I think it also really brought out this aspect of collaboration and working with people, which I was just starting to do in my photography. And now that's really the center of the work for me, I think.

WELLING: It's so ironic. I wanted to work in film before I realized I'd have to collaborate with people to make films.

LOCKHART: And then you walked away.

WELLING: My problem was that I didn't want to work with labs. The idea of having to assert what I wanted to a lab technician who, I imagined, would be generally unsympathetic to anything I wanted to do seemed like such a terror that I moved over to photography, where I can control everything myself.

LOCKHART: You mean to do experimental things?

WELLING: Yes. You know, after looking at Snow and Frampton I realized that to be a filmmaker you have to have a relationship with a lab.

LOCKHART: Yes, those relationships are problematic for me too. I feel as if I'm always pushing them beyond their normal standards. I love working with the subjects of my films and photographs, though. The experience of creating something with them is the most satisfying part of the process for me. I was looking through the books I have of your work and I think the only figure that appears is the woman at the lace factory.

WELLING: There are other figures. I took a group of photographs in the Wolfsburg VW factory, and there are a number of portraits.

LOCKHART: Of workers?

WELLING: Groups of workers posing for the camera or doing things, welding, conferring, etc.

LOCKHART: What about the subject in your work? I mean, when's the last time you photographed a person?

WELLING: I'm doing a book for Steidl of my 1992-2002 *Light Source* photographs and there are quite a few portraits in the book. Almost all are formal portraits.

LOCKHART: When you first came to Los Angeles and I was teaching at UCLA, I remember an image you were printing of students from I think a workshop in Sweden or somewhere. It really stayed with me.

WELLING: In Vienna at the academy; they were my seminar students. I posed them in a video studio. There are various group portraits and individual portraits in *Light Sources*. When I first started taking photographs in 1976, I made a number of portraits: Jack Goldstein, David Salle and other friends. I've always made a few portraits every year. In the *Railroad Photographs, Calais Lace Factories,* and in the *Wolfsburg* book I photograph people working.

LOCKHART: I guess I was just looking at those books and remembering the student portraits.

KLEIN: Is that where you first met, at UCLA?

LOCKHART: Yes.

WELLING: Yes.

LOCKHART: I first saw Jim's work when I was in the New England School of Photography. Alex [Slade] and I were talking about it last night because we both took a history of photography class. It was a technical school where you start with a 4 by 5 camera and you learned the zone system. We were being taught the history through the

Beaumont Newhall book, and at some point the teacher showed a slide of your work and a black-and-white photograph of you standing at a locker. Do you know what photograph it is?

WELLING: Yes, it's a portrait where I'm standing next to my wooden view camera.

LOCKHART: Yes, but we've never seen it since.

WELLING: It's not a self-portrait. An interesting New York-based photographer Peter Bellamy, took photographs of artists in the 1980s and that was published in his book.

LOCKHART: I remember your work being unlike any of the other works we were looking at. I think the slide was from the foil series.

WELLING: The draperies.

LOCKHART: It was the drapes, yes. We both were thinking, wow, this is really different. It didn't really make sense under the dominant aesthetic terms our teacher was describing.

WELLING: I think I first saw your work at the show at MOCA where you had your own room with the pictures of the kids kissing.

LOCKHART: The *Hall of Mirrors* show? They were in the cinema show.

WELLING: No, it was another show. It could have been a collection show. I don't think it was *Hall of Mirrors*. It was before that. It was a collection show of people working with photography.

LOCKHART: It's the *Auditions*.

WELLING: Is that your first or one of your earliest works?

LOCKHART: Yes it was the first piece I made out of grad school. And it was my first show in Berlin.

WELLING: Can you talk about the *Auditions* and beginnings? It's nice because it's both an early work and a work about a "first time." When you spoke at UCLA a few years ago I remember you said that you went to a couple of different high schools. Is that right?

LOCKHART: I found a public school in Los Feliz and I asked the drama department if I could work with the students and talk about French film and [François] Truffaut. I did these little workshops in the drama class. In the end I asked if someone would be interested in recreating the moment right before the first kiss from *Small Change*. Nine children were interested so I asked their parents. It seems audacious to me now. I can't imagine that a school would be so welcoming. It seems everything is so much more paranoid and bureaucratic these days.

WELLING: When Jane Weinstock made *Easy*, she filmed a prequel set ten years before the movie starts. The main character is nine and she is supposed to kiss a boy. It was an incredibly traumatic scene to shoot because neither of the child actors had ever kissed anyone. The boy ended up crying in the bathroom. He couldn't do it. In your pictures there is both an incredible anxiety and tenderness in the photographs.

LOCKHART: Thanks so much for saying that. That was exactly what I wanted from those photographs. I had worked with a few children already in the film I did for my thesis show at Art Center and enjoyed it very much. That was why I thought it wouldn't be a problem with *Auditions*. I work hard to create a situation children feel comfortable in. I still love the series when I see them hanging. Probably because it touches on a lot of the topics I'm still interested in, such as duration, portraiture, the anthropological, and fiction. I'm also still close with a lot of the children so it's nice to look back together.

WELLING: And also they're very specific. The staircase they stand in is so real. It's not a studio. For me the great thing about *Lunch Break* is the reality of the space you are filming in. The physicality of that corridor is incredible.

LOCKHART: As soon as I saw that corridor I knew it would be the center of the project. It was unlike any space I'd ever seen. All the equipment and the colors reminded me of the old Kodachrome images I had been looking at for research. I like how it almost looks like a photograph that's continually reframing itself through the film.

WELLING: It's so smooth. How did you do that?

LOCKHART: It's a hand-pushed dolly. That's all. I think it is just a result of going so slowly and the film being slowed down so much we had to build 9 frames for every frame of image (or something like that).

WELLING: Did you do any post work where you took out the bumps and jiggles?

LOCKHART: There are still bumps; you can see them when it goes slowly out of focus and then it comes back. I like those things now, which surprises me still. At the beginning of the post-production I was having a problem with the digital medium and the artifacts it creates. I love the look of "film" and was worried the final piece would look so different, but I was amazed by what we accomplished with the labs, and now I'm excited by the possibilities of digital image-making.

WELLING: You must have rehearsed this shot a number of times to get those guys to be completely oblivious to the camera.

LOCKHART: Oh yes, I was there for a while. I was there a

month of lunches before we shot.

WELLING: How many takes did you do of that?

LOCKHART: We did three during the thirty-minute lunch break.

WELLING: The same day?

LOCKHART: Yes, the same day, but I didn't want it to be about them coming into the hall for lunch or exiting after lunch. I really wanted it to be centered on the break. A lot of people aren't even eating. They're sleeping or doing their crossword puzzles and reading. And my assistant, Carly Short, she's really a great young filmmaker who helped me all the way through the project. She and I would go there and bring books and show them different images that I was researching. Not of my work, but others, like a lot of the WPA stuff. We wanted to get them used to us and for them to have a clear picture of what we were doing. They also brought us things to see a lot of the time.

WELLING: And where was that?

LOCKHART: At the Bath Iron Works.

WELLING: And where's Bath? It's in the middle of the state?

LOCKHART: It's a few miles up the Kennebec River from the ocean. It's about an hour north of Portland. They are one of the largest employers in Maine. I think they employ something like 6,000 people.

KLEIN: And how did you get entry?

LOCKHART: That was through the union. The shipyard said no for almost a year. Somehow the union found out about it through someone in the town, and they invited me for an appointment with the union leaders, which was incredible.

I wish I took a photograph of me sitting at the table with them because it was a huge, generic table with a beautiful hand-painted sign behind it of the union when it was formed and all these guys were sitting around the table with their hardhats. I had prepared packets of research images, and I started to try to present my project and they said, "We love it. Don't worry, we'll get you in." I really had the workers on my side and after that the company let me in and they bent over backwards to give me access. There were some great people on the inside, too, though. The labor relations guy was incredibly supportive. He actually had a Lewis Hine image in his office. The public relations office was also very helpful in the end.

WELLING: But do you think being from Maine helped?

LOCKHART: Yes, for sure it helped. My family knew some of the workers and relatives of workers, so I wasn't a complete outsider. I have a picture my mother took of my sister and me in the shipyard in the 1960s at a launch. I think it also helped that I really did understand them and it was just my assistant Carly and me (until the shoot day). She's from Boston and her dad's a tugboat operator, so she really fit in with everybody. We also shared their sense of humor. I think that was the most important of all. They're so funny. There are so many hysterical videos of Carly with the video camera timing out the dolly shot. In one video she's going down the hallway, trying to measure the time. And she shouts out, "Hey, Joe, whatcha got there today? Oh wow! That's a nice beef stew." Then someone else yells, "Hey, Carly, aren't you going to sit down and have lunch?" And she says, "I can't today. I'm timing up the hallway, but I'll come back later." Her personality was perfect. I couldn't have made that work without her, but they are really funny documentations of the process and the easy relationship we had with the workers.

WELLING: But you wouldn't ever show those, would you?

LOCKHART: No, God, they're really embarrassing and not

that interesting to anyone but us.

WELLING: Like sketches.

LOCKHART: Yes, studies. I always do lots of them but I keep them out of the final work. But recently I've been more open to showing research snapshots. I did that in the *Pine Flat* book for the Guggenheim Museum Bilbao. The photos show the relationships I had with the kids over a long period of time. So, I think with *Lunch Break* I'm going to do just a book with all the research and snapshots. I'm still working that out . . .

WELLING: Yes, I think that would be fantastic, because there's so much on the periphery that you see in that film. It would be nice to expand that out.

LOCKHART: Yes, one of the photographic projects I did is of independent businesses. Some of them are along the sides of the hallway. They all have great names like "Dirty Don's Delicious Dogs" and "Gordon's Java Hut". They sell things like candy bars, coffee, hot dogs and soda. In these photographs you see some of the culture of the place, but I agree that you can just expand out in all directions from that hallway. That was part of the problem in making photographs there. I just wanted to photograph everything. But I wanted to ask you about a particular picture of yours. I'm so curious because it's a re-photograph, and I had seen it many times in books but never noticed it was. It really surprised me and is exciting to the project.

WELLING: The McVeigh house in Chicago.

LOCKHART: Yes. I didn't know that was part of your practice but after I noticed that one it made perfect sense to me.

WELLING: When I did the H. H. Richardson project I went up to Harvard and looked at their archives of Richardson drawings and photographs. Later I took a monograph on

Richardson to the Polaroid studio in New York and I made 20 by 24 inch Polaroid prints of reproductions of destroyed buildings. So this is one of those destroyed buildings. And there are other buildings, train stations, houses, other types of images that I wish I could have photographed, but could not because they no longer exist.

I'm in a show at The Metropolitan Museum of Art that opens in April called *The Pictures Generation.* There are some early image appropriations that I made when David Salle and I shared a loft together. We were both very interested in advertisements and reproductions. Some of my appropriated images are going to be in that show.

LOCKHART: Has anyone ever seen them?

WELLING: No one's ever seen them since 1974.

LOCKHART: And what were they photographs of?

WELLING: One piece used Winston cigarette ads and another group of works paired photographs of famous artists. At the time I was struggling with the idea of what a photograph could be. I collected tons of images from ads, art reproductions, lots of different types of pictures. I exhibited a few and the others I used as my image bank. When I left grad school, I started halfheartedly painting them, but in very short order began to take my own pictures that looked a lot like those in my image bank.

LOCKHART: Were you inspired by Frampton's photographic portraits of artists?

WELLING: No, not directly, but his film *Nostalgia* was important to me.

LOCKHART: I think that was a big influence for me, too. So, what do you think of his photographs?

WELLING: You know, they seem a bit commercial. I think

he improved them by burning the photos. His film work is more interesting than his still photography, as it should be, because he's a fantastic filmmaker.

KLEIN: It's interesting you both mention that one film, *Nostalgia,* because that piece is so much about photography: the way that the voiceover matches up with the photograph that comes after the image shown on the screen. It's all about that slippage of meaning in photography and memory. I wonder if in that film there's a catalyst for some of your own photographic projects.

WELLING: As I said, the big Frampton film for me was *Hapax Legomena*. The title is Greek for words without context. Each of the seven films is very different from the other. My favorite, *Traveling Matte*, deals with the phenomenon of seeing. The filmmaker walks around a snowy college campus with a video camera and looks through his bunched up hand placed right in front of the camera. Now that I think about it, my *Lake Pavilion* owes something to that film with its pacing in the snow!

LOCKHART: Yes, that's a perfect match for you, actually.

WELLING: Didn't Stephen Prina show all of Frampton's films recently?

LOCKHART: He showed everything Frampton made when I was in school in '91, and he showed all of Straub-Huillet's films. And Morgan Fisher came in; Morgan was incredible. I think he showed all of his films, too.

KLEIN: I think that brings up an interesting point about an East Coast/ West Coast kind of way of working, and I'd be curious to hear you both talk a little bit about what the context of Los Angeles has done for your work. Even just the obvious point about the apparatus of Hollywood that's available to artists to use here, which I think applies specifically to some of Sharon's earlier works like *Shaun* and *Auditions*.

LOCKHART: Funny, because I wrote this question to Jim last night. I said "Do you think of yourself as a West Coast artist?" I was thinking about how we both are New Englanders, but that we grew up artistically here in California.

WELLING: Yes.

LOCKHART: But I always thought of you as a New Yorker until I saw the MOCA show [*James Welling: Photographs 1974–1999*]. That's when I saw the L.A. architecture images. Before that, I always pictured you as the East Coast photographer in your studio making setups with tin foil, drapery and phyllo dough.

WELLING: Coming out to California was very important for me to understand my East Coast sensibility. I don't think I would have recognized it if I hadn't come out here. So, I colonized my sensibility out here. I could understand these weird East Coast images better in California.

KLEIN: Such as?

WELLING: Well, in *Los Angeles Architecture,* I photographed houses that reminded me of the East Coast. I still find myself driving down a street and thinking, "That's a bizarre colonial building that reminds me of the East Coast." The idea of ventriloquism in architecture is one that I don't think I would have understood if I'd stayed close to home.

LOCKHART: Right, it heightens your awareness of it.

WELLING: I think it's interesting that we're both from the East Coast. I mean you're even more of an East Coaster than me; you're super-East Coast: you're "Down East."

LOCKHART: One of the reasons I was drawn to *Pine Flat*

was that it reminded me of Maine. The rural town and its people were very much like places I grew up in. It was very familiar. When I went back to the East Coast to make *Lunch Break* I thought I might stay, but by the end I couldn't wait to get back to California. Coming back here, I see California so differently. I'm so much more aware of the landscape and the light. When you mentioned the landscape outside of CalArts, that pastoral scene that no longer exists, that burnt, yellow, rolling hillside is exactly what is so refreshing to see again when you return.

WELLING: But I really formed my aesthetic after moving back to New York from Los Angeles. So, I don't completely think of myself as a West Coast artist. I'm in-between.

LOCKHART: I have one more question, and it's a quote from an old interview you did in *Bomb*. You said, "I prefer photographing emotional things. Maybe they don't appear emotional at first glance. On the other hand, I do like to control things . . . "

WELLING: I said that?

LOCKHART: Yes. I thought it was really great. You said you liked to photograph emotional things.

WELLING: For me, the abstract photographs are very emotional. With the drapery and phyllo dough it's extremely hard to put a literal description on them, but they seem like pure emotion. Maybe not "pure," but strong emotions.

LOCKHART: What about the representational thing; what about the landscapes?

WELLING: I think that all landscape photographs are a stand-in for abstract art, which is a stand-in for emotion in art. To me it seems very obvious that I'm photographing emotions. It's not something that I talk about much. There doesn't seem to be much to say about it apart from the emotion that is right there. But, you know, I also like to take pictures of things that look good in photographs. And there are only a certain number of things that to me are part of my photographic vocabulary. So, even though I might seem to work on a lot of different subjects, I photograph them relatively the same way. They are transformed into my own symbols.

I'm going to do a conversation with Jan Dibbets this fall and when I was at CalArts I was very interested in his work and in photo conceptualism. I was thinking about the distance on the world Conceptualism takes; Dibbets, for instance, made a work for the Guggenheim International where he took a picture every five minutes on the shortest day of the year. I was curious to know, first of all, how did he get to that point of using photography as this kind of remote-controlled machine? Obviously, it was a response to Henri Cartier-Bresson and heroic, Modernist photography that he must have seen in the 1950s, subjective photography, etc.. So the camera, for Dibbets or for Bernd and Hilla Becher, was a mute recording device. A few weeks ago when I put together some of my early work for *The Pictures Generation,* I realized that the muteness of the camera was one of the things that I rebelled against as a student. My attitude was, "Is that all the camera can do? Well, I think it can do other things as well."

KLEIN: And you didn't study with Douglas Huebler? He was after your time at CalArts, right?

WELLING: I met him in Boston in 1971. I shook his hand at an opening and talked to him a little bit but he was still in Massachusetts when I was at CalArts. He came out a few years later. I remember seeing his work at Castelli in New York, and I was very taken by the photographs, especially those pieces he did in New York where he'd put a sticker on an elevator, on a truck, etc.

KLEIN: It's like dematerialized sculpture that comes out of the *Primary Structures* era work.

WELLING: Yes, or the piece where he photographed ice along the road, melted the ice, and processed the film with the ice water. It's a wonderful physical and temporal thing that all comes together in a photograph.

KLEIN: Did you see the *New Topographics* show here?

WELLING: Yes, Otis Art Institute was one of the stops on the *New Topographics* tour. I remember taking the bus downtown to see it. That show changed my life.

KLEIN: And were you working in photography at that point?

WELLING: I think I was just on the edge of buying a camera. I remember being very, very taken by Stephen Shore's work. It was in color. And it was just really beautiful. He's someone who has got a great eye, as we all know. So that work was very important. It moved me more towards thinking seriously about photography. Progressing from Dibbets to Shore, I wanted to keep going and move on to another way of working with the photograph.

KLEIN: Well, to slightly just change the subject, you both have mentioned the influence of people whom you studied with. Sharon, you were looking at Morgan Fisher; Jim, you studied with John Baldessari, and I'm curious to hear more about your views on influence. Maybe this question is partially because I was Jim's student, but mainly it is because you are both influential teachers here in Los Angeles. I was wondering if you would like to share any reflections having both been schooled in L.A. and now being prominent pedagogues here in the art community?

LOCKHART: I never really thought about my influence as a teacher but I've had some great students over the years. Lately, I've realized that one of my strengths as a teacher is in organizing things where students learn by participating. I try to create an environment where students learn that the process is in their hands. You try to expose them to things and see where they take it. I think that as a teacher you hope you've had an influence on students but at the same time you are hoping to give them their own voice so, especially at the graduate level, it becomes hard to see exactly what you've done.

Another question I have that relates to this question is: I was thinking about this recent movement away from representation in photography. It could have something to do with digital, but also it just seems like there's a kind of skepticism within image-making, and I wonder what you think of that scenario and do you see yourself as starting a movement? You know, when I look at the multiplicity of someone like Wolfgang Tillmans, I can't help but think of your work.

WELLING: Going back to Alex's point for a moment, we are both really lucky to teach in L.A., and to have such great students. I think there is a dynamic where a lot is happening in L.A. People want to come out here and study. It's great to have interesting students coming to us.

LOCKHART: From everywhere, yes.

WELLING: I think the materialist bent in photography seems both very important today but also very worrisome—there's nothing more tedious than a bad abstract photograph.

LOCKHART: Well, it does seem like it's maybe not your movement, but it wouldn't have been possible without the work you've done.

WELLING: What interests me is looking at various modalities of image-making and that there can be multiple ways of working with photography.

LOCKHART: One of the great things about your practice is that one day you are making a photogram and the next day it's a landscape. Your work is always surprising and experimental with the materials. I feel like I've been very outside of the debate around representation but I'm so curious why there's so much of this kind of photography out there right now.

WELLING: You mention that it might have something to do with changes in visual technology.

LOCKHART: Yes, I think it does have to do with that.

WELLING: I think it is a fascinating moment right now. Photography has always depended on technological change, but where is digital technology going to take us? To me it's not at all clear where it's going to lead. So, I think this moment is exciting because it boosts all the capabilities of image-making, traditional and otherwise. Apart from just making sharper, crisper and more accurately colored photographs, digital ushers in different ways of thinking about image-making.

LOCKHART: Yes, I think I told you when we had dinner the other night that I think my last show, the Secession show, was probably my last analog show. I mean, I love to print analog, but it's just becoming harder and harder. In the past I've only used digital when I had to. I think of you as being more experimental with it.

WELLING: Well, were the *Pine Flat* pictures printed digitally?

LOCKHART: Yes, but I had to do that. It's not using it really as a tool the same way you are, I don't think.

WELLING: What were those pictures you made of Brussels sprouts? Were those in the *Pine Flat* show?

LOCKHART: Those are analog, too, and older, from 2003. They went along with the film I did on farming, *NO*. I was inspired by a radical ikebana artist who revolutionized the art of Japanese flower arranging. She was trained professionally to make arrangements and her husband was a geologist. He would go to farms for his job and she would always go with him. She would encourage the women farmers to make ikebana with their leftover roots or vegetables and teach them that it didn't have to be limited to the rules and structures of traditional ikebana. She called it "NO-no Ikebana," which means ikebana of agriculture. "No" means agriculture. I was interested in meeting these women farmers that she taught, so I went to this area to make a film and a series of photographs. In the end, I worked with a farming couple to make the film component. The *NO-no Ikebana* was an arrangement of Brussels sprouts, photographed over a month, yellowing. Then the photographs are put into groupings that are nonlinear. The whole thing was very analog. It would have been so much easier to make digitally, but we tested background colors and glaze colors for the base so everything would match. Then we had to make all of the prints match, which was also difficult.

KLEIN: When do you decide to make a film versus a photograph?

LOCKHART: The film projects require so much planning; I usually have them in mind when I go to make a companion photographic project. I like to do them at the same time or think about them at the same time because I'm interested in the difference between the two mediums and the way photography does something that film does not. So, *Goshogaoka* was done at the same time as *Goshogaoka Girl's Basketball Team,* but they do such different things. The photographs are so theatrical and lit, and the compositions look like Baroque paintings or sculptures. The film is comparatively clinical. It's the actions of the girls and their relation to the space of the gym that drives the film.

KLEIN: But your films also have a kind of photographicness to them. They usually have a single lock-off shot that you hold on to, and that's really interesting.

LOCKHART: Yes, I was always interested in making films that behave like photographs. I think that for the film viewer it creates an uneasy relationship. You are used to the moving camera and a lot of cuts, so when you are confronted with the static picture you have to change all your assumptions and establish a different relationship to duration. In the photographs, I've tried a bunch of different approaches. I think in a lot of ways Jim and I are similar because we're constantly looking for new ways to approach things. I remember when I did *Teatro Amazonas,* a lot of people were saying, "She's making documentary photos; what is this about?" But for me it was just a continuation of thinking about anthropology, or a medical image, or science, and how they work together.

WELLING: Did you study anthropology?

LOCKHART: No, but sometimes I think I do now. I get so nervous interviewing you, but I constantly interview people in the world. I'm always asking questions. For *Teatro Amazonas* I interviewed around 600 people, just to make up an audience because I wanted to learn about them. I found Jean Rouch after grad school, and he had a really big influence on me because of the way he participated with his subjects and collaborated. He was looking at other cultures and showing something very real, but through a fictional frame or character. Once I found him I had already done *Auditions* and started researching ethnography more. By the time I got to Japan, I was fully immersed in all of that. I think sometimes it seems like there are two or three different artists, and I wonder if people think that about you, Jim. Reading some of the essays about you, I thought it was so curious how some writers argue with other writers, like Rosalyn Deutsche and Michael Fried. And I thought, "Oh, Jim must have really enjoyed that."

WELLING: No, I don't enjoy it. Not at all.

LOCKHART: No? Not enjoy it, but that there are these

completely different takes on your projects.

WELLING: It's like divorced parents fighting. I'm friends with both sides of the discussion, so it's a little weird sometimes at openings.

You know, I was thinking about when you made *Lunch Break* you must have been thinking about that Duane Hanson work. That's a "lunch break," too, isn't it?

LOCKHART: Yes, Hanson's piece from 1989 is called *Lunch Break, Three Workers with Scaffold*. I became interested in him because of his many representations of the working class.

WELLING: There's that uncanny quality of the lifelike figure. And then in *Lunch Break* you're really slowing down the film, so it becomes very close to a photograph. I just thought of that Duane Hanson piece you did in 2003. I remember you had all those problems around adding the floor in postproduction. Even though I knew that Jeff Wall worked digitally, your Hanson piece was the first time I'd seen someone working with digital compositing. You were really testing the limits of the medium at that point with that floor addition. It was fascinating because no one knows it's a digital composite.

LOCKHART: Thanks so much for saying that, Jim. I wasn't trying to test the limits. I just couldn't figure out any other way to make the image I wanted. To get the whole sculpture in one shot, I would have had to distort it, and I hated doing that to the work. So, we shot several and put them together. I did a show at Blum and Poe in 1996 in which there was a photograph of a young boy in Germany and he had a red sweater. I remember I changed the perspective of the background. No one ever noticed and I never talked about it. But it was the first time I used digital photography. I mean digital manipulation. And the only person that noticed was Jeff Wall's assistant. I thought that was so curious.

KLEIN: That actually leads to another question that I have that's not exactly formulated. You both have made work that looks at other artists' work. Sharon, I'm thinking of the Hanson and the Morris Louis work and even the Disfarmer references; Jim, you've done a lot of work with architecture and photographing sculpture. It's just an observation really, but it's something that's interesting.

WELLING: Well, there's a truism that nothing good comes out of art about art; you know, the photographer should only look at the "real stuff" out in the "real world." One of the New Topographers said, "I'm not interested in opinions about the world, but in the world itself." But to me, it's all intermixed—our opinions about the world create the world. Looking at art that is looking at how we look at things is a valid way of seeing. I am interested in work that looks at forms of representation, of which art is probably the most interesting and profound form of representation.

LOCKHART: What are you looking at now?

WELLING: In addition to architecture, I've been photographing sculpture.

LOCKHART: And what sculpture?

WELLING: *Charles Ray's Log* two years ago. I photographed Michael Asher's show at the Santa Monica Museum. When I was in Paris for the Glass House show I shot Brancusi's studio. I'm interested in photographing *Smoke,* the gigantic Tony Smith that's here at LACMA. Because I did so much work about color over the last ten years, I want to work with the flipside of color, which is form.

LOCKHART: More like your *Torso* photos?

WELLING: They are halfway between sculpture and photography.

LOCKHART: Those are beautiful and moving.

WELLING: They are extremely tactile and that is something I associate with sculpture. So I want to do a black-and-white project about sculpture.

LOCKHART: 4 by 5, black-and-white?

WELLING: Different cameras. Film and digital.

KLEIN: It's interesting because they're all kind of impossible objects in a way. You can't really take them in from one vantage point.

WELLING: Charlie was taking thousands of pictures of his log piece. And so, I thought, "Hey, I'm going to get into the act." Michael Asher's show was a huge event for Los Angeles and for me and I thought that I needed to shoot it.

LOCKHART: How did you photograph that?

WELLING: 8 by 10 and digital. That was a lot harder than Charlie's log.

LOCKHART: Yes, so did they become abstractions because there are so many lines?

WELLING: I'm still editing the photos. When I photographed Brancusi's studio, it was extremely nerve-racking and difficult. Everything is precariously balanced in there. I was afraid I'd knock over something! For the past four years I've been working photographing in and around the Philip Johnson Glass House using an array of colored filters. As I said, the flip side of these photos would be a sculpture project.

LOCKHART: The sculpture project you're working on sounds great. I've made a few pieces, too, that reference other artists or their work. The first was the On Kawara piece. Did you ever see that one? It's called *On Kawara: Whole and Parts . . .* It shows the museum guards in an On Kawara retrospective in Japan. And then there's the Morris Louis conservator trying to recreate Morris Louis. It was so interesting because Morris Louis painted in his dining room, right? I wanted to go photograph the dining room. His wife still lives there. She's remarried. It was a small room. I can't remember the exact measurements, but we recreated the dimensions of the dining room for the studio that our conservator used to make the paintings for the photographs. We were trying to figure out how the hell Louis made these paintings every day, rolled them up, put them away, and got the dining room furniture back in order before his wife came home from work. I mean, it's such an incredible thing to try and figure out because most of the assumptions that people have made are completely wrong. I also made a photograph of Hollis Frampton's front door. I can't remember which movie showed him walking through the snowy landscape in the last shot. I think it was in *Zorns Lemma* and it's the view outside his front door.

WELLING: Oh, you went to Eaton, New York.

LOCKHART: Yes, and I tried to find where he lived. I found the house that I thought was his, but I wasn't sure. No one was home. So, I went next door and this old woman answered and said, "Oh, yes, Hollis, he loved martinis! He used to have dancers over here all the time." I was showing my films upstate when this all happened. They have such a hardcore film community. Everyone would always tell stories about other filmmakers who came through because there are all these universities like Cornell and Colgate, and Utica, with strong film departments. Hollis was always the center it seemed. And so, I just thought, all right, go try and find it.

WELLING: I'm still interested in my observation about you going back and forth between childhood and then the adult world. I think it's an interesting way to look at your work. What do you think? What are you working on next?

LOCKHART: I'm making a film and some photographs of a woman clam digger in Maine. She's an independent seasonal worker and she's also a self-taught artist. She does pencil drawings of workers and fishermen, and they are very much related to her own working life. It's reminiscent of the *NO* film, but it's much more organic, not choreographed. So that's what I'm working on now.

WELLING: So, she'll be working in this?

LOCKHART: Yes, and she's really working. It's hard physical labor, but it's also the most beautiful landscape. She's just such a strong, independent woman, and I find her very interesting to work with.

To answer your question about going back and forth between adulthood and childhood, I think it is a really interesting observation. I think there is something about each of those worlds that helps me work between them. In both cases, I think I work best when I make my subjects real partners. For children that means finding some middle ground where they are not treated as children, but as equals. For adults it often means engendering a spirit of real exchange where they feel a part of something.

CONTRIBUTORS

KEN ABBOTT received his MFA in photography from the Yale University School of Art in 1987 and has pursued independent projects in fine art ever since, also working in editorial and commercial photography. He is a 2006 North Carolina Arts Council Fellowship recipient, and is currently working on a book and film project entitled *Useful Work: The Legacy of Hickory Nut Gap Farm*, in Fairview, North Carolina. Abbott's work was included in the 2009 Museum of Modern Art (MoMA) exhibition *The Printed Picture*, in New York.

AMY ADLER lives and works in Los Angeles. She has shown her work internationally since 1998 and has presented one-person shows and projects at institutions such as the Museum of Contemporary Art (MOCA), Los Angeles; University of California, Los Angeles (UCLA), Hammer Museum; and the Photographers' Gallery, London. In 2005, Twin Palms Publishers released a monograph of her work entitled *Amy Adler Young Photographer* (2005). She is represented by ACME, Los Angeles; Galleria Massimo De Carlo, Milan; Taka Ishii Gallery, Tokyo; and c/o Atle Gerhardsen, Berlin. She is currently an associate professor in the Department of Visual Arts at the University of California, San Diego.

FIA BACKSTRÖM is a New York–based artist, born in Stockholm. She has exhibited work at Serpentine Gallery, London; Institute of Contemporary Art (ICA), Philadelphia; United Nations Plaza, Berlin; Sculpture Center, the Kitchen, White Columns, Andrew Kreps Gallery, and Elizabeth Dee Gallery, all in New York; and Marabouparken, Stockholm. She has had texts published in *Pacemaker*, *North Drive Press*, *Artforum*, and *Art on Paper*. Backström has served as visiting lecturer at New York University, Columbia University, and Rhode Island School of Design (RISD), and currently teaches in the School of Visual Arts (SVA) Photography Department.

GEORGE BAKER is an associate professor of art history at UCLA, where he has taught modern and contemporary art and theory since 2003. An editor of the journal *October* and its publishing imprint, October Books, he also writes as a critic for *Artforum*. Among his many publications are *The Artwork Caught by the Tail: Francis Picabia and Dada in Paris* (2007), *Gerard Byrne: Books, Magazines, and Newspapers* (2003), and *James Coleman: Drei Filmarbeiten* (2002). Baker is currently completing a book on the work of three female artists—Zoe Leonard, Tacita Dean, and Sharon Lockhart—to be entitled *Lateness and Longing*, part of a larger project that Baker has termed "photography's expanded field," detailing the fate of photography and film works in contemporary cultural production.

CHRIS BALASCHAK is a PhD candidate in the Program in Visual Studies at the University of California, Irvine. His research considers the social and institutional history of photography, with particular attention to photobooks, depictions of landscape, and issues of authorship. Balaschak's writing has appeared in *Frieze*, *Art Review*, and the UCLA Hammer Museum's Project series, among other publications.

CHRISTOPHER BEDFORD is curator of exhibitions at the Wexner Center for the Arts. Current curatorial projects include a mid-career survey of Mark Bradford (2010), a group exhibition tentatively titled *Hardware: Machine Aesthetics in the Digital Age* (2010), and a Chris Burden retrospective (2012). In addition to exhibition catalogues, his writing appears regularly in a range of magazines and scholarly journals, including *Artforum*, *Frieze*, *October*, the *Burlington Magazine*, and *Art in America*.

ADAM B. BELL is a photographer living in New York. His work was included in the Art+Commerce Festival of Emerging Photographers in both 2004 and 2005, and has been exhibited and published internationally. He is the coeditor and coauthor, with Charles H. Traub and Steven Heller, of *The Education of a Photographer* (2006). His work has been published in the *New York Times*, *New York Magazine*, the *Village Voice*, *Esquire*, *Me Magazine*, *Print*, and various other publications. Clients include HBO Pictures, THINKFilm, Journeyman Pictures, Pace/MacGill Gallery, Per Se, Brooklyn Museum of Art, Foundation for Architecture, and others.

WALEAD BESHTY was born in London in 1976. He is a Los Angeles–based artist and writer, and associate professor in the Graduate Fine Art Program at Art Center College of Art and Design. His work has been exhibited widely, including the Whitney Museum of American Art and MoMA, both in New York; Tate Britain, London; and Museum of Contemporary Art, Chicago; with solo exhibitions at the UCLA Hammer Museum; University of Michigan Museum of Art, Ann Arbor; and Hirshhorn Museum and Sculpture Garden, Washington, D.C. Beshty is a regular contributor to *Texte zur Kunst* and *Afterall*.

GIL BLANK is a photographer and writer. He is a contributing editor to *Art on Paper*, and was the founding editor of *Influence* magazine. His writing on photography has also been published as part of the monographs *Raised Eyebrows/Furrowed Foreheads*, by John Baldessari (2010); *White Planet, Black Heart*, by Torbjørn Rødland (2006); and *Freischwimmer*, by Wolfgang Tillmans (2004).

NATALIE BOOKCHIN is an artist with a background in photography and film. Her work has been shown widely, including such venues as P.S.1, New York; Massachusetts Museum of Contemporary Art, Boston; Generali Foundation, Vienna; Walker Art Center, Minneapolis; Centre Pompidou, Paris; and MOCA, Los Angeles. She has been written about in *Artforum*, the *New York Times*, *Flash Art*, *Art News*, *El Pais*, *Liberation*, the *Los Angeles Times*, *Glamour Magazine*, and *La Repubblica*. Bookchin lives and works in Los Angeles, where she is codirector of the

Program in Photography and Media in the School of Art at the California Institute of the Arts (CalArts).

DEBORAH BRIGHT was born in Washington, D.C., in 1950, and received her MFA from the University of Chicago in 1975. Her works have been shown internationally at the Victoria and Albert Museum, London; the Museet for Fotokunst, Odense, Denmark; Nederlands Foto Instituut, Rotterdam; Museum Folkwang, Essen, Germany; Canadian Museum of Contemporary Photography, Ottawa; Cambridge Darkroom, U.K.; and Vancouver Art Gallery. Her works can be found in the permanent collections of such institutions as the Whitney Museum of American Art, New York, and National Museum of American Art, Washington, D.C. She is a professor at RISD in the Departments of Art History, Architecture, and Photography.

JOHANNA BURTON is an art historian and critic living in New York. She is associate director and a senior faculty member at the Whitney Independent Study Program.

KATHERINE BUSSARD is assistant curator of photography at the Art Institute of Chicago and author of the exhibition catalogue *So the Story Goes: Photographs by Tina Barney, Philip-Lorca diCorcia, Nan Goldin, Sally Mann, and Larry Sultan* (2006). Bussard completed her doctoral dissertation on street photography at the City University of New York (CUNY) in 2009. She is currently cocurating a 2011 exhibition on the history of American color photography.

DAVID CAMPANY is an artist and writer, as well as a reader in photography at the University of Westminster, London. He is the author of *Art and Photography* (2003) and *Photography and Cinema* (2008).

MELISSA CATANESE received her MFA from the Cranbrook Academy of Art. She is represented by Sasha Wolf Gallery, New York, and her work can also be viewed as part of the Midwest Photographers Project at the Museum of

Contemporary Photography, Columbia College Chicago. The Humble Arts Foundation also included her work in the book, *The Collector's Guide to Emerging Art Photography* (2009). Catanese currently lives in Brooklyn.

PHIL CHANG received his MFA from CalArts, and his work has been exhibited in both Los Angeles and New York. He is currently a visiting faculty member at UCLA and at Otis College of Art and Design. Chang lives and works in Los Angeles.

SARAH CHARLESWORTH is a visual artist and photographer who has exhibited widely in the U.S. and abroad, with over forty individual exhibitions, a traveling museum retrospective (organized by SITE Santa Fe), and presence in major museum shows and collections. Her work has explored issues concerning the language of photography within contemporary culture. In addition to her photographic work, Charlesworth has taught photography for several years in the graduate programs at RISD and SVA. Her work appears in the collections of such museums as the Whitney Museum of American Art and MoMA, both in New York; Museum of Fine Arts, Boston; MOCA, Los Angeles; and Walker Art Center, Minneapolis. She is the recipient of two National Endowment for the Arts grants and a Guggenheim Fellowship. Charlesworth lives and works in New York.

JOSHUA CHUANG is the assistant curator of photographs at the Yale University Art Gallery. Most recently, he curated the exhibition *First Doubt: Optical Confusion in Modern Photography* (2008) and authored its accompanying catalogue. He has also organized monographs on American photographers Judith Joy Ross and Mark Ruwedel, and is currently at work on a retrospective of the work of Robert Adams.

JACOB CIOCCI is a founding member of the Paper Rad art collective. His work is concerned with the relationship between popular culture, technology, and notions of transcendence. In his paintings, comics, performances, net art and videos, contemporary and recently forgotten cultural symbols confront one another in a frenzied cartoon universe that is at once celebratory and critical.

JÖRG COLBERG is a writer and photographer, best known for Conscientious (www.jmcolberg.com/weblog), one of the most widely read and popular photography blogs. His work has been published by numerous magazines and websites, both nationally and internationally.

MILES COOLIDGE is an artist and a professor of photography at the University of California, Irvine. His work has appeared in solo exhibitions at Casey Kaplan, New York; ACME, Los Angeles; and Galerie Gisela Capitain, Cologne, Germany; among other venues. Group shows in which his work was displayed include *Now Is the Winter*, Projekt Fabrika, Moscow; *Been Up So Long it Looks Like Down to Me*, Presentation House Gallery, Vancouver; *Art in America Now*, Shanghai Museum of Art; *First the Artist Defines Meaning*, Kunsthaus Graz, Austria; and *Modern Photographs from the Collection*, the Metropolitan Museum of Art, New York.

CHARLOTTE COTTON is the National Media Museum's creative director for their future London galleries, and was formerly curator and head of the Wallis Annenberg Photography Department at the Los Angeles County Museum of Art (LACMA). She also served as curator of photographs at the Victoria and Albert Museum from 1992 to 2004. Cotton is the author and editor of several books, including *Imperfect Beauty: The Making of Contemporary Fashion Photographs* (2000) and *The Photograph as Contemporary Art* (2004).

ZOE CROSHER is a Los Angeles–based artist whose work has been exhibited internationally, in Vancouver, Rotterdam, Los Angeles, and New York, among other cities. In addition to her exhibition practice, Crosher released a monograph, *Out the Window LAX*, examining space and transience around the Los Angeles airport, in 2007, and is currently working on a book on her newest project, *The Reconsidered Archive of Michelle duBois*. Crosher recently served as visiting faculty at UCLA and was an associate editor at the journal *Afterall*.

MOYRA DAVEY is the editor of *Mother Reader: Essential Writings on Motherhood* (2001) and author of *The Problem of Reading* (2003). In 2008, the Fogg Art Museum presented *Long Life Cool White*, a twenty-year survey of her photographs. She is currently participating in the International Residencies program at the Cité des Arts in Paris.

TIM DAVIS is an artist and poet living and working in both New York City and Tivoli, New York. He graduated from Bard College and earned his MFA from Yale University. He is the author of several monographs, including *Lots* (2002), *Permanent Collection* (2005), and *My Life in Politics* (2006), as well as a book of poetry titled *American Whatever* (2004). He is represented by Greenberg Van Doren Gallery and Sikkema Jenkins & Co. in New York, and teaches in the Photography Program at Bard College. Davis was awarded the Joseph H. Hazen Rome Prize from the American Academy in Rome in 2007.

JOHN DIVOLA's work has been featured in more than sixty solo and two hundred group exhibitions internationally at galleries and institutions such as LACMA and Gallery Luisotti, both in Los Angeles; MoMA, Whitney Museum of American Art, and Charles Cowles Gallery, all in New York; San Francisco Museum of Modern Art (SFMOMA); and Centre Pompidou, Paris. His recent publications include *The Green of this Notebook* (2009), *Three Acts* (2006), *Dogs Chasing My Car in the Desert* (2004), and *Isolated Houses* (2000). Divola taught at CalArts from 1978 to 1988, before taking up his current professorship in the Department of Art at the University of California, Riverside.

SHANNON EBNER was born in New Jersey in 1971 and currently lives and works in Los Angeles. She received her MFA from the Yale University School of Art in 2000 and her BA from Bard College in 1993. A 2009 artist's book of Ebner's work entitled *The Sun as Error* was published by LACMA and coordinated by Dexter Sinister.

JASON EVANS is a multi-disciplinary photographer with a diverse range of outputs, typified by an experimental approach to image-making. Known for his work in different media, he has enjoyed a career that engages with the fashion, music, and editorial industries. He currently teaches at the University for the Creative Arts.

HARRELL FLETCHER has worked collaboratively and individually on a variety of socially engaged, interdisciplinary projects for over fifteen years. He was a participant in the 2004 Whitney Biennial and his work has been shown at such institutions as the Drawing Center, Socrates Sculpture Park, SculptureCenter, and Wrong Gallery, all in New York; DiverseWorks and Aurora Picture Show, both in Houston; Portland Institute of Contemporary Art (PICA), Oregon; Center on Contemporary Art, Seattle; Seattle Art Museum; Signal, Malmö, Sweden; Domaine de Kerguéhennec, Bignan, France; and Royal College of Art, London. His work is held in the collections of the MoMA, Whitney Museum of American Art, and New Museum of Contemporary Art, all in New York; SFMOMA; de Young Museum, San Francisco; Berkeley Art Museum, California; and the Regional Contemporary Art Collection (FRAC), Brittany, France. In 2002, Fletcher started Learning To Love You More, an ongoing participatory website, with Miranda July. He is the professor of art and social practice at Portland State University.

STEPHANIE FORD is a Los Angeles–based editor, teacher, and poet. Formerly an editor at the J. Paul Getty Museum, she currently directs the creative writing program at Campbell Hall in North Hollywood.

JASON FULFORD is a photographer, graphic designer, and co-founder of J&L Books. He is also a contributing editor to *Blind Spot* and a critic on the Yale MFA Photography graduate review panel. His monographs include *Sunbird* (2000), *Crushed* (2003), and *Raising Frogs for $$$* (2006). He lives in Scranton, Pennsylvania.

PETER FRASER was born in Cardiff, Wales, in 1953. He studied photography in Manchester, England, graduating in 1976. He has been exhibiting internationally since 1983, a year after a fateful visit with William Eggleston. He was shortlisted for the Citigroup International Photography Prize in 2004, and recently finished a photography residency at Oxford University. Fraser is currently living and working in Wales and London.

MARK GODFREY is a curator at Tate Modern. He is the author of *Abstraction and the Holocaust* (2007) and essays on artists such as Anri Sala, Ceal Floyer, Christopher Williams, Pierre Huyghe, Tacita Dean, Zoe Leonard, and Sharon Lockhart. He curated the exhibitions *Matthew Buckingham: Play the Story* at Camden Arts Centre in 2007 and *Roni Horn aka Roni Horn* at Tate Modern in 2009. He is currently working on an exhibition of work by Francis Alÿs and a book about Alighiero Boetti.

PAUL GRAHAM is a U.K.–born photographer currently based in New York. His work has been exhibited internationally and is in the collections of numerous institutions, including the Metropolitan Museum of Art, Guggenheim Museum, MoMA, and Whitney Museum of American Art, all in New York; Tate Gallery and Victoria and Albert Museum, both in London; Stedelijk Museum, Amsterdam; and Fotomuseum Winterthur, Switzerland. In 1996, his work was the subject of a Phaidon monograph. Other publications include *A1—The Great North Road* (1983), *Beyond Caring* (1986), *Troubled Land* (1987), *New Europe* (1995), *American Night* (2003), and *A Shimmer of Possibility* (2007).

KATY GRANNAN received her BA from the University of Pennsylvania and her MFA from the Yale University School of Art. She has exhibited at the 2004 Whitney Biennial, New York; Guggenheim Museum, Bilbao; and LACMA, among other venues. Grannan has been featured in *Artforum*, *Frieze*, *Art on Paper*, and the *New York Times*. Her monograph, *Model American*, was published by Aperture in 2005.

CATHERINE GRANT is a visiting lecturer at the Courtauld Institute of Art and Goldsmiths College. Her research interests include the representation of adolescence and femininity in photography, the theorization of spectatorship and identification in relation to the photographic portrait, and the intersection between queer theory and feminism. She completed her Ph.D., entitled *Different Girls: Performances of Adolescence in Contemporary Photographic Portraits*, at the Courtauld in 2006, and was the Courtauld Research Forum Postdoctoral Fellow in 2007. She authored an article on Anna Gaskell in *Feminism Reframed* (2007) and has written on contemporary art for various magazines and books, including *Flash Art* and *Vitamin Ph* (2006).

NICHOLAS GRIDER is an artist and curator living in Milwaukee. He has had solo exhibitions at Sea and Space, Los Angeles, and Portrait Society, Milwaukee, as well as venues in Los Angeles and Boston.

KARL HAENDEL received a BA from Brown University in 1998 and an MFA from UCLA in 2003. He also studied at the Whitney Museum Independent Study Program and the Skowhegan School of Painting and Sculpture. His work has been featured in group exhibitions at the Whitney Museum of American Art and MoMA, both in New York; Astrup Fearnley Museum of Modern Art, Oslo; and Serpentine Gallery, London; among other venues. He was the subject of a one-person exhibition at MOCA, Los Angeles, in 2006. Haendel is represented by Harris Lieberman Gallery, New York, and Susanne Vielmetter Projects, Los Angeles.

KAREN HELLMAN is a doctoral candidate in the history of photography at the CUNY Graduate Center and is currently writing a dissertation on the early London daguerreotype portrait studio of the Frenchman Antoine Claudet. She has worked at MOCA, Los Angeles; in the Department of Photographs at the J. Paul Getty Museum; and she organized the exhibition *André Kertész: Seven Decades*. Hellman is also research curator for a forthcoming exhibition at the Yale Center for British Art on the daguerreotype studios of Claudet and Richard Beard.

LESLIE HEWITT uses photography, sculpture, and film to challenge the representation and organization of social meaning. Hewitt uses the camera as a tool to reposition one's view, subtly disrupting the window effect and other expectations of a photographic document. She engages architectural space and the fragmentation of time through photographic and sculptural means. In exploring the "revolution" embedded in photography and film, her work addresses how cultural material is documented, classified, and preserved. Hewitt was recently named a 2008-2009 Radcliffe Fellow by Harvard University.

TODD HIDO is a Bay Area–based artist whose work has been featured in *Artforum*, the *New York Times Magazine*, *Eyemazing*, *Metropolis*, *The Face*, *i-D*, and *Vanity Fair*. His photographs are in the permanent collections of such institutions as the Whitney Museum of American Art and Guggenheim Museum, both in New York, SFMOMA, and LACMA. His award-winning monograph, *House Hunting*, was published in 2001 and a companion monograph, *Outskirts*, was published the following year. His other books include *Roaming* (2004), and *Between the Two* (2007), focusing on portraits and nudes. Hido is an adjunct professor at the California College of Art, San Francisco.

DARIUS HIMES served as founding editor of *photo-eye*, a quarterly magazine devoted to photography books, from 2002–7. He is a founding member and current editor of

Radius Books, a non-profit, Santa Fe–based organization launched in 2007 that publishes books on the visual arts. He is also a lecturer, consultant, educator, and writer, having contributed to *Blind Spot*, *Bookforum*, *BOMB*, *PDN,* and *American Photo*.

WILLIAM E. JONES's films and videos been shown at the Cinémathèque Française and Musée du Louvre, both in Paris; Whitney Museum of American Art and MoMA, both in New York; Tate Modern, London; and the 53rd Venice Biennale. His books include *Is It Really So Strange?* (2006), *Tearoom* (2008), *Selections from* The Anatomy of Melancholy *by Robert Burton* (2008), and *Heliogabalus* (2009), as well as his current engagement writing a book about Fred Halsted. Jones has worked in the adult video industry under the name Hudson Wilcox. He teaches film history at Art Center College of Design under his own name.

SIRI KAUR received her MFA from CalArts and her BA from Smith College. Her photographs have been exhibited in group shows at numerous venues, including 401 Projects, New York; Hayworth Gallery, Los Angeles; Torrance Museum of Art, California; and the UCLA Wight Biennial. Kaur's work is in the permanent collections of the National Gallery, Washington, D.C., and the University of Maine. She lives and works in Los Angeles, where she is currently a visiting lecturer at Otis College of Art and Design.

MATT KEEGAN's collaborations with Leslie Hewitt have been exhibited at venues such as Altman Siegel Gallery, San Francisco; Midway Contemporary Art, Minneapolis; Anna Helwing Gallery, Los Angeles; and D'Amelio Terras, White Columns, and Wallspace Gallery, all in New York. He is cofounder and publisher of the annual publication *North Drive Press*. Keegan lives in Brooklyn.

SOO KIM is a Los Angeles–based artist and curator. Her work has been included in numerous solo and group exhibitions internationally, and is held in several collections, both public and private. She received her MFA from CalArts, where she studied in the Schools of Art, Critical Writing, and Film and Video. Kim is currently professor and director of the Photography Program at Otis College of Art and Design.

ALEX KLEIN is an artist based in Los Angeles. She received her MFA from UCLA, her MA in the history of art from the Courtauld Institute of Art, and her BA from Columbia University. In Spring 2007, she co-organized, with James Welling, the Around Photography conference at the UCLA Hammer Museum. Klein is a co-founder of Oslo Editions and is currently the Ralph M. Parsons curatorial fellow in the Wallis Annenberg Photography Department at LACMA and a lecturer at the University of Southern California (USC) Roski School of Fine Arts.

SHANE LAVALETTE is a photographer, writer, and the founding editor of *Lay Flat*, a publication on contemporary photography and writing. He lives in Cambridge, Massachusetts, where he is completing his undergraduate studies at Tufts University and the School of the Museum of Fine Arts, Boston.

JOHN LEHR received his MFA from the Yale University School of Art in 2005 and his BFA from the Maryland Institute College of Art in 1998. His work has been included in exhibitions at MoMA, Yancey Richardson Gallery, and Kate Werble Gallery, all in New York; Walker Art Center, Minneapolis; Carnegie Museum of Art, Pittsburgh; and Corcoran Gallery of Art, Washington, D.C. Lehr is currently a lecturer in photography at the Yale School of Art.

SZE TSUNG LEONG is a Mexico City–born artist currently living in New York. His work has been exhibited internationally, and is held in the permanent collections of institutions, including the Brooklyn Museum of Art and MoMA, both in New York; SFMOMA; High Museum of Art, Atlanta; Yale

University Art Gallery, New Haven, Connecticut; and Santa Barbara Museum of Art, California. Leong is the recipient of a Guggenheim Fellowship and his book, *History Images*, was released in 2006.

MIRANDA LICHTENSTEIN received her MFA from CalArts. She has exhibited in numerous museums and galleries in the U.S. and abroad, including the UCLA Hammer Museum; Whitney Museum of American Art at Philip Morris, New Museum of Contemporary Art, and Elizabeth Dee Gallery, all in New York; Yerba Buena Center for the Arts, San Francisco; Renaissance Society, Chicago; Hirshhorn Museum and Sculpture Garden, Washington, D.C.; Stadthaus Ulm, Germany; Gallery Min Min, Tokyo; and Mary Goldman Gallery, Los Angeles. Lichtenstein lives and works in New York.

SHARON LOCKHART has, since 1994, been making films and photographs that frame moments of everyday life while questioning assumptions about documentary truth and narrative structures. Her project, *Lunch Break*, opened the Vienna Secession in November 2008, and the filmic elements were featured at both the Sundance Film Festival and Berlinale in 2009. Her work is held in the collections of LACMA; MoMA and Whitney Museum of American Art, both in New York; Tate Modern, London; Art Institute of Chicago; and Museum Boijmans, Rotterdam, the Netherlands; among others. Lockhart lives in Los Angles and is an associate professor at USC's Roski School of Fine Arts.

ALLAN MCCOLLUM lives and works in New York. He has spent over thirty years exploring how objects achieve public and personal meaning in a world inundated with mass production, focusing most recently on collaborating with small-community historical societies and museums in different parts of the world. He has had over one hundred solo exhibitions, including retrospectives at the Musée d'Art Moderne, Villeneuve d'Ascq, Lille, France; Sprengel Museum, Hannover, Germany; Serpentine Gallery, London;

Rooseum Center for Contemporary Art, Malmö, Sweden; IVAM Centre del Carme, Valencia, Spain; Stedelijk van Abbemuseum, Eindhoven, the Netherlands; and Portikus, Frankfurt. His works are held in the collections of over seventy museums worldwide, including the Metropolitan Museum of Art, MoMA, Whitney Museum of American Art, and Guggenheim Museum, all in New York; Art Institute of Chicago; and MOCA, Los Angeles.

TOM McDONOUGH is an associate professor of art history at the State University of New York, Binghamton, where he teaches contemporary art, spatial theory, and urban culture. His publications include *"The Beautiful Language of My Century": Reinventing the Language of Contestation in Postwar France, 1945–1968* (2007), and the anthology *Guy Debord and the Situationist International: Texts and Documents* (2002). He is an editor at *Grey Room*.

KEVIN MOORE is an independent scholar and curator whose work is focused on the history of photography and contemporary art. He has worked in the Department of Photographs at both the Metropolitan Museum of Art and Fogg Art Museum at Harvard University, and has taught at Boston University. He is the author of *Jacques Henri Lartigue: The Invention of an Artist* (2004), and co-author, with Michael Lorenzini, of *New York Rises: Photographs by Eugene de Salignac* (2007), as well as a contributing author to *The Oxford Companion to the Photograph* (2005); *L'Art de la photographie: 1839 à nos jours* (2007); *American Paintings at Harvard, Volume Two* (2008); and *More Than One: Photographs in Sequence* (2008). Moore is currently working on an exhibition and catalogue of color photography from the 1970s.

REBECCA MORSE received her MA in the history of photography from the University of Arizona. She is currently assistant curator at MOCA, Los Angeles.

CARTER MULL was born in Atlanta in 1977, and is

currently a Los Angeles–based artist. His work has been exhibited widely, including such venues as Presentation House Gallery, Vancouver; Domaine Départemental de Chamarande, Paris; The Approach, London; the Contemporary Art Center, Cincinnati; and Harris Lieberman Gallery and Gagosian Gallery, both in New York. His work is held in the collections of the Walker Art Center, Minneapolis, and the UCLA Hammer Museum, and has been featured in publications, including *Art on Paper*, *Blind Spot*, the *Los Angeles Times*, the *New Yorker*, *Artforum*, and *Art in America*. In 2009, Mull took part in MoMA's *New Photography* exhibition. He currently teaches photography at the USC.

MARISA OLSON is an artist, critic, and curator. Her work has recently been presented by the Whitney Museum of American Art and New Museum of Contemporary Art, both in New York; Centre Pompidou, Paris; National Museum of Contemporary Art, Athens; Edith Russ-Haus für Medienkunst, Oldenburg, Germany; Nederlands Instituut voor Mediakunst/Montevideo, Amsterdam; British Film Institute, London; and at the 52nd Venice Biennale. Olson is also a founding member of the Nasty Nets "internet surfing club," whose new DVD recently premiered at the New York Underground Film Festival and was the subject of an exhibition at the 2009 Sundance Film Festival. Her work has been written about in *Artforum*, the *New York Times*, *Art in America*, *Folha de S. Paolo*, *Liberation Paris*, and the *Village Voice*. Her critiques of contemporary art and digital visual culture have been published in *Flash Art*, *Art Review*, *Afterimage*, *Planet*, and *Art on Paper*. Olson has curated programs at SFMOMA; SF Camerawork, San Francisco; and Guggenheim, White Columns, Artists Space, and the Performa Biennial, all in New York. Olson is currently the curator-at-large at Rhizome.

CATHERINE OPIE is an artist specializing in issues within documentary photography. She is currently a professor of photography at UCLA, and her works are displayed in both museums and galleries internationally. Opie has had numerous catalogues published alongside museum exhibitions, including *Catherine Opie*, MOCA, Los Angeles, 1997; *Skyways and Ice Houses*, Walker Art Center, 1999; *In and Around Home*, Aldrich Museum, 2006; and *Chicago* Museum of Contemporary Art, Chicago, 2006. In 2008, she was the subject of a mid-career survey, *Catherine Opie: American Photographer*, at the Guggenheim Museum, New York.

ARTHUR OU is an assistant professor at Parsons The New School for Design. He received an MFA from the Yale University School of Art in 2000, and his work has appeared in exhibitions in Los Angeles, New York, Chicago, London, Vancouver, Beijing, and Dresden, Germany.

ED PANAR received his MFA from the Cranbrook Academy of Art in 2005 and, in 2007, he earned a fellowship from the Pennsylvania Council on the Arts. His first book, *Golden Palms,* was recently published by J&L Books. He currently lives and works in Brooklyn.

TOD PAPAGEORGE began to photograph during his last semester at the University of New Hampshire in 1962. In 1970, he received his first of two Guggenheim Fellowships in Photography and, in 1979, Papageorge was appointed Walker Evans professor and director of graduate studies in photography at the Yale University School of Art. Two collections of his photographs—*Passing through Eden: Photographs of Central Park* and *American Sports, 1970, or How We Spent the War in Vietnam*—were published in 2007 and 2008, respectively. He was recently shortlisted for the 2009 Deutsche Börse Photography Prize.

MARTIN PARR's boyhood interest in photography was encouraged by his grandfather, George Parr, himself a keen amateur photographer. Parr studied photography at Manchester Polytechnic from 1970 to 1973. He earned an international reputation for innovative imagery and his oblique approach to social documentary, becoming a member of Magnum in 1994. After the 2002 publication of the monograph, *Martin Parr*, a large retrospective of Parr's work was initiated by the Barbican Art Gallery, London, which has since traveled to the Museo Nacional Centro de Arte Reina Sofía, Madrid; Maison Européenne de la Photographie, Paris; and the Deichtorhallen Hamburg, Germany. Parr was appointed professor of photography at the University of Wales in 2004, and was guest artistic director for Rencontres d'Arles the same year. In recent years, he has developed an interest in filmmaking and has started to use his photography in different contexts, such as fashion and advertising.

EDITH MARIE PASQUIER is a London-based artist who received her MFA in photography from the Royal College of Art in 2008. Her interdisciplinary work has earned awards and commissions from Film London, Artsadmin, Soho Theatre, and Serpentine Gallery, all in London; and Nuffield Theatre, Southhampton, U.K. Her practice includes moving-image, photography, sound/music, and text work. Pasquier has also contributed as a writer and critic to numerous publications, including *Unknown Public*, *a-n Magazine*, and catalogues by the Women's Art Library and Museum of Modern African Art, New York.

ANTHONY PEARSON has had solo exhibitions of his art presented at David Kordansky Gallery, Los Angeles; Midway Contemporary Art, Minneapolis; and Marianne Boesky Gallery, New York. A monograph of his photographs, *Solarizations,* was published in Spring 2009. Pearson lives in Los Angeles.

LESTER PLEASANT's work has been exhibited widely to his friends and family, in his studio, and on his website. No longer a recent graduate, he is currently navigating the wilderness of the "real world" on a quest to develop his work and bring it to an even larger audience. He is currently based in Los Angeles.

PHILLIP PRODGER is the curator of photography at the Peabody Essex Museum. Previously, he was the Lisette Model/Joseph G. Blum fellow in history of photography at the National Gallery of Canada, and the assistant curator of prints, drawings, and photographs at the Saint Louis Art Museum. His books include *E. O. Hoppé's Amerika* (2007), *Impressionist Camera: Pictorial Photography in Europe, 1888–1918* (2006), and *Time Stands Still: Muybridge and the Instantaneous Photography Movement* (2003). Prodger's writings on photography and art have been published in six languages. He is currently completing a book on Charles Darwin and photography and organizing a major retrospective of the photographs of Jerry Uelsmann.

LAUREL PTAK is a New York–based independent curator. She is the founder of popular blog about contemporary photography, iheartphotograph.com. Ptak frequently teaches, lectures, and writes about photography, the Internet, and image culture, all in addition to her work curating "off-line" exhibitions based on her blog.

ELIZABETH PULSINELLI is an artist and editor in Los Angeles. She is executive editor of the contemporary art quarterly *X-TRA* and has worked on a variety of catalogues and books for museums, galleries, and artists. She received her MFA in photography from CalArts.

ADAM PUTNAM was born in New York in 1973. Most recently, his work appeared in the 2008 Whitney Biennial, Whitney Museum of American Art, New York; Art Statements, Basel; and the Busan Biennial, South Korea. He is represented by Taxter & Spengemann and lives and works in Queens, New York.

MICHAEL QUEENLAND received an MFA from UCLA in 2002. In 2005, his work was featured in *Michael Queenland: Photographs, Sculptures and Shaker Classics* at the Institute of Contemporary Art at Maine College of Art, Portland, Maine, and Massachusetts College of Art and

Design (MassArt), Boston. From 2004–5, Queenland was a resident artist at the Studio Museum in Harlem. His exhibitions include *Civil Restitutions*, Thomas Dane Gallery, London; *Trace*, Whitney Museum at Altria, New York; *Frequency*, Studio Museum of Harlem, New York; and the 2008 Whitney Biennial, Whitney Museum of American Art, New York. Queenland was named a United States Artists Fellow in 2006.

EILEEN QUINLAN is a graduate of the School of the Museum of Fine Arts/Tufts University and Columbia University. She has had solo shows presented at Miguel Abreu Gallery, New York; Sutton Lane, Paris; and Galerie Daniel Buchholz, Cologne, Germany. Quinlan's first solo museum exhibition was *Momentum 13: Eileen Quinlan*, at ICA, Boston.

DAVID REINFURT runs O-R-G inc., a small design practice; co-operates Dexter Sinister, a workshop and one-day-a-week bookstore; and coedits and publishes *Dot Dot Dot* magazine from a basement in New York's Lower East Side.

OLIVIER RICHON was born in Lausanne, Switzerland, in 1956. He studied at the Polytechnic of Central London, where he was taught by Victor Burgin, and graduated with a BA in film and photographic arts in 1980, and later a masters of philosophy in 1988. In 1991, he received the Camera Austria Award for Contemporary Photography. His work has been exhibited internationally since 1980, and is held in many public collections, including those of the Victoria and Albert Museum, London; Musée d'Art Moderne de la Ville de Paris; Museum Folkwang, Essen, Germany; National Museum of Modern Art, Kyoto; Brooklyn Museum; and National Gallery of New South Wales, Australia. A monograph of his photographic work, entitled *Real Allegories*, was published in 2006. He is currently professor of photography at the Royal College of Art, London.

NOEL RODO-VANKEULEN is a photographer and writer who holds a BFA in visual arts from York University. Currently living and working in Brampton, Ontario, Rodo-Vankeulen's work has been exhibited internationally and resides in numerous collections. Though he continues to work on various photographic projects, he is also editor of the *We Can't Paint Network* (wecantpaint.com), which includes the online magazine *Wassenaar*.

ALLEN RUPPERSBERG's work has been the subject of over sixty solo exhibitions and is in the permanent collections of such international museums as the Whitney Museum of American Art and MoMA, both in New York; MOCA, Los Angeles; de Appel Arts Centre, Amsterdam; and Museum für Moderne Kunst, Frankfurt. He is the subject of several monographs, including *Allen Ruppersberg: The Secret of Life and Death. Volume I: 1969–1984* (1985), *Allen Ruppersberg: Books, Inc.* (2001), and *Allen Ruppersberg: One of Many—Origins and Variants* (2006). His solo exhibitions include *Allen Ruppersberg: You and Me or The Art of Give and Take*, Santa Monica Museum of Art, California (2009); *Allen Ruppersberg*, Camden Arts Centre, London (2008); and *Selected Works*, Margo Leavin Gallery, Los Angeles (2008).

AARON SCHUMAN is an American photographer, editor, writer, and curator based in the U.K. He has exhibited his photographic work internationally, and has contributed to publications such as *Aperture*, *ArtReview*, *Modern Painters*, *Foam*, *HotShoe International*, *Photoworks*, the *British Journal of Photography*, *Creative Review*, the *Guardian*, the *Observer*, and the *Sunday Times*. He is a research fellow and senior lecturer in photography at the Arts Institute at Bournemouth, and a lecturer in photography at the University of Brighton, both in the U.K. Schuman is also the founder and editor of the online photography journal, *SeeSaw Magazine* (seesawmagazine.com).

BENNETT SIMPSON is associate curator at MOCA, Los

Angeles, where he has organized the recent exhibitions *MOCA Focus: Lisa Lapinski* and *Dan Graham: Beyond* (cocurated with Chrissie Iles). Prior to MOCA, Simpson was associate curator at ICA, Boston, as well as ICA, Philadelphia, where he organized *Make Your Own Life: Artists in and out of Cologne*, *Shoot the Singer: Music on Video*, and solo exhibitions with Philip-Lorca diCorcia, Roe Ethridge, and Justine Kurland, among others. Simpson's writing has appeared in *Artforum*, *Parkett*, and *Texte zur Kunst*.

ALEX SLADE received his MFA from CalArts in 1993. Since receiving his degree, he has been looking at various aspects of landscape with an eye turned toward the urban system, its economy, and the perceptual field it engenders. His work was included in *Eloi: Stumbling Toward Paradise*, California Museum of Photography, Riverside; *Utopian Mirage: Social Metaphors in Contemporary Photography and Film*, Vassar College, Poughkeepsie, New York; *Tomorrowland, CalArts in Moving Pictures*, MoMA, New York; as well as the 1999 Liverpool Biennial, 2003 Prague Biennial, and the first of UCLA Hammer Museum's mini-Biennials, *Snapshot-New Art from Los Angeles*. In 2006, Slade received a fellowship from the California Community Foundation and was the recipient of the City of Los Angeles Individual Artist Fellowship the following year. He is a faculty member in Otis College of Art and Design's Fine Arts program.

JASON SMITH is a faculty member in the Graduate Studies in Art MFA program at Art Center College of Design. His work has been published in *Artforum*, *Critical Inquiry*, *Rethinking Marxism*, and *Il Manifesto*. Smith cotranslated and introduced Jean-Luc Nancy's *Hegel: The Restlessness of the Negative* (2002). He is currently working on a manuscript devoted to the films of Guy Debord.

A.L. STEINER is a Brooklyn-based artist who uses constructions of photography, video, installation, collaboration, performance, writing, and curatorial work as seductive tropes channeled through the sensibility of a cynical, queer, eco-feminist androgyne. She is a member of the Chicks on Speed collective, collaborates with choreographers robbinschilds, cocurates the project *Ridykeulous* with Nicole Eisenman, founded Working Artists and the Greater Economy (W.A.G.E.), and teaches at SVA. Steiner is represented by Taxter & Spengemann.

HITO STEYERL is a filmmaker and writer based in Berlin. She is a guest professor in experimental media creation at the Universität der Künste, Berlin. Steyerl's writing focuses on documentary art forms and her exhibitions include the 2008 Shanghai and Pancevo Biennials, Documenta 12 (2007), 3rd Berlin Biennial (2004), and Manifesta 5 (2004).

SCOTT TENNENT is a writer and editor living in Los Angeles. He has edited books for Princeton Architectural Press, and written and edited projects for both LACMA and the University of Texas, Austin.

BOB THALL was born in 1948 and received a BA and MFA in photography from the University of Illinois, Chicago. He has been a professor of photography at Columbia College Chicago since 1976 and is currently chair of the Photography Department. Thall was the recipient of a 1998 Guggenheim Fellowship. His *The New American Village* pictures were shown in a solo exhibition at the Museum of Contemporary Photography, Columbia College Chicago, in 1999. His photographs are held in many collections, including those of the Bibliothèque Nationale de France, Paris; Canadian Centre for Architecture, Montreal; J. Paul Getty Center for the History of Art and the Humanities, Los Angeles; Library of Congress, Washington, D.C.; MoMA, New York; and Victoria and Albert Museum, London.

CHARLES H. TRAUB is a photographer and chair of SVA's MFA Photography, Video, and Related Media Department. His work has been exhibited in galleries and museums across the country and has been published in *Fortune*, *Newsweek*, *U.S. News & World Report*, and *Popular Photography*, among other publications. He lives in New York.

ANNE WILKES TUCKER received a BA from Randolph-Macon Woman's College and an MFA from the Visual Studies Workshop. She became the founding curator of photography at the Museum of Fine Arts, Houston, in 1976 and has curated over forty exhibitions, many with catalogues.

PENELOPE UMBRICO attended the Ontario College of Art and Design and received her MFA from SVA. She has had solo exhibitions of her work at numerous venues, including the International Center of Photography and Julie Saul Gallery, both in New York; Bernard Toale Gallery, Boston; and p/m Gallery, Toronto. Her work has been included in group shows at MoMA and Art in General, both in New York; Center for Curatorial Studies at Bard College, Annandale-on-Hudson, New York; Gallery of Modern Art, Brisbane, Australia; MassArt and Photographic Resource Center, both in Boston; Gallery 44, Toronto; Dazibao, Montreal; Ansel Adams Center for Photography, San Francisco; and Santa Barbara Museum of Art, California. Umbrico's work is included in the collections of the International Center of Photography, MoMA, and the Metropolitan Museum of Art, among others. She is the recipient of a New York Foundation for the Arts Catalogue Project Grant, a New York Foundation for the Arts Artists' Fellowship, and a Harvestworks Scholar Fellowship. She is currently the chair of MFA photography at Bard College, as well as core faculty in the SVA MFA Photography and Related Media Department.

DAVID WEINER's photography has been exhibited and published in the U.S. and Europe.

JAMES WELLING has worked to explore the materiality of

photography as a medium for over thirty years. Originally associated with postmodern photography in New York in the early 1980s, Welling worked and exhibited extensively in Europe in the following decade. In 1995, he moved to Los Angeles to become area head of the photography program at UCLA. His exhibitions include the 2008 Whitney Biennial, Whitney Museum of American Art, New York; *The Pictures Generation 1974–84*, Metropolitan Museum of Art, New York, and *Anos 80: Uma Topologia*, Museu de Arte Contemporânea de Serralves, Porto, Portugal.

RICHARD WEST is editor of *Source Photographic Review*, a quarterly magazine of contemporary photography based in Belfast, Ireland.

COLIN WESTERBECK is the director of the California Museum of Photography at the University of California, Riverside, a position he assumed in the fall of 2008. After moving to Los Angeles in 2003, Westerbeck wrote a weekly column on photography for the *Los Angeles Times* and taught photographic history at both UCLA and USC. From 1986 to 2003, he was a curator of photography at the Art Institute of Chicago. Among his publications are *Bystander: A History of Street Photography* (2001), coauthored with Joel Meyerowitz, and *Irving Penn, A Career in Photography* (1997).

CHARLIE WHITE, a photographer and filmmaker based in Los Angeles, is associate professor at the USC Roski School of Fine Arts, where he is also director of the MFA program. White's work has been exhibited internationally; recent monographs of his work include *Monsters* (2007) and *American Minor* (2009).

MARK WYSE received an MFA from the Yale University School of Art in 2001. His work has been featured in publications, including *Art in America*, the *New Yorker*, the *New York Times*, *Art on Paper*, *Blind Spot*, the *Los Angeles Times*, and the *Village Voice*, and was featured in his 2005 monograph, *18 Landscapes*. Wyse's work is held in the collections of the Metropolitan Museum of Art, New York; MOCA, Los Angeles; Yale University Art Museum, New Haven, Connecticut; and La Salle Bank Photography Collection, Chicago. He is represented by Wallspace. Wyse currently teaches at USC and Otis College of Art and Design.

AMIR ZAKI is an artist living in Southern California. He received his MFA from UCLA in 1999. Zaki exhibits his photographs and videos internationally; he has had solo shows at the Mak Center Schindler House, West Hollywood, California; Perry Rubenstein Gallery, New York; James Harris Gallery, Seattle; and Roberts & Tilton, Los Angeles. He has been included in group exhibitions at venues, including the 2006 California Biennial, Orange County Museum of Art, Newport Beach; Whitney Museum of American Art and Harris Lieberman Gallery, both in New York; Grimm/Rosenfeld Gallery, Munich; California Museum of Photography, Riverside; and San Jose Museum of Art, California. Zaki's work is held in numerous collections across the country, including those of the Whitney Museum of American Art and New Museum of Contemporary Art, both in New York; Henry Art Gallery, Seattle; Orange County Museum of Art, Newport Beach, and Santa Barbara Museum of Art, both in California.

ACKNOWLEDGMENTS

We wish to thank everyone who shaped and entered into the spirit of Words Without Pictures. A huge measure of thanks goes out to all of the contributors listed in the previous pages whose essays, responses, discussions, conversations, and questionnaire answers are published in these pages. We would also like to sincerely acknowledge all of the people who participated in the online forums and live events, and without whose support and enthusiasm this project would not have been possible:

Andy Adams, Darsie Alexander, Tim Atherton, Tim Barber, Hylan Booker, Liz Deschenes, Tim Druckery, Tiffany Fairey, Mary Fagot, Andrew Freeman, Thomas Frick, Jennifer Goldstein, Shigeo Goto, Clare Grafik, Sunil Gupta, Sophie Howarth, Farrah Karapetian, Elizabeth Lui, Lesley Martin, Liliana Martinez, Deepak John Matthew, Dave Miko, Mougin, Lisa Naftolin, Carol Norcross, Sara Nordstrom, Michiko Ohki, Kaycee Olsen, Mike Osborne, Niclas Ostlind, Mark Owens, Carolyn Peter, Walid Raad, Edward Robinson, Aaron Ryan, Britt Salvesen, Eve Schillo, Allan Sekula, Allan Sekula's MFA CalArts students, James Shashin, Sally Stein, Juan-Carlos Watkins, Sarah Bay Williams, Donna Wingate.

DESIGN NOTE

Rewinding now to page 1 and quoting the editors:

> The essays were proposals, from which the respondents picked up and created new strands of inquiry, thereby demonstrating the multidimensionality of each topic.

Likewise, the design has also developed in several directions at once over the course of more than one year. First, the website at www.wordswithoutpictures.org refused to archive past essays or conversations, its contents were completely replaced each month. Then, a mirror website at www.pictureswithoutwords.org mined the original site, programmatically producing a series of abstract images based on word frequencies. Finally, this book becomes a *de facto* archive—funneling the contents of the Internet project and live events into an explicitly chronological organization. The first edition of the book was printed-on-demand and offered as a PDF download via the original website, essentially closing the circuit. Perhaps all of this suggests that these kinds of conversations don't necessarily move forward only in a straight line, but progress in bumps, in fits and starts, looping back and moving forward in so many parallel streams.

David Reinfurt

Editor: Alex Klein
Initial concept: Charlotte Cotton
Questionnaires: Lester Pleasant
Publication Copy Editor: Elizabeth Pulsinelli
Website Copy Editor: Stephanie Ford
Additional copyediting: Scott Tennent
Design: O-R-G inc., David Reinfurt

The staff for the Aperture edition of *Words Without Pictures* includes: Juan García de Oteyza, *Executive Director*; Lesley A. Martin, *Publisher, Books*; Jenny Goldberg, *Assistant Editor*; Susan Ciccotti, *Senior Text Editor*; Nima Etemadi, *Assistant Editor*; Matthew Pimm, *Production Director*; Inger-Lise McMillan, *Design Manager*; Simone Eißrich, *Design Work Scholar*

First Aperture edition
Printed by Edwards Brothers in the United States
10 9 8 7 6 5 4 3 2 1

LACMA

Library of Congress Control Number: 2010921332
ISBN 978-1-59711-142-3

This volume is part of Aperture Ideas: Writers and Artists on Photography, a series devoted to the finest critical and creative minds exploring key concepts in photography.

Aperture Foundation books are available in North America through:
D.A.P./Distributed Art Publishers
155 Sixth Avenue, 2nd Floor
New York, N.Y. 10013
Phone: (212) 627-1999
Fax: (212) 627-9484

Aperture Foundation books are distributed outside North America by:
Thames & Hudson
181A High Holborn
London WC1V 7QX
United Kingdom
Phone: + 44 20 7845 5000
Fax: + 44 20 7845 5055
Email: sales@thameshudson.co.uk

aperturefoundation
547 West 27th Street
New York, N.Y. 10001
www.aperture.org

The purpose of Aperture Foundation, a non-profit organization, is to advance photography in all its forms and to foster the exchange of ideas among audiences worldwide.